Third Edition

Sociology in Everyday Life

David A. Karp
Boston College

William C. Yoels
University of Alabama, Birmingham

Barbara H. Vann
Loyola College, Maryland

WAVELAND

PRESS, INC.

Long Grove, Illinois

For information about this book, contact:
Waveland Press, Inc.
4180 IL Route 83, Suite 101
Long Grove, IL 60047-9580
(847) 634-0081
info@waveland.com
www.waveland.com

Photo credits:
    (p. 34) © Network Productions/The Image Works
    (p. 58) © Arlene Collins/The Image Works
    (p. 94) © Corbis
    (p. 130) © Corbis
    (p. 212) © Charles Orrico/SuperStock
    (p. 244) © Marilyn Humphries/The Image Works
    (p. 282) © Corbis
    (p. 352) © Corbis

For my parents,
Abraham and Rose, who taught love and respect
for learning through word and example.
—David A. Karp

In loving memory of my parents,
Harriet and Irving, for their lifelong support
and encouragement.
—William C. Yoels

For my parents,
William and Claradel Holcombe,
and my son Jesse, for always believing in me.
—Barbara H. Vann

CONTENTS

PART TWO
ESTABLISHING SOCIAL ORDER 91

PART THREE
DISORDER AND CHANGE IN EVERYDAY LIFE 279

PREFACE

During the course of our teaching careers we have become increasingly dissatisfied with the focus of most introductory level textbooks. Nearly exclusively, they are structured around macrosociological, institutional issues. If everyday interaction is treated at all, it is usually dealt with as a subheading in chapters on socialization, culture, or small-group study.

This is a serious omission for two reasons. First, the study of social interaction has always been a central concern of the sociological enterprise. Second, as we have come to learn very well, students taking introductory sociology courses are intent on learning something *immediately applicable to their everyday lives*. We have written *Sociology in Everyday Life* for those instructors who want to ground their treatment of traditional introductory topics in the stuff of daily life. This Third Edition is a completely revised and updated book. We think its title communicates the relevance of sociology for understanding our ongoing social experiences.

A key assumption underlying this book is that sociology's value lies in its ability to provide fresh insights into events and situations that students might ordinarily take for granted. In each chapter we show that there are underlying patterns to everyday life. These patterns become "obvious" only when we begin to look very hard at everyday phenomena and then apply sociological concepts to them. While our focus is fundamentally on processes of interaction, we are careful to indicate the mutually transformative connections between social structures and everyday face-to-face encounters.

To accomplish our goals, the book is divided into three main parts. Part One, consisting of three chapters, introduces key concepts in sociology (culture, socialization, roles, power, self, and the like) as well as the theoretical perspective that is maintained throughout the book. Most of our analysis of everyday life is derived from the symbolic interaction perspective, though the studies we refer to represent a variety of sociological viewpoints. The first three chapters, like all those in the book, are filled with examples that are resonant with the daily experiences of college students. Part Two centers on the construction and maintenance of order in social life. This section includes chapters on urban life and relations among strangers, the construction of intimacies, the distribution and use of power in daily life, everyday life within bureaucracies, and the experience of illness. Part Three speaks to questions of disorder and change in everyday life. It includes chapters on deviance, aging, and contemporary social movements, including the search for self.

We have constructed the book so that the topics parallel those discussed in most introductory sociology courses. Instructors will find that it can be used flexibly—in conjunction with other core texts or as the central book in the introductory course, along with a number of shorter texts or one of the many excellent readers organized around microsociological principles.

Acknowledgments

Peter Hall of the University of Missouri, Jack Kamerman of Kean College, Del Samson of Montana State University, John Stimson of William Paterson College, and Louis Zurcher of the University of Texas carefully and most professionally reviewed earlier versions of the book. Their sophisticated knowledge of symbolic interaction and their sensitivity to the subtleties of everyday life helped us in expanding and clarifying our thoughts. Long association with the late Gregory P. Stone of the University of Minnesota also had an important influence on the development of the ideas in this book.

The Third Edition of *Sociology in Everyday Life* reflects the valuable contributions of students in "Self & Society" at Loyola College in Maryland during the Fall 2001 and 2002 semesters. It would not have been possible without the endeavors of Beth Barnyock and Marta Ziolo, the best research assistants one could hope to have!

David A. Karp
William C. Yoels
Barbara H. Vann

ABOUT THE AUTHORS

David A. Karp received his Ph.D. in 1971 from New York University. He is currently Professor of Sociology at Boston College. Professor Karp has coauthored the following books: *Sociology in Everyday Life* (1993, 1986); *Being Urban: A Sociology of City Life* (1991, 1977); *The Research Craft* (1982); *Experiencing the Life Cycle: A Social Psychology of Aging* (1993, 1982); *Symbols, Selves, and Society* (1979); *Speaking of Sadness* (1996); and *The Burden of Sympathy* (2001). He has published work in *The Gerontologist, International Journal of Aging and Human Development, Qualitative Sociology, Symbolic Interaction,* and *The Journal of Contemporary Ethnography.*

William C. Yoels received his Ph.D. in 1971 from the University of Minnesota. He is currently Professor of Sociology at the University of Alabama-Birmingham. Professor Yoels has coauthored the following books: *Sociology in Everyday Life* (1993, 1986); *Being Urban: A Sociology of City Life* (1991, 1977); *Experiencing the Life Cycle: A Social Psychology of Aging* (1993, 1982); and *Symbols, Selves, and Society* (1979). He has published work in *The American Journal of Sociology, Qualitative Sociology, The Sociological Quarterly, Sociology of Education,* and *Symbolic Interaction.*

Barbara H. Vann received her Ph.D. from the University of Arizona in 1987. She is currently Associate Professor of Sociology at Loyola College in Maryland. She has published work in *Communication Quarterly, Cultivating the Sociological Imagination: Concepts and Models for Service-Learning in Sociology, Dreaming, Hawaiian Medical Journal, Journal of Sociology and Social Welfare,* and *Transformations.*

Part One

DEVELOPMENT OF THE PERSPECTIVE

The focus of this book is on everyday life. Our work is based on the belief that a key measure of sociology's value and vitality is its ability to provide insight into the underlying structure of day-to-day life. Certainly, sociology should provide you with a way to understand how society as a whole is organized and ordered. At the same time, a sociological way of looking at things should be immediately applicable to your everyday life. We propose to show that there is an order and predictability to everyday life which becomes visible once you begin to look very hard at behaviors and situations you might otherwise take for granted. Sociological analysis has the power to let you see everyday behaviors and situations in a new way. Talking, using space, waiting, relating to members of the opposite sex, choosing clothing, presenting images of yourself to others, touching, behaving in classrooms, and meeting strangers are all behaviors that happen in culturally predictable ways.

The first part of this book, consisting of three chapters, is designed to accomplish three broad goals: (1) to introduce the study of everyday life as a legitimate concern in the study of sociology; (2) to provide you with knowledge of some of sociology's key concepts; and (3) to lay out the theoretical perspective that is most helpful in analyzing everyday events.

While close observation is required in order to comprehend how daily life is organized, you also need some tools to help you know what to do with your observations. Concepts and the theories built from them provide a blueprint for identifying underlying patterns in social life. In the first three chapters you will learn how such standard sociological concepts as culture,

1

norms, values, roles, status, power, socialization, self, impression management, and interaction both direct the analysis of daily life and provide insight into its management.

In these chapters we also elaborate on a theoretical perspective in sociology called *symbolic interaction*. We will employ this theoretical view throughout the text as we investigate the various contexts of everyday life.

Chapter 1 presents a rationale for the study of everyday behavior. The notion that clear cultural expectations underlie daily activity is illustrated with examples of regularities in the use of time, space, and gesture. Beyond this, we emphasize how people's interpretations and definitions of social situations direct their behaviors. The questions of how individuals give meaning to various social situations are central to the perspective of symbolic interaction. An additional concern in chapter 1 is to show the significance of everyday behavior in studying how society itself is ordered. By the time you finish the first chapter you will possess several helpful ideas for looking at daily life in new ways.

Social life would be impossible without people's ability to define situations in shared ways. Chapter 2 elaborates on the important notion that human beings are symbol-using animals who collectively give meaning to the objects, events, and situations that make up their lives. We consider in detail the human capacity to symbolize, the socialization processes through which "selves" emerge, and the crucial importance of role-taking in human communications. The ability to engage in symbolic communication, we argue, not only makes social order possible, it also constitutes a continual source of nonconformity in social life. Chapter 2 can give you a deeper understanding of the symbolic interaction perspective and a better ability to use it yourself.

Chapter 3 shows how the assessment of meaning in interaction depends on information about others. Here we describe the kinds of information used to evaluate the people you physically encounter. We explain how such master attributes as sex, age, and race affect everyday relations and describe how people interpret each other's clothing, body type, and gestures. The chapter concludes by describing a view of interaction that stresses how individuals control information and foster impressions of self in everyday life. Chapter 3 builds on some of the key principles learned in earlier chapters.

one

CULTURE AND THE ORGANIZATION OF EVERYDAY LIFE

A story is told about a man who became a fixture on the streets of Edinburgh, Scotland. He would stop people on Princes Street, a main thoroughfare, and ask them if they were sane. "If any replied Yes, he would retort—ah, but can you *prove* it? And, if they could not, he proceeded triumphantly to show them that *he* at any rate could prove his sanity, by producing his own certificate of discharge from a mental hospital" (Gellner, 1975:431). This little anecdote raises significant questions about how we show that we are sane and the criteria we use in deciding whether others are insane. Mental illness is a social construction. A pivotal issue seems to be whether a "competent authority" will state for the record that an individual is "sane" or normal, or "insane" and abnormal (Curra, 2000). At the root of this difficulty is the fact that people's behaviors can only be seen as appropriate or inappropriate in terms of the societies and situations in which they take place. "Definitions of mental disorder are culture-bound; what is labeled crazy in one society or social context may be seen as perfectly normal in another—or possessed, extraordinary, saintly, inspired by the holy spirit" (Goode, 2001:381–82).

The American Psychiatric Association (APA) adopted guidelines in 1995, in response to growing concern about cross-cultural misunderstandings, that explicitly recommend considering cultural and ethnic factors when diagnosing or treating patients. With the rise in immigration to the United States during the last several decades, doctors increasingly must diagnose and treat patients whose symptoms do not appear in Western textbooks (Goleman, 1995). For example, whereas Americans sometimes fear that they will be embarrassed by their bodies, Japanese people sometimes experience disabling fears, known as "taijin kyofusho," that their bodies will embarrass *others*. Malaysian men may be stricken by "koro," the sudden and intense fear that their penises and testicles will recede into their bodies and kill them. Latin Americans can succumb to "boufee delirante," sudden outbursts of excited, confused, violent, or agitated behavior (Weitz, 2001:193).

Odd behaviors? Only in the context of U.S. cultural definitions of "normal" behavior (see box).

Female Circumcision? Or Female Genital Mutilation?

The topic of female circumcision, or female genital mutilation (FGM),[*] continues to be hotly debated among academics, governmental and nongovernmental organizations, and in the popular press. Defenders of the practice (including women) say it is a *cultural* issue, and that the Western world simply does not understand. Western opposition to the practice has become part of United States policy on human rights. Female circumcision has been performed since ancient times and continues to be commonly practiced throughout much of Africa. For example, although the most severe forms were banned in the Sudan in 1946, roughly 80 percent of ever-married women of reproductive age interviewed in 1989 and 1990 reported having undergone the most radical form of the ritual (Demographic and Health Surveys, 1991).

The primary purpose of female genital mutilation is to protect a girl from sexual temptations and thereby preserve her marriageability. There are firmly entrenched beliefs about the insatiable nature of female sexual desire in most practicing societies. The uncut are considered "dirty" and unmarriageable. Many parents say that if they fail to have their daughters cut, no respectable men will associate with the girls, who will end up "running wild like American women" (Dugger, 1996b; MacFarquar, 1996). In fact, many immigrants to the U.S. make tremendous sacrifices to save enough money to send their daughters back to their home country to have the operation performed (Dugger, 1996b). (The practice was made illegal in the U.S. in 1997.)

Westerners have difficulty understanding women's desire to continue this tradition. Critics of Western *ethnocentrism*—applying standards of our own culture to other cultures—point out that genital surgery increases women's status in societies where it is practiced. What might come as a surprise is the fact that clitoridectomies were not uncommon in the United States and Europe through the latter part of the nineteenth century. The practice was based on the belief that elimination of all sources of female sexual sensation would "cure" masturbation and prevent nymphomania—not to mention orgasm, which was considered an "ailment" that could be cured by removing the clitoris (Dreifus, 2000). Until the mid-1940s, clitoridectomies were routine for female patients in many mental hospitals. Views that women should be sexually "pure" are not limited to non-Western cultures.

Ethnocentrism notwithstanding, FGM is troubling. Women who have undergone FGM, often at a very young age, report that it is excruciatingly painful. FGM is seldom practiced under sterile conditions, with anesthesia and precise surgical instruments. The "surgery" is performed most frequently by untrained individuals who use sharp rocks, razor blades, kitchen knives, broken glass, or even their teeth. Short-term effects include excruciating pain, hemorrhage, tetanus, gangrene, and blood poisoning; long-term effects include sterility, increased difficulty in childbirth, permanent incontinence, painful intercourse, and lack of sexual pleasure.

The practice of FGM is waning. Senegal, Togo, and at least five other African countries have banned clitoridectomy. Although African women have been working to eliminate the practice in their own countries, there is considerable resistance from both women and men, who strongly object to having Western values imposed on them (Dugger, 1996a; MacFarquar, 1996). Waris Dirie, a Somali woman who underwent FGM at age 5 and later fled Somalia to escape an arranged marriage to a 60-year-old man, becoming a fashion model in London and UN special ambassador on FGM, says Westerners should not try to change African customs; changes must come from within countries themselves.

Will the practice continue? Williams and Sobieszczyk (1997) analyzed data from the Demographic and Health Surveys (1991) to discover to what extent circumcision rituals are performed on the current generation of young girls, and to ascertain which parents were most apt to choose to have their daughters undergo some form of the practice. They found that close to 90 percent of all women in the Sudan survey either had or planned to have their daughters undergo some form of circumcision, with roughly half favoring the most severe procedures. It seems likely, then, that this practice will continue.

*Use of the term "circumcision" to describe the range of procedures performed on females is objectionable to some on the grounds that it suggests a less severe procedure. Use of the term "genital mutilation" is offensive to others, particularly in instances in which no permanent alteration of the genitalia occurs (Williams and Sobieszczyk, 1997).

Cultural Expectations and Everyday Interactions

As Americans, we are born into an exceedingly complex **culture.** By culture we mean the totality, including knowledge, beliefs, customs, and morals, shared by members of a society. Our culture becomes so familiar to us at an early age that we tend to take it for granted. We normally do not question what we do and why we do it. Everyday life appears to be a reality that rarely requires explanation. It simply exists. The social world confronts us as an ordered and intelligible fact. We generally know which behaviors are proper and which would be improper in a given situation. Indeed, social life would be chaotic if we had to question at length the meaning of every behavior before we engaged in it. When we pull up beside a car at a red light, we know we should not stare at the occupants. When we meet a person for the first time, we do not need to ask ourselves how long we ought to shake hands. We do not expect new acquaintances to reveal their life problems to us. We would be likely to fear a stranger who boarded a nearly empty bus or train and deliberately sat next to us. There are, in short, an extraordinary number of **cultural expectations** which we learn virtually from birth and which lend order and organization to our daily interactions with others. Such "background expectancies" constitute the fundamental rules in accordance with which people normally act. These rules, sometimes difficult to specify, reflect our mutually held assumptions about proper and conventional behavior.

The central goal of this book is to analyze **everyday interactions** or communications from a sociological point of view. This first chapter provides a rationale for the study of routine social encounters in which everyone participates. The authors will also begin to outline the theoretical perspective we consider to be most valuable in exploring how transactions with others are accomplished. This is the **symbolic interactionist perspective** (see Fine, 1993; Hewitt, 2003), which centers attention on how individuals interpret and give meanings to the daily interactions that make up their **social worlds.**

To begin our presentation of this perspective, we will first consider the numerous social conventions which serve as guides for human behaviors and the maintenance of social order. Beyond that, they also serve as the basis on which everyday interactions are analyzed and interpreted by individuals. They therefore have a bearing on both the power of society to influence individuals' behaviors and the power of individuals to change or manipulate society.

Social Conventions as Guides for Social Order

There are thousands of cultural expectations which guide the minute details of our everyday interactions with others. These expectations are expressed as social conventions, or **norms,** which make up the rules for acceptable behaviors. Several volumes would be needed to describe all the norms in American society, ranging from proper table manners to the enormously complex regularities of verbal discourse. Together these norms make our daily encounters reasonably predictable, so we know what is expected of us and what to expect of others. Conventions such as those governing use of space, time, and posture or gesture also provide indications of the relative power, prestige, and status among the individuals taking part in interactions.

The authors of this book maintain that social life would be utterly unmanageable if there were no broadly shared consensus about how members of the society ought to conduct themselves in the myriad situations encountered in daily life. Social conventions or shared norms based on cultural expectations make everyday life possible and, by extension, constitute the basis for order in the society.

Spatial Conventions

The study of spatial conventions or norms regarding space between people in everyday behaviors has been labeled **proxemics.** Our **personal space,** "that piece of the universe you occupy and call your own" (Samovar and

Porter, 2001), is contained within an invisible boundary surrounding the body. With few exceptions, we do not allow others to violate this personal territory. Cultures that stress individualism (England, the United States, Germany, Australia) generally demand more space than do collective cultures. Africans, in contrast, "get physically close to complete strangers and stand even closer when conversing" (Richmond and Gestrin, 1998:95). This **territoriality** is evident in numerous types of daily encounters in American life. The next time you are waiting in an airline (or bus, or train) terminal, notice how people have arranged their luggage to create a zone surrounding them. Or on public transportation, when people go to great lengths to prevent someone from sitting in the seat next to them. Students in many classrooms soon develop a proprietary interest in their seats, for example. They lay claim to a particular seat early in the term which they thereafter feel they own for all practical purposes!

Appropriate Distances in Everyday Interactions

Spatial conventions serve as an ordering device that sets rules and limits for most everyday interactions. In American society, normal conversational distance is about two feet, for example. We become increasingly uncomfortable should anyone come closer. Imagine how you would react if a stranger came up to you and began to talk to you with his face only inches from yours.

The conventions about appropriate distance often work in conjunction with use of the eyes. In the elevator in a public building, for example, the occupants may avoid eye contact with one another by looking either at the floor or at the flashing numbers over the door. A plausible explanation is that eye contact is an invitation to verbal contact, and we do not wish to make verbal contact with strangers in a situation where our personal space might be violated.

Four common distances used in interpersonal communication were distinguished by Edward Hall, an anthropologist. He used observation and interviews with middle-class adults, mainly in the northeastern United States, as a basis for categorizing the spatial conventions that govern the distances people maintain between themselves in their communications with one another.

The closest encounters, according to Hall (1969), take place at 0 to 18 inches, or within **intimate distance.** They include activities such as lovemaking, wrestling, or whispering, which involve either actual body contact or very close proximity. At this distance, Hall says, "the presence of the other person is unmistakable and may at times be overwhelming because of the greatly stepped-up sensory inputs. Sight (often distorted), olfaction, heat from the other person's body, sound, smell, and feel of breath all combine to signal unmistakable involvement with another body" (p. 116).

Encounters at 1.5 to 4 feet take place at **personal distance** in Hall's terms. The space between individuals at this distance can be thought of as "a small protective sphere or bubble that an organism maintains between itself and others" (p. 119). Most daily conversations take place within this range.

Encounters which occur from 4 to 12 feet apart are said to take place at **social distance.** Interactions at casual social gatherings generally occur within this range. Encounters more than 12 feet apart are said to occur at **public distance,** "well outside the circle of personal involvement." In political addresses or theatrical performances, for example, "the voice is exaggerated and amplified, and much of the communication shifts to gestures and body stance" (p. 106).

In American society, conceptions of appropriate distance and personal space expand and contract, depending on the situation. How close to one another two people stand often is considered evidence of the degree of intimacy between them. Business conversations are carried out at one distance, talks between friends at another, and intimacies between lovers at still another. The relative status or position of different people also can be inferred from the spatial distances they maintain. The distance between the teacher and students in a classroom, for example, is a mark of the *differences* in their power and prestige. As the traditionally rigid status distinctions between teacher and student have been reduced in recent years, the way space is planned and used in classrooms also has changed. In many schools raised platforms and fixed rows of seats have been replaced by movable chairs and circular arrangements, in hopes of facilitating more direct and informal interactions between students and teachers.

Hall and Hall's (1990) work details cultural variations in the use of and response to space. They show that perceptions of private territory, conversational distances, and public distances maintained by Americans, Germans, the French, Japanese, and Arabs are quite different. The arrangement of offices provides a good example of how culture affects use of space. In Germany, where privacy is stressed, office furniture is spread throughout the office. In Japan, on the other hand, where group participation is encouraged, desks may be arranged hierarchically in the center of a large, common room with no walls or partitions (McDaniel, 2000). Supervisors and managers are positioned nearest the windows. "This organization encourages exchange of information, facilitates multitask accomplishments, and promotes the Confucian concept of learning through silent observation" (Samovar and Porter, 2001:187).

The way furniture is arranged in the home also communicates something about the culture. Visitors to the U.S. from France, Italy, and Mexico are often surprised at living rooms with furniture pointed toward the television. For them, conversation is important—facing seating toward a television hardly encourages people talking to one another (Samovar and Porter, 2001).

Spatial conventions constitute only one aspect of the cultural expectations which lend order and predictability to everyday interactions. Inferences about differences in power, prestige, and status among individuals based on their use of personal space must be confirmed or rejected by other aspects of their behavior, such as regard for time, facial expressions, posture, and verbalization.

Time Conventions

Seconds, minutes, and hours are not simply measures of time with a constant meaning. They assume different symbolic values in different contexts, different circumstances, and in front of different audiences. The meanings we attach to time are specific to particular situations and may, like spatial conventions, attest to differences in power, prestige, and status among persons. Students place a greater subjective value on a professor's time than on their own, for example. Entering a professor's office, students often begin their conversations with the declaration "I know you're probably busy, but . . ." and during the conversation they look for cues to determine whether they are exceeding an "appropriate" time limit in the office.

While time is measured in such absolutely defined units as seconds, minutes, and hours, each interval is not experienced in an identical fashion. The time spent on an important job interview will carry a different meaning from the same amount of time spent on the tennis court, for example. Albert Einstein once commented on the relativity of time by saying that two minutes in an uncomfortable situation seems like two hours. Like all other features of any culture, time is experienced subjectively.

Time Concepts in Contemporary Societies

There are clear understandings about most time conventions in American society. Imagine the reaction if you shook someone's hand for 60 seconds instead of the conventional 4 to 5 seconds, for example. Americans often plan their behavior to occur in a particular time sequence (see box). As with other social conventions or norms, however, there is considerable variation in expectancies about time within the society, depending on circumstances and the individuals involved.

Temporal (time-related) conventions and perceptions are linked to a society's level of urbanization and industrialization. The more complex, rationalized, bureaucratized, urbanized, and industrialized a society is, the more rigorous, concrete, and linear its conception and treatment of time will be. In a highly developed urban-industrial society, precision of timing is of great importance (see chapter 11). In fact, there is a classic argument that an orientation to time, rather than to task or social activities, becomes the crucial characteristic of industrial capitalist societies (Thompson, 1967).

This argument is based on the classical writings of Karl Marx and Max Weber, two of the nineteenth-century thinkers who helped lay the groundwork for sociology. Marx believed that the regulation and exploitation of labor time is the central characteristic of capitalism; that is, the exchange of commodities is in effect the exchange of labor time. Capitalism entails the attempts by the bourgeoisie either to extend the working day or to work labor more intensively. Later writers have demonstrated just how much conflict in industrial capitalism is focused around time—capital's right to determine hours of work and labor's attempt to limit those hours (see, for example, Walsh and Zacharias-Walsh, 2001).

Weber demonstrated that the Protestant Ethic encouraged people to develop themselves as subjects oriented to saving time and maximizing activity: "Waste of time is thus the first and in principle the deadliest of sins. . . . Loss of time through sociability, idle talk, luxury, even more sleep than is necessary to health...is worthy of absolute moral condemnation" (Weber, [1904–5] 1930:158). As Benjamin Franklin said, "Time is money"—to waste time is to waste money ([1904–5] 1930:48).

The sociologist Georg Simmel ([1905] 1950), writing at the onset of the twentieth century, described how life in the new "metropolis" required extensive use of clocks and watches in order for people's travel arrangements and appointments to occur efficiently.

Virtually all Americans, including many children, consider it essential to have a wristwatch. (In fact, many people have more than one!) Americans often must know exactly what time it is. The city dweller's constant preoccupation with time and punctuality has been identified as a central characteristic of urban life.

Generalization about the connection between time perception and extent of urbanization notwithstanding, we should still be clear on the idea that the

---

On Timing a Farewell: "Here's Looking at You, Kid"

One of the great lines of all time was spoken by Humphrey Bogart to Ingrid Bergman in the climactic scene at the airport at the end of *Casablanca*: "Here's looking at you, kid," Bogart's toast to Bergman, was his way of convincing her at that point that their affair was over. The seemingly offhand comment signaled the end of a dramatic sequence of events which moved inevitably to a farewell heightened by the dangers and uncertainties of war.

Erving Goffman (1971) used a similar example of a person seeing a close friend off at the airport to illustrate how we time our behaviors to fit a particular sequence. The highly ritualized farewell is timed so that its effusiveness increases in intensity as the time of departure gets closer. It reaches its emotional high point with a tearful embrace just prior to departure time. The display of emotion cannot occur too early or too late.

A great deal of interactional work is necessary in the case of a "failed farewell," when the plane fails to take off. The scenario might be as follows: We have reached the climax of our farewell only to hear that because of some technical difficulty our friend's plane will be delayed. Through no fault of our own, our farewell has failed and we must now go through the awkward process of restructuring the timing of our behaviors. We must backtrack from the intimate situation of high emotional involvement to an earlier stage of nonaffective, nonemotional talk. We must then begin to move once more through the expected time sequence leading up to yet another emotional display. Imagine how difficult this restructuring process would be if there were no reliable information as to how long the plane would be delayed or if, as in the case of Bergman and Bogart, the farewell represented the end of an interrupted love affair.

meaning of time varies from culture to culture. Differences in time orientation have a number of analogues in the way international business, for example, is handled and in the way people relate to each other. There is much more to business than just business in many parts of the world. Cultural distinctions in terms of protocol regarding appropriateness of jumping right into business discussions before a get-acquainted interlude can lead to problems. This cultural distinction is the greatest area of difference between American and Guatemalan styles of doing business, for example. In Guatemala, a strong personal relationship precedes solid business opportunities, which is also the case for Latin America in general. According to an article in *Business America*, an inexperienced American visitor often tries to force a business relationship:

> The abrupt "always watching the clock" style rarely works in Guatemala. A better informed business executive would engage in small talk, indicate an interest in the families of his or her business associates, join them for lunch or dinner, and generally allow time for a personal relationship to develop. (*Business America*, 1994:8)

Think about the way Americans talk about time: "losing time," "saving time," "making time," "killing time," and so on. Life in industrialized society is so enmeshed with the clock that its inhabitants are often oblivious to how eccentric their temporal beliefs can appear to others (Levine, 1997). Robert Levine describes an exchange student from Burkina Faso in eastern Africa who found the concept of "wasting time" confusing, because there is no such thing as wasting time in that country. What is truly wasteful, perhaps even sinful, is to not make sufficient time available for the people in your life (Levine, 1997). One of your authors has traveled to this country and observes that in this highly "relational" culture it would be seen as improper not to greet neighbors and have fairly lengthy conversations about their families, and so on. No one rushes, and the sort of frantic American relationship with time is nonexistent, at least in the villages.

As an exercise, you might pay attention over the next week or so to the way you think about and treat time. As you plan your study assignments, for example, do you devote one evening's study to your sociology, another evening for a second subject, and so on, or do you read in several subject areas each day? Which mode of studying do you find most comfortable and why? As you travel to your classes in the morning do you leave extra time in order to ensure that you won't be late for class? If you should arrive late, how do you feel upon entering the room and what do you imagine is running through the mind of your professor? As you leave class and proceed to the cafeteria for a lunch date do you quickly excuse yourself from an unexpected conversation with a friend or do you presume that the person waiting for you at the cafeteria will understand if you are late? How late can you be without expecting your friend to be upset? Will he or she be angry if you are 30 seconds late, 2 minutes late, 5 minutes late, 10 minutes late, half an hour late? If you are the one waiting, how long will it be before you become angry with a tardy friend? It might even be interesting to do a small informal poll with students you know from abroad. Do they feel as you do on these matters?

The Power to Make Others Wait

Bureaucracy, a predominant influence in modern society (see chapter 7), demands that much time be spent waiting for others or for goods and services. The study of delay in a mass-consumption society is a significant area of sociological inquiry because so much time must be spent waiting.

In the most immediate sense, delay may be caused by the relations between supply and demand for goods and services. Analysis of waiting, however, uncovers delay strategies used to exercise power and status in social interactions. The scarcity or monopolization of valued services creates situations which allow workers to exercise power over clients and customers, for example. Bureaucrats have notoriously abused their power to make people wait. They might not themselves possess anything of value, but in their work roles they control access to resources people need. We cannot even drive our automobiles without first acquiring licenses and registration papers from bureaucrats who, in fact, have low status within their organizations.

Others may keep us waiting because of the perceived importance of the services or knowledge they have to offer. Doctors usually have patients waiting for them, but a patient who fails to show up for an appointment will be charged for the unused time. Executives may regularly keep visitors waiting, "cooling their heels" in an outer office. Barry Schwartz observes: "In general the more powerful and important a person is, the more others' access to him must be regulated. Thus, the least powerful may always be approached at will; the most powerful are seen only by appointment" (1974:847).

Facial, Posture, and Gesture Conventions

Since 1980 the study of **nonverbal communication** has become a major area of inquiry in the social sciences and has engaged the attention of researchers in the fields of sociology, psychology, anthropology, communications, linguistics, and neuroscience. Much of the research on facial expression, for example, is concentrated on the universal presentation of such emotions as interest, surprise, disgust, anger, fear, and sadness (c.f., Keltner, 1995). Findings from a study on the ability to interpret facial expression of emotion may be of particular interest to you (especially if you are trying to convince your parents that studying abroad is beneficial!). Using student populations from the United States, Germany, South Africa, and Japan, researchers found that those who had traveled outside their home country were better receivers of nonverbal cues than were others (Swenson and Casmir, 1998).

Research on nonverbal communication shows that meanings conveyed by people's gestures and postures vary from context to context (c.f., Carroll and Russell, 1996) and cross-culturally (see box). **Kinesics,** the sociological study of body movement and gesture, is concerned with the shared cultural meanings attached to nonverbal behaviors. Consensus about the significance of postures, gestures, and expressions enhances our ability to explain and predict our own and others' behaviors in daily interactions.

Ray Birdwhistell (1952, 1970), a pioneer in this field, maintains that the majority of interactions utilize nonverbal communication. We give cues to our meanings by the way we stand, our facial expressions, and the position of our heads. We control most of these expressions and consciously use them to express a range of emotions from anger to disappointment to love. All com-

---

"V" is for Victory?

One of the arguments in this chapter, consistent with our social psychological viewpoint, is that behaviors carry quite different meanings in different settings. To be sure, assuming that certain nonverbal gestures carry the same meaning in other cultures can get you into a lot of trouble. Dane Archer, who is known for his use of video to explore cultural differences in gestures, states emphatically, "Gestures are definitely NOT a universal language, as people who have worked, lived, or studied abroad may have noticed" (Archer, 1997b:79). Travelers sometimes learn this the hard way, inadvertently committing offense by using the culturally "wrong" gesture. Archer urges travelers to practice "gestural humility"—"the assumption that the gestures we know from home will not mean the same things abroad, and also that we cannot infer or intuit the meaning of any gestures we observe in other cultures" (p. 80). Even prominent political figures can blunder. President George Bush (Sr.) greeted a group of Australians with a gesture he assumed was Churchill's famous "V" for victory gesture. However, President Bush had the gesture *backwards* (his palm facing his own face), effectively flashing the crowd with the British Commonwealth equivalent of the American "finger" (or "screw you") gesture. The Australians were more dumbfounded than insulted, not quite believing that a head of state would stoop to such an unpresidential act (Archer, 1997b:80). Bush isn't the only one to get it wrong—Margaret Thatcher did the same thing when she was Prime Minister!

Archer has videotaped hundreds of hours of ESL (English as a Second Language) students demonstrating gestures, resulting in the documentary videos, *A World of Gestures: Culture and Nonverbal Communication* (1991) and *A World of Difference: Understanding Cross-Cultural Communication* (1997a). These documentaries provide numerous examples of nonverbal communication with different cultural meanings. Perhaps the most famous is the American "OK" sign, which means "money" in Japan, "zero" in France, "homosexuality" in Ethiopia, and is regarded as an obscenity in Latin America! Similarly, the American raised thumb gesture of "good luck" is a vulgar gesture meaning "sit on this" in Sardinia and "screw you" in Iran (Archer, 1997a). Other examples of nonverbal communication with different meanings in different cultures include holding hands, shrugging, silence, and use of eyes in interpersonal expressions (Singh, McKay, and Singh, 1998).

If, however, you wish to avoid miscommunication, there is one gesture that carries virtually universal meaning. Most people will know that you mean to express appreciation when you smile.

municative expressions are not easily controlled, however. We find it hard to control such physiological responses as a red face in an embarrassing situation or involuntary hand tremors during high anxiety. Often we look for these expressions in others with whom we are interacting as a check on their emotions or attitudes.

An interesting example of the way our internal emotional states are reflected in outward appearance is the case of lying. Nonverbal behaviors that are significantly more frequent with lying include blinking and an increased number of what have been termed *adaptors*. These are nervous habits such as scratching or twiddling one's hair (Ford, 1996). Other physical cues believed to be associated with lying include an increased incidence of leaning forward, licking the lips, touching the nose, averting gaze, and handling objects (Henahan, 1999).

Raising the hand to the nose has been reported in many cultures as a movement associated with lying. This may be related to the fact that the nose contains erectile tissues that engorge when a person is lying, sort of a "Pinnochio effect" (Henahan, 1999).

The simplest nonverbal gestures can communicate a great deal. Think of a skier or skater who falls and then exaggerates the effect by lying on the cold ground longer than necessary with arms and legs flung out. Through such exaggeration the person may wish to communicate: "I know I look kind of silly, but understand that I am really a quite competent person and you should not take this momentary awkwardness very seriously." Sometimes gestures of this sort are used in conjunction with verbal utterances, as when a woman runs headlong to catch a bus or elevator before it leaves, only to have the doors close in her face. At this point she might stand, hands on hips, moving her head from side to side, muttering. Her comments are supposedly made to herself, but they also may be meant to be heard by anyone within earshot. They might be intended to communicate: "Understand that although this has happened, I remain fully in control of myself."

Avoiding Communications

Nonverbal communication can be instrumental in avoiding communication. Moore (1998) observed "courtship rejection signaling" by women attempting to discourage the attention of males in singles' bars. This is an interesting study, given that most research on courtship focuses on behaviors that individuals use to attract partners (see chapter 5). The women Moore observed used 17 behaviors to demonstrate disinterest or rejection, including facial expressions such as yawning, frowning, and sneering; gestures such as negative head shaking or putting hands in pockets; and posture patterns such as arm crossing or holding the trunk rigidly. A number of signals involved the eyes, for example *gaze avoidance*. This occurred when the woman did not make eye contact with the man, despite the fact that he was looking directly at her. She looked at other people or at another point in the room, or made eye contact with someone else at the table. Other eye signals that functioned as rejection signals included *upward gaze*, when she looked at the ceiling, and *hair gaze*, when she drew her hair across her face and looked at the ends (Moore, 1998).

People often use props as an aid in such situations. We would be hard-pressed to explain why some people wear sunglasses on the subway, for example, unless we considered their use in shielding the "improper" use of eyes. Other props such as newspapers—Goffman (1963) calls them "involvement shields"—are also used to avoid any kind of contact with others. Avoidance may itself be a form of social interaction—we must sometimes communicate to others that we do not wish to communicate. Particularly in urban interactions with strangers, we must systematically take one another into account in order to avoid unwanted encounters (see chapter 4).

Rules for Physical Contact

There also are clear conventions regulating actual physical contact between individuals (Henley, 1986). A commonplace behavior such as hand holding is a highly regulated activity, for example. A few questions suggest the range of these regularities: Who can hold hands with whom? Is it more appropriate for women to hold hands in public than it is for men? Why? Is there an age-related factor influencing who can hold hands with whom? Would a female in her 20s feel uncomfortable holding her father's hand while walking down the street? Would a male of the same age feel self-conscious holding his mother's hand in a restaurant?

We share clear expectations about who may touch whom, on what part of the body, and in what context. Different meanings and symbolic significance are attached to different parts of the body. On the field, male athletes pat each others' bottoms after significant plays or outstanding personal efforts, but this same behavior elsewhere would hardly be interpreted as a display of male camaraderie. You might seek others' attention by lightly tapping them on the shoulder, but you would not grab them by the thigh. Sometimes it is considered appropriate for one person to touch another, but not vice versa. A teacher may, while explaining a point to a student, touch the student's shoulder. The student would hesitate to do the same to the teacher. Sometimes even the slightest touch (touching another's foot under a dining table, for example) requires an immediate apology. Other times . . .

As with the other normative conventions detailed in this chapter, rules about touching vary considerably from culture to culture. Americans who normally do not touch other people unless they are on a fairly intimate basis will feel comfortable in Japan, England, Scandinavia, and Australia, where similar rules prevail. Americans who travel to Middle Eastern countries, Latin countries, Italy, Greece, Spain, Portugal, and Russia may have to adjust to encounters, even among strangers, where people routinely touch each other. People from some Mediterranean cultures often hold the elbow of the person to whom they are speaking. For many Americans, this uninvited touching is nearly unbearable (Archer, 1997b).

A Blueprint for Everyday Life

This section has described only a small fraction of the types of rules and expectations that constitute a critical part of any culture. As the members of a society together acquire knowledge, beliefs, art, customs, morals, and other capabilities and habits, the culture evolves over time. A pattern of norms or conventions about what one can and cannot do in a given society emerges. A society is possible only because its members share these standards and cultural expectations.

Commonly held ideas about how one ought to behave provide members of the same culture with a blueprint for conducting their everyday lives. Knowledge of cultural rules and social conventions is not itself enough to ensure social order, however. Human beings constantly interpret and negotiate such rules.

Beyond Social Conventions:
The Interpretation of Everyday Life

The sociologist's job—to explain human behavior—would be quite simple if behaviors were the product only of the types of social conventions we have mentioned. Were that the case, we would only have to set about cataloging all of the rules to which people in American society normally conform. Alas, things are not quite so simple! It would be more accurate to say that these conventions or shared norms constitute the *boundaries* within which people interact. Alone they are not sufficient to explain how daily encounters are managed. Beyond knowledge of background rules, successful interaction requires engaging in a **process of interpretation** through which a situation is assessed and meanings are assigned to a person's own behaviors and those of others.

Assessing Meanings and Formulating Behaviors

It may very well be true that you know what to do when entering a new classroom for the first time because you have learned from an early age the general rules applicable to classroom behavior. You are unlikely to sit down in the chair behind the desk at the front of the room, for example. You have learned not to speak unless directed to do so by the teacher. Should you want to talk, you would probably raise your hand and wait to be acknowledged by the teacher. And so on. Knowledge of these rules alone, however, will not allow you to predict fully the meanings and patterns of behavior that will become central in any particular classroom. That is, the rules which govern classroom behavior will be products of ongoing actions by the particular teacher and students involved, all of whom must constantly take the others' actions into account when formulating their own lines of action (Karp and Yoels, 1976).

As in any other setting, participants in the classroom will be engaged in an ongoing assessment of each others' actions. Students will soon define the situation as to whether in a particular class the teacher *really* wants discussion, whether it is safe to make one's opinion known, whether one ought to laugh at the teacher's jokes and, if so, how raucously. Decisions of this sort cannot be anticipated or determined solely through knowledge of the general and learned conventions applicable to most classrooms.

Interpretation in the Acting Situation

Behavior is always produced via interpretation in the **acting situation.** The expectancies surrounding behavior in any situation always emerge from the interaction itself. They may be in a state of continual transformation. According to Herbert Blumer, "In the flow of group life there are innumerable points at which participants are redefining each other's acts" (1962:184).

Suppose someone approaches you and asks for a light for a cigarette. This is an apparently simple request, but, in fact, it is not immediately clear how you would respond. You probably would believe the other person's motives to be different under different circumstances. What situational factors or variables might influence the meaning you attach to this request? Would the gender of the person make any difference in your interpretation? Would you possibly attribute different motives to a stranger and a close friend making the same request? Would it make any difference where the request was made (at a friend's house or a bar)? What role might such factors as the time of day, the age of the requester, or his or her dress, race, demeanor, and facial expression play in your interpretation of the request? Even the most apparently simple human transactions may call forth quite different meanings which we confer on them by piecing together bits of information in the situation.

Virtually all our behaviors depend on our ability to assess features of the situation in which we are acting and then define it. Some situations may require more extensive interpretation than others, however. In some situations we realize that we must be quite strategic in formulating our behaviors. In these situations we might engage in extensive mind work or mental gymnastics prior to acting. We might consciously try to manipulate those with whom we interact in order to control the **definition of the situation** they will come to have. These may be situations that we consider risky or in which we perceive obstacles to the realization of our goals.

The Individual-Society Relationship

The social conventions described in the preceding section lend support to a central idea in the symbolic interactionist approach to the study of sociology: The capacity of humans to interact and communicate effectively with each other is a truly extraordinary ability and worthy of in-depth investigation. The explanation of how social conventions reflect the social order and influence the interpretation of everyday events has brought out a number of general points. First, although we may not think much about it, there is a clear ordering to our everyday lives. There are underlying dimensions to everyday social life that can be discovered. Second, the coherence of everyday life depends on our possession of a truly remarkable range of knowledge. Third, our behaviors are a product of our ability to interpret social situations and confer meanings on them. Fourth, rather than being regarded as a given, social order should be considered a human accomplishment that requires explanation. Fifth, if we seek to understand how, in the broadest sense, a society is possible and how it operates as an ongoing concern, it is a good strategy to begin by exploring how we carry out our day-to-day interactions.

This approach also supports an even more general sociological theme: the relationship between the individual and the society. We live in a society which significantly influences our behaviors through numerous social conventions. At the same time, we exercise substantial freedom of action. It is a paradox of human existence that while societies influence human behaviors, humans sometimes also transform societies. We must entertain simultaneously the apparently contradictory thoughts that humans are social products and that society is a human product.

Understanding Freedom and Constraint in Social Life

The abiding theoretical questions of sociology flow from consideration of the individual-society connection: How do individuals become functioning members of a society? How and why do they become responsive to the demands of a society? Why do they conform to society's rules? How is it that some people refuse to do so? To what extent is behavior determined by **social structure?** Just how much can individuals change societies?

Nearly all the great classical social theorists were intrigued by these questions. On the whole, their theoretical work may be read as attempts to understand the nature of the **social bonds** existing between individuals and the bonding of individuals to the society (see box). Those who are considered the founding figures of sociology—Karl Marx (1818–1883), Émile Durkheim (1858–1917), Georg Simmel (1858–1918), Max Weber (1881–1961), Ferdinand Tönnies (1855–1936), and William Graham Sumner (1840–1910), among others—all broached questions of order and disorder, change and stability, deviance and conformity. These questions, of course, do not allow for single, definitive answers. They still are the guiding questions for sociological work, and sociologists collectively are still in the business of trying to understand just how societies and individuals influence one another. One thing seems clear, however. Comprehension of everyday life requires a conception of the individual-society relationship in which primacy is placed on neither the society nor the individual.

Émile Durkheim (1858–1917)

French sociologist Émile Durkheim was instrumental in establishing sociology as a social science, distinguishing "the scientific study of society and human behavior" from the field of philosophy and other social sciences. Central to Durkheim's work was the notion of society as a reality in its own right: Despite the variety of people within a society and the fact that some die and others are born, there is an order that exists above and beyond its specific components. Durkheim spoke of a "collective conscience;" the shared beliefs of members of a social unit. Perhaps most importantly, Durkheim showed that this order can be examined scientifically, through observations. These observations produce social statistics, or *social facts*, numbers that characterize a collectivity. For example, the birthrate of a society, although composed of thousands of individual births, is a statistic that exists at the level of society as a whole. Durkheim's emphasis on statistics reflected his personal concern to make sociology respectable to the ruling intellectual elites of the day. Then, as now, "science" was associated with numbers, with *quantitative* measurement. His classic work, *Suicide* ([1897] 1951), is based on a comparison of official statistics and historical records across groups.

Durkheim observed patterns in the data: Suicide rates in all the countries he examined tended to be higher among widowed, single, and divorced people than among married people; higher among people without children than among parents; and higher among Protestants than among Catholics. Rather than interpret this in terms of psychological states, Durkheim felt that the nature of *social* life was involved. He concluded that when group, family, or community ties are weak, people feel disconnected and alone. When these ties are strong, people have a supportive network that could protect to some extent against the individualism and alienation of life in modern society (see chapter 11).

Durkheim was a pivotal figure in the establishment of sociology in the French university system. His ideas had a profound impact not only in France, but also played a major role in shaping American sociology.

The Approach of the Authors

The authors of this book are convinced that any attempt to understand the operation of society that neglects the processes governing social interaction will be theoretically unsatisfying. Ultimately a society is composed of people interacting with one another. All explanations of human behavior must in some way account for individuals' intentions, motives, and subjective understanding of the situation in which they act. All human behavior is constructed from everyday **shared meaning structures.** We presume, in other words, that any effort to understand the operation of society as a whole must begin with and be built upon analysis of individuals' everyday life worlds. We agree with Peter Adler, Patricia Adler, and Andrea Fontana who, in their review of critical works on the sociology of everyday life, comment: "Naturally occurring interaction is the foundation of all understanding of society. Describing and analyzing the character and implications of everyday life interaction should thus serve as both the beginning and end point of sociology" (1987:219). This is not to suggest that sociologists should give up the study of social structure in favor of the study of human interaction. Instead, we believe, along with a number of sociological theorists (see, for example, Maines, 2001) that the most fruitful sociological inquiries are based on an integration of the two levels of analysis, society and the individual. Too much sociology, we think, makes the mistake of accepting the **reification** of social structures, regarding them as having a life of their own independent of individuals. Much sociological work is based on the supposition that institutions are more than the sum of their parts and, once created, exert a force on individuals over which they have little control.

There is no question that institutions exert a strong force on individuals. Ample evidence of this can be found in the bureaucratic systems (see chapter 7) which provide a structure for the lives of college and university students. There are certain things you are required to do if you wish to remain within the system. You must show up for exams, you must pay your tuition, you must follow certain course registration procedures, and so forth. In that sense the structure is real, powerful, and has an obdurate quality that transcends the existence of any particular student. The university has an independent life in the sense that it existed as an institution before any of you were born and will, in all likelihood, continue to exist after you are dead.

Does this mean that your behaviors are utterly controlled by the academic bureaucracy? Does it mean that sociologists need not be concerned with the interactions among individuals within the institution and the definitions and meanings they give to their lives in it? Of course not! It should not come as news that students manipulate academic institutions. Through interaction with others, you determine just how hard you will work in your courses. You and your fellow students could collectively choose to make life difficult for your instructors by such strategies as choosing not to participate in class discussion or conning them into letting you turn in late term papers.

We are committed to the idea that, in large measure, human beings act according to the *interpretations* they make of social life. Individuals are not merely puppets pushed around by forces over which they have no control. Substantially, they make their own worlds. Unlike atoms, molecules, or stable elements of the physical universe, they think, construct meanings, and respond creatively to their environments. Consequently, the social world is in a state of continual process, change, and production. Values and attitudes change. Behaviors once thought taboo become incorporated into the repertoire of conventional behaviors. New social forms are created to meet needs better, and unpredictable fads are devised.

Humans thus experience choice and discretion in their everyday lives. But it would be misleading to minimize the significance of the constraints within which they must act. The dramas of daily life occur within larger historical and institutional settings. Because people are born into a world that is itself a product of the actions of previous generations, many areas of social existence have already been staked out for them. There are understood limits on their behavior. Societies have moral as well as geographical boundaries. And every society has its caretakers (e.g., police, judges, psychiatrists) who are entrusted with the responsibility for maintaining the integrity of those boundaries and the power to do so (see chapter 8).

The Dynamic Interplay of Expectations and Interpretations

In our view, therefore, human behavior must not be seen exclusively as either the product of the social structures enveloping people or a matter of individual will and choice. There is a dynamic interplay between society's expectations for individuals and their own responses in situations.

The nature of the relationship between individuals and social structures is beautifully captured in a statement by sociologist Wendell Bell. Some people, he says, rather than following along like rats in a maze, view the social structure as tentative and proceed by experimentally testing to learn what parts of it can be manipulated. In his words,

> At the extreme, such persons may decide that the social structure, the maze itself, is subject to some extent to their will and may decide to shape it, as best they can, to suit themselves. . . . Usually in cooperation with others, some people try to manipulate the real world to conform more closely to their images of the future; push out some walls, add some new openings, widen the passageways, create some new opportunities. (1968:163)

Thus, while society sets the ground rules within which we act, we do not unthinkingly respond to society's expectations. Behavior is also partially the result of our personal, subjective interpretations of the situations we face. The most appropriate conception of daily life, therefore, requires that we understand human behavior as an ongoing interchange, or a *dialectic,* between freedom and constraint.

The Sociology of Everyday Life

The authors of this book advocate the study of everyday interactions as a central area of sociological study *in its own right.* We believe sociologists cannot afford to neglect the study of everyday life. On theoretical grounds, we maintain that the study of such interactions is necessary in order to understand social order and change in society. In a still broader sense, as we analyze various aspects of everyday lives in later chapters, we will be exploring the limits and potentialities of human beings' relations with each other. This is, by any standard, an important endeavor.

You may wonder, if the study of everyday interaction is as important as we believe it to be, why is it necessary to argue for its merits as an area of sociological investigation? The fact is that the processes governing everyday life and accounting for its order have been largely ignored by many sociologists who consider them as, at best, only the starting point for their own broader, more **macrosociological investigation** of large-scale processes and social structures. Much sociology, in this respect, leaves wholly unattended the grounds on which it is constructed. The sociologist Harold Garfinkel made this point some time ago when he said: "Although sociologists take socially structured scenes of everyday life as a point of departure they rarely see, as a task of sociological inquiry in its own right, the general questions of how any such commonsense world is possible" (1967:36). Garfinkel is arguing that efforts to understand society as a whole depend upon the **microsociological investigation** of individuals' daily interactions (see box).

Garfinkel's Ethnomethodology

Harold Garfinkel developed *ethnomethodology* (literally, people or folk methods) as a technique for looking beneath the "taken-for-granted" surface of daily life. His goal is to understand how people produce meaning out of their experiences. First we must consider the "seen but unnoticed," expected background features of everyday scenes that members of a society use as a scheme of interpretation. People respond to background expectancies, but are at a loss to say of what the expectancies consist. For these background expectancies to come into view "one must either be a stranger to the 'life as usual' character of everyday scenes, or become estranged from them" (1967:37). He is most famous for his "demonstrations," designed to "produce reflections through which the strangeness of an obstinately familiar world can be detected" (1967:38). That is, by doing something that turns this world upside down the unspoken reality is revealed.

Garfinkel sent his students out to expose this unspoken reality by "breaching" it. They entered elevators and stood facing the other occupants, rather than turning around to face the door. On visits home they acted as if they were strangers, asking permission to eat food, for example. In everyday conversations ("Hi, how are you?") they refused to respond in the expected manner ("What do you mean, 'how am I'? Physically? Emotionally?"). As you might expect, people's reactions were anything but positive, ranging from questioning the person's sanity, to anger. The point was not to upset people, but to upset the balance of everyday life, thus proving beyond doubt that certain taken-for-granted norms had been violated. According to Garfinkel, "there *is* order in the most ordinary activities of everyday life" (1996:7). The preoccupation in ethnomethodology's studies is "to find, collect, specify, and make . . . observable the . . . production and natural accountability of immortal familiar society's most ordinary organizational things in the world" (1996:6).

Why the Study of Interactions Has Been Neglected

A central reason why sociologists have failed to study everyday interactions systematically is their concern for conventional methods of scientific inquiry. Virtually since sociology's inception in the nineteenth century, sociologists have modeled their discipline after the natural sciences. They have been intent on using the same tools the natural scientist uses in their investigation of human behavior. This has meant a central concern with the establishment of causal laws about human society.

Moreover, social scientists have frequently embraced a version of scientific inquiry in which precise measurement of variables and the rigorous testing of propositions are the standard for judging scientific work. The notion that there is only one proper form of scientific inquiry is a somewhat naive conception of science, in our view. It immediately restricts the range of phenomena that may be investigated to those variables that are clearly quantifiable and hence measurable. Such a bias is reflected in the definition of a true behavioral *scientist* as a person who, when asked if he loves his mother, replies that he cannot answer until he has done an analysis of their correspondence.

We surely would not argue with attempts to measure accurately the variables of interest to social scientists. But the demand that social scientists be concerned only with observable, quantifiable, and measurable phenomena has directed attention away from basic processes of human communication which often defy precise "measurement." Our idea of interaction is that people act in awareness of each other and mutually adjust their responses in light of the actions of others. We therefore want to consider such factors as their motives, their goals, the meanings they confer on the gestures of others, their identities, their self-concepts, and the processes through which they define social situations. These necessary elements for understanding social interaction are resistant to precise measurement. We must be concerned with what goes on in a person's head, his/her mind work, so to speak.

An appropriate metaphor might be the operation of a clock. We cannot fully comprehend how a clock works by looking only at the outside casing or examining only the regularity of the minute, hour, and second hands. Certainly it is easier to describe these visible outer mechanisms, just as it would be simpler only to document and measure actual behaviors. The study of interaction requires more: concern with the inner dialogue that people have with themselves both before they act and while they are acting.

A second reason why sociologists have generally neglected the study of routine, everyday social encounters may be their longstanding preference for investigations of issues that have social policy implications. Sociologists have shown a preference for research areas which might persuade the public that sociologists have something to say about "important" issues. Understandably, they have concentrated their efforts on areas where they are likely to receive funding for their study. Such social problems as juvenile delinquency, poverty, race relations, health delivery systems, aging, prostitution, drug addiction, and homosexuality have always been issues for sociological study. These areas provide much rich information on day-to-day interactions, but they have not typically been investigated with this goal in mind. As we will see in the following chapters, this is no longer the case.

What the Study of Interactions Should Accomplish

If the analysis of everyday interactions is to be accepted as a central area of sociological study, it must be able to accomplish specified goals. Our efforts ought to produce some type of new knowledge about human behavior.

Discovering Underlying Social Forms

In some respects, the facts of everyday life are obvious and accessible to anyone who carefully observes. For that reason, our goal is never simply description of everyday life. Certainly our analysis begins with careful description, but beyond that we seek to appreciate how the facts of everyday behavior reveal deeper, often hidden dimensions of social life. The trick of sociological analysis is to identify recurring patterns of social life reflected in a range of behaviors. If we are successful, our analyses will let us see a familiar set of facts from new angles, and this will add new dimensions to our understanding. Another way to express the same thought is that our analyses should "penetrate" the obvious and thereby reveal underlying aspects of social life.

Ever since the first trees bore fruit, it has no doubt been obvious to everyone that apples fall from trees. Before Sir Isaac Newton purposely observed this event, however, no one had ever related the falling of apples to the motion of the planets. Newton's contribution was the conceptual breakthrough that revealed the laws of gravity. Once that underlying dimension of the physical world was uncovered, the fact that apples fall from trees became somewhat insignificant. Newton's law allowed scientists to understand the behavior of any falling body. The discovery of underlying dimensions that reveal commonalities in a whole class of events is the real task of scientific inquiry. Scientists are less concerned with the *content* of events than with the common forms taken by apparently dissimilar events.

The "obvious" empirical facts of social life are important in the same way. It is our job to make plain how the facts of everyday life reflect underlying social forms (Simmel, 1950) or dimensions. To illustrate the point, social scientists interested in a phenomenon such as "religious devotion" should not just investigate what goes on in churches. They would do well to study also such seemingly diverse phenomena as labor union meetings, behaviors on national holidays, football games, and punk rock concerts. Each of these are events that could profitably be understood as expressions of religious devotion. The same intensity and reverence associated with religious rituals underlie these phenomena. Clearly, contexts or situations which differ widely in content (the content of church services is quite unlike the content of football games) can nevertheless display common social forms.

A phenomenon such as embarrassment is interesting, but we do not suggest studying it only to describe embarrassing situations. Our broader intention is to use these descriptions as a starting point for thinking clearly about more general issues such as risk, identity, performances, and deviance in interaction (see chapter 9). To use an earlier example in this chapter, we might be interested in detailing conventions of "touching" behavior in order to gain insight into patterns of intimacy in society, elements of body image, and power relations (see chapter 6).

If we wish to investigate how people behave in stressful, anxiety-related, or uncomfortable situations, we could focus on contexts where we expect them to experience stress, anxiety, and discomfort. We might choose to observe students in dormitories before final exams, for example. It would be true that we were observing behaviors in a dormitory, but we would not be concerned with the context per se. We would be motivated to study dormitory life as a convenient context in which to develop an analysis of stress interaction. This analysis has significance far beyond the dormitory itself. In other words, sociological analysis must always carry us beyond the specific context we are investigating. The specific case of dormitory behavior becomes as incidental as apples falling from trees once we discover underlying elements of how humans behave under stress.

A danger faced by sociologists who study everyday life phenomena is the criticism that they are concerned with trivial events. We maintain, however, that sociological analysis of the routine events and worlds of everyday life often provides important insights and concepts that have a larger relevance for understanding social life. Throughout the following chapters we will be citing studies that we feel provide powerful explanation of human behavior. However, we can mention here a few examples of the kinds of topics we have in mind. Gary Fine (1996) has studied the organizational culture and structure of restaurant kitchens. Arlie Russell Hochschild (1997) examines what happens "when work becomes home and home becomes work." And Mitch Duneier and Harvey Molotch's (1999) study of urban street vendors uncovers the process of "interactional vandalism" in which street men are able to breach the norms of urban interaction. Studies such as these affirm the necessity of looking at everyday life settings and interactions in order to understand the bases of social order and change in society at large.

Some of the most exciting/promising work is in the area of social inequality. Philippe Bourgois (1995) shows how the urban drug trade offers a path to status and economic success for young men who have no chance for industrial work nor the cultural capital to break into middle-class service jobs. Katheryn Edin and Laura Lein (1997) interview mothers on welfare to discover how they "make ends meet." Elijah Anderson (1999) shows how the desperate search for respect influences the everyday lives of young African Americans in the inner city. Mitch Duneier (1999) describes the interaction between New York street vendors and the women passing by in terms of race, class, and gender.

Developing Sociological Skepticism

Unfortunately, there is no set of rules we can give that will allow you to discover the underlying forms of social life. What we can do in this book is to let you see how social scientists think about everyday phenomena, the particular imagination or consciousness they bring to the study of everyday events, and the kinds of questions that guide their analyses. The production of good ideas is not a mechanical process, as Stanislav Andreski (1972:108) notes:

> The so-called methods of induction are in reality methods of verification; they tell us how to test hypotheses *but not how to arrive at them.* Indeed, the latter process is just as much a mystery as it was in the days of Socrates: all that is known is that, *in order to conceive fruitful original ideas, one must have talent, must immerse oneself in the available knowledge, and think very hard.* (emphasis added)

In the chapters that follow we will familiarize you with the ideas of those who have written about everyday behaviors and share the knowledge they provide. We also will continue to detail the elements of the theoretical perspective—symbolic interaction—that we consider most useful for analyzing everyday events. The central goal of this volume, however, is to force you to begin thinking very hard about how your daily interactions are organized and made sociologically intelligible.

At the risk of sounding too dramatic, we want to develop in those who read this book a kind of sociological skepticism. Good sociology demands a degree of skepticism. It is the sociologist's obligation to question those features of reality that appear quite obvious. Sociologists must strive to become strangers to the events and phenomena in their daily lives that they most take for granted. As a sociologist, therefore, you must step outside your "normal" roles as a member of the society and ask how your behaviors are structured and endowed with meaning. Good sociology requires you to be skeptical enough to believe that things are not always as simple as they appear to be.

We presume, in other words, that those things "everybody already knows," those apparently obvious aspects of the society that you have grown up with from infancy, can be subjected to sociological analysis. It is, we will show, an analysis that provides insight into the way people produce and construct their everyday existences. In this respect, we take on the professional obligation of questioning aspects of social life that may seem obvious and unproblematic. Our subject matter does not have anything mysterious about it—we certainly grant that. The questions we ask about familiar life phenomena and the analyses deriving from these questions are intended to advance and deepen your understanding of the sociological topics to be discussed in the following pages.

Conclusion

The focus of this book is on the application of sociological principles, concepts, and ideas to your everyday life. It begins with the assumption that the value of sociology lies in its ability to provide fresh insight into events and situations that might ordinarily be taken for granted.

Space, time, gesture, and posture norms are examples of the underlying patterns in everyday life. These patterns become obvious only when we begin to look very hard at everyday phenomena. Moreover, social order persists only because we share knowledge of an extraordinary range of cultural expectations. Beyond knowledge of the norms of social conventions based on these expectations, however, the meanings we attach to behaviors vary from context to context. Social norms only provide the boundaries for our encounters. We must, in addition, interpret the meanings our behaviors have in a particular setting.

While much of the analysis in this book concentrates on face-to-face interaction, we also point out that the dramas of daily life are played out within larger institutional and historical settings. As members of schools, families, churches or synagogues, and a multitude of other bureaucracies, we are obliged to behave in certain ways. Social structures certainly diminish personal choice and discretion. At the same time, people manipulate social structures. Human behavior therefore is the product of neither the social structures enveloping individuals nor the individual's free will and choice. Rather, it is the result of a dynamic interplay between cultural expectations and people's interpretations of situations.

The notion that people must define and interpret the meanings of both their own and others' behaviors is basic to the perspective that guides our inquiry in this book—symbolic interaction. An important idea in this perspective is that individuals collectively shape, mold, and refashion their social worlds through the process of communicating with others and responding to their communications. Because the analysis of interaction must be based on some clear set of ideas about human encounters and communication, our development of this perspective continues in the next chapter with consideration of the following issues:

1. What is the significance of interpretation in human interaction and communication?

2. How do objects take on meaning?

3. How do individuals come to evaluate the meaning of their own and others' acts?

4. What are the sources of innovation and unpredictability, and thus of nonconformity, in social life?

DEFINITIONS

Acting situation   The immediate place or circumstances of an interaction (for example, a classroom) considered by individuals as they give meanings to their own and others' behaviors.

Cultural expectations   Broad and widely shared cultural rules that reflect mutually held assumptions about proper and conventional behaviors in different social contexts.

Culture   The complex whole which includes knowledge, beliefs, art, customs, morals, and any other capabilities and habits acquired and shared in common by the members of a society. A group's culture provides a blueprint for living which is transmitted to future generations.

Definition of the situation   W. I. Thomas's concept, "What people believe to be real is real in its consequences" (Thomas and Thomas, 1928), which refers to an interactant's understanding of a particular setting.

Everyday interactions   Those patterns of communication with others that regularly comprise our everyday lives.

Intimate distance   The area around a person within which the most intimate encounters take place. In American society intimate distance is between 0 and 18 inches.

Kinesics   A field of inquiry in the social sciences in which people's communication through body gesture and posture is studied.

Macrosociological investigation   Social science research that centers attention on the ways social structures function or society as a whole operates.

Microsociological investigation   Social science research that centers attention on the ways in which people's daily, face-to-face communications are organized.

Nonverbal communication   Any of the modes of communication (such as gesture or facial expression) other than verbal language.

Norms   The range of rules, both written and unwritten, which dictate appropriate ways of acting in different social situations. Most social norms are unwritten and once learned are followed virtually automatically. Laws are norms of sufficient importance to society that they are written down. Social conventions are synonyms for shared norms in a society.

Personal distance   The space maintained between a person and others during most routine interactions (such as conversations with friends). In American society personal distance is between 1.5 and 4 feet.

Personal space   The space that immediately surrounds a person's body. Others normally do not violate this space without permission. People's sense of personal space varies in different cultures and may expand or contract in different social situations.

Process of interpretation   The internal dialogues people have with themselves about the meanings of their own or others' behaviors in various acting situations.

Proxemics   A field of inquiry in the social sciences in which the rules that govern people's use of space in their everyday relations are studied.

Public distance   The space maintained between an individual and the audience for presentations such as public speeches. Public distances are those beyond 12 feet.

Reification   The concept that social structures have a life of their own, independent of the individuals that ultimately create those structures.

Shared meaning structures   The range of consensually held meanings about the world held by the members of a group or society. A shared meaning structure constitutes a group's view of reality.

Social bonds   The connections of individuals to their societies that create feelings of loyalty, belonging, and integration.

Social distance   The space maintained between a person and others during such casual gatherings as cocktail parties. In American society social distance is between 4 and 12 feet.

Social structure   The totality of social institutions such as government, the family, and religion which influence how individuals behave in a society.

Social worlds   The totality of the various social locations individuals occupy in society. Members of different classes and racial, religious, and ethnic groups inhabit different social worlds.

Symbolic interactionist perspective   A theoretical perspective in sociology that focuses attention on the processes through which people interpret and give meanings to the objects, events, and situations that make up their social worlds.

Territoriality   The space which individuals or groups feel they "own." Groups will take measures to protect their territory from "invaders." Studies of animal groups show that they too operate within territories which they protect from outsiders.

DISCUSSION QUESTIONS

1. Do you agree that there are no behaviors which are intrinsically deviant, that what we mean by deviance, mental illness, or insanity is a thoroughly cultural product?

2. What are some of the background expectancies concerning space, time, and gesture that operate in the classroom for this course?

3. Under what kinds of conditions do you feel people become most strategic in formulating their behaviors? What do they have to gain or lose in such situations?

4. In which aspects of your own life do you feel you have greatest freedom of choice, and in which areas do you feel most constrained by social structures? How much do you think people, individually or collectively, can change institutions such as universities?

5. What is your definition of science? What special problems does the social scientist studying human communication face?

6. Suppose your instructor asked you to observe behaviors in a local bar frequented by college students. What kinds of behaviors might it be important to record? What kinds of things might you be able to learn about interaction by observing behavior in a context like this? What general issues about human behavior could be examined by observing bar behavior? Where else might you investigate these same issues?

REFERENCES

Adler, P., P. Adler, and A. Fontana. 1987. "Everyday life sociology." *Annual Review of Sociology* 13: 217–35.

Anderson, E. 1999. *Code of the Street*. New York: W. W. Norton & Company.

Andreski, S. 1972. *Social Sciences as Sorcery*. New York: St. Martin's Press.

Archer, D. 1991. *A World of Gestures: Culture and Nonverbal Communication* (video). Berkeley: University of California Extension Center for Media and Independent Learning.

————. 1997a. *A World of Difference: Understanding Cross-Cultural Communication* (video). Berkeley: University of California Extension Center for Media and Independent Learning.

————. 1997b. "Unspoken diversity: Cultural differences in gestures." *Qualitative Sociology* 20(1):79–105.

Bell, W. 1968. "The city, the suburb, and a theory of social choice." In *The New Urbanization,* edited by S. Greer et al. New York: St. Martin's Press.

Birdwhistell, R. 1952. *Introduction to Kinesics.* Louisville, KY: University of Louisville Press.

———. 1970. *Kinesics and Context.* Philadelphia: University of Pennsylvania Press.

Blumer, H. 1962. "Society as symbolic interaction." In *Human Behavior and Social Processes,* edited by Arnold Rose. Boston: Houghton Mifflin.

Bourgois, P. 1995. *In Search of Respect: Selling Crack in El Barrio.* New York: Cambridge University Press.

Business America. 1994. "Recognizing and heeding cultural differences can be key to international business success." 115 (October 15):8–11.

Carroll, J., and J. Russell. 1996. "Do facial expressions signal specific emotions? Judging emotion from the face in context." *Journal of Personality and Social Psychology* 70:205–218.

Curra, J. 2000. *The Relativity of Deviance.* Thousand Oaks, CA: Sage Publications.

Demographic and Health Surveys. 1991. *Sudan Demographic and Health Surveys 1989/ 1990.* Khartoum, Sudan: Department of Statistics, Ministry of Economics and National Planning, and Columbia, MD: Institute for Resource Development/ Macro International.

Dreifus, C. 2000. "A conversation with Nawal Nour." *New York Times,* July 11:D7.

Dugger, C. 1996a. "A refugee's body is intact but her family is torn." *New York Times,* September 11:A1, B6–7.

———. 1996b. "Tug of taboos: African genital rite vs. U.S. law." *New York Times,* December 28:1, 9.

Duneier, M. 1999. *Sidewalk.* New York: Farrar, Straus and Giroux.

Duneier, M., and H. Molotch. 1999. "Talking city trouble: Interactional vandalism, social inequality, and the 'Urban Interaction Problem.'" *American Journal of Sociology* 104(5):1263–95.

Durkheim, E. [1897] 1951. *Suicide.* New York: The Free Press.

Edin, K., and L. Lein. 1997. *Making Ends Meet: How Single Mothers Survive Welfare and Low-Wage Work.* New York: Russell Sage Foundation.

Fine, G. 1993. "The sad demise, mysterious disappearance, and glorious triumph of symbolic interactionism." *Annual Review of Sociology* 19:61–87.

———. 1996. *Kitchens: The Culture of Restaurant Work.* Berkeley: University of California Press.

Ford, C. 1996. *Lies!, Lies!!, Lies!!!: The Psychology of Deceit.* Washington, D.C.: American Psychiatric Press.

Garfinkel, H. 1967. *Studies in Ethnomethodology.* Englewood Cliffs, NJ: Prentice Hall.

———. 1996. "Ethnomethodology's Program." *Social Psychology Quarterly* 59(1):5–21.

Gellner, E. 1975. "Ethnomethodology: The re-enchantment industry or the California way of subjectivity." *Philosophy of Social Sciences* 5: 431–50.

Goffman, E. 1963. *Behavior in Public Places.* New York: Free Press.

———. 1971. *Relations in Public.* New York: Basic Books.

Goleman, D. 1995. "Making room on the couch for culture." *New York Times,* December 5:C1.

Goode, E. 2001. *Deviant Behavior.* 6th ed. Upper Saddle River, NJ: Prentice Hall.

Hall, E. 1969. *The Hidden Dimension.* New York: Doubleday.

Hall, E., and M. Hall. 1990. *Understanding Cultural Differences.* Yarmouth, ME: Intercultural Press.

Henahan, S. 1999. "Science of lying." *Access Excellence.* Washington, D.C. <http://www.accessexcellence.org/WN/SU/lying599.html> Accessed 10/11/02.

Henley, N. 1986. *Body Politics: Power, Sex, and Nonverbal Communication*. New York: Simon & Schuster.

Hewitt, J. 2003. *Self and Society: A Symbolic Interactionist Social Psychology*. 9th ed. Boston: Allyn & Bacon.

Hochschild, A. 1997. *The Time Bind*. New York: Henry Holt and Company.

Karp, D., and W. Yoels. 1976. "The college classroom: Some observations on the meanings of student participation." *Sociology and Social Research* 60: 421–39.

Keltner, D. 1995. "Signs of appeasement: Evidence for the distinct displays of embarrassment, amusement, and shame." *Journal of Personality and Social Psychology* 68:441–54.

Levine, R. 1997. *A Geography of Time*. New York: Basic Books.

MacFarquar, N. 1996. "Mutilation of Egyptian girls: Despite ban, it goes on." *New York Times,* August 8:A3

Maines, D. 2001. *The Faultline of Consciousness: A View of Interactionism in Sociology*. New York: Aldine de Gruyter.

McDaniel, E. 2000. "Nonverbal communication: A reflection of cultural themes." In *Intercultural Communication*, 9th ed., edited by L. Samovar and R. Porter. Belmont, CA: Wadsworth.

Moore, M. 1998. "Nonverbal courtship patterns in women: Rejection signaling—an empirical investigation." *Semiotica* 118(3/4):201–14.

Richmond, Y., and P. Gestrin. 1998. *Into Africa: Intercultural Insights*. Yarmouth, ME: Intercultural Press.

Samovar, L., and R. Porter. 2001. *Communication between Cultures*. 4th ed. Belmont, CA: Wadsworth.

Schwartz, B. 1974. "Waiting, exchange and power: The distribution of time in social systems." *American Journal of Sociology* 79:841–70.

Simmel, G. [1905] 1950. "The metropolis and mental life." In *The Sociology of Georg Simmel*, edited by K. Wolff, pp. 409–24. New York: The Free Press.

———. 1950. "The study of societal forms." In *The Sociology of Georg Simmel,* edited by K. Wolff. New York: The Free Press.

Singh, N., J. McKay, and A. Singh. 1998. "Culture and mental health: Nonverbal communication." *Journal of Child and Family Studies* 7(4):403–9.

Swenson, J., and F. Casmir. 1998. "The impact of culture-sameness, gender, foreign travel, and academic background on the ability to interpret facial expression of emotion in others." *Communication Quarterly* 46(2):214–30.

Thomas, W. I., and D. S. Thomas. 1928. *The Child in America: Behavior Problems and Programs*. New York: Knopf.

Thompson, E. P. 1967. "Time, work-discipline, and industrial capitalism." *Past and Present* 38:56–97.

Walsh, J., and A. Zacharias-Walsh. 2001. "Working longer, living less: Understanding Marx through the workplace today." In *Illuminating Social Life*, 2nd ed., edited by P. Kivisto, pp. 7–44. Thousand Oaks, CA: Pine Forge Press.

Weber, M. [1904–5] 1930. *The Protestant Ethic and the Spirit of Capitalism*. London: George Allen and Unwin.

Weitz, R. 2001. *The Sociology of Health, Illness, and Health Care*. 2nd ed. Belmont, CA: Wadsworth/Thomson Learning.

Williams, L., and T. Sobieszczyk. 1997. "Attitudes surrounding the continuation of female circumcision in the Sudan: Passing the tradition to the next generation." *Journal of Marriage and the Family* 59:966–81.

SOCIALIZATION AND THE CONSTRUCTION OF SOCIAL REALITY

In chapter 1 we stressed the idea that humans are not simply rule-following creatures. Norms or social conventions set the boundaries within which human interactions may occur, and situations are grounded in cultural expectations that the participants will interact in conventional ways. Through the process of interpretation, however, individuals may redefine situations while reinterpreting the behaviors expected of them. The symbolic interactionist perspective provides a picture of social life which neither reifies social systems nor sees individuals as perfectly free to fashion society (Hewitt, 2003). Perceived meanings of behaviors are always liable to revision as individuals piece together information about themselves, others, and the arenas in which they interact. The social world cannot be seen as independent of people's definitions of it. Symbolic interactionists see meaning as variable and emergent. Meaning arises and is transformed as people define and act in situations. It is not merely dictated by culture. These points are cogently captured in Herbert Blumer's statement of the central premises of symbolic interaction (1969:2):

1. Human beings act toward things or situations on the basis of the meanings that the things or situations have for them.

2. These meanings are derived from or arise out of the social interactions individuals have with others.

3. These meanings are handled or modified through the interpretive process used by individuals in dealing with the things or situations they encounter.

These three premises (the first one in particular) call attention to the fact that things as such have no inherent meaning. Whatever meanings they have derive from the responses individuals make to them. It is in this sense that humans live in a world of symbols and interact through **symbolic communication.**

The sociological study of everyday interactions analyzes how people through their communication with others socially construct and use the meanings which they then confer on things. The existence of shared meaning structures, that is to say, common definitions of **social reality,** must be assumed, but not all social groups construct identical versions of reality. Behaviors that deviate widely from what is expected become defined as **nonconformity.** In this chapter we will examine how symbols are used in the social construction of multiple social realities. Particular reference will be made to the process of *socialization*, which informs us about behaviors expected or considered deviant in our society.

Symbolic Communication

You may be sitting on a chair while reading this book. In order to know the "meaning" of a chair you might reasonably rely on the definition of it as an object "on which you sit." That is what a chair is—something to sit on. An object's meaning, in other words, is defined in terms of how it is used. But there is nothing inherent in the object called a chair that dictates you must respond to it by sitting on it. Indeed, there are other uses; in western movies, for example, chairs are used as weapons in barroom brawls.

Our range of responses to an object is dependent on the social and cultural circles in which we live our daily lives. Should strangers from a planet where chairs are nonexistent land on Earth, they would have difficulty figuring out that this object called a chair is something to sit on. We have to learn such meanings through symbolic communication with others.

The Difference between Symbols and Signs

Symbols are words, acts, and objects used intentionally to communicate and represent something. When we say that symbols represent something we are saying that they are, in Mead's terms, "meaningful" acts—they make sense to the person using them. This quality of symbols makes communication possibilities infinitely greater, complex ideas possible, and thinking (talking to oneself) a central characteristic of the symbol user (Charon, 2002).

Words are symbols; in fact, the only function of words is to be symbolic. Objects also can be made into symbols; for example, the U.S. flag symbolizes patriotism, a gold ring symbolizes marriage, a dove symbolizes peace. Acts also can be symbolic, such as shaking a fist at someone to indicate anger.

The physical characteristics of symbols can be irrelevant to their meaning. To Christians, a crucifix has meaning because it represents (or better, re-presents) a historical event, the crucifixion of Christ, which they have designated as a divine event. Whether a crucifix is made of gold, iron, or wood is irrelevant to Christians, who define it as a holy object and respond to it reverently. As in the example of the chair, however, if strangers from another culture, never having heard of Christianity, were to happen upon a crucifix, there is no way that the physical characteristics of the object would indicate to them what it represents. They would have to learn that through communication with others. The crucifix also evokes a different response (that is, has a different meaning) for non-Christians, such as Jews, Muslims, or atheists.

Only humans assign meanings to things. Symbols mobilize our responses to the environment and help us bring together, or conceptualize, aspects of it. In contrast, animals live in a world of signs. A **sign** differs from a symbol in that its meanings remain constant. Its meaning is identified with its physical form and may be grasped through the senses (Becker, 1962:20). Animals, in short, can respond to their environments only in terms dictated by their physiology. Only humans, through symbolic behavior, are able to transcend the limits of our bodies through the development of such phenomena as technology and science. In so doing, we transform the environment through the meanings which we collectively, in communication with others, confer on it. As Ernest Becker put it: "Nature provides all life with H_2O, but only man could create a world in which 'holy' water generates a special stimulus" (1962:20).

The claim that human beings' capacity for symbolization distinguishes us from the lower animals is often disputed (see box). This is even more true in regard to animals higher in the evolutionary scale, such as chimpanzees and other primates.

Can Animals Communicate?

One of the most interesting and hardest-to-solve puzzles in the social sciences is whether primates are capable of any form of symbolic communication. As early as 1748, based on the notion that possession of language alone distinguished humans from other animals, Julien de La Mettrie proposed the experiment of teaching a young chimpanzee language through sign and vocal instruction. Although he published anonymously and his publisher, when hauled before the authorities, claimed not to know him, La Mettrie had to flee France and Holland (Leiber, 1995). It was not until the twentieth century that systematic attempts to teach apes to speak were carried out. The question of whether apes can use language, however, remains unanswered.

In the 1960s, Beatrice and Allen Gardner, realizing that chimps in the wild appear to communicate mainly through gestures, began to teach American Sign Language to a chimp named Washoe. The Gardners never used verbal speech in Washoe's presence, only sign language. By the age of five Washoe had acquired a vocabulary of 160 signs and could put together "words" to form new "sentences" (Gardner and Gardner, 1969). Since then, many other chimpanzees have been taught sign language and to use other word symbols. A chimp named Lana at the Yerkes Primate Research Center in Atlanta learned to use various symbols on a computer keyboard to ask for food, companionship, and music. A bonobo named Kanzi, described as "the ape at the brink of the human mind" (Savage-Rumbaugh, 1998), learned his first words by merely watching his mother. Perhaps most famous is Koko, a gorilla who rhymes and jokes, makes up words when she does not know the name for an object ("finger bracelet" for ring), and clearly expresses emotions—you've probably heard about her love for kittens, and the sadness she experienced when her kitten "All Ball" (who was named by Koko) was killed.

In spite of such accomplishments, some researchers have questioned whether the apes had learned to use language the way humans do. Although

---

There's No Such Thing as a Bad Dog

You may have had success teaching your dog to sit or to bark when it wants to go outside, but this does not mean you have an obedient pet. At the same time, a dog that ignores the command to sit or soils the carpet is not being disobedient. The reason is that the lower animals cannot be held responsible for either following rules or breaking them. Teachers often find it difficult to convince students that animals have no regard for rules. The following dialogue from one of our classes illustrates the rationale for the argument that animals react to the physical properties of objects (signs) without endowing them with the meanings attached to them (symbols).

Teacher: Let me try to illustrate this distinction between animal and human behavior by asking you this question: Can animals be deviant?

Student A: Sure, don't we punish animals for doing things we don't like? I have a dog that used to urinate in the house. After I gave the dog a few whacks with a rolled-up newspaper, he stopped doing it. Now all he's got to do is see the paper and he runs under the bed.

Teacher: But is the dog really responding to your commands in terms of symbols? Or is it merely responding to a particular physical stimulus without giving it any meaning? Let me try to make myself clear on this. You can get a dog to stop at a red light, a traffic light, by physically punishing it if it doesn't. But you must understand that that red light, like your rolled-up newspaper, can never be more than a sign to the dog. When we stop at a red light, on the other hand, we can think about the meaning behind the light. Why is it there? What would happen were it not there? You see, we understand the necessity for stopping at the red light. We recognize that people's safety depends on it. That's the essential difference.

Student B: I still don't understand why it's not possible for a dog to be deviant. The dog is breaking rules. Isn't that deviance?

Teacher: Deviance itself is a symbolic phenomenon. I mean, what is deviance? Is there any social act that is intrinsically deviant? Like anything else, it's human beings who confer the label *deviance* on a particular act. After all, people establish the social rules in the first place, and the departures get labeled as deviance. Can animals establish those rules?

Most students eventually acknowledge that animals neither make nor break the rules governing their conduct.

they had clearly learned to use hand signs or symbols ("words") in appropriate situations, did they understand what the signs or symbols represented?

The PBS series *Nature* ran a miniseries called "Inside the Animal Mind" (2000), which explored the topics "Are Animals Intelligent?", "Do Animals Have Emotions?", and "Animal Consciousness." Some of the more intriguing findings included the following:

1. Honeybees deprived of their normal route between hive and nectar source complete their missions anyway, suggesting that they are able to form pictures in their minds of the land surrounding the hive—a sort of mental map.

2. Ravens have the ability to solve difficult puzzles, such as untangling a knotted string to free up a treat or figuring out how to steal fish by hauling in an angler's untended line.

3. Chimps and elephants appear to be aware of death, grieving when family members die (as did Koko the gorilla when her kitten was killed).

4. Dolphins appear to recognize themselves in mirrors, and exhibit a keen awareness of the status and identity of other dolphins in their highly social groups (<http://www.pbs.org/wnet/nature/animalmind/consciousness.html> accessed 1/13/00).

While examples of this sort are certainly intriguing, they do not resolve the question of whether animals are self-aware in the way humans are. The debate is not whether animals can learn. The ongoing controversy is whether animals are capable of picturing the future, planning, improvising, and symbolically communicating with each other. There is no doubt that animals have managed to learn a code that includes some of the characteristic features of human communication. Nevertheless, there remains an unbridgeable gap between human language and communications of the sort demonstrated in research studies. Animals are essentially limited to the symbols they have been taught by humans. This is, of course, very different from the manner in which humans continually create new, more complex verbal communications.

Language as an Aspect of Human Culture

One way to frame this argument is to say that the major distinction between humans and nonhumans is that only human beings possess a culture, or collectively shared ideas, concepts, beliefs, and knowledge which can be transmitted to succeeding generations (see chapter 1). Lower animals may be said to operate within *social structures* in the sense that there is an order and predictability to their behaviors. This is a consequence of biological instinct, however. Culture, in contrast, is a symbolic creation, and language has an important role in its construction.

In one of a series of early studies, Wolfgang Kohler (1927) placed a stack of bananas outside a chimpanzee's cage, just beyond its reach. He also placed a number of sticks inside the cage that could be fitted together to make a longer stick, thus enabling the animal to reach the fruit. Now it might be said that when, after much trial and error, the monkey fits the sticks together to reach the bananas, it has at that moment gained insight into a very abstract idea—the concept of addition. But—and this is the important point—without verbal language the monkey cannot transmit that abstract idea to others of its species. If a particular monkey has discovered the principle of addition, it remains, without language, forever its individual possession. It never becomes a collective, cultural possession that can be elaborated on to produce new mathematical principles and eventually such revolutionary discoveries as computers. In this respect, language reflects and is part of human culture. Language is also essential to the continuance of a culture and ongoing changes in it.

We are not suggesting that animals do not communicate. They do. For example, bees can, with great precision, communicate the location of food via physical movement, and sea animals (whales and dolphins) communicate danger warnings over long distances. Such communications are rooted in instinct, however. There is never any variation or elaboration of the available messages that can be transmitted. The content of the messages is genetically determined.

In contrast, it is the essence of human communication that there is no intrinsic or built-in meaning to the words constituting the language used. The very same words can carry different meanings for different persons and groups, and certain words, used in particular contexts, can be considered either obscene or acceptable. The meanings of words are constantly subject to change. A good example is the word *gay*, which now is more apt to mean "homosexual" than "happy and excited," an earlier definition.

The Liberating Effects of Symbolic Communication

Symbolic communication (or symbolic behavior) also permits us to, in effect, liberate ourselves from the physical constraints of time and space. If we create a word, or verbal symbol, such as *house* to refer to the physical object called a house, we are free to talk about, think about, and refer to houses without the necessity of having a house in sight. It is possible to refer to houses that existed in the past as well as to conjure up houses that might exist in the future, not just in the United States, but elsewhere—even on other planets! The range of possible habitats for humans is limited only by our imaginations rather than by our physiology, as space trips to the moon and experiments in living under the oceans have demonstrated.

The use of symbols not only permits us to step outside the particular physical setting in which we find ourselves but, more importantly, it permits us to step outside ourselves. We can look at ourselves from the standpoint of others, put ourselves in their place, and anticipate how they are going to react to us. We can, in effect, look at ourselves as if we were objects and anticipate how others are going to respond to those objects. Verbal symbols (language) are critical in this situation, since the spoken word is heard simultaneously by both the speaker and those to whom it is addressed. The speaker can react to the word while monitoring the responses of others to what is being said.

George Herbert Mead, a major formulator of symbolic interaction, described symbolic communication as a "conversation of gestures," initiated by one individual giving a significant symbol—a gesture that arouses a similar response both in the one employing the gesture and in those who perceive it. Significant symbols may be behavioral, but humans rely for the most part on language. Humans produce responses in themselves and others by using words, and thus signaling their intentions or plans of action to one another. The key to this process is the fact that significant symbols arouse the same or a very similar response in the one using the symbol and those who perceive it. Thus it is the significant symbol that is the basis for shared meanings in human life. For example, when you say to someone that you are sad, not only do you presumably arouse in that person an attitude of sympathy toward you, but you also stimulate yourself to feel sympathetic toward yourself. By thus arousing the same or a very similar response in self and other, both see things in the same way (Hewitt, 2003).

The ability to evaluate our own behaviors objectively, from the perspective of others, is necessary if we are to become "normal" functioning members of society. Once we acquire that ability, we possess what Mead calls **the self.** This conception of self underlies the symbolic interaction perspective.

Development of the Self through Interaction with Others

Just as symbolic communication requires an audience to which communications can be directed, so is the self formed and transformed through interaction with others. You were not born with a preformed self. Through the use of symbols you have learned to take on the attitudes, values, and moods appropriate to the particular social circles in which you participate. Through the reflected appraisals of others, you have come to define yourself as a certain kind of person.

Charles Horton Cooley used the metaphor of a looking glass to characterize this process:

> A self idea . . . seems to have three principal elements: the imagination of our appearance to the other person; the imagination of his [sic] judgment of that appearance; and some sort of self-feeling, such as pride or mortification. (1902:152)

As people interact, based on their respective identities, they develop images of one another. People imagine their own appearance to others in terms of these images. That is, the person forms an image of the other, then imagines their appearance to the other from the standpoint of that image and feels good or bad accordingly. Cooley explained the **looking glass self** with the couplet: "Each to each a looking glass, reflects the other that doth pass" (Cooley, 1902).

Another way to think about it is as follows:

I am not what I think I am.
I am not what you think I am.
Rather, I am what I think you think I am.

In fact, you have many identities which are established and validated (or invalidated) through the responses others make to you. The psychologist William James suggested in 1892 that humans have as many selves as they have memberships in various social groups. We belong to numerous social circles simultaneously—the family, a church or synagogue, friendship cliques—and adjust our behaviors to take into account the particular situation and the others with whom we are interacting. Others do the same with us. One does not act in a classroom, for example, as one does in a morgue—at least, most of the time! As Mead notes:

> We carry on a whole series of different relationships to different people. We are one thing to one man and another to another. We divide ourselves up into all sorts of different selves with reference to our acquaintances. We discuss politics with one and religion with another. There are all sorts of different selves answering to all sorts of different social reactions. (1934:142)

Role-Taking

The capacity to adjust one's behavior in response to particular social situations is termed **role-taking** by Mead. From the symbolic interaction perspective, the development of the self is inextricably bound up with the capacity to take the role of others (see box). Every act of role-taking simultaneously involves two dimensions: (1) people anticipating the responses that others are going to make toward them, and (2) people evaluating their *own behavior* in terms of the anticipated responses of others.

Such expressions as being proud of yourself or being ashamed of yourself illustrate the principle of role-taking. There is no way to experience such reactions as shame or guilt without introspectively evaluating and appraising our own behavior while taking into account the actions of others. It is in this sense that the self is both the subject and the object of our own acts. We engage in a behavior as an acting subject. We then introspectively evaluate the meaning of that behavior to ourself and to others based on the responses they have made to it—that is, we reflect back on our own behavior, viewing it much like an "object" to be studied and evaluated. Such internal evaluations then influence our future course of action. If, after thinking about our own behavior and how others have responded to it, we feel ashamed of something we did, for example, we will probably try to avoid acting that way again. We also can imagine how our doing something might appear to others—we might look foolish in their eyes, for example—before we actually engage in such actions. Based on our interpretations of how others might respond to that behavior, we can then modify our course of action to avoid possible

---

Put Up Your Hands! (Know What I Mean?)

In order for two people to interact or communicate, each must understand the point of view of the other. This may mean you have to put yourself in some unlikely positions. If a robber tells you to put your hands in the air, for example, you have to think like the robber as well as the victim in order to behave as you are expected to. If you don't, you may save your wallet but not your skin.

Blumer (1969) suggests that a robbery can only occur if both the robber and the victim can put themselves in the place of the other person. The robber, for example, can only understand the logic of his own demand for the victim to put his hands in the air by being able to imagine what it means to face the barrel end of a gun. In fact, the robber could not even make the verbal demand ("Put your hands up in the air") unless he understood the meaning it would have for the victim. The victim, likewise, "has to be able to see the command from the standpoint of the robber who gives the command; he has to grasp the intention and forthcoming action of the robber" (p. 10). Interaction is always oriented to the future, to what the other person will do, and the only way to anticipate the future is through this kind of mutual role-taking.

A newspaper account told how robbers broke in on a party and demanded that everyone turn over their valuables. The guests, thinking it was a put-on, refused to cooperate and dismissed the situation as a harmless spoof. They told the robbers to cut it out and stop joking, while they continued to joke about it themselves. Faced with this totally unexpected reaction, the robbers were stymied in their efforts and finally fled the party empty-handed. They were arrested later trying to break into another house. Still confused, they told the police of their experience at the party.

Thus, even robbers must count on the mutual understanding of their victims if they are to make a success of their way of life. When the victim refuses to validate the robber's identity as a robber and defines him instead as a prankster, the robber must be willing to assume a new identity—even that of murderer—if the robbery is to succeed.

---

embarrassment. In the final analysis, the ability of people to both act and reflect on their actions from various perspectives lies at the root of what is distinctively human.

There is an important difference between role-taking and role-playing. Role-taking—the process of imaginatively putting yourself in another's place and considering what they expect of you, or how they might respond to behaviors you are thinking of enacting—precedes role-playing. It is on the basis of role-taking that we fashion the roles we actually play and the role performances we undertake.

The Socialization Process

The process through which individuals learn what society expects of them is called **socialization.** According to Mead, the development of the self occurs in childhood in two distinct phases of this process: the play stage and the game stage. Mead's writings on childhood play are probably the most important interactionist statement on self-development.

The Play Stage

The **play stage,** according to Mead, is the period in which children develop the ability to actually take on the characteristics associated with others in particular roles. They become able to look at themselves from the point of view of others. During this stage a girl, for example, learns to put herself in the role of a mommy, doctor, teacher, or TV star. She is able to cast herself as a social object and then respond in the role of others to that object. In playing doctor, for example, she may talk to others as she interprets how a doctor might actually talk to her. During this period the child also realizes that there is a direct linkage between a person's status (mother, father, police officer, and so on) and behavior. The importance of "child's play" in creating durable male and female roles has been noted by social scientists (c.f., Cahill, 1994).

For Mead, the most important quality of children's role-playing during the play period is its unorganized character. During this period children pass from playing one role to another in a very inconsistent and erratic fashion. They have proceeded beyond sheer imitation of others' behaviors, but they do not yet have any *unified* conception of themselves. In referring to the play stage, Mead notes:

> The child is one thing at one time and another at another, and what he is at one moment does not determine what he is at another. That is both the charm of childhood as well as its inadequacy. You cannot count on the child; you cannot assume that all the things he does are going to determine what he will do at any moment. He is not organized into a whole. The child has no definite character, no definite personality. (1934:159)

In the play stage children may be able to take the roles of particular others toward themselves, but as yet they fail to see how the behavior of others toward them represents the expectations of larger social groups. They are unable to view themselves from the point of view of the community or, even more abstractly, the society. They may understand, for example, what parents mean when they tell them to be good. They will learn later that it is not only their parents who expects them to be good, but others in the neighborhood, the school, and the larger society as well.

The Game Stage

After children have mastered the ability to take the roles of particular others, they are presented more and more with the task of responding to the expectations of several persons simultaneously. According to Mead, it is participation in the **game stage** that equips the child for this task. Games are distinguished from play by the presence of an organized body of *rules* to which the participants must orient their responses. Rather than reacting to particular individuals, as in the case of play, children must now begin to see themselves in relation to *all* the roles played by the other participants.

In order to play baseball, for example, a girl must know how her position (third base, let's say) relates to those of every other person on the team. When a ball is hit to her, she must realize that she should throw it to first base, not because she likes the person on first base but because that is what the rules of the game dictate. She must also conceptualize how her team stands in relation to the opposing team. She must throw to first base to put the batter out. That is what the game is all about.

In effect, then, in order for the game of baseball to be played, all the participants must have a conception of how to act vis-à-vis their own team and the opposing one. In doing so each player develops a conception of how a particular position is really part of a larger social organization called "the team." Mead observes that in the game stage, "a definite unity . . . is introduced into the organization of other selves!" In the play stage, by contrast, there is "a simple succession of one role after another" (1934:158–59).

If you think of the baseball game as a metaphor for the organization of society in general, you can see that we are truly functioning members of a social order only when we know the basic "ground rules" and can organize our actions with reference to the whole group. Mead's terms for all of those countless others whose behaviors and expectations are considered and interpreted by individuals in formulating their own behaviors is the **generalized other.** The generalized other, it should be stressed, does not refer to any particular, concrete person. Rather, it is an abstract configuration of all the relevant *roles* and *rules* that we must take into account in order to function successfully in any social environment. In the case of the baseball game, the team constitutes the most important generalized other to which the players must orient their actions.

The socialization process through which the child eventually comprehends societal expectations can be illustrated by an example from Peter Berger and Thomas Luckmann's classic, *The Social Construction of Reality* (1967). They note:

> [T]here is a progression from "Mummy is angry with me now" to "Mummy is angry with me *whenever* I spill the soup." As additional significant others (father, grandfather, older sister, and so on) support the mother's negative attitude toward soup-spilling the generality of the norm is subjectively extended. The decisive step comes when the child recognizes that *everybody* is against soup-spilling, and the norm is generalized to "*One* does not spill soup"—"one" being himself as part of a generality that includes, in principle, all of society insofar as it is significant to the child. (1967:132–33; emphasis in original)

Components of the Self: The I and the Me

If we were to look at Mead's conception of the socialization process and the development of the self uncritically, we might be led to believe that all our behaviors are totally determined by others, leaving no room for us to do anything but conform completely to their expectations. This robotlike image does not square very well with either our knowledge of people or our own life experiences, however. Although we are certainly constrained by society, we do have some freedom of action. Mead takes this into account by introducing the idea that the self has two components—the I and the me.

In chapter 1 we emphasized that everyday life must be analyzed in a way that takes into account both the expectations of society and the unique, individual interpretations of the world that people make. On the one hand, we formulate our behaviors in terms of our interpretations of the broad expectations of others in general, represented by the concept of the generalized other. Ultimately a society is possible only because the individuals in it carry around a picture of that society in their heads. People's behaviors constructed in terms of that picture of the generalized other reflect what Mead termed **the me**. The me represents the more conventional aspects of the self—those aspects which respond to social conventions. At the same time, because we are self-conscious, reflective beings, we can never completely predict what our own responses will be in any situation. **The I**, in contrast to the me, consists of those particular idiosyncratic, personal factors that enter into our communications with others.

In the example of the baseball game, the third baseman, like every other player on the team, no doubt wants to play well. She wants her team to win. In that sense she organizes her own behaviors (her me's) in terms of trying to follow the rules of the game and meet the expectations of fellow team members (the generalized other). But just how well she will play in a game cannot surely be predicted in advance. Her mind may wander, for example, and she may drop an easy pop-up. She might get angry enough at the umpire to show it and get thrown out of the game. The range of such unanticipated, novel, subjective responses reflects the operation of the I.

Development of the self is thus an ongoing process in which our actions are shaped by the continuous conversations we have with our "selves." These conversations have two components. We ask ourselves (1) what does society (the generalized other) want me to do in this situation, and (2) how do I personally feel about these expectations? Do I respond enthusiastically, angrily, halfheartedly? We are, in sum, only partially the product of the roles we learn from childhood onward. Our behaviors are affected not only by all our various learned social roles, but by our personal, subjective interpretations of the situations we face. This is the essence of the self as process. There is an impulse to act, imagined responses to such an act, imagined alternative actions, and some eventual resolution of the inner dialogue into some overt course of action. We can see this process in what takes place when, for example, we feel caught between what we want to do and what others want us to do. Suppose you have been invited to a party, but would really rather spend a quiet evening at home. You might say to yourself, "If I go I won't have a good time because I'm tired and don't feel like partying. But if I don't go, I'll hurt my friends' feelings. Maybe they'll understand if I explain that I'm tired. But what if they remember that I didn't go out with them last weekend? I guess

I'll go but not stay long." You can hear the alternation between the "I" and "me" in this internal conversation (Hewitt, 2003).

Gender Identity

Through taking the role of the generalized other, children learn the rules of public conduct and acquire skills in applying those rules in everyday interaction. A fundamental aspect of this process is the acquisition of **gender identity**.

In keeping with the premise that identity is socially anchored, interactionists reject the idea that gender identity is biologically determined. Rather, it is a product of social interaction.

> Gender identity is constructed as others reproduce sexually differentiated behavior by reinforcing interaction that is in keeping with gender ideals. The social construction of gender continues as children respond to others' expectations in a process of unwitting participation—a process that centers on children's active, but unaware, participation in fashioning gender. (Musolf, 1996:311)

To a great extent, children learn to become self-regulating participants in society. By displaying masculine and feminine behavior—that is, claiming a gendered identity—individuals conform to the gender ideals of society. Thus, notions of gender not only are socially constructed, but are reproduced. Gender-segregation behaviors are rehearsed in childhood and performed in adulthood (Cahill, 1994). Assuming that the world as we know it is what we want to reproduce, gender ideals remain relatively static as conforming behavior is rewarded. To the extent that nonconformity (deviance) is no longer subject to punishment, gender ideals become more flexible and social change occurs. Each generation modifies gender ideals. That is, today men in U.S. society may wear earrings; however, we are not ready to accept men in makeup and a dress!

Socialization in general and gender socialization in particular vary across racial/ethnic lines and social class boundaries. Earlier perspectives on race tend to be assimilationist, assuming that African Americans embrace and pass on to their children the gender norms of the dominant white society. An Afrocentric perspective challenges this view, maintaining that the unique historical experiences of blacks have worked to de-emphasize rigid gender distinctions, and that relative gender neutrality exists in black families' child-rearing practices. Research by Hill and Sprague (1999) supports this. Whereas working-class whites in their study emphasize obedience/respect for boys, and lower-middle-class whites emphasize happiness and self-esteem for girls, blacks seem to make fewer gender distinctions overall. Other research on early childhood socialization suggests that Hispanic parents differ from parents of other ethnic groups in their child-rearing values and the interpersonal behavior they want their children to display at home and school (Zayas and Solari, 1994). And research on social class differences continues to find greater gender stereotyping among parents who are lower in social status, less educated, and full-time homemakers (Hoffman and Kloska, 1995). It seems clear that race and social class interact to shape the intergenerational construction of gender in families. Parents operate within their own specific economic and social constraints. In struggling within these constraints and with gendered expectations—both their own and the ones they read in others—they draw on the values they learned from their own families and communities, which are marked by race and class. "In parenting, and probably in the rest of life, race, class, and gender dynamics interact" (Hill and Sprague, 1999:497).

The Interdependence of Self and Society

Mead's conception of the self refers, in the fullest sense, to the interdependence of the individual and the society. He locates the self in society. The creation of the self is an ongoing process that emerges from the person's interactions with others in society. There is a point in the development of the self when people can view themselves from the perspective of others. At this point the person is able to treat the world as a symbolic entity—to endow the world with meaning. This capacity for symbolic behavior makes it possible for humans to coordinate their actions with those of others and thereby modify or even substantially transform society. The self is simultaneously a reflection of society as it exists and a source of change in it.

Our daily lives are describable in terms of these theoretical distinctions. Everyday behaviors represent a combination of conformity and novelty, of response to the expectations of others and more impulsive personal reactions to situations. In any situation, we cannot ourselves know exactly how we will act. We know the parameters within which we are expected to act, but such knowledge does not guarantee complete predictability of behavior. In a fundamental way we really do not know how we are going to respond in any situation until we actually begin to act. We cannot, for example, fully anticipate feelings and expressions of anger, pleasure, relief, indifference, confusion, and the like as we move through even the most routine day-to-day situations.

Human behavior, in Mead's terms, is constructed through the interchange of the two aspects of the self—the I and the me. The me encourages conformity to societal expectations and reinforces existing social arrangements. By contrast, the I permits personal interpretations which allow for nonconformity, the construction of multiple social realities, and ultimately social change (see box).

Social Reality and Nonconformity

Social reality should not be thought of as a "thing" existing objectively "out there" in the world. Rather, reality is something that human beings continually negotiate, re-create, alter, and disagree on. Humans construct so much of the reality within which they live that it is difficult to identify one reality that exists for all people (Sarbin and Kitsuse, 1994). In a very real sense reality is the product of a political process in which different individuals and groups vie to have their idea of reality become accepted as *the* reality for everyone (see chapter 6). The successful definition of alternate realities as inauthentic, pathological, or deviant reinforces the dominant view of reality and makes it appear more immutable and concrete than it actually is (Berger and Luckmann, 1967).

In our daily activities, we assume that we are responding to the same realities as others. Suppose, for example, that the clock radio wakens you with a news report. Simply in order to understand the news, you must assume that the words being used to describe the events mean roughly the same thing to

In the Absence of Human Interaction

In November 1970, a nearly blind woman appeared at a Los Angeles welfare office with her 13½-year-old daughter. From about 20 months of age, "Genie" had been kept in a back room by her 70-year-old father (who later committed suicide), isolated from language (and significant human interaction), and frequently restrained on a potty chair. Genie was incontinent, could not chew solid food, spat indiscriminately, walked with a "bunny-like" gait, and could not speak. She was placed in the Children's Hospital of Los Angeles where she flourished amidst the attention of psychiatrists and psychologists. She learned words, became more outgoing, and was able to communicate emotionally. Susan Curtiss, the linguist who worked with Genie, was particularly interested in testing the "critical period" theory of language acquisition, which is premised on the belief that if language is not learned by puberty, normal language development will not occur. Her book, *Genie: A Psycholinguistic Story of a Modern "Wild Child"* (1977), is a scientific account of Genie's development during the four years when federal grants provided support. Although Genie acquired many words, and some grasp of syntax, she left out prepositions, articles, and had difficulty using pronouns. One of the most interesting aspects of Genie's speech was her use of "I," "me," and "you" interchangeably. Compare this to Helen Keller:

> When I learned the meaning of "I" and "me" and found that I was something, I began to think. Then consciousness first existed for me. Thus it was not the sense of touch that brought me knowledge. It was the awakening of my soul that first rendered my senses their value, their cognizance of objects, names, qualities, and properties. Thought made me conscious of love, joy, and all the emotions. (1904/1908:117)

Keller's choice of "I" and "me" is significant, "for the pronouns form a system, a framework of consciousness and personhood; the words 'girl' and 'Helen' had come long before" (Leiber, 1997:336).

Genie never reached this point. After a period of flourishing, she reached a plateau and made little advance beyond, reinforcing the conclusion that there is a critical period for language acquisition. Unfortunately, Genie's story does not have a happy ending. After the four-year period during which federal grants provided support (when Genie was both nurtured and exposed to extensive language work and testing), Genie lived with her mother for a brief period. She was then placed in a succession of foster homes, and later was permanently institutionalized, regressing to a point where she was distant and nonverbal.

the newscaster as they do to you. The newscaster makes the same assumption. In reporting some catastrophe such as an earthquake or tornado, for example, it is assumed that the listener knows what the phenomenon is. Rarely does a newscaster attempt to define such words as *tornado* or *earthquake.*

Having been bombarded with the morning's scoreboard of human misery and happiness, you probably still have enough fortitude to leave your home and go out, entering the world of anonymous others. Consider the assumption of trust you must make in order to navigate your way through the day's activities. In going to your job or class, for example, you must assume that others share your understanding of the social conventions relating to personal safety. As a pedestrian, you assume that others know how to move their bodies or control their cars to avoid bumping into you (Whyte, 1988). Other pedestrians or drivers make the same assumption about you. If you are driving, you must assume that other drivers also know the meaning of green lights, stop signs, railroad crossings, and so forth. Think what driving in any metropolitan area would be like without such understandings—suddenly Boston comes to mind!

While smooth daily functioning depends on the assumption of a commonly shared social reality, there is also an element of uncertainty in the construction of reality. You must anticipate that your own version may not be totally shared by others. You also cannot be completely sure how you and others will behave in an anticipated or ongoing interaction. In any social situation, allowances must be made for the unexpected behaviors of the participants.

Sources of Nonconformity

When behaviors seriously deviate from societal expectations, they are defined as deviance (see chapter 9) or nonconformity. In the interactionist perspective, nonconforming behaviors can be explained in terms of the human ability to symbolize and the existence of multiple social realities within the society. Generational differences also encourage the existence of deviant or nonconforming behaviors.

The Ability to Symbolize

From the interactionist perspective, society is formed through the symbolic communication occurring between two or more persons. Since, as we have noted, there is no inherent meaning in an object, it is always possible for individuals, through their symbolic activity, to redefine objects in ways that challenge existing definitions of reality. The transformation of the meaning of *Negro* to *black* in racial terms provides dramatic evidence of this. As a consequence of the 1960s civil rights movement, blacks began to think of the former term as something imposed on them by whites. The label *black* or *African American*, carrying the meaning of racial pride and a rich cultural heritage, now is widely used. Similar changes have occurred in the definitions of gender as a result of the feminist movement (Epstein, 1997).

Symbolic behavior makes it possible to reject the symbols used by those in one's immediate physical surroundings and to identify with symbols used by others elsewhere. A person's **reference groups** (those groups providing standards for the person's behaviors) need not be confined to others who are physically present. In that sense, the ability to symbolize provides humans with a continual source of nonconformity. Ward Abbott illustrates how symbolic activity can lead to nonconformity in his statement about the relationship of the artist to the state:

> The artist is doubly subversive in that only a bullet can stop him. He feeds on changes as others shy away from them. Josip Brodsky, exiled in Siberia, infuriated officials by *enjoying his life there.* Unlike a banker, the artist carries his work in his mind. To express it, he needs only a stub of a pencil and a scrap of paper, or charcoal and any surface. One of the last acts of Gaudier-Brezka in the trenches of World War I, surrounded by death and desolation, was to carve, out of a bit of blown-up rifle butt, a splendidly Brezkian sculpture. (1975:89; italics added)

The example of the subversive artist suggests that individuals are, to a substantial degree, responsible for determining their environments. The term *environment,* it is important to stress, encompasses *both* physical objects as well as our ideas about those objects. Like any symbolic construct, the meaning of an environment is something created and conferred on it by human beings acting through social communications with others. Even physical objects such as mountains and rivers can have vastly different meanings for members of different groups, based on how those groups intend to use such objects. For some Native Americans, for example, a mountain may symbolize a holy place where the spirits of one's ancestors reside. For modern recreationists, by contrast, the mountain may be a setting for sport and athletic activities such as mountain climbing and skiing. So physical objects, then, take on significance in people's lives as meanings are conferred on them, based on how those objects will be used.

There are, however, real limits to our capacity for totally determining what the nature of our immediate environments will be. However much the artists Brodsky and Gaudier-Brezka were able to redefine their lives in Siberia and World War I trenches, they still had to cope with both the physical features of their wartime surroundings as well as the socially constructed decisions made by powerful "others"—such as politicians and military officers—who put them in those trenches in the first place. Thus it can be argued that we both determine the environment and are determined by it.

Despite the physical and social constraints we face, the self-reflecting character of interactions makes nonconformity a continual possibility. To use Jean Paul Sartre's term, it is "bad faith" to claim that we are utterly without choice in a particular situation. Even individuals being tortured decide when, or indeed whether, to give in to their tormentors. The choice in an extreme situation might be death, but it is an available choice.

The Existence of Multiple Social Realities

In highly diverse, stratified societies such as contemporary American society, several realities exist concurrently. People at different levels or locations in the society, possessing more or less power, prestige, and wealth, have very different images of the world. Definitions of reality adhered to by people are influenced by their position in the social structure, as Berger and Luckmann (1967) and, most notably, Karl Mannheim (1952) have suggested. Various racial, ethnic, and religious groups also engage in different responses, and therefore give different meanings to their worlds. Moreover, individuals develop commitments to their distinctive values, attitudes, and lifestyles. They may even take action against those representing alternative or contrary versions of reality, particularly if the others' reality is perceived as threatening to their own (Scott, 1990).

Differences in power influence morality, values, and therefore the behaviors that are deemed socially acceptable. Everyone does not have an equal role in the development and maintenance of society's dominant or official versions of reality. In our society, for example, the medical profession's authoritative definitions of illness commonly prevail over those of Christian Scientists; psychiatrists' definitions of subjective experience prevail over those of patients; social service providers' definitions take precedence over clients' definitions of their own problems, and so on (Cahill, 1998). Psychiatrists, for example, have exercised substantial power in defining mental illness. Erving Goffman's (1961) classic piece on "the moral career of the mental patient" describes how mental institutions and their staffs convince patients to internalize the psychiatric view of reality and of themselves. In the "politics of reality" of the mental institution, patients are virtually powerless.

There are always some people who are unwilling to accept others' notions about proper behavior. If they seek each other out and agree to act collectively, they may decide to challenge the dominant version of reality. Sometimes these challenges are successful, and new expectations for behavior become institutionalized over time. The women's movement, for example, influenced legislation prohibiting gender-related discrimination in jobs and education, and it has altered in many ways the relations of men and women as friends, lovers, and colleagues. More often, however, challenges to established reality fail. Those with a strong investment in the status quo react quickly, vigorously, and sometimes violently to any threat to their reality. In every society, agencies (such as prisons and mental hospitals) and roles (such as shamans, psychiatrists, clergy, police officers) are created to manage reality disrupters.

Goffman, in his numerous works (1959, 1961, 1963, 1971), describes the construction of social realities as a fluid affair. The maintenance of these realities is subject to the continual negotiation of the participants. If the term *subversion* were stripped of its political and negative connotations, it could be applied more broadly to everyday interactions. Individuals constantly bend or subvert established rules and expectations to their own purposes. They include students who turn in papers late and pedestrians who jaywalk, as well as drug users who steal to maintain their habit.

A continual source of nonconformity in society is the actions of people and groups seeking to have their versions of reality either accepted by others or translated into the accepted version of reality. Deviance and nonconformity arise from the variety of perspectives produced in different social worlds. We could say that when a person raised in one social world, equipped for travel on a particular symbolic highway, enters another world's symbolic thoroughfares, the result could be a multisymbol accident!

The Nature of Generational Differences

Another source of nonconformity, in social terms, lies in the different viewpoints of the various generations in a society. Biologically, a generation may be thought of as a group of people who were born at about the same time. Sociologically, a **generation** should be regarded as people who have experienced similar *historical* events at similar points in their lives. Others who have not undergone such experiences at the same time in their own lives find it difficult to understand the meanings conferred on particular events by those who have. Depending on the nature of the historical situation, members of different generations may be thought of as inhabiting different social worlds and recognizing different social realities.

Different generations establish collective memories based on their members' unique experiences of historical events occurring during adolescence and early adulthood. One study found that people's memories of World War II and the Vietnam War, for example, were strongly influenced by their age at the time of the event, with the memories being "strongest for those in their youth at the time of the event" (Schuman and Scott, 1989:366). While youth is no doubt a critical time period for all generations, the nature of the memories that each generation collectively retains will certainly differ since young people in one generation experience different events than those who are young in other historical eras. We can only wonder what the collective memories of the September 11, 2001, terrorist attacks on the World Trade Center and Pentagon will be.

The development of different generational styles is one reason the socialization process is not a completely repetitive one. New generations do not adopt the behaviors expected of them by society without question. Because they have not themselves had a hand in the creation of the reality they are expected to appropriate as their own, they are bound to experience it differently than do older generations. The older generations are confronted with the problem of legitimating their reality to the new generations, and the newcomers may well challenge the assumption that they will accept it. Not being satisfied with the explanations of their elders, they may proceed to subvert that reality—through symbols of dress, music, language, and so on—in the course of their daily lives. At some point they may succeed in constructing a new reality which they must then legitimate to their own children, and so on.

The concept of generation calls attention to a socially derived process related to the "rhythm" of social life. Because of its effects on the construction of social reality, it represents another continual source of nonconformity and change in society.

Conclusion

Our concerns in this chapter have been primarily theoretical, and the discussion has been somewhat abstract. To conclude that there is no relationship between the issues discussed and your everyday life would be to miss an important point, however. You cannot begin to understand how associations with others are ordered and made predictable and sensible unless you have some theoretical understanding of human relations.

As we noted in chapter 1, sociological analysis, particularly the analysis of everyday events, requires more than simple description. To get beyond description and discover underlying forms of social interaction, sociologists adopt different theoretical perspectives. The authors of this book have adopted the perspective of symbolic interaction. In this chapter we have introduced the central concepts in the interactionist perspective: symbolic communication, the emergence and development of the self through interaction, the process of role-taking, the existence of multiple social realities, and the sources of nonconformity in social life. We believe that these ideas provide a foundation for an understanding of human interaction and communication, and we will refer to them throughout this volume.

Symbolic communication provides a means of predictable interactions in a world where things and situations have no fixed meanings. Symbols mobilize our reactions to the world and help us coordinate our actions with the actions of others through socially shared meanings. They help us conceptualize the social world in which we live. By conferring meanings, we can transform our environment in concert with others.

The symbolic interactionist perspective stresses the interconnections between people and society. As originally conceived by George Herbert Mead, it provides a picture of social life in which individuals make their own interpretations of the situations in which they are involved, while simultaneously taking societal expectations into account. Analytically, this idea is expressed in Mead's description of the relationships between the generalized other, the I, and the me. The components of the self operate together to maintain a balance between conventional behavior and nonconformity. The social self thus both reflects society as it exists and provides a means of changing it.

Any social encounter requires role-taking, or understanding the positions of other people. In order to role-take successfully, we must continually assess available information about others. We cannot engage in meaningful communication with others without first identifying who they are. Knowledge of others' social attributes, such as their age, sex, and occupation, strongly affects our judgments about the type of people they are. In the next chapter we will examine the central role of information in role-taking efforts.

DEFINITIONS

Game stage   The stage of the socialization process during which children become able to understand the morality of their own behaviors. The game stage is distinguished from the play stage in that children orient themselves to a body of rules that spell out proper behavior.

Gender identity   A sense of self in terms of femininity or masculinity; i.e., as feminine or masculine.

Generalized other   An abstract configuration of all the relevant rules and roles that we must take into account to function successfully in any social environment. In the most abstract sense, the generalized other is society as a whole.

Generation   A group of people who have experienced similar historical events at similar points in their lives. Members of different generations inhabit different social worlds and recognize different social realities.

Looking glass self   Cooley's notion that our self is based on our interpretation of others' appraisals of us. That is, others are like a mirror in which we see ourselves reflected. However, that reflection is what we *imagine* others think of us, not necessarily what they might really think.

Nonconformity   Behaviors that deviate from generally held cultural expectations or social norms.

Play stage   The stage of the socialization process during which children learn certain roles by playing at them, as when they play doctor, nurse, police officer, and so on.

Reference groups   Any social group used by an individual as a standard for evaluating his or her behavior. One need not officially belong to a group to have it as a reference group.

Role-taking   The process through which individuals imaginatively put themselves in the positions of other people in order to evaluate how others see them and their behaviors. Individuals ordinarily modify their behaviors on the basis of their role-taking efforts.

Sign   An object to which a fixed, unchanging response is made. In contrast to a symbol, a sign is characterized by the fact that its meaning is identified with its physical form. Animals generally respond to objects as signs, not as symbols.

Social reality   The totality of meanings about the world on which the members of a group or society agree. It is possible that different individuals and groups will hold quite different pictures of reality. In any complex society there are multiple realities.

Socialization   The process through which people learn the behaviors required by their cultures. It is also the process through which culture is transmitted from one generation to the next. Without the process of socialization, society could not exist.

Symbol   An object to which any meaning can be assigned. The meanings assigned to symbols can be arbitrary and are not determined by the physical characteristics of objects or the sensory experiences they may cause.

Symbolic communication   Communication that involves people's ongoing interpretations of each other's action.

The I   One of two aspects of the human self. It is the spontaneous, creative, unpredictable part of the self. The I consists of subjective, idiosyncratic, and unanticipated factors that enter into our communications with others.

The me   One of two aspects of the human self. It is that part of the self that is conventional; the conforming, rule-following part.

The self   The view of oneself derived from the ability to evaluate one's behaviors from the point of view of others, ultimately from the point of the standards of society as a whole. The self is capable of both acting (as a subject) and then, through an ongoing internal conversation, reflecting on its actions (as an object).

Discussion Questions

1. Do you think that human beings are uniquely different from other animals because of their symbol-using capacity? What does it imply about the distinctiveness of human communication that we can discuss this and other questions in class?

2. Can anything you do (or think, for that matter) have any meaning apart from your assessment of how some other people are likely to evaluate your behaviors?

3. Reflect on your activities during a typical day. To what extent do your behaviors represent a combination of conformity and novelty, of your responses to the expectations of others and more impulsive reactions to situations? In which kinds of situations is it hardest for you to anticipate just how you will behave? In which situations is it easiest?

4. Think of a time when you did not conform to some person's or group's expectations. Now think of a situation in which you did not want to conform to the expectations of others but did so anyway. What distinguished the two situations? In what way were your behaviors constructed in response to symbols?

5. What is the relationship between the kinds of games people play as children and the kinds of roles they later perform in adult life?

6. The authors suggested that every generation is confronted with the problem of legitimating its view of reality to the next generation. In what areas do you feel that your own conception of reality is fundamentally different from that held by your parents? Describe some of the symbols that reflect the different generational realities.

References

Abbott, W. 1975. "Begin by shooting the poet." *Nation* 221 (August 2):88–89.

Becker, E. 1962. *The Birth and Death of Meaning.* Glencoe, IL: Free Press.

Berger, P., and T. Luckmann. 1967. *The Social Construction of Reality.* New York: Doubleday.

Blumer, H. 1969. *Symbolic Interaction: Perspective and Method.* Englewood Cliffs, NJ: Prentice Hall.

Cahill, S. 1994. "And a child shall lead us? Children, gender, and perspectives by incongruity." In *Symbolic Interaction: An Introduction to Social Psychology,* edited by N. J. Herman and L. T. Reynolds, pp. 459–69. Dix Hills, NY: General Hall Press.

_____. 1998. "Toward a sociology of the person." *Sociological Theory* 16:131–48.

Charon, J. 2002. *The Meaning of Sociology.* 7th ed. Upper Saddle River, NJ: Prentice Hall.

Cooley, C. H. 1902. *Human Nature and the Social Order.* New York: Charles Scribner's Sons.

Curtiss, S. 1977. *Genie: A Psycholinguistic Story of a Modern "Wild Child."* New York: Academic Press.

Epstein, C. 1997. "Sameness and difference between men and women." *Journal of Social Issues* 53(2):259–78.

Gardner, R., and B. Gardner. 1969. "Teaching sign language to a chimpanzee." *Science* 165:664–72.

Goffman, E. 1959. *The Presentation of Self in Everyday Life.* New York: Doubleday.

———. 1961. *Asylums.* New York: Doubleday.

———. 1963. *Behavior in Public Places.* New York: Free Press.

———. 1971. *Relations in Public.* New York: Basic Books.

Hewitt, J. 2003. *Self and Society.* 9th ed. Boston: Allyn & Bacon.

Hill, S., and J. Sprague. 1999. "Parenting in black and white families: The interaction of gender with race and class." *Gender & Society* 13:480–502.

Hoffman, L., and D. Kloska. 1995. "Parents' gender-based attitudes toward marital roles and child-rearing: Development and validation of new measures." *Sex Roles* 32:273–95.

Keller, H. 1904/1908. *The World I Live In.* New York: Century.

Kohler, W. 1927. *The Mentality of Apes.* New York: Harcourt Brace.

Leiber, J. 1995. "Apes, signs, and syntax." *American Anthropologist* 97(2):374.

———. 1997. "Nature's experiments, society's closures." *Journal for the Theory of Social Behavior* 27:325–43.

Mannheim, K. 1952. *Essays on the Sociology of Knowledge.* London: Routledge & Kegan Paul.

Mead, G. 1934. *Mind, Self, and Society.* Chicago: University of Chicago Press.

Musolf, G. 1996. "Interactionism and the child: Cahill, Corsaro, and Denzin on childhood socialization." *Symbolic Interaction* 19(4):303–21.

Sarbin, T., and J. Kitsuse. 1994. *Constructing the Social.* Thousand Oaks, CA: Sage.

Savage-Rumbaugh, E. 1998. *Kanzi: The Ape at the Brink of the Human Mind.* Cambridge: Oxford University Press.

Schuman, H., and J. Scott. 1989. "Generations and collective memory." *American Sociological Review* 54: 359–81.

Scott, R. 1990. *Domination and the Arts of Resistance.* New Haven, CT: Yale University Press.

Whyte, W. H. 1988. *City.* New York: Anchor Books.

Zayas, L. H., and F. Solari. 1994. "Early-childhood socialization in Hispanic families: Context, culture, and practice implications." *Professional Psychology: Research and Practice* 25:200–6.

Suggested Audiovisuals

PBS. 1994. *Secret of a Wild Child.*

PBS. 2000. *Nature: Inside the Animal Mind.*

The Gorilla Foundation. *A Conversation with Koko.* (VHS and DVD)

Sociology on the Web

You might enjoy checking out www.koko.org, the Web site for The Gorilla Foundation/Koko.org, P.O. Box 620530, Woodside, CA 94062.

three

UNDERSTANDING
INTERACTION

Living in a modern society and engaging in everyday activities involve virtually constant interactions in a variety of settings and with a multitude of different people, each of whom may demand a different posture. A person's attempts to get along with others or to get his or her own way with them in these various social arenas can require an astounding amount of practical and social knowledge. There also must be reasonable agreement among the people involved on their view of social reality. Otherwise human communication—and society itself—would be impossible.

The Need for Communication in Role-Taking

The process through which we act in awareness of others and continually adjust our own behaviors in accordance with the way others are acting depends on our distinctively human ability to role-take, as we noted in chapter 2. In order to infer correctly the intentions, motives, and goals of others, and therefore to predict their future behaviors, we must put ourselves in their place and attempt to view the situation as they do. We cannot gauge the meanings of others' acts and then respond appropriately unless we achieve some understanding of the way others are interpreting and making sense of the situation. Such role-taking is, of course, mutual. All people in any particular interaction are simultaneously formulating their behaviors in accordance with their assessments of the perceptions and expectations of others.

Failed Communications

This does not mean that the capacity for role-taking necessarily ensures that all interactions occur smoothly and without difficulty. In many everyday encounters, role-taking leads to incorrect inferences about others. We frequently find it difficult to understand why others act as they do. There is the possibility that our attempts at role-taking will lead us to formulate a definition of the situation that varies from the definition held by those with whom we are communicating. When this happens, a **failed communication** can result.

The college classroom is a setting which offers numerous possibilities for failed communications. Teachers often proceed under one set of assumptions about "intellectual work" while students operate under another. Teachers tend to value critical thinking. They may respond critically to comments made by students and push students to defend their own points of view. The teacher's goal—to help students think more analytically—may be misperceived by the students, however. They may consider teachers to be flaunting their superior knowledge or, worse still, to be putting the students down. The authors have identified this situation as the beginning of a vicious circle of sorts. The more that teachers try to instill in students a critical attitude toward their own ideas, the more students come to see faculty members as condescending (Karp and Yoels, 1976). In the classroom, as elsewhere, a host of misunderstandings may arise when people define the situation differently.

The greatest difficulty in assessing the meanings of another's actions ordinarily arises in those situations where we know very little about the other person. Differences in experiences, biographies, and cultural backgrounds increase the likelihood that two people will not understand one another. Those who have traveled in foreign countries should recognize the difficulty of role-taking with cultural strangers. In our own country, we tend to regard with caution the members of ethnic, class, or racial groups whose patterns of speech, grooming, dress, and demeanor vary from our own. The French historian Fernand Braudel (1981) argued that the most visible cultural differences between the elite, or ruling classes, and the masses have always involved speech, etiquette, protocol, and even body language. Poor people who manage to achieve high rank may still find it difficult to overcome cultural barriers that exclude them from full membership in higher social circles. They may not immediately know how to talk, walk, and generally act "correctly."

Several studies on the subjective experience of social mobility illustrate this. David Karp's (1986) study of professionals who came from working-class circumstances suggests that our original class position is a status requiring negotiation throughout our life. People do not shake off their original class position as a snake sheds its skin, but continue to feel the lingering effects of their inherited class membership. Despite having risen into the ranks of professional workers, respondents in Karp's study reported continued feelings of marginality, discomfort, and inauthenticity. In a study of working-class students in elite law schools, Granfield (1991) found that although these students entered law school with class pride, this began to diminish fairly quickly. The students came to define themselves as different from non-working-class students and began to view their class backgrounds as a burden, leading them to experience a "crisis in competency." Granfield describes this as a "hidden injury of class" (Sennet and Cobb, 1973), a psychological burden that working-class students experienced as they came to acquire the "identity beliefs" associated with middle-class society. Working-class students dealt with class stigma by managing information about their backgrounds using such strategies as adopting the dress code of higher class students and developing different interpersonal skills. As one author explains, "Working-class people do not have the quiet hands or the neutral faces of the privileged classes" (Zandy, 1995:5). Academics are not exempt— Diane Reay (1997), who has written about working-class women who become academics, suggests that these women are unlikely ever to feel at home in academia. In her own case, she vacillates between getting angry about middle-class privilege and feeling guilty because she is now implicated in it. According to Reay, her own experience of growing up working-class has left vivid memories of the heritage and history of her social origins imprinted on her consciousness. However, "that consciousness, rooted in working-class affiliation, appears increasingly to be a misfit; a sense of self both out of place and out of time . . ." (p. 79).

We can never experience exactly what another person is experiencing because we cannot be that person. We can only approximate through imagination what it must be like to be a given person in a given situation. Moreover, everyone is not equally able or willing to see the world as others do. In some cases the people involved are simply insensitive. In other situations they make little effort to take others' roles. In chapter 6 we will elaborate on the difference in role-taking between those in more powerful and less powerful positions.

The Importance of Information

In theoretical terms, role-taking requires us to distinguish between identification *with* and identification *of* others (Stone, 1962). In role-taking, one person tries to identify *with* another person or group and tries to imagine how others are seeing and conceiving a given situation. Before such identification with others can be made, however, it is necessary to place, categorize, or define them. Knowledge or identification *of* others' social class, gender, age, race, and the like is a requisite of the role-taking process. In other words, successful role-taking is heavily dependent on the *information* we pick up about others during the course of our interactions with them.

The building up of information is essential to the continuance of interactions. If we incorrectly assess both the information we possess about others and the amount and nature of the information they possess about us, the communication is likely to fail; that is, both persons in an interaction may incorrectly judge how much information of the other they actually possess. Further, the information they believe they have may be wrong. In either case, the result could be a "fractured interaction" as individuals act either out of ignorance or on the basis of incorrect information. Such interactions may result in embarrassment (see chapter 9) or, in the extreme case, the alienation of people from one another.

This chapter explores more deeply the relationships among information, role-taking, and the attribution of meanings in interactions. We will consider in detail the categories of information employed in assessing others, the manner in which information is processed, and the ways in which these assessments of others affect daily interactions. We will also consider how information is controlled to create favorable definitions of self in various situations.

Gathering and Processing Information about Others

When we confront others, particularly those about whom we have little biographical information, we form a total picture of them—a kind of gestalt—by considering simultaneously and fitting together a number of highly visible cues or clues about them. The specific meanings we attach to any attribute of a person may be modified as we assess it in conjunction with the person's other attributes. In most situations, we identify or form a more or less definite picture of others by taking into account their social attributes, such as age, gender, and race; their physical attributes, such as attractiveness, posture, facial expressions, and body type; their clothing; and their discourse, or what they say.

Information Provided by Social Attributes

Meaningful social interaction is rooted in the definitions of ongoing situations arrived at by the people involved in them. Participants in any encounter must be mutually oriented to the social expectations concerning the setting, to the purpose of their communications, and to any available information about others. Certain **social attributes** have informational significance because they help define the identities of self and others.

Individuals bring with them to all social encounters their own expectations about what to anticipate from other people with certain attributes. As a result of the socialization process Americans have experienced, for example, we have learned the significance in our society of being male or female, black or white, young or old. We have learned how to deal with these categories of people and, on occasion, how to manipulate them. Our interactions depend on our images or categorical conceptions of persons possessing such social attributes. For better or worse, we begin our interactions with culturally given conceptions of the ways that women and men; blacks, whites, Hispanics (etc.); Jews, Christians, Muslims (etc.); and teenagers or the elderly, to name a few categories, are likely to behave.

A large number of attributes may define a person socially or indicate a person's **social status.** A woman might, for example, simultaneously occupy the statuses of mother, Republican, member of the Better Business Bureau, Phi Beta Kappa, CEO, and so on. Sociologists make a useful distinction in discussing the properties of social attributes by differentiating between ascribed and achieved statuses. **Ascribed statuses** are those which are acquired at birth (such as gender and race), and **achieved statuses** are acquired during the course of a person's life (such as educational, organizational, and occupational statuses). This distinction alone, however, does not indicate the relative importance of the many statuses a person may occupy.

The Master Attributes

Some statuses are substantially more central than others, both to the way individuals view themselves and the way others view them. Such highly visible, essentially unalterable attributes as race, gender, and age sharply define a person in any situation. Because these attributes are so powerful, tending to supersede any other definitions of self that an individual might present to others, they are referred to as **master attributes**. Feagin and Sikes (1994) recount numerous examples of ill treatment experienced by middle-class blacks in restaurants, banks, and other public settings that illustrate the primacy of race over class. Even individuals of high status are not exempt from such treatment, as in the case of movie star/television producer Debbie Allen who was refused service by a white clerk in a Beverly Hills jewelry shop. Clearly her ascribed racial status took precedence over her achieved class status. In an incident that resulted in considerable media attention, black secret service agents sued Denny's restaurants because of their treatment in a Denny's in Annapolis, Maryland. They waited nearly an hour to be seated while white agents and other white patrons were seated.

One strategy used by African Americans in all income classes to cope with racism is to put on their defensive "shields." Feagin and Sikes (1994) describe a conversation with a retired music teacher in her 70s who is black. She contrasts her life with that of a white woman, who, like her, bathes, dresses, and puts on cosmetics before leaving the house each morning. Unlike the white woman, however, this black woman must put on her "shield" just before she leaves the house; that is, she has to be prepared psychologically and to steel herself in advance for racist insults and acts, and she has to be prepared even if nothing adverse happens on a particular day.

The information provided by such master attributes as gender, age, and race is so familiar that we can easily lose sight of its importance for the conduct of our everyday affairs. We may recognize just how dependent we are on such knowledge only when we are confronted by a situation where it is not available. Our interactions with others would be considerably complicated if their gender suddenly became unclear, for example. Our role-taking ability depends heavily on our ability to assess others' genders, and we would become disoriented in the absence of this information.

The overwhelming significance of gender as a strategic piece of information in guiding interactions is illustrated by transsexuals. These are individuals whose biological sex does not match their self-identification in terms of gender—"a girl brain in a boy body" (or vice versa) (Mason-Schrock, 1996). Presentation of self becomes the determining factor in being able to fully "pass" in society as a member of the opposite sex; that is, the transsexual individual must be able to cue correct gender identity. Transsexuals must learn to dress as a member of the opposite sex, walk, talk, use gestures and so on. Much time, attention, and effort is given to learning the ways of presenting oneself differently from the gender identity in which one was socialized as a child. It is on the basis of this presentation of self that others respond to the individual.

Much early socialization is directed toward recognizing the significance of gender and the appropriate behaviors associated with sexual differences. Conceptions of manhood and womanhood are cultural products acquired through interaction with others. Gender is one attribute that is ordinarily considered to be fixed and unchangeable. This piece of identity information pervades our lives in countless ways. It is questioned only in the unusual case of those who seek to alter that status (see box).

Names are also a central feature of a person's identity. Like gender, name is a piece of information that grounds the person's identity in the eyes of society. Both gender and name are "identity pegs" that become part of a person's official, documented identity:

> Whether an individual's biographical life is sustained in the minds of his intimates or in the personnel files of an organization, and whether the documentation of his personal identity is carried on his person or stored in files, he is an entity about which a record can be built up. . . . He is anchored as an object for biography. (Goffman, 1963b:62)

Kate Bornstein's (1994) experience as a transgendered individual illustrates the extent to which gender and name "anchor" biographies and social identities:

> Changing my name from Al to Kate was no big deal in Pennsylvania. It was a simple matter of filing a form with the court and publishing the name change in some unobtrusive "notices" column of a court-approved newspaper. Bingo—done. The problems came with changing all my documents. The driver's license was particularly interesting. Prior to my full gender change, I'd been pulled over once already dressed as a woman, yet holding my male driver's license—it wasn't something I cared to repeat. (p. 28)

She goes on to describe the reactions at the DMV. The first officer she encountered, not noticing that the name on the license is a male one, assumes the reason for her name change is marriage or divorce. He flirts with her and calls her "honey." When another officer notices that the name on the license is a male one and points this out to the first officer, he is, according to Bornstein, "crestfallen."

"I Don't Know How I'm Supposed to Refer to You"

Alice Myers was a tomboy growing up who dreamed of playing goalie for the U.S. Olympic hockey team. Her hair was so short and spiky that a sixth-grade teacher told Alice's parents, "Your son is doing well in my class." By the summer after her junior year in high school, Alice had realized that she was transgendered. When senior year began, Alice had become Alex, who wore a coat and tie to class. According to Myers, it confused his teachers, who were unable to control the class at times. He reported that one teacher took him aside and said, "I don't know how I'm supposed to refer to you." When Myers applied to Harvard, his college interview ended abruptly when the interviewer noticed the name Alice on a form, while Alex, in coat and tie, sat before him. (Alex explained his change of gender.) A week later, Myers was called in for another interview because the alumnus who interviewed him had been unable to give a fair opinion.

Myers legally changed his name during the summer of 1996 when he turned 18. He managed to keep his biological sex (female) secret for his first two months at Harvard, but the presence of so many of his former classmates made anonymity impossible. According to Myers, "For the first few weeks people were treating me as a nerdy, sort of conservative white guy." In November, he came out to other dorm residents. Although there was no open hostility, according to one of his dormmates, ". . . some of the guys here don't know what to make of him. . . ."

At Harvard, Myers sparked a campus-wide argument that reflects a larger debate in American society, and in the medical community, about the boundaries of gender and sex. And there has been some success. Myers successfully lobbied Harvard's student government to add protections for transgendered undergraduates to its constitution and appealed to the administration to change its discrimination policy to protect transgendered individuals. At the same time, the Cambridge city council voted unanimously to include protections for "gender expressions" in the city's Human Rights Ordinance.

Myers describes himself as a living, breathing example of the notion that gender and sex don't naturally go together, that gender is a construct. "Man and woman—those are societal molds," says Myers. "I think it's a big trap. I believe gender and sex are two different things. They are not complimentary forces. . . . And I'm hardly the first person to feel this way" (Mathews, 1997:1E).

The way medical teams manage the gender assignment of intersexed infants (hermaphrodites who are born with ambiguous genitals) illustrates the idea that gender is as much a social as it is a biological reality. Kessler (1996) has criticized physicians who rush to surgically "correct" genital ambiguity, pointing out that their decisions are influenced as much by cultural factors as by medical ones: medical technology is used to convert the non-normative (intersexuality) into the normative (either male or female). According to Kessler, this "correction" is not done because it is threatening to the infant's life, but because it is threatening to the infant's culture. By preserving gender "normalcy," people won't have to deal with those whose gender does not neatly fit into one of two categories. However, the growing visibility of the transgender movement indicates that there is a segment of the population that feels recognition of a "third gender" (intersexual) is more important than people's discomfort in interactions with those who "don't fit the model" (Coventry, 1998).[*]

[*] For more information, contact the Intersexual Society of North America (ISNA), P.O. Box 31791, San Francisco, CA, www.isna.org.

Processing Master Attributes

The case of transsexualism illuminates the extraordinary importance of gender as part of our self-definitions, the definitions that others have of us, and the implications these normally mutual definitions have for the way we order our encounters. Much the same case can be made with regard to the other master attributes, age and race. Like gender, they are aspects of others upon which we rely in making judgments about the kinds of people they are, the kinds of behaviors we might expect of them, and the attitudes and values they are likely to hold. Therefore, they help us judge the kinds of behaviors in which we might properly engage in our encounters with others.

The manner in which we use the information revealed by these attributes to formulate our behaviors is somewhat complicated. It is not simply a matter of attributing significance to these attributes *one at a time*. We do not consider them singly and in isolation from each other. Instead, we formulate a conception of people based on a **configuration of attributes,** or the statuses they simultaneously occupy. People are not just male or female, they are *young* males, *old* males; *young* females, *old* females; *young, black* males, *young, white* females; and so forth. Because these statuses are possessed in combination, the number of categorical conceptions we must store in our minds is quite large. With such a simple example, you could conjure up in your mind a different picture of the kind of person represented by each of these categories. We have purposely chosen the simplest case, treating each of the three statuses as a dichotomy, or two mutually exclusive groups. Such an assumption is reasonably safe with respect to gender. With the exception of such unusual cases as transsexuals or hermaphrodites, a person is either male or female. It would be an oversimplification to treat age and race as dichotomies, however.

Our conceptions of age, for example, are more specific than just young or old. If we only add the frequently used category of middle-aged, the number of combinations of age along with race and gender increases. The issue is further complicated because age is a continuous variable with values that can range from 0 to over 100 in a series of steps. Our assessment of someone's age is therefore quite sophisticated. A matter of even a few years can influence our judgments about what a person can and cannot or should and should not do (see chapter 10).

There are also many racial distinctions within the black-white dichotomy. Distinctions are made between light- and dark-skinned blacks in the United States, for example, and in countries such as South Africa even finer distinctions constitute the basis for racial oppression. Studies suggest that in the United States, employers view darker African American men as violent, uncooperative, dishonest, and unstable (Kirschenman and Neckerman, 1998), thus excluding them from employment and blocking their access to rewards and resources (Thompson and Keith, 2001). Black women of all ages tend to prefer lighter skin and believe that lighter hues are perceived as most attractive by black males (Chambers et al., 1994; Robinson and Ward, 1995). Since, like age, race is also a continuous variable, the number of possible combinations of the attributes of gender, age, and race is very large.

The Ongoing Search for Information

We can quickly make inferences about people who possess different configurations of these master attributes. In the presence of other people for the first time, we assess virtually instantaneously their age, gender, and race, and on this basis we form some preliminary judgment about them. Our evaluation of these attributes sensitizes us to what we can generally expect from such people. The judgments we make after picking up this **face information** cannot be final, however. Our preliminary conceptions of others may prove incorrect as the interaction proceeds, and we must be prepared to make continuous revisions in light of their actual behaviors.

The search for salient or conspicuous information about other people does not begin and end with assessment of the master attributes. Once we make a preliminary judgment about others based on these attributes, we begin to search out additional information to help us confirm, reject, or modify these early judgments. In most encounters other central sources of information are available from which we can make inferences about these people. The information provided by social attributes is complemented by information from such attributes as physical appearance and clothing, which are easily observed and therefore serve as important cues for role-taking.

Information Provided by Physical Attributes

Advertising attests to the enormous emphasis placed on physical appearance in American society. If our teeth are not white enough, our haircut is not in the latest style, our bodies do not have an agreeable odor, we weigh too much or too little, or our complexion is not clear, we are told that we are unattractive and our interactions with others will suffer. We may be convinced that if our appearance is unattractive or incorrect we will be denied opportunity for intimacy with others.

Physical appearance—height, weight, facial characteristics, posture, mannerisms, and grooming—certainly plays a large part in nearly all social interactions. These features of self provide cues as to what we can expect from others and they from us. Like age, race and gender, **physical attributes** also serve as a basis for judging the kinds of people others are or appear to be.

The importance of physical attributes in our assessments of self and others emphasizes the significance of symbols in the person-perception process. In chapter 2 the distinction between signs and symbols was described in terms of a crucial difference between fixed and socially conferred meanings. We do not respond to the attributes of others merely as signs. It is not, for example, the physical characteristics of clothing as such that we respond to, but the meanings given to certain types of clothing. In the same way, no intrinsic meaning is attached to shortness, tallness, thinness, or fatness. The meanings conferred on these physical attributes are culturally and historically established, and there are wide variations in the values attached to them.

Appearance and Attraction

Body image and physical appearance affect our perceptions of ourself and others, as well as our interactions with one another (see box). Our awareness of the influence our physical appearance has on others' perceptions of us is illustrated in the care and preparation involved in the way we present our-

---

What Is Beautiful Is Good—Still True?

In a landmark study, Dion, Bersheid, and Walster (1972) showed participants photographs of attractive and unattractive individuals and asked them to rate these people on a series of personality traits. They found that attractive individuals were perceived as more sensitive, kind, sociable, interesting, outgoing, strong, poised, and exciting than less attractive people. These findings stimulated more than 25 years of research into the physical attractiveness stereotype. The attractiveness stereotype has become so pervasive in frequency and strength that Dion and colleagues' (1972) suggestion that "what is beautiful is good" has become axiomatic (Perlini, Bertolissi, and Lind, 1999). In addition, perceptions of physically attractive individuals are often influenced by halo effects—others judge them as having other actually unrelated positive characteristics, such as social skills (Ashmore and Longo, 1995). Physical attractiveness affects our perceptions of ourselves and others, as well as the quality of our social relationships. The following findings are typical:

1. Women in U.S. society are held to certain beauty standards; physical appearance continues to play a large part in how women's worth is assessed (Wood, 2003); in many contexts, physical attractiveness is valued more in women than men (Buss and Kenrick, 1998).

2. Women who undergo cosmetic surgery imagine they are being perceived more favorably than they were prior to the operation, and begin to behave in a manner that they believe appropriate for "attractive" women (Gimlin, 2000).

3. In personal ads, men continue to seek young, attractive partners; women are more likely to seek financial security (Lance, 1998).

4. There is a negative bias toward unattractive women in hiring decisions (Marlowe, Schneider, and Nelson, 1996).

5. Girls have a greater likelihood of being negatively affected by the feminine ideal of physical attractiveness than boys have of being negatively affected by the masculine ideal (Franzoi, 1995).

6. More attractive persons are perceived to have more achievement-related traits and greater initiative (Chia et al., 1998).

7. Women of color are especially disadvantaged by the dominant culture's beauty norms, for a central component of idealized beauty is whiteness. Nonwhite women go to great lengths to more closely resemble the idealized image of white beauty (Rooks, 1996). Creams for lightening skin and chemical treatments to straighten hair are two common techniques used by black women; Asian women are turning to cosmetic surgery to "Caucasianize" their eyelids (Kaw, 1994).

selves in public. When in a public setting, as Goffman (1963a) pointed out, individuals are expected to have their "faculties in readiness for any face-to-face interaction that might come his [sic] way in the situation" (p. 24). One of the most evident means by which individuals express such readiness is "through the disciplined management of personal appearance or 'personal front,' that is, the complex of clothing, make-up, hairdo, and other surface decorations" that they carry about on their person (p. 25). In a classic study of "the interaction order of public bathrooms," Spencer Cahill and colleagues (1985) observed that individuals often enter public bathrooms with no apparent purpose other than the management of their personal front. Most public restrooms are equipped for this purpose, offering coin-operated dispensers of a variety of "personal care products" and almost all have at least one mirror to aid individuals in reconstructing their personal front in what Lofland (1972) termed a "readiness check."

We respond to mirrors as if they represent an unseen audience. The reflected appraisals of ourselves which we get from mirrors allow us to anticipate the responses others may make to us. In terms of the discussion in chapter 2 of the self as both the subject and the object of our actions, we present ourselves to the mirror and then stand outside this presented object, trying to view it from the perspective of others.

The extent to which people worry about their physical appearance is, to some degree, a function of the situation. In some contexts physical appearance affects the nature of interactions more than in others. This is evident in the case of physical disability. The image of a disabled person as one who is weak and disempowered is a potent image, one from which disabled individuals may choose to distance themselves. One individual, who thinks of herself as "just a person with an impairment" and who "feels normal" in that her self-awareness is not premised on who people think she is, but on what she feels herself to be (Watson, 2002:516), describes her frustration when nondisabled people fail to see this: "That really gets my goat. You know, when you are trying to live a normal life and every time you achieve something they sort of pat you on your head and say 'Ain't that good?' and you don't need that" (p. 516).

For some disabled individuals, being disabled is about "living in a system in which people with an impairment are subordinated through relations that are contradictory to their own views of their self" (Watson, 2002:521). Rather than accepting this, however, they challenge this by refusing to define themselves as "other."

Appearance and Character Assessment

Not only do we discriminate or rank people in terms of their physical attributes, we also make inferences about the "kinds" of people who display particular physical attributes. That is, we make inferences about others' personalities and even their moral characteristics as we assess them physically. Warranted or not, we form preliminary conceptions of others as confident, strong-willed, prudish, sentimental, withdrawn, happy, jolly, evil, tough, honest, sincere, dangerous, intellectual, stupid, and the like.

Our evaluation of others' facial expressions is especially crucial in our "reading" of their attitudes and emotions (c.f., Eckman, 1992). Our assessment of others' faces is central to the view we come to have of them. In most interactions we spend a good deal of time looking directly at faces. Facial expressions, purposely or unwittingly, express an enormous variety of attitudes and emotions (c.f., Carroll and Russell, 1996). For example, research shows that people's different expectancies for emotions according to gender are used to interpret facial expressions. Plant and coauthors (2000) found that women and men posing the same negative ambiguous facial expression were attributed "feminine" and "masculine" emotions, respectively. That is, men were thought to be expressing anger, whereas women were thought to be expressing sadness.

Other physical characteristics such as posture and gesture are also used as a basis for inferences about others' emotions, attitudes, and character. People are viewed as being more or less open, accessible, aloof, rigid, and so forth depending upon their gestures and stance.

Goffman's classic study of stigma (1963b) provides the underpinnings for much of the research on physical appearance. His work focused on the negative social consequences of visible disabilities and other socially devalued attributes. Individuals with visible physical differences are at greater risk of being perceived as unattractive and viewing themselves as unattractive.

Obesity is a stigmatized characteristic in American society. Natalie Allon's classic work on obesity describes it as "a central target for human vindictiveness and puritanical zeal." According to Allon, "The public condemns and scorns the overweight, who are viewed as handicaps to themselves" (1971:217). A number of studies on public reaction to obesity support the idea that obese persons are held in low esteem, criticized, and stigmatized precisely because they are considered responsible for their own condition. Overweight is viewed as a voluntary condition because such people are thought to have control over the condition of their own bodies. The stigmatization of obese individuals comes full circle when they accept the legitimacy of others' negative definitions of them. Overweight people are in a peculiarly disadvantaged position because (1) they are discriminated against, (2) they are made to feel that they deserve such discrimination, and (3) they may come to accept their treatment as just.

Overweight individuals come to view themselves as fat by internalizing societal conceptions about weight that lead to the recognition of one's body as something other than "normal." These individuals are forced to appropriate a "fat" identity and deal with the difficult interactions that often result (Degher and Hughes, 1999). Nonacceptance of personal responsibility for overweight may be self-protective. A study of children age 9 to 11 found that children who attributed their overweight to an external factor had more positive self-esteem. This was also true of children who believed their weight did not influence social interaction outcomes (Pierce and Wardle, 1997).

People use various strategies to cope with the negative character of obesity, including avoidance, compliance, rejection of societal definitions, compensation, and accounts to explain their obesity (Degher and Hughes, 1999). Accounts in the form of excuses or justifications are given by people when social interaction is disturbed by rule violations (Scott and Lyman, 1968). Sometimes response to the stigmatization of obesity is in the form of rejection or resistance, such as verbal assertion, physical aggression, self-acceptance, activism, enlightenment, and even flamboyance (Joanisse and Synnott, 1999).

The stigma attached to obesity in American society makes it abundantly clear that assessments of others' morality and general worth are made on the basis of their appearance. The growth of dieting workshops, plans, and organizations, as well as low-calorie food industries on which Americans yearly spend billions of dollars, is persuasive evidence of the general concern with weight. A rigid cultural value is placed on thinness, and those who are very noticeably overweight are evaluated quite negatively. Children develop negative attitudes about overweight as young as six years old and may exclude fat children from play. They already associate obesity with a variety of negative characteristics such as laziness and sloppiness (Dietz, 1998), and these strong negative stereotypes about obesity are difficult to change (Anesbury and Tiggemann, 2000). Discrimination against overweight children begins early in childhood and becomes progressively institutionalized. This is particularly significant given that obesity is now the most prevalent nutritional disease of children and adolescents in the United States (Dietz, 1998).

There is some evidence of subcultural variation. White women appear to engage in a greater degree of negative stereotyping of large women, especially large white women, rating them lower on attractiveness, intelligence, job success, relationship success, happiness, and popularity than average or thin women. Interestingly, black women do not show the same denigration of large women, especially large black women (Hebl and Heatherton, 1998).

Obese individuals experience weight-related difficulties with their families, in romantic relationships, and at school or work. Feelings of loneliness and isolation stemming from discrimination by employers, health practitioners, and the general public are common patterns (Joanisse and Synnott, 1999). Obese individuals must cope not only with the stigma of being fat and the interactional difficulties that occur because of this but also face employment discrimination (Paul and Townsend, 1995). Women in particular pay a penalty for being obese (Pagan and Davila, 1997), suffering lower pay in entry-level managerial positions and lower occupational status (Haskins and Ransford, 1999).

Based on our discussion thus far it should not be surprising that cultural standards of beauty are more critical criteria for evaluating the worth of women in our society than for evaluating men. Cultural messages about the rewards of thinness and the punishment of obesity are everywhere. Most women accept society's standards of beauty as "the way things are," even though these standards may undermine self-image, self-esteem, or physical well-being. Because women feel their bodies fail the beauty test, American industry benefits enormously, continually nurturing feminine insecurities. Images of the culturally desirable female body are presented through the media, and these images are everywhere—television, movies, billboards, in print. Women's magazines, with their glossy pages of advertising and beauty advice, hold up an especially devious mirror, offering "help" to women while at the same time presenting a standard nearly impossible to attain (Hesse-Biber, 1996).

Given the pervasiveness of the message that their self-worth is tied to "looking good" coupled with a nearly fetishistic "cult of thinness" in American society, women, more than men, are dissatisfied with their bodies. In fact, a meta-analysis of gender differences in attractiveness and body image based on 222 studies from the past 50 years showed dramatic increases in the number of women who have poor body image (Feingold and Mazella, 1998). Numerous studies have concluded that the prevalence of eating disorders has increased in the 1980s and 1990s, primarily among women, (c.f., Muth and Cash, 1997), and that this increase is a result of the erosion of body image (body satisfaction) engendered by heightened societal pressures on women to be thin and attractive (Garner and Kearney-Cooke, 1996). Young white women, for example, are likely to want to achieve an appearance portrayed in the media, even when they regard such images as unrealistic and largely artificial (Milkie, 1999). Despite powerful media images, research has consistently shown that African-American women worry less than women of other races about weight, dieting, or being thin (Molloy and Herzberger, 1998).

The cultural emphasis on thinness as an ideal for women carries another danger. When females are encouraged to focus so intensely on their bodies, they may give less attention to more important aspects of identity. Joan Brumberg claims that for many young women in America the body has become an all-consuming project, one that takes precedence over all others (1997).

Effects of Clothing on Appearance

The way people dress also provides information about them. Sociologists have focused on the status differentiation functions of fashion from the early days of the discipline—Veblen's (1899) conspicuous consumption; Simmel's (1904) insights into the social psychology of fashion—continuing to the more recent work of Bourdieu (1984) on cultural capital and Davis (1992) on ambivalence in the meaning of clothing. We make assessments of the ethnicity, social class, occupations, social values, moods, emotions, and even political ideologies of those we encounter on the basis of their clothing. The ways others are dressed provide cues we can use in formulating our behaviors toward them. Clothing also is a prop that helps us project the images of ourselves that we choose to present. It provides a way to manipulate the images we publicly present of ourselves and project the identity that the wearer wants to express (see box). This is simpler than is the case with other physical and social attributes. Gender and race, for example, are difficult or impossible to modify.

Racism and the other subtle badges of symbolic power are expressed through wardrobes and body language. Bourgois (1995) discovered that appearance and clothing were a significant barrier to middle-class employment for the inner-city youth he studied. It was not just that they did not have the money for clothes, but they had no idea what clothes to choose. They did not know when their clothes would elicit ridicule or anger. One individual was hurt when his supervisor accused him of "looking like a hoodlum" on the days when he thought he was actually dressing well. Another dropped out of an employment-training program because of the humiliation of having an inappropriate wardrobe. He feared he might appear to be "a buffoon on parade" on the days when he was trying to dress up. He admitted that the precipitating factor in his decision not to go back to the job-training program was when he overheard someone accusing one of his female friends of "looking tacky" after she proudly wore her new clothes at the first class. "As a matter of fact, Primo had thought she had looked elegant in her skintight, yellow jumpsuit when she came over to his apartment to display her new outfit proudly to him and his mother before going to class" (p. 162).

Dress for Success??? But I Don't Know What to Wear!!!

Dressing for work is a daily activity for many of us. Donning uniforms or particular work costumes helps us put on our role for the day. You might say we manage and construct our work identity at least in part through dress (Goffman, 1959). However, dressing for work may not be a simple routine for everyone anymore. For women who have entered management and executive levels in ever-increasing numbers during the last 20 years, "dressing for work is an exercise in politics and diplomacy" (Kimle and Damhorst, 1997) that requires substantial knowledge and effort (Rafaeli et al., 1997).

Although women are entering a widening array of careers in increasing numbers, women in higher management positions are still in the minority. Scholars have generally found that women's attire influences judgements of chances for success and promotion through the ranks of corporate business environments. John Molloy's (1977) "dress for success" uniform of a tailored business suit with a skirt, modeled after men's traditional suits, was widely adopted during the 1970s and 1980s. By the late 1980s, however, women's professional dress styles seemed to have changed, encompassing much more varied attire than the navy suit. Although this seems like progress, the elaborated code for women's business dress is now more complex—there are many choices and therefore more ambiguity.

How can women safely "dress for success"? Two researchers from Iowa State University interviewed women in professional and "white-collar" positions to identify "the ideal business image for women" (Kimle and Damhorst, 1997). One of the most striking findings was the discovery that the women were aware of presenting multiple meanings through dress. Although the participants in the study all agreed that there is an ideal business image for U.S. women today, there was a great deal of variety in the specific details of appearances which these women felt expressed this image. However, despite the absence of specifics, the concepts underlying the ideal image were evident.

Six concepts were identified as components of meaning that must be accommodated in women's ideal business image: Conservatism versus Fashion, Masculinity versus Femininity/Sexuality, Creativity versus Conformity. These appear on the surface to be three pairs of polar opposites which exert pull on the individual. The following quote from one participant illustrates the Masculinity versus Femininity/Sexuality dilemma:

> Well it's just—I think part of it is men wear suits and that's [that] and it's kind of back to the knight and the armor. You put on your armor, and you're ready for business; you put on your jacket, and you are going to work. The jacket is the pivotal piece in the wardrobe for women. Men just standardly wear suits. It's no nonsense. There is no room for frills. You're not there for ornament. (Kimle and Damhorst, 1997:57)

However, women must avoid looking *too* masculine, which could be perceived as a gender norm violation. At the same time, women must maintain an appropriate degree of femininity. Accessories such as gold jewelry, pearls, scarves, and small touches of lace are acceptable—some women thought that others in a business setting *appreciated* seeing these touches of femininity. On the other hand, extreme femininity—printed floral fabrics, pastels, styles with lots of ruffles and lace—can be detrimental to a business image. Participants felt that being overly feminine could lead to women being perceived as *frivolous*.

And then there's sexuality. The avoidance of blatant sexuality in the workplace was a strong theme for these women. They felt that, in every instance, women should be very cautious about looking "sexy." Sexiness was most frequently equated with body-revealing or body-hugging dress such as low-cut necklines, short skirts, and tight sweaters. These women thought looking sexy in business could cause many types of conflict and was never a wise approach:

> It's almost that people assume something else about your life if you wear something like that . . . to work. They might assume you were at work for a reason other than to be serious about your work. (p. 58)

Finally, women are expected to cultivate physical attractiveness in their business image. Most of the participants agreed that women who are attractive have greater chances for career advancement.

The authors conclude that "women's business dress in late twentieth-century American society has a degree of latitude in choice that allows women to embrace multiple roles and contexts in a single appearance" (p. 60), at least in one midwestern city. The women interviewed seem to locate themselves along a continuum between dichotomies. For example, conservatism was more important than fashion for some; for some, expressing femininity was important, and they were less interested in adopting the masculine aspects of business dress. At any rate, the authors conclude that "there is not a simple uniform for female executives that, in analogous manner to the men's suit, encodes a woman's work identity and is read similarly across business and other situational contexts. Women's identity work in the business arena requires effort" (p. 64).

Shopping, anyone?

Information Provided by Discourse

The necessary information for role-taking in interactions is not acquired solely by observing others' social (or master) and physical attributes. Interactions are accomplished through both appearance and discourse, which is the actual "text" of the communication or conversation. Gregory P. Stone suggests that appearance and discourse have at least equal significance in any theory of human communication:

> Appearance and discourse are in fact dialectic processes whenever people converse or correspond. They work back and forth on one another, at times shifting, at other times maintaining the direction of the transaction . . . In all cases, however, discourse is impossible without appearance which permits the requisite identifications with one another by the discussants. (1962:91)

The information on others provided by social and physical attributes sets the stage for verbal encounters. Before we can talk to people with different attributes, we use the information we have to decide what we can expect from them. This lends some predictability to our encounters. We make reasonable guesses about others' future behaviors. However, as you have no doubt learned through your own interactions, we cannot rely solely on such guesses. We must be prepared to modify our images of others as the interaction proceeds.

Much of the information considered important for predicting others' behaviors must be ferreted out during verbal discourse. The search for relevant information and the corresponding role-taking occur throughout the interaction process. Such aspects of others' identities as their occupation, social class affiliation, ethnicity, marital status, educational level, religion, prejudices, and political beliefs cannot be fully determined through observation alone. Verbal discourse furthers the search for such aspects of others' identities.

Many of our inquiries about others are designed to elicit this information. Consider the information-seeking intentions that lie behind the following types of verbal probes, which are often heard in the course of conversation:

Question Asked	Possible Information Sought
Does your wife work?	Are you married?
Did you belong to a college fraternity?	What is your education?
Where do you live?	What is your social class?
Did your kids learn about that in church?	What is your religion?
Do you find enough time away from your job to do that?	What is your occupation?
What do you think about politician X's position on that issue?	What are your political attitudes?

We not only seek out information about others, we frequently find it useful to provide selective information about ourselves. We deliberately present certain images of ourselves by the way we stand, our dress, and our general demeanor—what Goffman referred to as "sign vehicles" (Goffman, 1959). We also provide selective information about ourselves in our verbal communications. Jill Nelson (1994) describes the internal struggle she experienced during an interview with the *Washington Post* as she realizes that she—a black woman—is being stereotyped by her interviewer—a white man—rather than being seen for who she really is. She finally lets it drop that she spent three years at prep school and that her parents have a home in Martha's Vineyard. His response: "He grins. It's as if he's suddenly recognized that the slightly threatening black guy asking for a hand-out on the street is actually a Harvard classmate fallen on hard times. The bond of the Vineyard makes me safe, a person like him" (p. 6). She realizes that the job is hers. "Simply by evoking residence on Martha's Vineyard, I have separated wheat from chaff, belongers from aspirers, rebellious chip-on-the-shoulder Negroes from middle-class, responsible ones" (p. 6).

Goffman (1959) makes the distinction between **expressions given**—verbal symbols or their substitutes which one uses admittedly to convey information—and **expressions given off**—nonverbal, presumably unintentional conveyance of information. To illustrate, Goffman cites an incident from a novel in which an Englishman named Preedy who is vacationing in Spain makes his first appearance on the beach:

> But in any case he took care to avoid catching anyone's eye. First of all, he had to make it clear to those potential companions of his holiday that they were of no concern to him whatsoever. He stared through them, round them, over them—eyes lost in space. . . . If by chance a ball was thrown his way, he looked surprised; then let a smile of amusement lighten his face (Kindly Preedy), looked around dazed to see that there *were* people on the beach, tossed it back with a smile to himself and not a smile *at* the people, and then resumed carelessly his nonchalant survey of space. (Sansom, 1956:230, in Goffman, 1959:4–5)

This example suggests an important point about the interaction process: Human beings are capable of manipulating the information they provide others in order to present certain self-images. We conceal, control, and give off certain bits of information about ourselves in order to realize certain desired ends in our transactions with others. Since we carefully monitor the information we provide others, we must presume that those with whom we interact are doing the same. This knowledge certainly complicates our interactions, as we must sometimes question whether and to what extent others are presenting authentic or deceptive images of themselves.

Controlling Information and Managing Impressions

The communication and interaction process we have been describing in this chapter takes the following form. Two people come into each others' presence and immediately begin to assess one another. Each begins to pick up as much information as possible about the other's physical and social attributes. This information is important if each person is to have some degree of control over the interaction and to elicit a response from the other person that can be considered favorable. As the encounter proceeds, however, the participants do more than rely on the cues gleaned from one another. Beyond that, they begin to put on a performance and try to project certain identities of themselves. This part of the process is called **impression management.**

The idea that individuals systematically control the information they provide others about themselves in order to manage the impressions they are presenting is basic to a view of human interaction called the **dramaturgical view.** This view of interaction is most closely associated with the writings of Erving Goffman (1959, 1963a, 1963b, 1967), who is sympathetic to the idea we have presented that individuals must be capable of assigning meanings to their own and others' behaviors in order to communicate. Goffman's work falls within a symbolic interaction frame of reference because he agrees that individuals must learn to interpret, through role-taking, their transactions with others and to formulate the meanings of their encounters. However, in Goffman's work certain aspects of this process are emphasized. The dramaturgical view of interaction sees individuals not simply as *role-takers* but equally as **role-makers.** People do not merely interpret meanings, they also purposely create and manipulate meanings.

In the analogy suggested by the dramaturgical view of interaction, the essential reality of life is a series of fabricated roles, and society is a theater in which everyone is an actor engaged in a perpetual play. Goffman's view of human behavior indicates he takes seriously Shakespeare's claim that "all the world's a stage and all the men and women merely players"! Goffman's writings have had a profound effect on the way that social scientists think about the character of social interaction and have generated a body of literature around his ideas. These works include interpretations of Goffman's writings (Burns, 1992; Manning, 1992), research elaborating theoretically on the dramaturgical metaphor of behavior as performance (Kivisto and Pittman, 2001), applications of the impression-management notion to specific settings (Copp, 1998), and Lemert and Branaman's *The Goffman Reader* (1997). The general significance of Goffman's thinking for the sociology of everyday life is well stated by Spencer Cahill in Joel Charon's (2001) text on symbolic interaction theory:

> To Goffman . . . human beings act on a stage; they perform for others; they impress and they are impressed. They are both actors and audiences. And they often form a cooperative performance team that works to present a unified front to others. We know we do this; others know we do this; we know that others know we do this. Life is drama, and to understand interaction, self, or society we must consider this fact. (p.191)

Presenting the Right Impression

In the dramaturgical view, individuals construct their **presentations of self** in a calculated and often contrived way. They do this not only to give a favorable impression of themselves but to establish specific definitions of the acting situation.

> When an individual appears before others his action will influence the definition of the situation which they will come to have. Sometimes the individual will act in a thoroughly calculating manner, expressing himself in a given way solely in order to give the kind of impression to others that is likely to invoke from them a specific response he is concerned to obtain. (Goffman, 1959:6)

Although this may sound as if Goffman is reading a Machiavellian kind of manipulation into human interactions, he did not see contrivance and chicanery everywhere. According to Cahill, Goffman emphasizes the intrinsically cooperative and moral character of human interaction:

> . . . he shows us that mutual performance creates the mutually acceptable rules that form the basis of orderly social interaction. I perform for you and present myself in a way I choose. You perform for me and present yourself in a way you choose. Some of this performance is honest, some dishonest. Yet, if there is no clear evidence of deception, we agree to respect each other's performance and treat each other accordingly. Out of this agreement arises the morality that guides our acts and allows for the continuation of our interaction. (Charon, 2001:192)

By fabricating impressions, we try to control the definition of the acting situation others come to have, and in so doing we set the future course of the interaction.

The dramaturgical view also assumes that humans are approval-seeking animals. We wish to be applauded by others for the self-images we present. We are anxious to receive approval for our behaviors, opinions, and attitudes. We want to be seen as worthwhile, social, proper people, so we try to present our "best face" to others. To accomplish this end, we seek out information about others and systematically control information about ourselves. We particularly strive to exclude information we perceive as damaging to ourselves.

Sometimes we go to extremes to conceal biographical information about ourselves. This occurs when we believe the hidden information would somehow taint our identities. Given the tendency to map each other into racial and ethnic categories that trigger associated racial or ethnic meanings which influence interaction (Kang, 2000), some people seek to disavow their ethnic or racial statuses. Jerry Kang, an Asian-American law professor, describes several occasions when interactants' lack of knowledge of his racial status facilitated interaction. He has bought cars through a buying agent, mostly because he is too busy to negotiate with car dealers, but also because he worries that he may receive worse offers than a similarly situated white male. This effectively removes racialized negotiations from the car-buying ritual.

Another example comes from his finding housing for a college summer job over the telephone. He arranged to live with a graduate student, who agreed to pick him up at the airport:

> I told him my height, what kind of jacket I had, and that I wore glasses. He told me that he had red hair, which would make him easy to spot. I later learned that neither he nor my immediate supervisor knew that I was Asian American until we met face to face. My phone voice, grammar, and accent did not prompt them to flip out of the default assumption: white. As for my name, they somehow heard "Jerry *King*." (p. 1133)

The telephone inadvertently cloaked his race until the face-to-face meeting with his roommate: "If he were uncomfortable or particularly elated about living with an Asian, neither discomfort nor joy would have been triggered until we met at the airport" (p. 1134).

Other kinds of information may also be concealed. In order to present an integrated, consistent, and proper impression of ourselves in everyday situations, we carefully monitor our actual behaviors. We make use of various devices to conceal our participation in improper or unconventional activities. Goffman describes the "involvement shields" people use to give the impression of being properly involved, though they are not strictly conforming to the obligations of a social setting. They might use their hands to cover their eyes if they cannot keep them open when attention is demanded, or use a portable shield such as a newspaper to stifle a yawn. They may use their hands to cup a cigarette in places where smoking is not allowed. They sometimes sustain a pose of deep interest when they are, in fact, uninterested in a conversation. You no doubt have, at one time or another, nodded agreement to something you did not hear or understand (in class, perhaps?).

Contrary to a number of psychological models of the human being, Goffman does not view people as having one identity. Rather, individuals have **multiple identities,** a repertoire of identities, and can choose from among these available identities the one that they judge best suits the expectations of a given audience. Goffman describes humans as persons of *appearance.* It matters little what we actually are, therefore. What most matters is *what we appear to be.* And this is inevitably true because it is on the basis of our appearance—on the basis of the images, identities, impressions, and information we provide others about ourselves—that others will formulate their conceptions of us.

Mutual Protection

While we conceal certain aspects of ourselves so others will think of us as proper, there is another way in which information control is related to the appearance of propriety. The preservation of orderly interaction depends on the mutual protection of the individuals involved. The ultimate display of social morality is a person's attempt to protect the social images of others. Life, therefore, should not be viewed as an endlessly competitive struggle in which individuals aggressively protect only their own interests.

A basic feature of social interaction is that individuals tend to conduct themselves in encounters in such a way that both their own image and those of the other participants are protected. Both the construction of a favorable personal impression and the protection of others' fabricated impressions involve information control. In Goffman's terms, individuals "show respect and politeness, making sure to extend to others any ceremonial treatment that might be their due. They employ discretion; they leave unstated facts that might implicitly or explicitly contradict or embarrass the positive claims made by others" (1967:16).

Conformity

In the usual sociological view of conformity, when individuals internalize social norms, their behaviors conform to societal expectations. Society, in effect, gets inside their heads. The price of nonconformity, under the condition of internalization, is not simply the scorn of one's fellows but, more important, scorn for oneself. Individuals conform because not to do so engenders guilt. From this perspective, norms are not merely guidelines. They assume a moral force.

Goffman provides an alternative view of conformity, at least implicitly. The dramaturgical analyst sees most human behavior as highly stylized and ritualized. It is performed in accordance with the rules, but not necessarily motivated by a *belief* in the rules. As individuals move from one setting or situation to another, they may simply adopt the interactional posture most appropriate for that situation.

Cynicism and Sincerity in Role-Taking

If we do not believe in the rules but conform merely because we are expected to do so in the situation, the honesty and sincerity of our behaviors may be suspect. In the dramaturgical view, society is viewed as a stage on which the actors, with premeditation, manipulate and withhold information about themselves and sometimes offer false information. The question is to what extent the role-players or performers are being consistent with their own image of self. Indeed, the dramaturgical model raises the question of just where to locate the person's "real" self or even whether there is a real self. When you act one way in front of your same-sexed friends and an entirely different way in the company of the opposite sex, which of the two behaviors reflects your true self more accurately? When you display thoroughly proper table manners at a formal affair and the next day at dinner gruffly demand that your roommate "pass the goddamn butter," which of the two performances best reflects the kind of person you really are? Or are you both kinds of persons, simply alternating in a chameleonlike way from one situation to the next?

Everyday interaction is characterized by not only an expressive order, but an emotional order as well. Since the 1970s, sociologists have studied and written about the social shaping and consequences of human emotions. In particular, Arlie Russell Hochschild proposed that human emotions are shaped by learned but implicit "feeling rules." According to her, individuals manage not only their outward expression of emotions but also their very feelings in order to conform to such rules. That is, they not only express but also attempt to feel what they think they should be feeling. In a book titled *The Managed Heart* (1983), Hochschild notes that in postindustrial society more and more jobs are requiring workers to manage their feelings. Occupations such as flight attendant require constant smiles and cordial behavior, even when customers become nasty or abusive. Hochschild warns that the "emotional labor" required in the growing number of service occupations will take a heavy psychological toll from workers who are required to put on cynical role performances as a matter of course. A number of investigators have found this idea useful in examining emotion management in various contexts: Copp (1998) with instructors at a sheltered workshop for people with developmental disabilities; Hansen (1996) with temporary workers; Konradi (1999) with rape survivors in a courtroom setting; Leidner (1993) with fast-food workers; Pierce (1996) in law firms; Staske (1998) between close relational partners; Yoels and Clair (1994, 1995) with medical residents in an outpatient clinic, and others.

It would be a mistake to assume that everyone is always being cynical in the performance of their roles, however. The issue is not, we think, whether a person puts on performances, plays roles, or manipulates others. We all do that. The question of sincerity or cynicism in role-taking turns rather on whether performers *believe in their own performances.* We may think of role performances as sincere when individuals present themselves to others as they really believe themselves to be. Only when they rationally set out to deceive others by presenting false information about themselves can it be called a cynical role performance.

An observer of another's behavior cannot always determine whether the performance is cynical or sincere. Only the person producing the act knows whether he or she is being dishonest. Two different people could put on concretely identical performances, one of which would be sincere and the other cynical. As an example, in a program which provided shelter, food, and drug and alcohol rehabilitation to homeless men, the requirement to show a commitment to recovery in order to participate led to cynical as well as sincere role performances (Weinberg, 1996). Weinberg observed that it was widely assumed among program participants that many of their peers merely *pretended* commitment in order to remain sheltered, "feigning a desire for sobriety in order to enjoy the benefits of 'three hots and a cot' (three meals a day and a bed), to satisfy court orders or to escape the myriad other adversities of skid row street life" (p. 141). As a result, the enactment and appraisal of authentic commitment to recovery became a central organizing feature of the program and a source of interactional tension between clients. Although there was always the possibility that one was being hustled by a potential malefactor, the possibility that one was being offered a genuine self-expression by someone trustworthy and authentically committed to recovery was also there. Individuals dedicated to their own recovery had to develop techniques to protect themselves from betrayal by others in the program, as well as techniques to determine who was and was not worthy of emotional investment. If they were to be trusted by others in the program, they also had to develop techniques for convincing others that they themselves were authentically committed to recovery and worthy of trust.

The only time a cynical performance can be uncovered as such is when it fails—when it falls through, and the person's true intentions are therefore made plain. In Weinberg's study, if a client who professed commitment was discovered with alcohol or drugs, his cynical performance had failed.

A person may eventually come to believe in a performance that was originally cynical. For example, young people may act intellectually in order to gain the status associated with being considered intellectuals in some situation. At the outset they may sustain this performance even though they do not believe themselves to be intellectuals. If they are accorded the status of an intellectual by others and recognized for their intellectual performance, however, at some point they might come to believe in their own originally cynical performance. The music they once listened to, the books they once read, and the museums they once attended only to provide props for this particular performance become over time true sources of pleasure. Their image as intellectuals has been incorporated into their conception of self.

Modifying the Situational View of Self

The concept of self appears throughout this book. In chapter 2 we described Mead's conception of self as a process in which people objectively evaluate their behaviors from the perspective of the generalized other. This implies that a person presents quite different selves in different situations. To employ Mead's term, a person has not one me, but a number of me's, each corresponding to a situationally proper role.

Goffman also offers a highly situational view of the self. As people move from one acting situation to another, their self-presentations change, often dramatically. In this interactionist view, individuals construct and perform roles in terms of both the norms governing particular situations and the specific responses they want to invoke from others. According to dramaturgical theorists, individuals remain detached from the roles they perform, changing presentations of self each time they enter a new situation.

Critics have charged that the dramaturgical metaphor is committed to an overly fluid, changeable notion of the self. They have questioned whether the self is always discrete, called forth only by the situation and the audience. These critics suggest that there are order and stability in the self, as well as some consistency in presentations of self, which transcend particular settings. Some organizing attribute or unifying principle in the self keeps a person from being only a bundle of situationally constructed roles.

Personality theorists such as the psychologists Sigmund Freud, Abraham Maslow, Harry Stack Sullivan, and Erik Erikson argue for the development of a personality structure that controls or coordinates situational presentations of self. Although they frequently stress different themes and processes, all understand human beings as developing a distinct, bounded, identifiable conception of themselves (a personal identity, if you will) that has continuity through time.

Through interaction with others we appear to develop early in childhood a conception of ourselves—perhaps as intelligent, shy, confident, physically attractive, or clumsy. If people do develop an overriding, independent, and relatively stable view of themselves, we must somewhat amend or revise the situationalist stance of the dramaturgical model. We need not reject Goffman's emphasis on the performance features of interaction. We simply have to acknowledge that basic and pervasive elements of self-conception may lie behind and motivate the particular performances individuals choose, the images they project, and the manipulations they attempt. A complete explanation of behavior must incorporate both the immediate character and requirements of social situations and the unique, subjective conception of self that individuals bring to every situation.

Conclusion

In the first three chapters we have been asking: How do individuals organize, interpret, and give meaning to their own and others' behaviors? To answer this question we have analyzed how individuals form a conception of others to make judgments about their interests, motives, values, attitudes, and character. They also try to manage the impressions of themselves that they present in order to control social situations and appear proper.

Information gathering is an important part of the person-perception process and the basis for the theoretical idea that *identification of* others precedes *identification with* them. From the interactionist perspective, information is critical to role-taking and so to meaningful human communication and interaction. The master attributes—gender, age, and race—are especially significant in the definitions individuals come to have of others. The absence of these key pieces of information can create confusion and uncertainty in daily interactions.

Preliminary evaluations of others based only on these attributes may be incorrect, however. Individuals, therefore, continue to seek out information to refine their conceptions of others before and during their interactions. Elements of physical appearance such as height, weight, facial characteristics, posture, grooming, and clothing, as well as discourse, are noticed carefully. Beyond such information, which is immediately observable, verbal communications can provide knowledge of others' attitudes and values by seeking out information on their educational levels, occupations, and religions.

The dramaturgical model of interaction stresses the manner in which information is controlled to create definitions of situations. The idea that people present manufactured selves to each other, striving to appear proper in each other's eyes, rings true as a general statement about interaction. But presentations of self vary with particular settings. Some situations in everyday life require more extensive interpretation, calculation, and "self-work" than others do. There are some contexts in which individuals become especially concerned with the effects of their performances on others. In the following chapters we will examine how our relations with strangers and intimates involve us in different configurations of self, meaning, and informational analysis.

DEFINITIONS

Accounts   Excuses or justifications given by individuals when social interaction is disturbed by rule violations.

Achieved statuses   Those social statuses that are acquired during the course of individuals' lives and over which they may exert some control (for example, occupational level, educational attainment, or marriage into a higher social position).

Ascribed statuses   Those social statuses possessed by individuals over which they have no control (for example, race, gender, age, and circumstances of birth).

Configuration of attributes   The whole range of attributes about others that we take into account as we try to assess the kinds of people they are and the behaviors we might expect from them.

Dramaturgical view   A perspective that uses theatrical metaphors to describe and analyze social interaction. The basic idea is that individuals present themselves to others in a manner analogous to a stage actor's presentation of a role to an audience.

Expressions given   Verbal symbols or their substitutes which one uses admittedly to convey information.

Expressions given off   A wide range of actions performed for reasons other than the information conveyed, presumably unintentionally, but which nevertheless convey information.

Face information   Information about aspects of a person's identity that can be gleaned simply by observing them. Race, gender, demeanor, and clothing, for example, are normally visible as soon as we encounter another person. It is on the basis of face information that we make preliminary judgments about the likely behaviors of others.

Failed communication   An instance in which those interacting respond to each other on the basis of fundamentally different definitions of the situation.

Impression management   The process through which individuals consciously try to foster particular images of themselves in order to gain control of a situation or the approval of others.

Master attributes   Those statuses that are most central both to the way people view themselves and the way others view them. Race, gender, and age are three attributes that sharply define a person in any situation and tend to supersede other definitions of self that an individual might present to others.

Multiple identities   According to the dramaturgical view of interaction, individuals have several identities from which to choose in staging a particular performance. From the repertoire of identities at their disposal, they ordinarily choose to present the identity that in their opinion best suits the expectations of a given audience.

Physical attributes   Those aspects of self that define an individual's physical appearance. Height, weight, expression, posture, gesture, and so on provide cues to the expected behaviors of others.

Presentations of self   The ways in which individuals present themselves to others in order to evoke a favorable impression and control definitions of situations.

Role-makers   All human beings are role-makers to the extent that they do not unthinkingly act out socially prescribed roles. In addition, humans create and manipulate meanings through the roles they choose to perform.

Social attributes   Those aspects of self that define an individual's location in society. Among social attributes are race, gender, ethnicity, occupation, and religion. We build up a picture of others based on our knowledge of their various social attributes.

Social status   An individual's position in society based on social attributes, including the ascribed statuses of race, gender, and age as well as achieved statuses such as wealth, education, and occupation. Status indicates the degree of prestige, esteem, and power conferred on individuals because of these attributes.

DISCUSSION QUESTIONS

1. Think of a time when your attempts to role-take with another did not succeed. What happened to the interaction? How did it proceed? Why did you have difficulty role-taking? In what kinds of situations generally do people have the most difficulty assessing each other's meanings?

2. Which of your social attributes or statuses do you consider as most centrally defining your identity? Describe how you think those attributes affect the way others respond to you.

3. Describe some of the ways in which you feel that individuals' physical attractiveness influences their own behaviors and the behaviors of others toward them. Do you think that physical appearance affects the lives of men and women differently in American society? If so, how do you account for this difference?

4. Devise some simple experiments to demonstrate for yourself the significance of the clothes you wear in determining how others treat you in a variety of settings. Would you be treated differently by clerks in department, specialty, or discount stores, depending on your clothing, for example? What kind of experiment would you construct? Where would you conduct it? How would you alter the type of clothing worn by the experimenters? Which reactions would you particularly want to record?

5. Do you agree or disagree with Erving Goffman's picture of humans as strategic, manipulative, sometimes insincere managers of impressions? In what ways might contrived performances be necessary for maintaining social order?

6. Is there such a thing as a "real" self, or are we only a bundle of situationally constructed roles? What do you think is the linkage between someone's "stable" personality attributes and the particular self he or she presents in a given situation?

REFERENCES

Allon, N. 1971. "Group dieting interaction." Ph.D. dissertation, Brandeis University.

Anesbury, T., and M. Tiggemann, 2000. "An attempt to reduce negative stereotyping of obesity in children by changing controllability beliefs." *Health Education Research* 15:145–52.

Ashmore, R., and L. Longo. 1995. "Accuracy of stereotypes: What research on physical attractiveness can teach us." In *Stereotype Accuracy: Toward Appreciating Group Differences*, edited by Y. Lee, L. Jussim, and C. McCauley, pp. 63–86. Washington, DC: American Psychological Association.

Bornstein, K. 1994. *Gender Outlaw: On Men, Women, and the Rest of Us*. New York: Vintage Books (Random House).

Bourdieu, P. 1984. *Distinction*. Translated by R. Nice. Cambridge, MA: Harvard University Press.

Bourgois, P. 1995. *In Search of Respect: Selling Crack in El Barrio*. New York: Cambridge University Press.

Braudel, F. 1981. *The Structures of Everyday Life*. New York: Harper & Row.

Brumberg, J. 1997. *The Body Project: An Intimate History of American Girls*. New York: Random House.

Burns, T. 1992. *Erving Goffman*. Boston: Routledge & Kegan Paul.

Buss, D., and D. Kenrick. 1998. "Evolutionary social psychology." In *Handbook of Social Psychology*, 4th ed., edited by D. Gilbert and S. Fiske, Vol. 2:982–1026.

Cahill, S., W. Distler, C. Lachowetz, A. Meaney, R. Tarallo, and T. Willard. 1985. "Meanwhile backstage: Public bathrooms and the interaction order." *Urban Life* (14):33–58.

Carroll, J., and J. Russell. 1996. "Do facial expressions signal specific emotions? Judging emotion from the face in context." *Journal of Personality and Social Psychology* 70:205–18.

Chambers, J., T. Clark, L. Dantzler, and J. Baldwin. 1994. "Perceived attractiveness, facial features, and African self-consciousness." *Journal of Black Psychology* 20(3):305–24.

Charon, J. 2001. *Symbolic Interactionism: An Introduction, An Interpretation, An Integration*. Englewood Cliffs, NJ: Prentice Hall.

Chia, R., L. Allred, W. Grossnickle, and G. Lee. 1998. "Effects of attractiveness and gender on the perception of achievement-related variables." *The Journal of Social Psychology* 138(4):471–77.

Copp, M. 1998. "When emotion work is doomed to fail: Ideological and structural constraints on emotion management." *Symbolic Interaction* 21(3):299–328.

Coventry, M. 1998. "The tyranny of the esthetic: Surgery's most intimate violation." *On the Issues* 7(3):16–60.

Davis, F. 1992. *Fashion, Culture and Identity*. Chicago: University of Chicago Press.

Degher, D., and G. Hughes. 1999. "The adoption and management of a 'fat' identity." In *Interpreting Weight: The Social Management of Fatness and Thinness*, edited by J. Sobal and D. Maurer, pp. 11–27. New York: Aldine de Gruyter.

Dietz, W. H. 1998. "Health consequences of obesity in youth: Childhood predictors of adult disease." *Pediatrics* 101(3):518–25.

Dion, K., E. Bersheid, and E. Walster. 1972. "What is beautiful is good!" *Journal of Personality and Social Psychology* 24:285–90.

Eckman, P. 1992. "Facial expression and emotion." *American Psychologist* 48:384–92.

Feagin, J., and M. Sikes. 1994. *Living with Racism*. Boston: Beacon Press.

Feingold, A., and R. Mazella. 1998. "Gender differences in body image are increasing." *Psychological Science* 9:190–95.

Franzoi, S. 1995. "The body-as-object versus the body-as-process: Gender differences and gender considerations." *Sex Roles* 33(5/6):417–37.

Garner, D., and A. Kearney-Cooke. 1996. "Body image 1996." *Psychology Today* 29(March/April):55–61.

Gimlin, D. 2000. "Cosmetic surgery: Beauty as commodity." *Qualitative Sociology* 23(1):77–98.

Goffman, E. 1959. *The Presentation of Self in Everyday Life*. New York: Doubleday Anchor Books.

———. 1963a. *Behavior in Public Places*. New York: Free Press.

———. 1963b. *Stigma*. Englewood Cliffs, NJ: Prentice Hall.

———. 1967. *Interaction Ritual: Essays on Face-to-Face Behavior*. New York: Doubleday Anchor Books.

Granfield, R. 1991. "Making it by faking it: Working class students in an elite academic environment." *Journal of Contemporary Ethnology* 20(3):331–51.

Hansen, K. 1996. *Just a Temp*. Philadelphia: Temple University Press.

Haskins, K., and H. Ransford. 1999. "The relationship between weight and career payoffs among women." *Sociological Forum* 14(2):295–318.

Hebl, M., and T. Heatherton. 1998. "The stigma of obesity in women: The difference is black and white." *Personality and Social Psychology Bulletin* 24(4):417–26.

Hesse-Biber, S. 1996. *Am I Thin Enough Yet? The Cult of Thinness and the Commercialization of Identity*. Oxford University Press.

Hochschild, A. 1983. *The Managed Heart: Commercialization of Human Feeling*. Berkeley: University of California Press.

Joanisse, L., and A. Synnott. 1999. "Fighting back: Reactions and resistance to the stigma of obesity." In *Interpreting Weight: The Social Management of Fatness and Thinness*, edited by J. Sobal and D. Maurer, pp. 49–70. New York: Aldine de Gruyter.

Kang, J. 2000. "Cyber-race." *Harvard Law Review* 113(5):1131–63.

Karp, D. 1986. " 'You can take the boy out of Dorchester, but you can't take Dorchester out of the boy': Toward a social psychology of mobility." *Symbolic Interaction* 9: 19–36.

Karp, D., and W. Yoels. 1976. "The college classroom: Some observations on the meanings of student participation." *Sociology and Social Research* 60: 421–38.

Kaw, E. 1994. " 'Opening' faces: The politics of cosmetic surgery and Asian American women." In *Many Mirrors: Body Image and Social Relations*, edited by N. Sault, pp. 241–65. New Brunswick, NJ: Rutgers University Press.

Kessler, S. 1996. "The medical construction of gender: Case management of intersexed infants." In *Gender & Scientific Authority*, edited by B. Laslett, S. Kohlstedt, H. Longino, and E. Hammonds, pp. 340–63. Chicago: University of Chicago Press.

Kimle, P., and M. Damhorst. 1997. "A grounded theory model of the ideal business image for women." *Symbolic Interaction* 20(1):45–68.

Kirschenman, J., and K. Neckerman. 1998. "We'd love to hire them, but . . ." In *The Meaning of Race for Employers in Working America: Continuity, Conflict, and Change*, edited by A. Wharton. Mountain View, CA: Mayfield.

Kivisto, P., and D. Pittman. 2001. "Goffman's dramaturgical sociology: Personal sales and service in a commodified world." In *Illuminating Social Life*, 2nd ed., edited by P. Kivisto. Thousand Oaks, CA: Pine Forge Press.

Konradi, A. 1999. "'I don't have to be afraid of you': Rape survivors' emotion management in court." *Symbolic Interaction* 22(1):45–77.

Lance, L. 1998. "Gender differences in heterosexual dating: A content analysis of personal ads." *The Journal of Men's Studies* 6(3):297–305.

Leidner, R. 1993. *Fast Food, Fast Talk: Service Work and the Routinization of Everyday Life.* Berkeley: University of California Press.

Lemert, C., and A. Branaman, eds. 1997. *The Goffman Reader.* Malden, MA: Blackwell Publishers.

Lofland, L. 1972. "Self-management in public settings: Part I." *Urban Life* (1):93–108.

Manning, P. 1992. *Erving Goffman and Modern Sociology.* Stanford, CA: Stanford University Press.

Marlowe, C., S. Schneider, and C. Nelson. 1996. "Gender and attractiveness biases in hiring decisions: Are more experienced managers less biased?" *Journal of Applied Psychology* 81:11–21.

Mason-Schrock, D. 1996. "Transsexuals' narrative construction of the 'true' self." *Social Psychology Quarterly* 59(3):176–92.

Mathews, J. 1997. "Is Biology Destiny?" *Baltimore Sun*, September 24: 1E, 5E.

Milkie, M. 1999. "Social comparisons, reflected appraisals, and mass media: The impact of pervasive beauty images on black and white girls' self-concepts." *Social Psychology Quarterly* 62:190–210.

Molloy, B., and S. Herzberger. 1998. "Body image and self-esteem: A comparison of African-American and Caucasian women." *Sex Roles* 38:631–43.

Molloy, J. 1977. *The Women's Dress for Success Book.* Chicago: Follet.

Muth, J., and T. Cash. 1997. "Body-image attitudes: What difference does gender make?" *Journal of Applied Social Psychology* 27:1438–53.

Nelson, J. 1994. *Volunteer Slavery: My Authentic Negro Experience.* New York: Penguin Books.

Pagan, J., and A. Davila. 1997. "Obesity, occupational attainment, and earnings." *Social Science Quarterly* 78(3):756–70.

Paul, R., and J. Townsend. 1995. "Shape up or ship out? Employment discrimination against the overweight." *Employee Responsibilities and Rights Journal* 8(2):133–45.

Perlini, A., S. Bertolissi, and D. Lind. 1999. "The effects of women's age and physical appearance on evaluations of attractiveness and social desirability." *The Journal of Social Psychology* 139(3):343–54.

Pierce, J. 1996. *Gender Trials: Emotional Lives in Contemporary Law Firms.* Berkeley: University of California Press.

Pierce, J., and J. Wardle. 1997. "Cause and effect beliefs and self-esteem of overweight children." *Journal of Child Psychology and Psychiatry and Allied Disciplines* 38(6):645–50.

Plant, E., J. Hyde, D. Keltner, and P. Devine. 2000. "The gender stereotyping of emotion." *Psychology of Women Quarterly* 24(1):81–92.

Rafaeli, A., J. Dutton, C. Harquail, and S. Mackie-Lewis. 1997. "Navigating by attire: The use of dress by female administrative employees." *Academy of Management Journal* 40 (1):9–45.

Reay, D. 1997. "The double-bind of the 'working-class' feminist academic: The success of failure or the failure of success?" In *Class Matters,* edited by P. Mahoney and C. Zmroczek, pp. 18–29. Philadelphia: Taylor & Francis.

Robinson, T., and J. Ward. 1995. "African American adolescents and skin color." *Journal of Black Psychology* 21(3):256–74.

Rooks, N. 1996. *Hair Raising: Beauty, Culture, and African American Women*. New Brunswick, NJ: Rutgers University Press.

Sansom, W. 1956. *A Contest of Ladies*. London: Hogarth.

Scott, M., and S. Lyman. 1968. "Accounts." *The American Sociological Review* 33:44–62.

Sennet, R., and R. Cobb. 1973. *The Hidden Injuries of Class*. New York: Random House.

Simmel, G. 1904. "Fashion." Reprinted in *American Journal of Sociology* 62 (May 1957):541–58.

Staske, S. 1998. "The normalization of problematic emotion in conversations between close relational partners: *Inter*personal emotion work." *Symbolic Interaction* 21:59–86.

Stone, G. 1962. "Appearance and the self." In *Human Behavior and Social Processes*, edited by A. Rose. Boston: Houghton Mifflin.

Thompson, M., and V. Keith. 2001. "The blacker the berry: Gender, skin tone, self-esteem, and self-efficacy." *Gender & Society* 15(3):336–57.

Veblen, T. 1899. *The Theory of the Leisure Class*. New York: Macmillan.

Watson, N. 2002. "Well, I know this is going to sound very strange to you, but I don't see myself as a disabled person: Identity and disability." *Disability & Society* 17(5):509–27.

Weinberg, D. 1996. "The enactment and appraisal of authenticity in a skid row therapeutic community." *Symbolic Interaction* 19(2):137–62.

Wood, J. 2003. *Gendered Lives: Communication, Gender, and Culture*. 5th ed. Belmont, CA: Wadsworth.

Yoels, W., and J. Clair. 1994. "Never enough time: How medical residents manage a scarce resource." *Journal of Contemporary Ethnography* 23(2):185–213.

———. 1995. "Laughter in the clinic: Humor as social organization." *Symbolic Interaction* 18(1):39–58.

Zandy, J., ed. 1995. *Liberating Memory: Our Work and Our Working-Class Consciousness*. New Brunswick, NJ: Rutgers University Press.

Part Two

Establishing Social Order

Part two demonstrates how the elements of face-to-face communication can be employed to analyze aspects of everyday life. Our concern centers on the ways in which people establish predictable, meaningful patterns of behavior in a wide variety of daily settings. The four contexts discussed in this part are contacts between strangers, or urban public encounters; contacts between intimates; relationships in the world of work in bureaucracies; and the institutions that shape our experience of health and illness. We also consider the definitions of the situations people create through their participation in various social arrangements, and we examine how power and status differences affect face-to-face encounters. The chapters in part two will help you understand that the meanings of any human relationship are socially constructed; that is to say, people establish meanings through their daily communications with one another.

Chapter 4 is concerned with how people perceive and interact with others in anonymous public places. Our analysis proceeds from the observation that people in public places are strangers to one another. They employ various adaptations to cope with the huge volume of stranger contacts experienced in cities and may adopt strategies to avoid direct communication. The consideration of stranger relations in chapter 4 describes the connections among information, trust, and risk in *any* interaction.

The substance of chapter 5 is intimate relations. This chapter begins with the argument that intimacy is a socially constructed, symbolic phenomenon. The meanings of intimacy vary both historically and in terms of individuals' personal attributes. The building of relationships is an ongoing process, and strangers go through typical stages in their transformation into intimates. The last sections of chapter 5, which look at the literature on living together, staying single, and divorce, give you some idea of recent changes in the meanings given to intimacy, sexuality, and commitment.

In our analyses of relations among strangers and intimates, we touch on questions of power only briefly. Chapter 6 provides an important addition to our treatment of social interaction by stressing the differences in access to decision-making processes for various individuals and groups. As a result of these differences, some individuals are in more strategic positions than others to have their definitions of the situation translated into actuality. There is also a relationship between role-taking ability and the power accorded the positions occupied in society. You will see that such daily behaviors as staring, pointing, crowding, touching, and interrupting others' conversations are all functions of power differentials between people.

Chapter 7 expands on the importance of the positions a person occupies in the social order by focusing more specifically on everyday life in bureaucratic organizations. Contacts between people in modern societies are increasingly mediated by the intervention of third-party agencies such as insurance companies, government bureaus, and the courts. Our treatment of bureaucratic life emphasizes the concepts of multiple realities, the processes of negotiation, and the symbolic foundations of social structures. You will be shown how people's locations in the organizational hierarchy of a work organization shape their conceptions of their jobs. You will also learn how workers strive to achieve some degree of autonomy in their work lives.

The last chapter in part two examines the meanings attached to health and illness in America. Here, as throughout this book, we demonstrate that every human experience must be viewed from the subjective perspectives of the individuals going through it. Illness would seem at first glance to be thoroughly an objective fact. Either one is sick or one is well. Rather, health and illness are in large measure the product of ethnic, class, and cultural differences, as well as an outcome of the negotiations between "patients" and the health care system. In the second part of chapter 8 we present a case study of one "illness"—depression—which exemplifies the notion that the experience of illness, like everything else, is a product of meanings arising out of human communication.

EVERYDAY URBAN RELATIONS
CONTACTS AMONG STRANGERS

When we were children, we were taught to avoid strangers and even fear them, for our own protection. Who knew what a stranger might really want who stopped you on the street asking for directions, approached to sell you something, or chose a seat next to you on a bus? Because we cannot know for sure what the motives of strangers are, we learn to regard them with suspicion.

Strangers are strange precisely because we know little or nothing about them. Their lives may be guided by symbol systems different from our own, and they may not share our concept of social reality. In such a case the essential meanings they give to objects, events, and situations will be different from our own. This difference is what makes communication and interaction with strangers so difficult.

Sociological Definitions of the Stranger

The stranger has always intrigued sociological theorists. Georg Simmel, for example, was concerned not with one-to-one relationships between strangers but with new relationships between an individual and a larger social system (a group, an institution, a community). Simmel (1950b) conceived of the special quality of the stranger status as always remaining peripheral or marginal to groups with which interactions are being sought. The best example is the successful trader or merchant who has direct dealings with a number of groups but does not seek assimilation into any of them. The stranger's distinctive position is to be near and distant to a group at the same time.

95

In American sociology, the stranger as a social type has often been equated with what Robert Park referred to as **marginal man.** He applied the idea to immigrant racial and ethnic groups in the city who remain marginal members of urban society because they are in the process of giving up their old cultures without having fully assimilated the culture of the new. The marginal man stands between the two cultures as "one who lives in two worlds, in both of which he is more or less a stranger" (Park, 1928:892). The wandering Jew, historically without a homeland, was the best example of the stranger or marginal man by Park's definition.

Alfred Schutz (1960) also speaks of the stranger in terms of an individual's relationship to organized group life. His analysis focuses on the definition of the stranger as one who is not knowledgeable about the cultural pattern of the group to which admission is sought. For a stranger approaching a group, the relevancies of everyday life are not the same as for the group's members. The stranger therefore is not sure how to interpret social situations, events, and behaviors. The stranger, puzzled by the apparent incoherence and inconsistency of the group's cultural pattern, is likely to question elements of group life that full-fledged members take for granted. In Schutz's words, "The cultural pattern of the approached group is to the stranger not a shelter but a field of adventure, not a matter of course but a questionable topic of investigation, not an instrument for disentangling problematic situations but a problematic situation itself and one hard to master" (1960:104).

For Peter Berger and Hansfried Kellner (1970), an essential element of the concept of strangeness is the fact that unacquainted individuals come from different face-to-face contexts and **areas of conversation,** with different biographies and life experiences. Their pasts have a similar structure, but because they do not have a shared past they are likely to define situations quite differently.

Biographical and Cultural Strangers

Sociologists have defined the stranger concept in very specialized ways. We will adopt a more conventional use of the term and differentiate between those who are **biographical strangers,** because we have never before met them and have no information about their pasts, and those who are **cultural strangers,** because they occupy symbolic worlds different from our own. We are cautious in the presence of both those whom we have never met before and those who do not share our values, attitudes, or lifestyles.

Much of a person's time is spent in front of an audience of strangers. Public thoroughfares are crowded with people who are biographical and often cultural strangers to one another. Each time you enter a subway, stand in a line, go jogging in a city park, attend a concert, or shop in a discount store, you are in effect performing in front of an audience of people you have never seen before and whom, in all likelihood, you will never see again.

When biographical or cultural strangers confront one another, they typically put on a performance that reflects the uncertainties in such encounters. In this chapter we will explore the uncertainties that accompany relations with strangers and the strategies which can be employed to take them into account. Patterned and predictable presentations of self are necessary if individuals are to manage and make sense of their daily lives in public places.

The Paradox of Doubt and Trust

Social life could not proceed in an orderly fashion if a **norm of trust** did not underlie our behaviors with others (Semmes, 1991). By and large, we trust that others' spoken words and actions really represent the kinds of individuals they are. Each day we face situations that demand such trust. For example, in dealing with bank tellers, store clerks, or waitresses, there is a moment when we hand them our money and must trust them to complete the transaction honestly by returning with the proper change. What could you do in a restaurant if the waitress claimed you gave her a $10 rather than a $20 bill? Normally we must, in order to get through the day, trust that others mean us no harm, that we are not being purposely misled in our encounters with them. Social life would be intolerably complicated if we had to routinely suspend the norm of trust.

While trust is essential in order to maintain an ordered social life, there is always some measure of doubt about the true motives, goals, and intentions of others. This is because role-taking efforts can never be perfect; we can never identify absolutely with others. All social interactions, even those between intimates, therefore involve some measure of doubt or risk. Our inability to suspend doubt fully in our social interactions presents the paradox that we must doubt and trust others at the same time. It is true that ordered interaction proceeds on the general assumption of trust, *but we can never be certain that such an assumption is perfectly safe*. A comment by a Greenwich Village resident interviewed by Mitch Duneier (1999) in his study of life on city sidewalks reflects the conflict surrounding the issue of trust: "That's what cities are about . . . You want to be able to trust in the kindness of everyone around you . . . [but] you can't ever look anyone in the eyes, you have to be really guarded and it actually ends up being sort of rude . . ." (p. 199).

Trust is an aspect of everyday life with which we must deal all the time. However, it is one of those "taken-for-granted" aspects that we seldom analyze. Sometimes we are sharply aware of our distrust of others and the reasons for this distrust. At other times we may be only vaguely aware that we are uneasy and distrustful in the presence of certain people.

Uncertainty in Interactions with Strangers

We are most likely to distrust others, as a general rule, when they obviously have different social attributes than we do. An unshaven, slovenly man approaching a woman who does not know him on a dark city street could be assumed to be a mugger, for example. Those who try to initiate encounters when there are discrepancies in their attributes are likely to find their motives misinterpreted. We depend heavily on immediate observation of others to determine whether we can trust them and whether interaction with them is therefore permissible. We carry around pretty clear expectations about the appropriateness of interactions between people with particular attributes.

Race, for example, may particularly affect interaction between people who do not know one another. Elijah Anderson (1999) describes the importance of race in determining people's reactions to black males in public encounters in his study of a racially mixed neighborhood in Philadelphia. Although the white residents do not think that the black people they ordinarily see on the streets are bound to rob them, the fact that there have been several incidents of black people robbing a bank and committing other crimes in the area gives "a peculiar edge to race relations between blacks and whites" (p. 17). Both blacks and whites are aware that young, black males are disproportionately involved in crime. "A black male walking into the stores, especially a jewelry store, can see this phenomenon. The sales personnel pay particular attention to people until they feel they have passed inspection, and black males are almost always given extra scrutiny" (p. 17).

Jerry Kang, an Asian-American lawyer, describes his own reactions:

> After a long conference, I am walking in a strange downtown, late at night, looking for a taxi. I see two people approaching me. From a distance, I ascertain their rough size. From their clothing and body shape, I guess that they are male. As they walk closer, I see that they are Black. For reasons I cannot explain, my heartbeat quickens, and I become anxious, glancing around for other people. I begin taking a few steps to cross to the other side of the street but decide against it. Instead, I grip my briefcase more tightly, closer to my body, then walk at a faster pace. As I pass the Black men, I peek over my shoulder just to make sure that they have walked on by. (Kang, 2000:1140)

Encounters with strangers pose special trust problems because we have no information about them, other than face information, or that which is obtainable through immediate observation. Sometimes a person's general appearance or location can tell us a good deal about him or her. In the presence of strangers, however, information of this sort is usually incomplete and possibly unreliable. To judge with assurance the genuineness of others' performances and the meaning of their behaviors, we must know about their "areas of conversation." The more we know about others' biographies and life experiences, the better we are able to role-take with them. To illustrate the point, knowing that a woman is diabetic helps us to interpret what she is doing by injecting some substance into her arm with a hypodermic needle. If we have knowledge of her biography as a diabetic, the interpretation "maintaining her health" is a far more credible explanation of her behavior than "maintaining her habit." Sometimes people may deliberately attempt to create an atmosphere that affirms trust when surface signs might indicate otherwise. Brent Staples (1992) describes the measures he has adopted in his nighttime walks through New York streets to thwart perceptions of those who may fear he is a "dangerous black man"—he whistles classical music!

How Cabdrivers Size Up Strangers

The relationship between face information and trust is especially crucial in some interactions with strangers. City cabdrivers, for example, who must be in continual contact with strangers, adopt certain strategies to assess which ones to accept as passengers. Henslin (1991) documented the informal criteria cabdrivers use in sizing up the trustworthiness of passengers. He conceptualizes trust in dramaturgical terms: "[T]rust consists of an actor offering a definition of himself and an audience being willing to interact with the actor on the basis of that definition" (p. 180). Like everyone else, cabdrivers must determine the conditions under which they have reason to question the performances put on by others. In deciding whether a passenger is to be trusted, they consider: (1) the setting in which the person is picked up, (2) the characteristics of the person as judged by his or her appearance, and (3) the individual's behavior. In other words, cabdrivers simultaneously consider the characteristics of the *person* they pick up, the *places* where they pick them up, and the *poses* adopted by their passengers.

Cabdrivers ordinarily accept a person's self-definition as a passenger who wishes to be taken to a particular destination. Sometimes, however, they have reason to distrust a person's performance as a legitimate passenger. Each time a passenger approaches, the driver must decide if it is safe to make the trip. The driver's trust judgments are made on the basis of the individual's age, race, gender, general demeanor, and social class; the neighborhood and the time of the day of the pickup; and the announced destination of the passenger. When the configuration of these factors indicates the need for distrust, the prudent driver usually decides to pass up the potential passenger.

Like people in general, when deciding whether to trust or distrust a stranger, cabdrivers rely heavily on commonly accepted stereotypes about social classes and groups in American society. The results of Henslin's study indicated that drivers expect comparatively less trouble from passengers in upper- and middle-class areas, females, whites, and the very young or very old.

The Case for Being Uncertain about Strangers in Public Places

Mutual strangeness puts limits on people's role-taking capacity and therefore on the ways they can and will relate to each other. The following propositions sum up the reasons why interactions between strangers have a large element of uncertainty in them.

1. There is a measure of uncertainty attached to *any* interaction since we can never be completely certain of another's motives.

2. The uncertainty of risk decreases as we acquire more information about others, since the accuracy of our role-taking increases.

3. Strangers in public places possess no biographical information about each other.

4. It follows that public relations between strangers carry particularly great uncertainties.

The Structure of Everyday Public Behaviors

Public behaviors seldom require more than a passing acquaintance, and strangers typically confront each other in highly anonymous situations. While the ability to remain anonymous increases the potential for individual freedom of action, it does not decrease the constraints imposed on individual behaviors by society. In fact, anonymity must be created and maintained through *social relationships,* and this is itself a social effort. Rather than being a state which *is independent* of social relationships, therefore, anonymity must be produced by people interacting with one another. The structure of public behaviors between strangers is reinforced by efforts to maintain the **norm of anonymity.**

Efforts to Remain Anonymous

The creation of anonymity through interaction can be seen in the efforts people make to avoid unnecessary encounters with unfamiliar others. As in many other public contexts, individuals engage in what Erving Goffman (1963) described as **civil inattention** when they are forced to recognize others' presence while trying to minimize the possibility of a "focused" interaction with them. In other words, they try to minimize the interactional claims that others might make on them. Lyn Lofland has argued that civil inattention may be viewed as the *sine qua non* of city life in that it "makes possible co-presence without co-mingling, awareness without engrossment, courtesy without conversation" (1998:30). But as Lofland notes, this is not because of the "stimulus overload" which concerned Simmel, or the psychological shutdown thought to result in the "typical" urban attitudes of emotional coldness and unconcern. "Civil inattention suggests that when humans in the public realm appear to ignore one another, they do so *not* out of psychological distress but out of a ritual regard, and their response is *not* the asocial one of 'shut down' but the fully social one of politeness" (1998:30) (emphasis in original). Candace West (1999) provides a great example:

> I notice a supreme test of civil inattention just outside the window of the shop. A man is walking down the street with black grease paint on his face, a hat with Viking horns on his head, and a huge spear, which he is carrying upright in his fist. . . . As he moves toward other pedestrians, they do their best to seem urbane—catching sight of him from about 8 feet away and averting their eyes as they near him—but whipping their heads around to stare at him, just after he passes by. (p. 8)

This interactional effort is, of course, reciprocal, as all the individuals in the situation are doing the same thing. Subway passengers choose seats that maximize their distance from fellow travelers. They limit their visual attention to props they may have with them (books, magazines, newspapers) or to advertising over the windows; they take great pains to avoid physical contact once the subway car begins to get crowded, and the like. These regulations, shared and known about by all participants, are designed to limit the accessibility of unacquainted individuals to one another. By utilizing knowledge of these regulations—or, as Lofland calls them, principles—along with a general understanding of what's expected in public behavior, "strangers are able to communicate to one another messages such as: 'I want my privacy and am not available to be spoken to or encountered in any way;' 'I know you are present and you know I am present but we are, of course, each invisible to the other;' or 'I am not intruding and will not intrude into your personal space; in fact, I am going out of my way to avoid doing so' " (Lofland, 1998:34–35).

There are, of course, circumstances when it is acceptable for civil inattention to be breached. Carol Gardner (1995) found in her observations that "stranger etiquette" permits someone with a dog or a child to be "approached at will" (p. 93). Duneier and Molotch (1999) observed that in Greenwich Village (as elsewhere), strangers pet one another's animals or ask about a toddler's identity ("Oh, is this your grandson?"). According to these authors, "Perhaps to the advantage of both parties, the dog or child serves to modulate intimacy, permitting, in effect, indirect communication via the dependent creature" (p. 1279). However, dogs (and children) can also induce and sustain unwanted interaction, as in the case of Keith, a homeless African-American street vendor, who calls to a dog being walked by a white woman:

> Keith: "Come here, Dottie." . . . Pulling on the leash, the dog tugs her owner over to Keith who begins playing with Dottie. Keith: "Sit down." The dog sits as Laura, the dog's owner, stands by looking distracted, pulling on the leash. (Duneier and Molotch, 1999:1281)

The interaction continues for a few minutes, with Keith primarily talking to the dog but attempting to engage its owner in conversation. "The woman has the dog by the leash, which means that when Keith gains access to the dog, he has the woman by the leash. Developing rapport with a dog who does not recognize class or race distinctions helps Keith entangle a woman who does" (p. 1282).

Efforts to Assure Public Privacy

The order of public life is clearly demonstrated in situations where a person's moral identity is called into question. David Karp (1973) studied the behaviors of customers of pornographic bookstores and movie theaters in Times Square, the ultimate example of the anonymous public place. Karp observed a number of strategies employed in these settings to assure a kind of **public privacy**. In the bookstore, shoppers maintain a strict impersonality toward one another. Under no circumstances do they make physical or verbal contact, and the clerks quickly eject anyone who interferes with the privacy of other customers. The normative structure appears to demand silence and careful avoidance of any focused interaction. Customers adopt techniques that allow them to complete their purchases as quickly and unobtrusively as possible. They are more likely to make a purchase if left alone. Customers strive to appear as uninterested as possible.

Similarly, efforts to maintain public privacy can be observed in a cigarette shop, "Now, the only store in town that allows smoking on its premises" (West, 1999). West describes the discomfort involved in this experience:

> Arriving at the doorway of this shop, I am aware of other pedestrians who studiously avert their eyes from me as I enter. Buying cigarettes these days feels like buying tampons did when I was 13—making an acutely stigmatizing purchase that you hope nobody notices. . . . Not only do nonsmokers look away from smokers as the latter enter this shop but also smokers themselves avoid looking at one another as they pull cartons from the shelves. Skulking out with my plain unmarked bag. . . . (p. 8)

Such settings encourage a highly structured social situation in which privacy norms are standardized and readily understood. The system works so that each person's bid for privacy is complemented by the behaviors of others. Even in anonymous public places such as Times Square, people are very much constrained in the production of their behaviors. Despite the impersonality and anonymity of daily life, and despite the fact that actions in the public domain are overwhelmingly performed in front of strangers, it is necessary to constantly engage in impression management. When it comes to maintaining a proper image of ourselves, everyone counts, both intimates and strangers. Impression management strategies used by customers in strip clubs, for example, seem to indicate that "more than relying on dress or body adornment, they depended on conversation, gesture, and facial expressions to try and convey whatever image they wanted to the strippers, or friends, or to other customers" (Wood, 2000:21–22). Customers seem to guard their expressions to keep other customers or the strippers from thinking they are enjoying it too much. According to one club dancer, "If they're even that much more attracted to you, that makes them kind of squirm and look around like 'someone's going to think I'm enjoying this too much,' you know, like 'I'm not supposed to be watching her like this' " (p. 21).

Abiding by the Rules

An example illustrating the sometimes elaborate strategies adopted by strangers in order to maintain a distinctive public privacy can be found in Laud Humphreys' classic *Tearoom Trade: Impersonal Sex in Public Places* (1970). Humphreys analyzed the behaviors of homosexual men meeting in public restrooms (known as "tearooms"). He describes these settings as well-organized places where the participants strictly abide by the rules. The activities of approaching the room, positioning oneself inside it, signaling one's availability, contracting for the nature of the sexual exchange, completing the sexual act, coping with intrusions, and finally leaving the situation are carefully patterned. Nearly all of these negotiations occur without any verbal interaction between the participants.

The importance of Humphreys' study goes far beyond description of the particular behaviors he documented. The fact that these kinds of behaviors can be accomplished at all serves as a broader commentary on the orderliness of everyday public activities. In Humphreys' words:

> Analysis of the highly structured patterns that arise in this particular situation increases our understanding of the more general rules of interaction by which people in routine encounters of all kinds manage their identities, create impressions, move towards their goals, and control information about themselves, minimizing the costs and risks in concerted action with others. (1970:ix)

Although Humphreys' book won a prestigious sociological award, it also gave rise to controversy, raising serious questions about ethics in sociological research.

New technology has the potential to change social relations in public places. Mobile phones, for example, raise interesting questions about public privacy: "Is it, for example, proper to talk about private matters on a mobile phone in public places?" (Persson, 2001). Perhaps more to the point: Why do people, who normally keep their private lives to themselves, sometimes reveal the most intimate details to strangers around them when speaking on mobile phones in public places? The mobile phone seems to make us feel as if we are alone, even in public places where we are surrounded by many other people. This suggests that the phones, in the same way as newspapers or books when one is dining alone in public, serve as "involvement shields" (Goffman, 1963); that is, objects used to make oneself seem inaccessible to others (Persson, 2001). Those within earshot engage in civil inattention, not showing that they hear what may be intimate details about the caller's life. It is no surprise, then, that modern etiquette books have a paragraph on mobile phone etiquette.

With technological innovation comes the need for new rules regarding civil inattention and public privacy. The use of video camcorders to videotape people may sometimes cross lines of propriety. Individuals who are taped without their knowledge or consent may feel that their privacy has been invaded. Such feelings can result when the behavior of the camcorder user violates or appears to violate the established social norm for visual behavior. This norm, as Goffman (1963) observed, holds that it is customary for people who are present in a public setting but are not interacting to engage in civil inattention. This ritual consists of a glance of acknowledgment that the other person is present, followed by restraint of further visual attention. Visual attention after the acknowledgment can be construed as a breach of etiquette or, more seriously, as an invasion of privacy (Crabb, 1996).

Crabb (1996) extends this definition to include such behavior when it occurs with technological devices, coming up with what he describes as a "viewing norm"; that is, "a rule that prohibits prolonged visual (or audiovisual) attention to another person who is present but with whom one is not interacting" (p. 806) (see box).

Impression Management with Strangers

The patterns of behavior followed in the situations described above not only maintain the norm of anonymity and assure public privacy, they also are designed to protect personal identities, minimize social risk, and give the

Video Voyeurism

Imagine that you are at a party. As you walk around, you spot a man and a woman who are dancing. You watch them for a few minutes.

Imagine that you are at a party with your video camcorder. As you walk around, you spot a man and woman who are dancing. You videotape them for a few minutes.

Imagine that you are walking around town. You spot a man and woman who are kissing passionately. You watch them for a few minutes.

Imagine that you are walking around town with your video camcorder. You spot a man and woman who are kissing passionately. You videotape them for a few minutes.

How much would you approve of watching (videotaping) the two people dancing (kissing)?*

Peter Crabb asked these questions of undergraduates in a study examining whether viewing with a camcorder would be met with higher approval than watching with the naked eye (1996). He chose these scenarios in an effort to include activities that varied in situational demand for privacy, and thus in the degree to which civil inattention should be exercised by potential onlookers. Not surprisingly, participants approved more of viewing in the low-privacy scenario (dancing) than in the high-privacy scenario (kissing passionately). Interestingly, males more than females approved of viewing in the high-privacy situation. Students who had experience with video camcorders were more approving of viewing than those who had not, suggesting that perhaps experience with camcorders may have broadened their acceptance of viewing behavior generally.

Crabb's findings appear to show that participants' evaluations of viewing behavior were affected by the use of a video camcorder. Videotaping was consistently seen as more tolerable than watching, suggesting that the viewing norm will be less effective in restraining a person's viewing behavior when a camcorder is used.

Crabb designed a second study to examine the effect of camcorders on subjective comfort during forced violation of the viewing norm. His prediction was that participants using a camcorder to videotape people would report higher levels of comfort than participants who watched without camcorders. This time he had students stand at a fixed point in a room and videotape or watch two confederates, a male-female dyad seated facing each other and conversing at a volume that was barely audible to participants. After five minutes, participants were instructed to stop and were asked, "How comfortable did you feel videotaping (watching) the couple?" and "How much privacy would you say the couple deserved?" As expected, participants who used camcorders were significantly more comfortable than participants who watched with the naked eye. This time, female and male participants were equally comfortable. In response to the question about privacy, participants believed the couple deserved a moderate amount of privacy, with no difference between conditions.

> The results of the second study appear to show that the relative comfort of viewing with a camcorder would, in theory, make it easier to engage in videotaping behavior that may be construed as rude or invasive of privacy. What worries Crabb are the implications of routine use of video camcorders (and other similar devices). A technology that can be used for audiovisual intrusion may affect the motivation for doing so; that is to say, might using video camcorders encourage potential intruders to invade others' privacy? Viewing behavior that was once proscribed conceivably could become an accepted cultural practice.
>
> * From Crabb, P. B. 1996. "Video camcorders and civil inattention." *Journal of Social Behavior and Personality* 11(4):805–16.

appearance of propriety. Thus they are examples of the impression management techniques people use to foster particular images of themselves in their interactions with others (see chapter 3). They also are examples of the **self-management techniques** people use to control the identities they present to others and to protect themselves when in the presence of strangers.

Lofland used an interactionist perspective to study the self-management techniques used by strangers in their everyday interactions. Her work was based on the assertion: "If a person is to exist as a social being, as an organism with a self, there must be some minimal guarantees that in interaction with others he will receive the affirmation and confirmation of himself as 'right'" (1971a:95). The risk for the self in confronting strangers in public places is that they may be unable to provide this confirmation. An encounter with a stranger may even *disconfirm* the other person's "rightness."

The State of Involved Indifference

In their efforts to maintain anonymity and protect public privacy, strangers in public places adopt elaborate strategies to avoid one another. This does not mean that they are entirely uninvolved with one another, however. Strangers in public places also adopt mechanisms to produce ordered relationships. Even the **avoidance behaviors** engaged in by strangers are highly coordinated social activities demanding some degree of cooperation. To suggest that humans are like atoms anonymously floating around each other at random is not a very insightful description of the public relationships of strangers. It fails to account for the means by which public life is managed and ordered. While strangers rarely talk with one another or exchange information of a private nature, it is nevertheless clear that public life is *ordered* rather than chaotic (see box).

Lofland (1998) has suggested that we think in terms of people carrying around and consulting (symbolically) guidebooks to help them define the situation and direct their own conduct. Some of her titles are: *Grammars of Motility*, which recommends rules of social and physical movement in the public realm; e.g., how to make one's way through crowded streets and intersections, choose a seat in a crowded bar or restaurant or bus, escape

Going with the Flow

What strikes researchers with the discipline and patience necessary for careful observation of public behavior is the orderliness and patternedness with which city denizens seem to conduct even their most fleeting and ostensibly "trivial" encounters (Lofland, 1998). "For order to be possible, people must behave like competent pedestrians and must expect copresent others to act accordingly" (Wolfinger, 1995:323). Clearly there are social conventions which order this commonplace behavior in an anonymous situation. Yamori (1998) describes the "banded structure" shown by a collectivity of pedestrians on a large crosswalk in Osaka, Japan:

> ... flows of pedestrians pass by each other, forming in orderly fashion into a few bands or lanes. Each band contains either one or the other of the two groups of pedestrians walking in opposite directions from each other. It achieves a smooth traffic flow of pedestrians without which they would bump and jumble into each other in a disorganized mass. (p. 530)

Once the structure is created at a macro level, it constrains individual behavior in a crowd. For example, after the banded structure has been established in a crosswalk, late-coming pedestrians are not likely to walk against or across the established stream of people. Instead, they are forced to follow preexisting traffic patterns even if for some reason they do not want to (p. 541).

It appears that pedestrian order depends essentially on two social rules: (1) people must behave like competent pedestrians, and (2) people must trust copresent others to behave like competent pedestrians. But why do people believe that other users of public places will indeed behave like competent pedestrians? Nicholas Wolfinger decided to find out by exploring a particular case in which pedestrian interactions may become problematic: rollerskating. Rollerskating presents many challenges to the normal order of public space interaction. For example, the characteristic weaving motion of a skater makes him or her seem out of control, and skaters move quickly which may surprise pedestrians. Collisions are potentially more consequential. Wolfinger surmised that the challenges rollerskating poses to pedestrians should allow special insight into the organization of public interaction.

Wolfinger engaged in first-person observation as he rollerskated approximately six miles several times a week commuting to and from the University of California, Los Angeles. He was able to create many situations where normal pedestrian order broke down (following Garfinkel, 1963), which provided diverse opportunities to examine the social dynamics of trust in public space.

Wolfinger observed that people usually looked uncomfortable in situations in which their trust was threatened (e.g., when caught by surprise because they hadn't seen him coming, or when he skated behind someone for a period of time without passing), indicating that people rely on safe passages as a matter of course. Troublesome situations test the trust that people generally take for granted. Pedestrian interaction is inherently social because it depends on the ritualized production of trust between copresent users of public space. When order is threatened, pedestrians often respond with specific remedial behaviors,

> such as apologies. When pedestrians apologize, they acknowledge an infraction of trust and reaffirm their commitment to the bargain.
>
> It is the ritualization of remedial measures that enables continued order in public places (à la Goffman, 1971). In this respect, pedestrian life is but a microcosm of social order. And public spaces are characterized to a great extent by order. The considerable attention paid to the disorderliness of America's public spaces "overlooks our day-to-day experiences; the great majority of our interactions with strangers in public places proceed comfortably and smoothly. We implicitly place confidence in scores of strangers every day, and they almost invariably oblige. Certainly, our streets are not devoid of hazards, but in sheer numbers they pale in comparison to the countless acts of trust we each experience every day" (Wolfinger, 1995:338).

unwanted attention, and so on; *Urban Visual Aids: Rules for Coding Space, Appearance, and Behavior*, "a book devoted to detailing the 'interpretation principles' by which urbanites make sense of the raw data emanating from their physical and social environment and thus define the situations in which they find themselves" (p. 28); *Verbal Sociability Customs*, "a volume that assists them in determining when, with whom, and how they may or may not try to engage their fellow urbanites in direct conversation" (p. 28).

Although this tells us much about interaction in the public realm, she suggests that what we know of the normative system of the public realm is probably more easily grasped if we conceive of it in terms of "overarching principles" rather than in terms of a plethora of narrowly focused rules (see box).

The authors of this book suggest that there is a fragile balance between noninvolvement and cooperation in the structure of public relationships. Strangers try to avoid involvement with others in order to protect themselves from unwanted and risky encounters. At the same time, they orient their behaviors toward others and cooperate enough to ensure some degree of order and sense in their everyday lives. Like the pedestrians on the sidewalk, they systematically take each other into account in public places in order to avoid unwanted encounters. In sum, we are offering a mini-max description of public encounters. Strangers are obliged both to *minimize involvement* and *maximize order*. They must take each other into account while simultaneously protecting their own and others' privacy. "What is everybody's business in the country is nobody's business in the city where people must see everything while averting their eyes" (Erickson, 2001:34).

The idea of **involved indifference** as a basis for interactions with strangers may seem contradictory. We use this term to communicate that although strangers may not engage in direct verbal interactions, they nevertheless produce their behaviors from a careful assessment of those around them. Everyday public life "works" because of the subtle blending of involvement, indifference, and cooperation.

Lofland's Principles of Public Face-to-Face Interaction

1. **Cooperative motility**. "[M]ost of us get through doors without incident, most pedestrians don't collide with other pedestrians, most buses and cars do not flatten human beings, and most people do not get body parts crushed by closing elevator doors. Most of the time our movement through the public realm is simply *uneventful*, and it is so because humans are *cooperating* with one another to make it so" (1998:29).

2. **Civil inattention**. According to Goffman (1963): "What seems to be involved is that one gives to another enough visual notice to demonstrate that one appreciates that the other is present (and that one admits openly to having seen him), while at the next moment withdrawing one's attention from him so as to express that he does not constitute a target of special curiosity or design" (pp. 83–84). "It is practiced on buses, in restaurants, on park benches, in airplanes, in hotel lobbies, even on that stereotyped symbol of urban alienation, the subway . . ." (Lofland, 1998:30).

3. **Audience role prominence**. " . . . humans often quite enthusiastically assume the audience role in the face of what are very serious problems, even catastrophes . . . " (pp. 31–32).

4. **Restrained helpfulness**. "Specifically targeted and clearly limited requests for mundane assistance and a response of restrained helpfulness . . . are a constant feature of life in the public realm. 'Could you tell me the time?' is answered by 'it's 5:12' " (p. 32).

5. **Civility toward diversity**. " . . . in face-to-face exchanges, confronted with what may be personally offensive visible variations in physical abilities, beauty, skin color and hair texture, dress style, demeanor, income, sexual preference, and so forth, the urbanite will act in a civil manner, that is, will act 'decently' vis-à-vis diversity" (p. 32).

From Lofland, L. 1998. *The Public Realm: Exploring the City's Quintessential Social Territory*. New York: Aldine de Gruyter.

The City as a World of Strangers

The volume of contacts between strangers is greatest in anonymous city places. According to Lofland, ". . . the city provides, on a permanent basis, an environment composed importantly of persons who are personally unknown to one another—composed importantly of strangers" (1998:xi). The connecting possibilities in the city make it a liberating place for many people. "The sheer mass of people allows for personal autonomy and creativity that is often chased out of less dense environments" (Erickson, 2001:34).

The Volume of Interactions in Cities

By definition, cities are places where large numbers of individuals with varied backgrounds live crowded together in a limited space. Urban areas are no longer limited to cities, however. They include the surrounding towns and suburbs in metropolitan areas and megalopolises, in which several adjacent cities are merged. Along the East Coast, for example, an unbroken metropolitan area with more than 100 people per square mile stretches from Kittery, Maine, to Quantico, Virginia. This megalopolis of over 40 million people, popularly known as Boswash, includes the cities of Boston, New York, Philadelphia, Baltimore, and Washington, D.C.

American society has become predominantly urban. In 2000, some 226 million people—accounting for 80 percent of the American population—lived in metropolitan areas. Almost one-third of Americans (30 percent) lived in metropolitan areas of at least 5 million people. In fact, between 1990 and 2000, the population within metropolitan areas increased by 14 percent, while the nonmetropolitan population grew by 10 percent. Metropolitan areas with populations of 2 to 5 million in 2000 grew the fastest, up 20 percent (Perry and Mackun, 2001). With modern transportation and communication, very few small towns are still considered rural. In large cities, however, the density of the urban population greatly increases the number of possible contacts between people. The population of New York City, for example, was more than 8 million in 2000 (U.S. Census Bureau, 2000). In midtown Manhattan you probably would not know intimately any of the thousands of people who would pass you by. Such a phenomenon constitutes an essential distinguishing feature of urban life according to Lofland, who refers to the "public realm" as "made up of those spaces in a city which tend to be inhabited by persons who are strangers to one another or who 'know' one another only in terms of occupational or other nonpersonal identity categories (for example, bus driver-customer)" (1998:9).

Social scientists have constructed explanations of everyday interactions based on the volume of potential interactions in anonymous urban settings. Georg Simmel argued that because urban dwellers are bombarded with far more stimuli than they can possibly manage, they must maintain superficial, impersonal relationships with fellow urbanites. He contrasts urban and rural life in this respect:

> With each crossing of the street, with the tempo and multiplicity of economic, occupational and social life, the city sets up a deep contrast with small town and rural life with reference to the sensory foundation of psychic life. The metropolis exacts from man as a discriminating creature a different amount of consciousness than does rural life. Here [in rural life] the rhythm of life and sensory mental imagery flows more slowly, more habitually and more evenly. . . . [T]he sophisticated character of metropolitan psychic life becomes more understandable as over against small town life which rests upon deeply felt and emotional relationships. (1950a: 410)

For Simmel, a central difference between the resident of the metropolis and the resident of the small town is the former's more rational response to the world. In his classic essay, "The Metropolis and Mental Life" he describes the urban person as reacting "with his head instead of his heart." In order to cope with the shower of highly varied stimuli characterizing urban life, individuals must be selective in terms of the stimuli to which they will respond. As the social psychologist Stanley Milgram (1970) put it, urban people, facing **stimulus overload,** must develop very clear **norms of noninvolvement**.

Behaviors in Urban Settings: Selectivity and Noninvolvement

Because of stimulus overload and the constant presence of biographical strangers in urban public places, urbanites must learn to set priorities for the events and people to which they will pay attention. Certain situations, in fact, become effectively invisible. Few people passing through an inner-city area pay much attention to the homeless down-and-outers on the street. They cannot, because if they stopped to get help for every such person they could accomplish little else.

The contexts of everyday life often carry different meanings for men and women. One useful way to think about variation in urban experience is in terms of the question, "Who can be where, when, and doing what?" We propose that urban places and times are not equally accessible to men and women. Any well-socialized urbanite knows that it is dangerous for women to be in certain city areas, especially at night. To the extent that men and women have different access to activities, places, and times, they have different subjective experiences of urban life. Moreover, while everyone is constrained to abide by norms of noninvolvement in public places, women are especially vulnerable to unwanted attentions by men and so must be more vigilant about protecting their privacy.

Goffman (1963) referred to women (also pets and children) as "open persons" who can be addressed without conventional opening devices (p. 63). This is clear in Duneier and Molotch's (1999) description of women's experiences with street men in Greenwich Village. They found that a common genre of street talk involves men calling out to women who do not respond. For example, as a woman passes by, one street man calls out, "I love you baby." Her response: "She crosses her arms and quickens her walk, ignoring the comment" (p. 1273). Gardner (1995) has called attention to these types of interaction as something women frequently experience as abusive (one particular example—not being able to pass by a construction site without being yelled at). She suggests that these interactions perhaps signal the oft-claimed fact of male privilege in public spaces, which is enforced at the extreme through women's physical vulnerability and the omnipresent threat of rape. The streets are areas in which gender, race, and class dominance are acted out.

The process of objectifying women is heightened when accompanied by racist and xenophobic remarks such as those experienced by the Latina teenagers interviewed by Madriz (1997). Not only does objectification serve to dehumanize, which is always a first step toward domination and violence, but it also provokes feelings of powerlessness and alienation (Madriz, 1997). The particular strategies women must adopt in public places to minimize being sexually harassed by men are reflective of power differences between men and women (see chapter 6). That is, men feel the right to stare (and often to make comments) at women passing on the street while women must carefully avert their eyes lest they be mistakenly seen as inviting the attention of men. Gardner comments:

> Women in public have their respectability to preserve. They may be in public but they are not supposed to be part of public life, not supposed to be out to strike up an acquaintance. If acquaintance happens, it must be under circumstances that do nothing to suggest that the woman has initiated it. . . . It is important to appreciate that avoiding the appearance of accessibility is routinely important to women in public places, not only to women attempting to prevent crime. (1988:387–88)

One of the Latina teens interviewed by Madriz told her:

> I try to be careful, that's all. [What do you mean by being careful?] I just dress conservative . . . no gold, no tight pants or sweaters. I wear my skirts all the way to my knees. . . . I also avoid going out at night by myself, avoid the wrong people. (1997, p. 46)

On the other hand, a group of poor Puerto Rican teenagers expressed the way they think a woman should dress:

> I dress the way I want . . . I even wear my gold. I love big earrings and gold chains. We should be able to dress the way we want . . . that is nobody's business. . . . If they think we look too sexy, that's their . . . problem, not mine. . . . Why is it that men can dress the way they want and women cannot? (p. 46)

However, Madriz reports that despite their belief that women have the right to dress the way they want, some are aware that if something happens to them, they are going to be blamed for their own victimization.

"Streetwise" middle-class people, women and men alike and across racial categories, develop skills—what Anderson (1990:209) has called "the art of avoidance"—to deal with their feelings of vulnerability to violence and crime.

Urbanites also use mechanisms in their homes to block off or filter out certain encounters with strangers before they have a chance to occur. Living in an apartment house with a uniformed attendant to monitor who goes into and out of the building or in a gated community with a security guard accomplishes this. Phone calls also may be monitored by having an unlisted phone number and/or using "caller ID" to restrict others' telephone access.

The mechanisms of selectivity and noninvolvement adopted by city dwellers in their daily interactions in a world of strangers are sometimes used as an explanation for their alleged detachment in public relationships. The popular stereotype of urbanites is that they are cold, indifferent, brusque, and generally uncaring. We question whether people who live in the city really have colder personalities than those who live in the country, however. The often-cited failure of people in the city to offer help to someone in trouble has been found to be due less to their indifference than to the **diffusion of responsibility** that results when there are many bystanders who might intervene (see box).

Interactionists, in fact, question the existence of unique rural and urban personality types as an explanation of behavior. They believe instead that people everywhere respond more coolly and with greater distrust to others they do not know. Any observed differences in the public behaviors of urban and rural residents can be understood in relation to the fact that urbanites are confronted much more often by strangers. As Milgram said, "Contrast between city and rural behavior probably reflects the responses of similar people to very different situations rather than intrinsic differences in the personalities of rural and city dwellers. The city is a situation to which persons respond adaptively" (1970:1465).

Somebody Ought to Do Something

An incident that took place over thirty years ago has been widely publicized as an example of the apathy and indifference of city people and their failure to get involved when help is needed. Kitty Genovese, returning to her home in Queens, New York, shortly after 3:00 A.M., was attacked by an assailant with a knife. In response to her screams, "Oh my God, he stabbed me! Please help me!" lights went on in a number of apartments and people peered out. One man called out, "Let that girl alone!" But no one called the police, though thirty-eight people later testified that they had heard her screams. The attacker was scared off but returned twice to finish the murder.

The assumption that these bystanders had failed to intervene because of their alienation or apathy to urban life was challenged by two social psychologists, John Darley and Bibb Latane. They conducted laboratory experiments in which the participants were led to believe that someone was being victimized or in trouble, and then their offers to help—or failure to offer it—were observed. Darley and Latane's results were summarized in a book entitled *The Unresponsive Bystander: Why Doesn't He Help?* (1970).

In one of Darley and Latane's ingeniously conceived studies, participants were placed in separate rooms and allowed to communicate only by microphone. In this way they could hear other study volunteers but could not see them. At some point the investigators played a recorded, staged tape of a person experiencing an epileptic seizure. The study participants believed the person heard on the tape was another volunteer. In one experimental variation each person was led to believe that she or he alone had heard the seizure. In other cases everyone was made to believe that a number of other people also heard the individual in trouble. The findings confirmed that subjects were far more likely to help when they thought no one else had heard the incident. Indeed, the greater the number of people who were thought to have heard it, the less likely each individual was to help.

These and similar studies by Darley and Latane offer strong support for the proposition that the *more* bystanders there are in an emergency, the *less* likely any one bystander is to intervene to provide aid. Each person, aware that others are witnessing the event, assumes that one or more of these others will take the responsibility to intervene. The result of this "pluralistic ignorance" is that no one steps forward. Darley and Latane suggest that this is how Kitty Genovese could have been murdered while others listened and looked on. It also helps explain how smashing windows of women motorists and grabbing their purses in full view of a crowd of onlookers, or extorting grade schoolers' lunch money on a busy playground, can become everyday interactions for would-be thieves.

Darley and Latane's work has generated a considerable body of research examining a large number of situational variables: ambiguity of the situation, severity of the victim's distress, victim's level of dependency, style of the request for help, degree of threat in the situation, and the physical attractiveness of the victim, among other factors (Laner, Benin, and Ventrone, 2001). With regard to bystanders, a large number of studies have found no differences between women and men in rates of helping; however, a few have found differences, perhaps due to the nature of help required in the situation. "Active, doing, spontaneous, and anonymous acts are more likely to be carried out by men than by women. Women are more likely to help than men (as a small number of studies have found) when helping is more planned, formal, personal, and less likely to involve direct intervention" (Laner et al., 2001:27).

Characteristics of the victim seem to make a difference in decisions to help strangers. Laner and associates (2001) included a dog, a child, and a woman as victims of violence in their study, assuming that the dog would have the least support for intervention because of the greater value placed on human life. Respondents were given vignettes portraying violence in a public setting, varying the victim, and were asked how likely they were to intervene on behalf of the victim. Although the findings were as expected (children had the highest likelihood for intervention, then women, then dogs), the authors were surprised by the closeness of the means and lack of significance for the differences. They surmised that perhaps intent to intervene has more to do with the bystander than the victim; that is, in a situation in which a person or a dog is being attacked, people who have the appropriate capacity and beliefs will report an intention to intervene, regardless of the victim. Another interpretation is that the norms regarding intervention are similar across victims (Laner et al., 2001).

This study did find that gender of the bystander interacts with the type of victim in predictions of whether a person will intervene. Men and women were equally likely to report an intention to intervene, but women were most likely to indicate they would help children, while men were most likely to indicate they would help women.

Other findings were that perceptions of self as strong and aggressive predicted intent to intervene, whereas actual physical size did not. Experience breaking up fights was found to be an important predictor of intent to intervene, and people who rated themselves as more sympathetic than others were also significantly more likely to say that they would intervene on behalf of a victim (Laner et al., 2001).

What do you think you would do?

While there is a situational basis for public behaviors, in most situations urbanites abide by the norms of noninvolvement. They rarely implicate themselves in each other's public lives. Strangers in public places appear, by and large, to avoid one another. In most public settings in American society we close ourselves off from interaction with others. We typically avoid excessive eye contact since we do not want to encourage others to talk to us. We make use of portable props ("involvement shields") such as newspapers to insulate ourselves from those around us. We try to maximize our personal space as we travel on buses, sit in waiting rooms or theaters, stand in lines, or simply walk along the street. As an editorial in the *New York Times* describes:

> So people wear sunglasses in the rain. They carry their eyes fixed in their skulls, immobile, unreflective. They let you see that they are purposely not looking. On the subways they bury their heads in books, in romances that turn on the erotic, expressive power of interlocking eyes, or they read the rum ads over and over again. (Klinkenborg, 2000:A26)

Most of our interactions are brief and highly impersonal—"fleeting" relationships that occur between or among persons who are personally unknown to one another and are of very brief duration. "Characteristically, although not necessarily, fleeting relationships involve no spoken exchanges and when such exchanges do occur, they are, by definition, brief and likely to be in the form of inquiry/reply" (Lofland, 1998:53); an accidental bump and an "I'm sorry," or, "Can you tell me the time?" and the reply, "It's just noon." These are, we might say, interactions without a "career." They have no past and virtually no possibility of future. In terms of sheer volume, fleeting relationships are the most representative of urban life. We can understand these as patterns of avoidance resulting from the need for city dwellers to protect themselves from stimulus overload and the uncertainties of interactions with strangers.

Tolerance for Alternative Lifestyles

The city not only provides the most opportunities for contacts with biographical strangers. It also is the context in which individuals are likely to have the most contact with cultural strangers, or members of groups that do not share their beliefs, attitudes, ideologies, or values. An urban society supports a great diversity of class, ethnic, racial, and **alternative lifestyle groups** such as homeless individuals. In managing their involvements with one another, members of culturally different groups must take into account the uncertainties and intolerance that arise when information about others is biased or incomplete.

Identification with individuals perceived as cultural strangers is more difficult than identification with those with whom we believe we share similar backgrounds. For example, the preexisting stereotypes of poor and homeless individuals held by many people often serve to cast these individuals as cultural strangers (Vann, 1999). This can lead to interactional difficulties, as when upper- and middle-class pedestrians are confronted by panhandlers (c.f., Duneier and Molotch, 1999), or when college students experience fear and perhaps even disgust prior to a community service experience with homeless individuals (Vann, 1999). It may also result in instances of "everyday" intolerance such as children on a school bus throwing pennies—and insults—at homeless men waiting outside the Salvation Army for dinner (Snow and Anderson, 1993). It can even lead to what we might call legally enacted intolerance—e.g., antipanhandling statutes such as those passed by New York City, Seattle, Atlanta, Cincinnati, Dallas, the District of Columbia, San Francisco, Santa Barbara, Long Beach, Philadelphia, New Haven, Raleigh, and Baltimore, among other places, in response to claims that, along with such things as unsanitary streets, crime, and graffiti, interactions between street people and pedestrians were eroding the city's "quality of life" (Duneier and Molotch, 1999).

Political groups quarrel, residents write angry letters to newspapers, and racial conflicts flare up (see box). Around certain issues, whether in rural or urban areas, it is difficult for groups to sustain a tolerant attitude toward other groups they have defined as adversaries.

Elijah Anderson's (1999) work illuminates the inner-city conflict between those who live by the "code of the streets"—a set of informal rules governing interpersonal public behavior, including violence—and those who identify more with mainstream values. This code is largely a cultural adaptation to a profound lack of faith in the police, who are viewed as representing the dominant white society and not caring to protect inner-city residents, and the judicial system. The code requires that people must—at least—give the impression that they are able to take care of themselves. This is accomplished by "going for bad"; that is, a presentation of self through facial expressions, gait, and verbal expressions that indicates a predisposition to violence. "Their manner conveys the message that nothing intimidates them" (p. 79). The object of the exercise is to prevent others from "messing with" him. "[F]or those who are invested in the code, the clear object of their demeanor is to discourage strangers from even thinking about testing their manhood" (p. 77). Although most people in inner-city communities are not totally invested in the code, a street-oriented demeanor is sometimes a necessity. The "decents" are trying hard to be part of mainstream culture, but the racism, real and perceived, that they encounter helps legitimate the oppositional culture of the streets, and so on occasion they adopt street behavior. The problem, according to Anderson, is that:

> A vicious cycle has thus been formed. The hopelessness and alienation many young inner-city black men and women feel, largely as a result of endemic joblessness and persistent racism, fuels the violence they engage in. This violence serves to confirm the negative feelings many whites and some middle-class blacks harbor toward the ghetto poor, further legitimating the oppositional culture and the code of the streets in the eyes of many poor young blacks. Unless this cycle is broken, attitudes on both

sides will become increasingly entrenched, and the violence, which claims victims black and white, poor and affluent, will only escalate. (p. 325)

Bourgois (1995) presents a similar picture of social marginalization in a neighborhood in East Harlem, "El Barrio," in his study of individuals involved in the underground crack economy. By embroiling themselves in the underground economy and proudly embracing street culture, these individuals are seeking an alternative to their social marginalization. Isolating themselves in inner-city street culture serves as a way to remove any danger of having to face the humiliations inevitably confronting them on venturing out of their social circle to seek legal employment.

Spatial (Dis)order

Perhaps the best indicator of underlying racial tensions that have the potential to erupt into an urban volcano are the riots and looting that occurred in April 1992 in the aftermath of the acquittal of the five Los Angeles police officers accused of beating black motorist Rodney King. The comments made by several L.A. gang members interviewed by Ted Koppel provide perspective:

> 3rd Gang Member: We still don't understand how it [the trial] get shipped from Van Nuys to Simi Valley, population majority Caucasian. Where do all the police live at? Simi Valley. How did that happen? The jury, was they from Simi Valley?

> 1st Gang Member: Why did it get moved? Is that the question, really? You're really asking me something that simple, that small? And we all know why it got moved. They could have had it downtown anywhere. Anywhere. Could have had it close to Rodney King's house, maybe he would have went to the trial then. White folk moved that for a reason. They want . . . they didn't have to move it . . . we could have had it right here. . . . They could have found them guilty on every charge, everything would have been fine. (ABC News, *Nightline*, April 30, 1992)

For several days after the acquittal of the police, citizens in South Central L.A. looted, trashed, and burned the businesses that provided jobs to their community. According to Alan Keyes (1992), it is too easy to assume that the rioters acted irrationally. It makes more sense to assume that what they destroyed (and what they rioted about) symbolized what they hated most—outside influences, outside powers, and the fact that outsiders dominate every aspect of their lives, "Because they have power over nothing, nothing in their environment reflects their own image. Because they see themselves in nothing, it is not long before they see nothing in themselves. And it is not long again until this emptiness itself becomes their identity" (p. 38). He continues:

> People can live side by side for generations without war and violence, if they feel secure in their identities. But when some feel their identity threatened by the actions or beliefs of others, the fear that results engenders hatred, which leads to war. (p. 38)

Intolerance is especially likely when the members of a group perceive, correctly or incorrectly, that their economic interests are threatened. Such a perception is a dominant factor in the animosity between the ethnic and racial groups that abound in the city. When working-class whites see increasing numbers of immigrants who are people of color, they may fear that they will be displaced in jobs and put at a disadvantage in the competition for scarce resources. As Rubin's (1994) analysis of working-class white ethnics demonstrates, when faced with the prospect that the in-migration of people of color could threaten their own hard-won advances, her respondents expressed clear anti-immigration and racist beliefs, perhaps best summed up by a remark made by one respondent: "Is this a white country, or what?" (Rubin, 1994:172).

The city also fosters tolerance for differences in behavior and group lifestyles, however. According to the sociologist Louis Wirth (1938), cities have historically been the melting-pot of races, peoples, and cultures, not only tolerating but rewarding difference.

Urban people are comparatively more sophisticated about lifestyle diversity. As we have noted elsewhere, it would seem that the basis of the difference between cities and towns, and between large, complex environments and small, relatively closed social circles, becomes clearer insofar as such differences are manifested in a social psychological way. In the small town one may easily lose one's individuality in relationship with others, whereas in the large city one establishes one's individuality *through* social relationships with others (Karp, Stone, and Yoels, 1991).

Social Contracts among Groups

It appears that urban tolerance is based on a specific type of interaction between members of different groups, what Becker and Horowitz (1972) referred to as a kind of *social contract*—a silent, unwritten bargain that minority group members will moderate their behavior to make them acceptable to other groups around them. Pattillo's (1998) study of a middle-class black neighborhood in Chicago which, although middle-class, is home to one of the top gang leaders and drug dealers in Chicago, offers support for this idea. Despite the fact that young people in the neighborhood are as easily introduced to the gangs and their drug business as they are to the neighborhood political organization, the two coexist and maintain what residents refer to as a "quiet neighborhood." Pattillo concludes: "There exists a system of interlocking networks of responsible and deviant residents that sometimes paradoxically, and always precariously, keeps the peace" (p. 747). Other authors agree, concluding that regardless of the social class and racial composition of a neighborhood, most people share a "common goal of living in an area relatively free from the threat of crime" (Bursik and Grasmick, 1993:15).

Lofland (1998) distinguishes between negative and positive tolerance. Negative tolerance is defined as "the capacity to 'put up with' another's difference from self because the different other is simply not perceived and/or because self and other do not intersect" (p. 238); in other words, out of sight, out of mind. As long as a meal program/transitional housing for homeless individuals is not in my backyard (NIMBY), I have no objection to feeding/housing the homeless. Positive tolerance, on the other hand, is "the capacity to 'put up with' another's *fully recognized* differences from self even under conditions of intersection and, perhaps, sometimes, to do so with a mild appreciation for our enjoyment of those differences" (p. 238). An excellent example of this is Laurie Stone's (1993) wonderful description of her interactions—and feelings about those interactions—with three homeless individuals she regularly encounters:

> I try to sort out how I feel. I started out meaning to save her [a homeless woman who is being beaten] from Jerry, but now I see that she is dealing with him herself. So what do I want with this trio? Not to reform or rescue them—or, if I do, I don't want to want those things. I feel an affinity. They tolerate my voyeurism. I allow for their self-destructiveness. And we all love the street. . . ." (p. 294)

Becker and Horowitz apparently have only a *positive* notion of tolerance, however. They imply that tolerance exists in cities because the different groups involved consciously value it and agree to ensure it. While this is undeniably often so, it may equally be the case that tolerance in cities is a by-product of avoidance; that is, city people may develop social procedures that minimize the probability that they will come into intimate contact with those with whom they do not agree.

The Spatial Ordering of City Activities

Social ecologists provide a picture of the city in which different groups are segregated and have little contact with one another. There are clear territorial groupings composed of people with similar characteristics or various national backgrounds who restrict their activities to well-defined areas.

In this view there is a **spatial ordering** to city activities (Harvey, 1989). Properly socialized urbanites know that certain types of people will be found in specific areas of the city. People can choose to be in areas of the city where they will come into contact with people engaging in certain behaviors or practicing different lifestyles, or they can choose to avoid such contact. They have, in other words, **controlled contact** with various lifestyles or marginal groups. If, for example, they want to avoid contact with prostitutes or those selling pornography, they can simply avoid areas of the city where such people are likely to be found. Tolerance is contingent on this controlled contact. The spatial segregation of groups and activities provides a comforting predictability in encounters with cultural strangers. It follows that tolerance is likely to break down when the conditions for controlled contact are not met. A public clamor is likely when members of certain groups begin to appear in areas where they "don't belong"; for example, when prostitutes appear in suburban commercial strips.

Of course, we do not always wish to avoid those whom we perceive as having unusual lifestyles. We may welcome the opportunity to observe the behaviors of cultural strangers or to participate in ethnic or neighborhood festivals. Every city has certain public parks or areas where representatives of a range of lifestyles and social types can come into contact and become familiar with one another. Perhaps one of the best examples of such an area is Manhattan's Greenwich Village, "a place of contemporary extremes of wealth as well as marked ethnic and racial difference" (Duncier and Molotch, 1999:1264). The Village's cultural tradition is well known across the world as arty, bohemian, and free thinking. It is a visitor destination for people coming from other parts of the world as well as other neighborhoods of the city, and a prime location for "people watching." William H. Whyte's (1988) study of urban space indicated how important public spaces are to the quality of urban life. He noted how people themselves determine the number that is right for a place, and they do it very well. "People need not worry that they might make a place too attractive, too overrun by people. It is the reverse that they should be worrying about. The carrying capacity of most urban spaces is far above the use that is made of them" (1988:172).

The spatial ordering of activities in cities allows urbanites to maintain a limited level of intimacy with cultural strangers. By being able to control the place and timing of contacts with others and by knowing what kinds of behaviors to expect of people in different city areas, urbanites can monitor the extent of their involvement with cultural strangers.

Middle-class society increasingly has been able to disassociate itself from the ethnically distinct, urban-based working poor and unemployed who inhabit the inner city. Budget cuts and fiscal austerity have accelerated the trend toward public sector breakdown in impoverished urban neighborhoods, while services improve, or at least stay the same, in Anglo-dominated, wealthy suburban communities. As Bourgois (1995) describes:

> The concentration of poverty, substance abuse, and criminality within inner-city enclaves such as East Harlem is the product of state policy and free market forces that have inscribed spatially the rising levels of social inequality. . . . More subtly, this urban decay expresses itself in the growing polarization around street culture in North America, giving rise to what some observers call a "crisis in U.S. race relations." (p. 241)

According to Bourgois, it is the institutionalized expression of racism— America's de facto apartheid and inner-city public sector breakdown—that government policy and private sector philanthropy need to address if anything is ever to change significantly in the long run.

According to Massey and Denton (1993), most Americans vaguely realize that urban America is still a residentially segregated society, but few appreciate the depth of black segregation or the degree to which it is maintained by ongoing institutional arrangements and contemporary individual actions. In their book, *American Apartheid*, these authors describe the relationship between spatial ordering and poverty:

> . . . segregation concentrates poverty to build a set of mutually reinforcing and self-feeding spirals of decline into black neighborhoods. When

economic dislocations deprive a segregated group of employment and increase its rate of poverty, socioeconomic deprivation inevitably becomes more concentrated in neighborhoods where that group lives. The damaging social consequences that follow from increased poverty are spatially concentrated as well, creating uniquely disadvantaged environments that become progressively isolated—geographically, socially, and economically—from the rest of society. (p. 2)

Establishing Relationships with Strangers

While the city provides a setting in which strangers can protect themselves from the intrusion of others, too much emphasis can be placed on their lack of direct interaction with one another. There are occasions when strangers come together and freely interact. There are situations in which people can begin to dissolve the strangeness between them. The usual conception of risk and uncertainty in interactions with strangers can be reduced in certain circumstances. A paradox of modern-day life is that, although information and interaction have been dislodged from physical location to a great extent due to electronic communication, there are unprecedented opportunities for connection. However, connection is not synonymous with community.

> Spontaneous and unprogrammed public life is perceived as risk laden. Public activity has moved into quasi-private physical public places such as shopping malls, gated communities, health clubs, and play zones. An attribute of such "public places" is surveillance, monitoring, and control, the very things decried in demands for privacy. In an age of increasing demands for protection of a right for privacy, Americans willingly give up privacy in exchange for safety, retreating into private worlds devoid of duty but filled with controlled contact. (Gumpert and Drucker, 1998:422)

Effects of Social Settings and Situations

As casual observation indicates, strangers are more likely to meet and begin relationships in some settings or situations than in others. In some settings, such as cocktail parties, such meetings are very likely, and in others, such as bus stops, they are very unlikely. Between these extremes there is a range of contexts where the likelihood of strangers meeting is greater or less (classrooms, ballgames, plays, laundromats, and so forth). Why is it easier for strangers at a baseball game to strike up conversations than those in, say, an elevator? To answer this question we will briefly consider the effects of settings, contexts, or situations on interactions with strangers.

Settings cannot be defined only in physical terms. A bookstore is a place with a lot of books, salespeople, cash registers, and so forth, but such a description would not capture the distinction between a college bookstore and a pornographic bookstore. Even if someone were to describe the contents of the books, we would not fully appreciate how the two places differ. A more accurate way to define these places would be in terms of the social conventions governing the nature of the interactions that occur in them.

Definitions of Behaviors

We cannot understand the meaning of another's behavior without considering the setting in which it occurs. For example, in order to assign a meaning to the behavior of one person striking another with a fist, we would have to know whether it happens in a neighborhood bar, the middle of Times Square, or a boxing ring in Madison Square Garden. The very same behavior can assume quite different meanings in different places.

We tend to excuse others for acting improperly with the explanation that they have never been in the situation before. In essence we are saying, "She should be excused because she does not know the rules here. She does not know the meaning her behavior carries in this setting." More directly still, "She thinks she knows the meaning of her behavior, and she is correct that it is the meaning of her behavior somewhere else, but she does not know that the same behavior carries a different meaning here." We use the phrase "acting out of place" to describe such improprieties.

Extraordinary events can change the character of settings. When the normal character of a setting becomes abnormal, or an ordinary setting becomes somehow extraordinary, and all involved recognize that fact, definitions of behavior change. It may be perfectly appropriate to begin conversations where ordinarily this would be considered improper. Conversations between strangers become allowable in stalled subway trains or elevators or when motorists are stuck in traffic, for example. Goffman notes:

> During occasions of recognized natural disaster, when individuals suddenly find themselves in a clearly similar predicament and suddenly become mutually dependent for information and help, ordinary communication constraints can break down. . . . What is occurring in the situation guarantees that encounters aren't being initiated for what can be improperly gained by them. And to the extent that this is assured, contact prohibitions can break down. (1963:36)

Information about Others

The context of a situation not only provides information which helps define the meaning of behavior. It also may indicate certain aspects of individuals' identities or details of their biographies, which can make it easier to initiate interactions. Sometimes a person's mere presence in a setting gives out a good deal of information about that person. When you encounter a group of strangers in a university classroom you can safely assume a good deal about them, such as their social class and values. Seeing a crowd of people standing on a street corner waiting for a red light to change would tell you very little about such strangers, however.

The difference that the social setting or context makes in an interaction is related to the amount of information it provides about the individuals taking part (see chapter 3). Some contexts provide more information about those in them than others do. In fact, an anonymous place can be thought of as one that provides little or no information about the people in it. *The likelihood of strangers meeting and beginning interactions is greatest in those settings that provide the most information.* The more information we possess about another, the more easily and correctly we can assess whether those with whom we begin a transaction will reciprocate in an acceptable fashion. Some settings give off enough information about the individuals in them to substantially reduce the uncertainties normally accompanying interactions with strangers.

How Strangers Meet

Once people decide to begin an interaction, they must find some way to initiate it. In the usual case, talk is preceded by a series of nonverbal gestures indicating the individuals' openness to interaction. This preparatory stage preceding verbal interaction is in effect a risk-reducing mechanism. Without directly committing themselves to an interaction, people use nonverbal communications to obtain a reading of others' willingness to respond. At this stage the level of their involvement is very slight, and if their own gestures are not positively responded to, they may gracefully disengage from their invitational efforts.

People who want to engage in interaction can let this be known with various types of nonverbal gestures. In full view of those around them and in a quite deliberate fashion, they may make a point of removing territorial markers (clothes, books, and so forth) from areas close to them. Thus they indicate that their personal space will not be violated should someone choose to approach them. They may engage others in eye contact and smile, or make a show of not being involved in any activity that demands their attention.

On occasion, people go beyond these purely nonverbal gestures by making statements aloud, ostensibly to themselves but clearly directed to those around them. The following occurrence in a laundromat, reported in a student term paper, is a typical example:

> One girl sat down next to me and started biting her nails. A few minutes later she opened a textbook of New Testament something or other and flipped through it. She put the book down, as if really bored with it, and she got up and read notices on the wall. Then she blurted out to no one in particular, "They [the machines] take forever."

Another laundromat conversation began this way:

> I sat down next to a guy who was reading something and I began reading an essay in *Time* magazine. Every once in a while this fellow would start to laugh out loud to himself.
> At one point he started to laugh very hard.
> "All right now, what's so funny? What are you reading?"
> "*Finnegan's Wake.* It's so full of puns . . ."

According to the norm of noninvolvement, the usual procedure for strangers in public places is to communicate systematically that they do not wish to become involved in an interaction. These kinds of nonverbal and verbal initiatives, however, which are also based on the commonly understood rules of noninvolvement, are designed to communicate just the opposite. They communicate to others an openness for interaction. When these moves for opening up interaction succeed, they do so precisely because the procedures for closing oneself off from interaction are so widely used and understood.

When conversations are begun, very ordinary issues such as weather, work, traffic, or the price of food are typical opening topics. No one can pretend ignorance of such things. People are normally constrained to respond when such issues have been raised, and just mentioning them is taken as an indication of openness for interaction. These openings are specifically used and understood as ritualized throwaway lines whose only purpose is to initiate conversation. Such topics also serve as vehicles for probing the willingness of others to engage in conversation. Should they decline, their reluctance can be communicated without personally discrediting or embarrassing those making the probe.

One strategy for those who wish to begin an encounter is to make things go wrong purposely. People may pretend to be lost when they are not; they may show puzzlement about what is happening around them; or they may purposely bump into another person, so some kind of remedial interaction is necessary. These strategies are used to create a situation where the ordinary becomes extraordinary and interaction is more acceptable.

As noted earlier in the chapter, pets and small children figure into interaction with strangers. Studies have found that being accompanied by a dog increases the frequency of social interactions, especially with strangers (Robins, Sanders, and Cahill, 1991; McNicholas and Collis, 2000). It is a particular type of interaction, however, that does not violate Goffman's notion of civil inattention (West, 1999). Of course, as Duneier and Molotch (1999) note, dogs (and children) can also induce (and sustain) unwanted interaction, as when a street person addresses remarks to a dog in order to force interaction with its female owner. According to these authors, this is what might be called "interactional vandalism" in that a subordinate person breaks the tacit basis of everyday interaction that is of value to the more powerful. In this case, the street person is depriving the woman of something crucial—"the ability to assume in others the practices behind the social bond" (p. 1290).

> Much more is going on than the breaking of conventional 'rules of etiquette.' . . . Through the pacing and timing of their utterances, the men offer evidence they do not respond to cues that orderly interaction requires. . . . That another cannot be presumed to, *of course*, socially collaborate . . . undermines trust. . . . Without it, the individual teeters on social vertigo. (p. 1290)

Conclusion

The manner in which people manage their public encounters is determined by the fact that public places are almost exclusively populated by people who are strangers to one another. They are biographical strangers who know nothing of each other's pasts, cultural strangers because they live in different social worlds, or both. Relationships between strangers pose special role-taking problems which make them uniquely risky and uncertain.

Every interaction carries a measure of uncertainty and risk. There is the chance that the images a person presents to others will be found unacceptable or that events will cast an unfavorable light on the individual. It also is never possible to be absolutely sure of others' attitudes, goals, and motives. The probability of doubt is greater in public encounters since strangers, as they try to role-take, must rely solely on information they can acquire through observation. Sometimes this face information is sufficient to persuade individuals that they can or cannot, should or should not, try to communicate directly with others. More typically, though, it is recognized as an incomplete basis for making these decisions.

City dwellers are confronted with public situations in which the number of potential encounters with strangers is enormous. They adapt to the volume of possible contacts and the role-taking problems inherent in urban relationships by structuring their public lives in ways designed to minimize the chances of unpleasant or unwanted encounters. More important, they adopt norms of noninvolvement that insulate them from unnecessary contact with strangers.

People in anonymous public settings adopt certain strategies to communicate their desire to maintain public privacy. Avoidance behaviors do not fully explain the complexity of ordered public life, however. People also are constrained to follow the norm of anonymity. They mutually orient their behaviors in order to construct a situation in which others' actions are intelligible, their own self-images are protected, and risky contacts are reduced. In public life, people seek to maximize order while minimizing involvement with others. They create a delicate balance between indifference and cooperation in their public transactions.

Unacquainted people may also adopt strategies to open up interactions. In some contexts, people relax their noninvolvement stance, enjoy communicating with others, and begin to establish long-lasting relationships. Situations vary in their capacity to support relationships among strangers.

Strangers comprise only one part of our social worlds, however. Relationships with strangers stand at one end of an interaction continuum, with intimate relationships characterized by deep commitment and trust at the other end. As Stanford Lyman and Marvin Scott have observed, a relationship is not established completely until the individuals involved "reciprocally regard one another as persons whom they know fully and for whom they have sincere affection, deep trust, and broad commitment" (1970:48). In the next chapter we will explore the processes involved in the transformation of strangeness to intimacy.

Definitions

Alternative lifestyle groups   Groups whose members exhibit a lifestyle that differs in significant ways from that adopted in mainstream, conventional society.

Areas of conversation   Topics of mutual interest to both participants. The participants also share a common understanding of the meaning of such topics.

Avoidance behaviors   The ways in which strangers seek to avoid involving themselves in the affairs of others.

Biographical strangers   People who have no knowledge of one another's life histories.

Civil inattention   The act of appearing to be uninvolved in the affairs of others. Individuals engage in this behavior when they are forced to recognize the presence of others but want to avoid interaction with them.

Controlled contact   The manner in which members of one group regulate the contact they have with members of other groups.

Cultural strangers   People who have no shared frameworks for interpreting social reality. They occupy different symbolic worlds.

Diffusion of responsibility   A phenomenon of behavior whereby no member of a group is regarded as clearly responsible for taking action in a situation which seems to demand it.

Involved indifference   A way of taking others' presence into account while avoiding intrusion in their affairs. Strangers are obliged to minimize involvement while they maximize public order.

Marginal man   A person who participates in the social activities of two different social groups without identifying completely with either group. A marginal person in a society is a stranger.

Norm of anonymity   A shared expectation that individuals will not intrude on each other's privacy.

Norm of noninvolvement   A shared expectation that strangers will not intrude on the activities of one another.

Norm of trust   A shared expectation that others will act in the ways we expect them to, and vice versa.

Public privacy   A situation in which strangers in public places try to maintain a strict impersonality in their interactions with one another.

Self-management techniques   The range of self-conscious strategies people use to ensure that they will project a positive image of self in front of any audience.

Spatial ordering   The ways in which various groups are associated with particular geographic areas. In the city, certain types of people and activities can be found in certain neighborhoods.

Stimulus overload   Bombardment with more stimuli than people can possibly respond to. Urbanites must develop very clear norms of noninvolvement to deal with the excess of stimuli they encounter.

DISCUSSION QUESTIONS

1. How do you interpret the authors' claim that we must simultaneously doubt and trust others as we interact with them? Would social life be impossible if it were not rooted in a general norm of trust? Under what conditions do you become most distrustful of others?

2. Suppose you are asked to try establishing a relationship with a stranger. In what settings would you find it easiest to do this? In what kinds of settings would you be unwilling to try meeting someone? Why? What characteristics or attributes of another would make a difference in your willingness to approach them? Why? What would you consider the biggest risks in carrying out such an assignment?

3. Do you think there is such a thing as a distinctive urban personality?

4. Describe some of the techniques you use to protect your privacy in public places. To what extent do you take others into account in formulating your own behaviors, even though you have no direct verbal communication with them?

5. Do you feel that cities provide greater freedom to practice unusual lifestyles than small towns do? If so, what is it about cities that fosters greater tolerance for strange lifestyles? When is such tolerance most likely to break down?

6. What behaviors can you think of that would constitute transgressions of noninvolvement norms in anonymous settings? How do you imagine people would react to such rule infractions?

REFERENCES

Anderson, E. 1990. *Streetwise*. Chicago: University of Chicago Press.
———. 1999. *Code of the Street*. New York: W.W. Norton & Company.
Becker, H., and I. Horowitz. 1972. *Culture and Civility in San Francisco*. New Brunswick, NJ: Transaction Books.
Berger, P., and H. Kellner. 1970. "The social construction of marriage." In *Recent Sociology*, edited by H. P. Dreitzel. Toronto: Collier Macmillan.
Bourgois, P. 1995. *In Search of Respect: Selling Crack in El Barrio*. New York: Cambridge University Press.
Bursik, R., and H. Grasmick. 1993. *Neighborhoods and Crime*. Lanham, MD: Lexington Books.
Crabb, P. 1996. "Video camcorders and civil inattention." *Journal of Social Behavior and Personality* 11(4):805–16.
Darley, J., and B. Latane. 1968. "Bystander intervention in emergencies: Diffusion of responsibility." *Journal of Personality and Social Psychology* 8:377–83.
———. 1970. *The Unresponsive Bystander: Why Doesn't He Help?* New York: Appleton-Century-Crofts.
Duneier, M. 1999. *Sidewalk*. New York: Farrar, Straus and Giroux.
Duneier, M., and H. Molotch. 1999. "Talking city trouble: Interactional vandalism, social inequality, and the 'Urban Interaction Problem.'" *American Journal of Sociology* 104(5):1263–95.
Erickson, V. 2001. "On the town with Georg Simmel: A socio-religious understanding of urban interaction." *Cross Currents* 51(1):21–44.

Gardner, C. 1988. "Access information: Public lives and private peril." *Social Problems* 35:328–56.

———. 1995. *Passing By: Gender and Public Harassment*. Berkeley: University of California Press.

Garfinkel, H. 1963. "A conception of, and experiments with 'trust' as a condition of stable concerted actions." In *Motivation and Social Interaction*, edited by O. Harvey, pp. 220–35. New York: The Ronald Press Company.

———. 1967. *Studies in Ethnomethodology*. Englewood Cliffs, NJ: Prentice Hall.

Goffman, E. 1963. *Behavior in Public Places*. New York: Free Press.

———. 1971. *Relations in Public*. New York: Harper & Row.

Gumpert, L., and S. Drucker. 1998. "The demise of privacy in a private world: From front porches to chat rooms." *Communication Theory* 8(4):408–25.

Harvey, D. 1989. *The Urban Experience*. Baltimore: Johns Hopkins University Press.

Henslin, J. 1991. "Trust and cabbies." In *Down to Earth Sociology,* edited by J. Henslin. New York: Free Press.

Humphreys, L. 1970. *Tearoom Trade: Impersonal Sex in Public Places*. Chicago: Aldine.

Kang, J. 2000. "Cyber-Race." *Harvard Law Review* 113(5):1131–63.

Karp, D. 1973. "Hiding in pornographic bookstores: A reconsideration of the nature of urban life and anonymity." *Urban Life and Culture* 4:427–51.

Karp, D., G. Stone, and W. Yoels. 1991. *Being Urban: A Sociology of City Life*. New York: Praeger Publishers.

Keyes, A. 1992. "After L.A." *National Review* 44(11):38–41.

Klinkenborg, V. 2000. "The city life: Eye contact." *The New York Times*, April 27:A 26.

Laner, M., M. Benin, and N. Ventrone. 2001. "Bystander attitudes toward victims of violence: Who's worth helping?" *Deviant Behavior: An Interdisciplinary Journal* 22:23–42.

Lofland, L. 1971a. "Self-management in public settings, Part I." *Urban Life and Culture I* (April):93–117.

———. 1971b. "Self-management in public settings, Part II." *Urban Life and Culture 2* (July):217–31.

———. 1973/1985. *A World of Strangers*. Prospect Heights, IL: Waveland Press.

———. 1989. "Social life in the public realm." *Journal of Contemporary Ethnography* 17:453–81.

———. 1998. *The Public Realm: Exploring the City's Quintessential Social Territory*. New York: Aldine de Gruyter.

Lyman, S., and M. Scott. 1970. "Game frameworks." In *A Sociology of the Absurd*, edited by S. Lyman and M. Scott. New York: Appleton-Century-Crofts.

Madriz, E. 1997. "Latina teenagers: Victimization, identity, and fear of crime." *Social Justice* 24(4):39–56.

Massey, D., and N. Denton. 1993. *American Apartheid: Segregation and the Making of the Underclass*. Cambridge, MA: Harvard University Press.

McNicholas, J., and G. Collis. 2000. "Dogs as catalysts for social interactions: Robustness of the effect." *British Journal of Psychology* 91(1):61–70.

Milgram, S. 1970. "The experience of living in cities." *Science* 167 (March):1461–68.

Park, R. 1928. "Human migration and the marginal man." *American Journal of Sociology* 33:888–96.

Pattillo, M. 1998. "Sweet mothers and gangbangers: Managing crime in a black middle-class neighborhood." *Social Forces* 76(3):747–75.

Perry, M., and P. Mackun. 2001. *Population Change and Distribution 1990 to 2000: Census 2000 Brief.* U.S. Department of Commerce, Economics and Statistics Administration. Washington, D.C.: U.S. Census Bureau.

Persson, A. 2001. "Intimacy among strangers: On mobile telephone calls in public places." *Journal of Mundane Behavior* 2(3). <http://www.mundanebehavior.org/issues/v2n3/persson.htm> Accessed 8/15/02.

Robins, D., C. Sanders, and S. Cahill. 1991. "Dogs and their people: Pet-facilitated interaction in a public setting." *Journal of Contemporary Ethnography* 20:4–25.

Rubin, L. 1994. *Families on the Fault Line: America's Working Class Speaks about the Family, the Economy, Race, and Ethnicity.* New York: HarperCollins.

Schutz, A. 1960. "The stranger: An essay in social psychology." In *Collected Papers: Studies in Social Theory.* The Hague: Martinus Nijhoff.

Semmes, C. 1991. "Developing trust." *Journal of Contemporary Ethnography* 19:450–70.

Simmel, G. 1950a. "The metropolis and mental life." In *The Sociology of Georg Simmel,* edited by K. Wolff. New York: Free Press.

———. 1950b. "The stranger." In *The Sociology of Georg Simmel,* edited by K. Wolff. New York: Free Press.

Snow, D., and L. Anderson. 1993. *Down on Their Luck.* Berkeley and Los Angeles: University of California Press.

Staples, B. 1992. "Black men and public space." In *Life Studies,* edited by D. Cavitch, pp. 29–32. Boston: Bedford Books.

Stone, L. 1993. "Perfect strangers." *Triquarterly* 86 (Winter 92/93):282–302.

U.S. Census Bureau. Census 2000 Redistricting Data (Public Law 94-171) Summary File (http://factfinder.census.gov). Accessed 6/30/03.

Vann, B. 1999. "Service-learning as symbolic interaction." In *Cultivating the Sociological Imagination: Concepts and Models for Service-learning in Sociology,* edited by J. Ostrow, G. Hesser, and S. Enos, pp. 83–92. Washington, D.C.: American Association for Higher Education.

West, C. 1999. "Not even a day in the life." In *Qualitative Sociology as Everyday Life,* edited by B. Glassner and R. Hertz, pp. 3–12. Thousand Oaks, CA: Sage Publications.

Whyte, W. H. 1988. *City.* New York: Anchor Books.

Wirth, L. 1938. "Urbanism as a way of life." *American Journal of Sociology* 44 (July):1–24.

Wolfinger, N. 1995. "Passing moments: Some social dynamics of pedestrian interaction." *Journal of Contemporary Ethnography* 24(3):323–41.

Wood, E. 2000. "Working in the fantasy factory: The attention hypothesis and the enacting of masculine power in strip clubs." *Journal of Contemporary Ethnography* 29(1):5–31.

Yamori, K. 1998. "Going with the flow: Micro-macro dynamics in the macrobehavioral patterns of pedestrian crowds." *Psychological Review* 105(3):530–57.

five

FAMILY, FRIENDSHIP, AND LOVE
CONTACTS AMONG INTIMATES

The need for intimate relationships is so strong it has given rise to an industry devoted to helping compatible singles make contacts with one another. Make no mistake, it is big business. A 1997 estimate put the amount spent annually on traditional print and voice mail personals at $300 million (Sprout, 1997). There are singles' bars and apartment complexes, as well as dating services and other operations designed to bring people together. Newspapers regularly run ads for singles events, such as "Celebrating single: Caribbean cooking demonstration and free wine tasting."

Operation Match, the first computer dating business in the United States, was organized by a Harvard sophomore during the late 1960s. The response was overwhelming, and thousands of college students happily spent $3 each on the chance that they would meet others whom they would find attractive and who would be attracted to them. The process has become more sophisticated and more costly as the intimacy industry has become more firmly established. The Internet revolutionized the singles industry. Online dating services blossomed—by 1997 there were some 200 sites on the Web offering online personals (Sprout, 1997), taking "dating agencies out of the classifieds" (Choat, 2000). According to a 34-year-old female New Yorker, online dating is more convenient and comfortable than scouring dreary Manhattan bars and haranguing friends to set her up. "As you get older you know fewer and fewer people who aren't married, but go online and there are hundreds of people who are single. It makes you feel a lot less alone" (*Newsweek*, 2001:46) (see box).

Finding Love on the Web

Technology is changing the way we do romance. Computer-knowledgeable singles are turning to the World Wide Web in increasing numbers for personal ads. One of the pioneers of online dating is U.S.-based Match.com, launched in 1995, which had 2.5 million members worldwide in 2000. According to Match.com's "vice president of romance," "The Internet addresses the problem that professional, single people face today. It's fast, affordable and convenient" (quoted in Choat, 2000:49). She continues, "Traditionally, you start seeing people on the basis of physical attraction. You then spend the next weeks, months, even years trying to work out whether you are really suited, whether you have the same values, and so on. Going through an agency you first look for compatibility and then the romance follows" (p. 49).

People feel very comfortable with the level of anonymity provided by Web sites. On the Web you can hide behind a handle and an e-mail address, giving out your phone number—or photo—only when you choose to (Sprout, 1997). The anonymity lessens the immediate risk of meeting another person, but comes with other risks, especially when moving a relationship from online to in person. According to the director of Cyberangels.org, an Internet safety watchdog group, "It's like going to a bar blindfolded and then going home with someone" (quoted in Anderson, 2001). At the time Anderson's article was published, the Cyberangels were handling about 600 cases of cyberstalking a day, and about ten rape reports in a month. According to the director, "It all happens because of a disconnect that makes people feel like they know a stranger intimately" (p. 38). Some services recognize these dangers and advise their users to proceed with caution. eHarmony, a Christian site, claims to eliminate 20 percent of its applicants due to their questionable emotional stability (Anderson, 2001). At least one magazine has published rules for online dating such as "practice common sense," "be honest," "take your time," and "pay attention to the signs" (Starling, 2000).

Another downside is that the seemingly perfect match on-screen may not live up to expectations when the individuals meet. One problem appears to be false advertising. Experienced Net daters urge honesty, but many confess to small exaggerations. Skeptics argue that the Internet doesn't convey the overall gestalt of a person, that impalpable physical essence. Without any information besides the text of e-mail, readers project their own fantasies onto other people. Worse still, users can carefully edit their e-mails and present themselves in the most flattering way (*Newsweek*, 2001). However, for some individuals, online romance erases the awkwardness of first meetings and makes communication easy. Disabled people, for example, prefer to use the Internet in looking for dates and potential partners. According to one user, it is a way to weed out people who are uncomfortable with disabilities. She says, "I am an attractive woman, I think men are just afraid to approach me [in person]. People are afraid of what they don't know. In my [online] ad, I try to make it clear I am a lot more than my disability. I want the reader to know although I am disabled my life is very enriched and I lead an active life" (quoted in Lynch, 1999).

Internet dating has also entered the daily fabric of life abroad. In China the practice is helping to break down the centuries-old tradition of parents selecting their children's spouses. One million people have signed up for Club Yuan, the dating section of Sina.com. A researcher in Britain predicts that one in five single Brits uses the Net or offline dating agencies to date, and expects that number to "explode" over the next five years as globalization brings American-length workdays to the rest of the world (*Newsweek*, 2001).

And then there's the international dating service called A Foreign Affair, at loveme.com, started by a group of guys in Phoenix, Arizona, in 1995. They ran ads in Russian newspapers asking women to send photos and vital statistics, then launched their Web site with 300 Russian "princesses." By 1999 they had profiles of 6,500 women from 49 countries, dozens of clients had married, and they had to hire more employees in Phoenix and Russia (*Time*, 1999).

There are sites for everyone, it seems. A limited sampling includes:

- for African-Americans, LoveNubianStyle.com (for black professionals); Blacksingles.com, which soared from 3,000 hits in its first month of operation to an average of 5 million by 2000; and BlackVoices.com with half a million regular users (Starling, 2000)
- for Jewish singles, JDate.com
- for Catholics, CatholicSingles.com
- for Ivy League graduates, GoodGenes.com
- for gay men, gay.com and the online company Gaydar, which also has its own internet radio station; for gays and lesbians, AOL's "Utopia Lesbian and Gay Village" (Clark, 1996) and Altmatch.com; and the computer bulletin board for lesbians called the Lesbian Café, "an electronic lesbian 'bar'" (Correll, 1995)
- for those with an interest in rural life, countrysingles.com (*Time*, 2000)
- and there's the offbeat TheSpark.com, which asks the sign-up question, "Which would you rather kill, Puppy or Kitten? (*Newsweek*, 2001).

So who uses these sites? The larger sites, like Matchmaker.com, SocialNet.com and Match.com, boast a tech-savvy, slightly male-skewed audience typically in their 20s and 30s and concentrated around major cities. The online-research firm Media Metrix reported that the number of people regularly using such sites increased from 3.4 million in December 1999 to 5 million in December 2000 (*Newsweek*, 2001). Mature singles have embraced the trend as well—one user is writing a book on online dating for seniors. The demographics of the typical BlackVoices.com user are interesting. Six of every 10 members are women, more than 80 percent attended college, and users range between the ages of 25 to 55 (Starling, 2000:46).

What does it all mean? According to one source, this is courtship as it once was, before the advent of the singles bar:

> There is plenty of conversation but no touching. With the computer serving as a chaperone, guaranteeing that no one gets too close, tastes are compared, as are family backgrounds, hopes and dreams. Much as sites such as Priceline and eBay encourage old-fashioned economic behavior—one bids, one negotiates, one doesn't pay retail—the dating sites serve as nineteenth-century parlors where couples sit in chairs and chat. Even the word chat is slightly antique, recalling porch swings and glasses of iced tea. (*Time*, 2000:73)

People of all ages devote considerable time to thinking about, worrying about, analyzing, developing, or trying to end intimate relationships. The advice columns of daily newspapers, television programming, films, and popular fiction all indicate the extent to which the quality of our relations with family, friends, and lovers occupies our time and thoughts.

It may not be an exaggeration to say that love has become a *social problem* of sorts in America. As a popular song not too long ago put it, many people may be "looking for love in all the wrong places." The urgency of the search is evidenced by a trip to any local bookstore, where the shelves in the self-help section are routinely filled with titles promising the formulae for the right ways and places to find love (see box).

According to Boston psychotherapist Mira Kirschenbaum's book, *Women & Love* (1999), fear of intimacy is almost like an epidemic in the lives of young women today. "The keynote of fear of intimacy is that falling in love feels like bad news. When your heart sends you that letter that you're falling in love, it feels like you've gotten a letter from the IRS telling you they're auditing you" (quoted in Duin, 1999).

Love and Relationships in the Bookstore

A trip to the "relationships" section of any of the large chain bookstores provides a lesson in the culture of relationships in contemporary America. Some of the titles that "jumped out" on a recent trip include books for every phase of a relationship. To get started, there's *Single No More: How and Where to Meet Your Perfect Mate* (Kreidman, 1999) or the *New York Times* million-copy bestseller, *The Rules: Time-Tested Secrets for Capturing the Heart of Mr. Right* (Fein and Schneider, 1995). It didn't take long to figure out that this is a book written for women—Rule #2 is, "Don't talk to a man first (and don't ask him to dance)"; Rule #7, "Don't accept a Saturday night date after Wednesday"; Rule #20, "Be honest but mysterious"—although some readers no doubt checked the date to make sure it was 1995 and not 1955!

If you do manage to find someone suitable to date, there's John Gray's *Mars and Venus on a Date* (1997). Actually, Gray has a book for every aspect of relationships: *Mars and Venus in Love* (1996), *Mars and Venus in the Bedroom* (1995), *Mars and Venus Starting Over* (1998), and so on.

If things do go wrong, there's plenty of help: *The Relationship Cure: A 5 Step Guide for Building Better Connections with Family, Friends, and Lovers* (Gottman and DeClaire, 2001); *The Relationship Rescue Workbook: Exercises and Self-Tests to Help You Connect with Your Partner* (McGraw, 2000), and if that doesn't work, there's *Heal Your Heartbreak: How to Live and Love Again* (Spezzano, 2000, 2001).

Judging from the number of titles that seem to be warnings (*Things Mama Should Have Told You about Men, When Your Lover Is a Liar,* or *Love: The Course They Forgot to Teach You in School*), relationships are fraught with difficulties, particularly for heterosexual women. The following are just a sample of titles aimed at women:

- *Secrets about Men Every Woman Should Know*
- *It's a Guy Thing: An Owner's Manual for Women*
- *Don't Call That Man*
- *Why Men Are the Way They Are*
- *Loving Him without Losing You*
- *What Smart Women Know*
- *Nasty Men: How to Stop Being Hurt by Them Without Stooping to Their Level*
- *101 Lies Men Tell Women and Why Women Believe Them* (e.g., "What attracts me to you is your mind" or "It doesn't matter that you make more money")
- *Men Who Can't Love: How to Recognize a Commitmentphobic Man Before He Breaks Your Heart*
- *Making Sense of the Men in Your Life: What Makes Them Tick, What Ticks You Off, and How to Live in Harmony*
- *If Men Could Talk . . . Here's What They'd Say*
- *What Men Don't Want Women to Know*
- *What He Can't Tell You . . . and Needs to Say*
- and Dr. Joyce Brothers' 1981 classic, *What Every Woman Should Know about Men*

There were only a few books aimed at heterosexual men, such as *How to Be a Great Husband*, and *What She Wants: A Man's Guide to Women*.

Whew. It makes you wonder if it's worth it!

Intimate Relationships in Contemporary Society

The idea that human beings require identity-sustaining relationships with intimate others is not new. The **need for affiliation** is a theme that has always been present in social science literature (Schacter, 1959). In nineteenth-century sociological theory, concern was expressed that industrialization and urbanization were destroying intimate bonds between individuals. Theorists such as Ferdinand Tönnies and Émile Durkheim sought to explain the effects of the transformation of social life from small pre-urban or peasant communities to large cities. Alexis de Tocqueville's *Democracy in America* (1835) warned that some aspects of the American character—what he was one of the first to call individualism—might eventually isolate Americans from one another and thereby undermine freedom. Although the theoretical conceptions of these writers vary, their ideas generally reflect agreement on these points:

1. Modern society is characterized by increased rationality and individuality.
2. People are less well integrated into modern society than they were in pre-urban communities.
3. Relationships between people in modern society become more contractual, artificial, and contrived.
4. Ties to primary groups (family, neighborhood, and friendship groups) are weaker in modern society.

Although some of these propositions have been questioned (c.f., Karp, Stone, and Yoels, 1991), there can be no doubt that contemporary society does impose a variety of unique pressures on human relationships. Both social science literature and the popular media have discussed the changing character of human relations in the twentieth century. Rapid social change, the urge toward achievement and social mobility, and the weakening of community associations are said to have produced a pervasive rootlessness in modern people (see also Bellah et al., [1985] 1996). The failure to sustain intimate relationships is often cited as a serious shortcoming in urban-industrial society (see box).

Intimacy thus not only dominates our everyday consciousness, it is also a yardstick against which we can evaluate the quality of our everyday lives. The level of intimacy we perceive in any encounter affects our presentations of self, impression management, and the kinds of information about ourselves we reveal to others. In general, the configuration of expectations, obligations, and reciprocities governing any relationship is bound up with the degree of intimacy between the people involved. How we allocate our time and the social circles we enter and leave cannot be understood apart from the networks of intimate relationships we sustain. Inquiry into the structure and operation of everyday life therefore demands serious consideration of the manner in which we define, interpret, and give meaning to relations of intimacy.

The Interactionist Perspective on Intimacy

Students often resist sociological analyses of personal relationships. When asked to describe some of the social factors that might account for the way intimate relationships are conducted in American society today, students in our courses have argued that it is impossible to generalize about intimacy. Among other things they say: "It depends upon the individual." "No two people relate to one another the same way." "You can't define what love is."

To some degree the students are correct: No two relationships are the same, even when the social characteristics of the participants are very similar. Each relationship emerges out of the unique context in which the individuals encounter one another. They also are correct that any attempt to provide an absolute, clear, permanent definition of intimacy, love, or friendship would be fruitless. We agree that a relationship is intimate only when the partici-

Alone in the Lonely Crowd

Intimacy plays a critical role in psychological growth and well-being, and a lack of intimate interactions has been associated with loneliness (Prager and Buhrmester, 1998; Reis and Shaver, 1997). According to a legion of columnists, therapists, and pastors, Americans have become starved for intimacy (Duin, 1999). In the words of one author, "In the been-there-done-that nineties, people crave intimacy" (Duin, 1999:28).

In 1950, David Riesman described Americans as living lonely lives in the midst of a crowd of lonely people. In a classic book titled *The Lonely Crowd*, he proposed that the American character changed from the *inner-directed* personality of the nineteenth century, motivated by an internalized set of achievement goals, to the *other-directed* personality of the twentieth century, motivated by a desire for the approval of peers and associates. The modern personality is sensitive to cultural expectations and responds to the cues others give about the behaviors they expect. Such people find it difficult to establish lasting intimate relationships with others because they have no firm values to base them on. Riesman describes the other-directed person as "at home everywhere and nowhere, capable of a rapid if sometimes superficial intimacy with and response to everyone" (1950:25).

Fifty years later, Robert Putnam's *Bowling Alone* (2000) echoes this theme. Putnam uses bowling as a symbol for the decline of American associational life; that is, between 1980 and 1993 the total number of bowlers in America increased by 10 percent, while league bowling decreased by 40 percent. He is concerned that we are in danger of becoming a nation of strangers to one another without adequate social bonds to tie us together. In a section of the book titled "So What?" Putnam describes the importance of connection: "People who have active and trusting connections to others—whether family members, friends, or fellow bowlers—develop or maintain character traits that are good for the rest of society" (p. 288). The effect of disengagement on our personal lives is particularly sobering; among adult Americans life satisfaction has declined steadily over the past four decades, at least partly due to social connectedness. "Young and middle-aged adults today are simply less likely to have friends over, attend church, or go to club meetings than were earlier generations" (p. 335).

Laura Pappano writes about the new loneliness of people who are overcommitting and underconnecting in *The Connection Gap: Why Americans Feel So Alone* (2001). This aloneness is played out in the way we eat (single-serving frozen meals), watch TV (with earphones), work (telecommuting), play (. . . bowling), fall in love (personal ads), marry (or don't), socialize (e-mail), and shop (online). Research on Americans' use of time over the past three decades shows that we now watch more TV and socialize less (Robinson and Godbey, 1997). The percentage of people driving to work alone rose from 76 percent to nearly 85 percent between 1980 and 1990; carpoolers dropped from 24 percent to 15 percent of commuters over the same period. More people today are single, either by choice or chance, than at any other time in history; there are as many single-person households as there are households of married couples with children.

Will the twenty-first century be different?

pants in the relationship define it that way. At the same time, we maintain that the criteria used in arriving at such a definition are *social* in origin.

Intimacy as a Social Construction

As we noted in chapter 2, social life would be impossible if there were no general consensus concerning the meanings people give to objects, events, and situations in their lives—if people were not generally agreed on the meaning of symbols. The definitions given to intimacy depend on both the general values of the society in which individuals live and the more specific values of the groups to which they belong or with which they identify.

These roots in socially shared definitions are what allow us to carry our analysis of intimacy beyond the assertion that each human relationship is unique. Relationships of love and friendship can only be understood as symbolic or **social constructions** which by themselves have no intrinsic meaning. For example, feelings of romantic love and passion surely have a physiological component to them. Scientists have discovered that oxytocin, a brain chemical known to stimulate lactation and mother-child bonding, may be partly responsible for romantic love as well (Brownlee, 1997). Anthony Walsh, the author of *The Science of Love: Understanding Love and Its Effects on Mind and Body*, describes love as a natural high, similar to being "hopped up on coke." The rush is fueled by elevated levels of neurotransmitters, brain chemicals such as dopamine, norepinephrine, and phenylethylamine (Price, 1999). However, the distinctions among such emotions as love, jealousy, anger, and anxiety are not based on our body reactions alone, but rather on the way we interpret and label our experiences (Thoits, 1989).

Consider what you might feel on "some enchanted evening." Your eyes meet the stranger's, you smile warmly at each other, and as you approach one another, oblivious to others in the room, you experience increased heart and respiratory rates, flushing of the face, dryness of the mouth, and slight body tremors. Aware of these physiological responses, you may decide that you are experiencing love at first sight. You have learned from your peers, from television, and from books and magazines that such feelings can be interpreted as love. The feelings we have described do not *have to be* interpreted as love, however. If we did not know the context in which the feeling occurred and simply knew that an individual had experienced higher heart and respiration rates, flushing, dry mouth, and body tremors, we could make a variety of interpretations concerning what was happening. It could be that the individual was high on drugs, suffering from the flu, or experiencing any one of a number of quite diverse emotions—fear, anger, anxiety, jealousy, embarrassment, or love. Our emotional states are symbolic states. As such, they require interpretation and labeling to establish their meaning.

The Social Meanings of Sexuality

Much the same point can be made concerning the meanings attached to sexuality. The ways in which individuals pursue and engage in sexual relationships reflect the social attitudes of both society as a whole and the groups with which the individuals are affiliated. Our capacity for intimate sexuality is in part a function of biological maturity, but we become sexual through a learning process. What turns us off or on reflects culturally defined and learned ideas about sexuality. There is evidence to suggest that culture profoundly affects how people perceive love, how susceptible they are to falling in love and with whom, and why they feel sexual desire. There are wide variations in the kinds of sexual behaviors that are forbidden, tolerated, or encouraged in various cultures, including clear differences between sexual practices in smaller, preliterate societies and the larger, more complex societies of developed countries (Kelly, 2001). For example, societies vary in terms of the type and appropriateness of foreplay, ranging from those in which men might fondle a woman's breasts only immediately prior to intercourse to those in which foreplay might last for hours. It might surprise you to learn that there are societies where kissing is thought disgusting. Oral sex is a routine practice in some societies and taboo in others. And cultures vary in terms of coital positions that are thought both desirable and permissible (see Hyde and DeLamater, 1997). In Sweden, for example, premarital sex is accepted, people are expected to be sexually knowledgeable and experienced, and Swedes are likely to associate sex with pleasure—what we might refer to as a "sex positive" society. In Ireland, however, Catholics are supposed to heed the Church's strict prohibitions against sex outside of marriage, birth control, and the expression of lust. The experience of sexuality in these two countries is different because the *rules* are different (Schwartz and Rutter, 1998). Even within a particular region or culture, various political, economic, and social changes can also affect people's sexual attitudes and behaviors (Hatfield and Rapson, 1996).

Another indication that social influences play a larger role in shaping sexuality than biology is the changing notions of male and female differences in desire through history. The norms governing sexuality are so powerful that it is impossible to imagine the absence of such norms. In fact, most examples of "liberated" sexuality involve breaking a social norm—for example, having sex in public rather than in private. The social norm is always the reference point. Because people are influenced from birth by the social context of sexuality, their desires are shaped by these norms (Schwartz and Rutter, 1998). Some norms are explicit, such as laws against adult sexual activity with minors. Others are implicit, such as norms of fidelity and parental responsibility. In a changing, complex society such as the United States, the rules may be in flux or indistinct at any given time. Perhaps this ambiguity is what makes some issues of sexuality so controversial today.

Throughout this book we have been sustaining the idea that the meanings of objects, events, and situations reside in our responses to them. The meanings attached to the body itself are illustrative of this point. As pointed out in chapter 3, standards of beauty are clearly culture-bound. While contemporary American women evaluate themselves in terms of a "cult of thinness," the paintings of Peter Paul Rubens and others indicate that historically there is nothing universal about this standard; indeed, most societies view larger women as more attractive. It is also the case that in different societies different parts of the body, especially female bodies, are eroticized. While female breasts are a focus of erotic attention in the United States, other societies may place greater erotic emphasis on the neck, arms, or ankles.

It is worth pointing out that a great deal more is known about the way that men respond to female bodies than vice versa. As some feminists suggest, the fact that specific body parts of women can be isolated as erotic objects may be related to the general objectification of women intrinsic to male-dominated societies. Those holding such a view feel particularly outraged about the image of women in materials ranging from magazine advertisements to *Playboy* to hard-core pornography.

Although researchers have not been able to conclusively establish a direct causal link between viewing pornography and violence against women, there is substantial evidence that pornography, especially violent pornography, is a factor that contributes to violence against women. Research with men, including sex offenders, shows that pornography helps shape a male-dominant view of sexuality, contributes to a user's difficulty in distinguishing between fantasy and reality, and is often used to initiate victims and break down their resistance to particular types of sexual activity. According to one author (Jensen, in Dines, Jensen, and Russo, 1998:119), pornography provides "a training manual for abusers" (see also Jensen, 1995). To be sure, not all pornography is violent, but the objective of pornography is the objectification and control of women—male dominance of the female body for the purpose of sexually arousing the male consumer—and often violence is one of the ways pornography accomplishes this (Dines et al., 1998). Objectification of the female body that occurs in everyday media also affects sexual attitudes and beliefs. In a study in which men and women were shown advertisements depicting female models as sex objects, or ads with female models competently performing various nontraditional roles, the men who saw the sexist advertisements increased their tendency to gender stereotype and also scored higher than other research participants on a scale measuring attitudes supportive of rape and sexual aggression (Lanis and Covell, 1995).

Our general point that the meanings attached to sexuality are social in origin is reflected in the vocabulary we use to describe people in terms of sexual behaviors, particularly the differential evaluation according to gender. The association of sex with female immorality starts in childhood, as is made clear by Orenstein's (1994) interviews with middle-school students which found the sexual double standard alive and well. According to the girls Orenstein interviewed:

> At Weston, girls may be "sluts," but boys are "players." Girls are "whores"; boys are "studs." Sex "ruins" girls; it enhances boys. In their youth, they may be snips and snails and puppy dogs' tails, but by adolescence, boys learn that they are "made of" nothing but desire. . . . Girls are, in fact, supposed to provide the moral inertia that (temporarily)

slows that force. . . . The Weston girls themselves participate in this dynamic, shunning sexually active girls, but excusing male behavior by saying, "Boys only think with their dicks." (Orenstein, 1994:57)

Despite the norm of "true love" currently accepted in our culture, personal choice and indiscriminate sexuality have often been construed as socially disruptive. Disruptions to the social order include liaisons between poor and rich; between people of different races, ethnicities, or faiths; and between members of the same sex (Schwartz and Rutter, 1998). As Schwartz and Rutter note, traditional norms of marriage and sexuality have maintained social order by keeping people in familiar and "appropriate" categories, with offenders punished by ostracism or curtailed civil rights and conformists rewarded with social approval and material advantages. They remind us that although it hardly seems possible today, mixed-race marriage was against the law in the United States until 1967. Committed same-sex couples continue to be denied legal marriages, income tax breaks, and health insurance benefits; heterosexual couples take these social benefits for granted.

Our discussion and various examples affirm that definitions of intimacy vary because they are social constructions with no fixed meaning. They have their roots in both general societal values and more specific values of the groups and people with whom an individual frequently communicates. The meanings also vary historically and according to the social attributes of the participants. Society's interest in controlling sexuality is expressed in the debates regarding sex education. Debates about sex education in elementary, middle, and high school illustrate the importance to society of both the control of desire and its social construction (Schwartz and Rutter, 1998) (see box).

Historical Changes in the Meaning of Intimacy

The social conventions concerning intimacy in a society have been different in various historical periods. In *Gone with the Wind,* Rhett Butler sweeps the protesting Scarlett O'Hara off her feet and carries her to an upstairs bedroom. According to Civil War era definitions of appropriate male-female relationships, Butler's behavior would be interpreted as intense passion. Men could plausibly disregard women's attempts to rebuff their sexual advances because men were expected to be aggressive in such situations and women were expected to protest. With the exception of black males, who could be lynched for improprieties as slight as looking the "wrong" way at a white woman, it would have been unthinkable to define behaviors like Rhett's as rape. Today there are quite different interpretations of such male-female interactions. In the context of present values, women's raised consciousness, and changed legal standards, it is unlikely that Rhett Butler's behavior would be interpreted today as mad passion or romantic devotion. However, changes in attitudes and conventions often happen very slowly. Today too many men still do not appreciate that having sex after a woman says no or when she is incapable of giving consent is, in fact, rape.

To Educate or Not? The Controversy over Sex Education

The question at the core of the debate over sex education is, "Does formal learning about sex increase or deter early sexual experimentation?" Those who favor sex education hold that children benefit from early, comprehensive information about sex. Providing young people with an appropriate vocabulary and accurate information both discourages early sexual activity and encourages safe sexual practices for those teens who will not be deterred from sexuality (Sexuality Information and Education Council of the United States [SIECUS], 1995). On the other hand, opponents of sex education are intensely committed to the belief that information about sex changes teenagers' reactions and values and leads to early, and what they believe are inappropriate, sexual behaviors (Whitehead, 1994). Conservative groups hold that sex education, if it occurs at all, should emphasize abstinence (Just say no!) as opposed to practical information.

What does the scientific research say? In June 2001, Surgeon General David Satcher issued a report that provoked an immediate strong reaction from the White House. The report, *The Surgeon General's Call to Action to Promote Sexual Health and Responsible Sexual Behavior*, was based on scientific review papers by experts and recommendations from national conferences. The report cited a number of sexually related public health problems, including:

- the infection of 12 million Americans each year with sexually transmitted diseases (STDs)
- 800,000 to 900,000 Americans living with HIV, with one-third of them unaware that they are even infected
- unintended pregnancies accounting for nearly one-half of all pregnancies in the U.S.
- an estimated 1.36 million abortions in 1996
- an estimated 104,000 children becoming victims of sexual abuse each year
- reports that 22 percent of American women and 2 percent of American men have been victims of rape (Satcher, 2001).

The report calls for strategies focusing on increased awareness, implementation and strengthening of interventions, and expanding the research base relating to sexual health matters. A key strategy for increasing awareness is the availability of school sexuality education that not only encourages abstinence from sex, but also talks about birth control. Evaluation evidence indicates that programs that include both either have no effect on initiation of sexual activity or, in some cases, delay the initiation of sexual activity (Kirby, 1999, 2001). Although a majority of Americans favor some form of sexuality education in the public schools and also believe that some sort of birth control information should be available to adolescents (Smith, 2000), "abstinence only" programs, which bar any talk of contraception, are the only ones supported by conservatives. The White House and conservative allies were not happy with the report's finding that there is simply no evidence that teaching abstinence from sex works (nor with the lack of evidence to support the religious right's assertion that gay individuals can become straight). According to a spokesman for President George W. Bush, "The president continues to believe that abstinence and abstinence education is the most effective way to prevent AIDS, to prevent unwanted pregnancy" (http://www.sunspot.net/news/health/bal-te.satcher30jun30.story).

According to Satcher, the primary purpose of the *Call to Action* is to initiate a mature national dialogue on issues of sexuality, sexual health, and responsible sexual behavior. He quotes an Institute of Medicine (IOM) report, *No Time to Lose* (IOM, 2000):

> Society's reluctance to openly confront issues regarding sexuality results in a number of untoward effects. This social inhibition impedes the development and implementation of effective sexual health and HIV/STD education programs, and it stands in the way of communication between parents and children and between sex partners. It perpetuates misperceptions about individual risk and ignorance about the consequences of sexual activities and may encourage high-risk sexual practices. It also impacts the level of counseling training given to health care providers to assess sexual histories, as well as providers' comfort levels in conducting risk-behavior discussions with clients. In addition, the "code of silence" has resulted in missed opportunities to use the mass media (e.g., television, radio, printed media, and the Internet) to encourage healthy sexual behaviors. (Satcher, 2001:17–18)

According to Satcher, we must all share the responsibility for initiating a national dialogue, working at every level of society to promote sexual health and responsible sexual behavior.

Rape is legally defined as sexual intercourse (vaginal, oral, or anal) that occurs by means of force or threat of force. Rape, however, need not involve physical force and legally applies to those situations in which the victim—by reason of unconsciousness, mental derangement, retardation, or intoxication—is incapable of giving consent to sexual relations.

Although this is a fairly straightforward definition, the crime of rape is still viewed in our society in terms of a collection of myths about rapists and rape victims, including the notion that some women enjoy "being taken" by force; that women initially say "no" to men's sexual advances to appear "respectable" and must be "persuaded" to give in; that many women provoke men by teasing them and therefore get what they deserve.

In recent years research has revealed that a sizable amount of violent crime, including rape, involves people known to one another. A rape case involving a victim who knows or is familiar with her assailant is known as *acquaintance rape*. At least 55 percent of rapes are acquaintance rapes. More than 33 percent of rapes take place at or in the victim's home; 21.3 percent occur at, in, or near the home of one of the victim's friends, relatives, or neighbors (U.S. Department of Justice, 1997). One form of sexual assault that almost always occurs in the victim's home is marital rape, the sexual assault of a woman by her husband. It was not until 1977 that the Oregon state legislature repealed the marital exemption to its rape statute, and two years later the first marital rape conviction occurred. Marital rape is now a crime in all 50 U.S. states, although in some states rape by a husband is defined more narrowly than rape by a stranger (Bergen, 1998). Research indicates that marital rape often accompanies other forms of family violence, and occurs in 9 to 14 percent of all U.S. marriages (Bergen, 1996). This is not a situation in which one spouse wishes to have sex and the other does not, but gives in out of love or to please. Marital rape is a brutal physical assault that may have a graver impact on a victim than stranger rape, given that the assailant is a person whom she knows and, at least at one time, loved and trusted (Bergen, 1996).

Acquaintance rapes are especially common on college campuses. Despite claims by some (c.f., Roiphe, 1993) that the term "date rape" is being misapplied to cases involving boyfriends verbally coercing their girlfriends to have sex, or to intercourse that occurs because the woman is intoxicated and becomes "sexually confused," empirical research indicates that the incidence of acquaintance or date rape on college campuses is a serious problem (see Schwartz and DeKeseredy, 1997, for a review of college date rape studies).

Acquaintance rape remains a controversial topic because of confusion around the definition of consent. In an attempt to clarify this definition, Antioch College in Ohio adopted in 1994 what has become "an infamous policy delineating consensual sexual behavior" (Curtis, 1997). According to the policy, the definition of consent is based on continuous verbal communication during intimacy—the person initiating the contact must take responsibility for obtaining the other participant's verbal consent as the level of sexual intimacy increases. Even if you have had a particular level of sexual intimacy before with someone, you must still ask each and every time (*The Antioch College Sexual Offense Policy*, in Francis, 1996). Although the policy was ridiculed and lampooned by many based on the criticism that it reduced the spontaneity of sexual intimacy to what seemed like an artificial contractual agreement, this attempt to remove ambiguity from the interpretation of consent was hailed by some as the closest thing yet to an ideal of "communicative sexuality" (Curtis, 1997).

Studies of college students have found that many young men and women believe that under some circumstances it is all right for a man to force a woman to have sex (Schwartz and DeKeseredy, 1997). These authors and others (Benedict, 1997; Sanday, 1990, 1996) have found that among all-male social networks, especially those such as fraternities and athletic teams where heavy drinking is the norm, certain women, particularly those who are intoxicated, are considered "legitimate sexual targets." Some men believe that when a woman says no to sex it is still proper to continue their sexual advances. Peggy Sanday's (1990) study of a college fraternity detailed how male definitions of consenting sexuality can become so stretched that instances of several men having sex with a nearly unconsciously drunk woman were thought legitimate (the men termed such events "pulling train" or "gang banging"). Their definition was that women who became drunk and acted flirtatiously were "asking for it," and that plying a woman with alcohol was one of several appropriate strategies used in "working a yes out" when a woman initially showed no interest in sex or explicitly said no. More recently, Boswell and Spade (1996) found differences between fraternities viewed by women students as "high risk" or "low risk" in terms of likelihood of being raped. "High-risk" fraternities were characterized by members who treated women as subordinates and kept them at a distance, active discouragement of ongoing relationships with women, routine degradation of women, and more participation in the "hook-up" scene, thus increasing the probability that women would become faceless victims. Hooking up, a phenomenon that seems to have replaced dating on most college campuses, was defined by men in this study as something that happens "when you are really drunk and meet up with a woman you sort of know, or possibly don't know at all, and don't care about. You go home with her with the intention of getting as much sexual, physical pleasure as she'll give you, which can range anywhere from kissing to intercourse, without any strings attached" (Boswell and Spade, 1996:139).

Women's version of hooking up differed. Women said they hook up only with men they cared about and described hooking up as kissing and petting but not sexual intercourse. Many women said that hooking up was disappointing because they wanted longer term relationships.

Not all men interviewed for this study held negative attitudes toward women; however they did say that, when together in groups with other men, they sensed a pressure to be disrespectful toward women. One senior man's statement pretty well sums things up: "In general, college-aged men don't treat women their age with respect because 90 percent of them think of women as merely a means to sex" (Boswell and Spade, 1996:141).

The Parent-Child Relationship

A clear example of historical change in the quality and nature of intimate relations involves the norms governing the relationships between parents and children. Here we can refer back to a theme raised in chapter 1 in which we argued that the meanings of everyday life must be understood within the broad frames of history and social structure. Even such a commonsense idea as what it means to be a child varies at different times and particularly as the economic structure of society changes. The place and meaning of childhood is different in an agrarian economy than in an industrial economy. In agricultural societies married couples had a large number of children because they needed the help to run their farms. In industrial societies fertility rates drop dramatically, and too many children may be seen as a hindrance to one's own mobility in society. In his pioneering work, *Centuries of Childhood* (1962), the French social historian Philippe Aries demonstrates that the meanings of children as a social category and of childhood as a life-cycle period are shaped by particular historical circumstances.

Aries argues that childhood was "discovered" as a separate life stage during the sixteenth and seventeenth centuries in Europe. He demonstrates that childhood carried a fundamentally different meaning in the Middle Ages than in the contemporary world. In the Middle Ages, children were considered to be small adults. The equality of their relationship with adults was reflected in numerous customs. Parents and children wore similar clothing, participated in identical work and play activities, and even exchanged sexual jokes. As the dominant form of the family institution changed from the **extended family**, which included several generations of a kinship network, to the **nuclear family**, which was composed only of a father, a mother, and their children, the father assumed absolute control over both mother and children. The extent of such domination is reflected in the laws of the period. In seventeenth-century Massachusetts children over 16 were subject to the death penalty for cursing or striking their parents or for refusing to obey their orders.

During the early period of industrialization in Europe and America, children came to be seen as an economic resource, valued in large measure by the contribution they could make to the family's well-being. In this period there were no child labor laws, and it was common for even young children to work 14 or more hours per day in the expanding factories of the industrial world. The meaning of childhood shifted yet again with the emergence of American cities, taking root first among the middle class in the early nineteenth century and spreading to encompass working-class children by the early twentieth century. "Not surprisingly, middle-class children were redefined as vulnerable innocents in need of full-time care and devoted attention in the same era as their mothers were being redefined as the guardians of virtue and morality, the ideal keepers of the domestic sphere" (Farrell, 1999:22). Despite class differences, which sharpened as the United States industrialized during the nineteenth century and produced clear distinctions in the life experiences of children, "the middle-class model of the vulnerable and defenseless child who required a mother's full-time care" gained dominance as the cultural norm, if not the behavioral reality, by the middle of the century (p. 23). Between the 1870s and the 1930s, working-class as well as middle-class children began to be sentimentalized and reinterpreted as innocent and vulnerable, a process that involved a significant cultural shift from a belief in the economic usefulness of children to one in which children were understood as economically useless but morally and emotionally priceless (Zelizer, 1985). According to one author, by the start of the twentieth century "American children were beginning to serve more the psychological than the economic needs of adults" (Cross, 1997:85).

Although expectations about parent-child relationships continue to vary with the ethnic, religious, and social class characteristics of families, most parents today seek to be friends with their children and try to foster mutual respect for all family members' behaviors and opinions. The family circle typically resembles a democracy in which the children have the right to participate in the decision-making process. It is, however, an imperfect democracy.

Because parents have full responsibility for their offspring, they have authority over them and are expected to exert strong control over their lives.

Although this section uses childhood as a convenient example, historical analyses would reveal similar changes in expectations concerning appropriate behaviors between siblings, friends, and lovers.

Social Status and the Meaning of Intimacy

The meanings attached to family, friendship, and love relationships also vary with a person's social status (see chapter 3). At various levels of the social structure of American society, there are variations in the definitions and meanings assigned to these relationships.

Friendships, for example, are distinguished from family relationships by their voluntary character. The saying, "You can pick your friends but you can't choose your relatives" contains much truth and has significant sociological implications. First, we expect friendships to be less binding than family relations. Indeed, one way we describe "close" friendships is to invest them with a familial status. A woman might affirm the closeness of her friendship with another woman by saying, "She is like a sister to me." "Kindred spirits," a quaint phrase in Victorian literature, carries the same sentiment as the more current phase "going for brothers" used by black men to describe friendships based on trust and mutual responsibility. Friendships, of course, vary in intensity. A range of terms is used to describe gradations of nonkin intimacy, from acquaintance to friend, close friend, and best friend.

The meanings we give to friendship and other intimate relationships reflect a person's social attributes, including the ascribed statuses of age, race, and gender, as well as achieved statuses such as occupation, education, and social class (see chapter 3). We will consider how two of these attributes, gender differences and social class, affect the maintenance of intimate relationships among friends and in the family.

Gender Differences

The voluminous social science literature on **gender roles** adds up to the conclusion that perhaps even more than class or age, gender, along with race/ethnicity, defines one's identity, opportunities, and constraints. Social definitions of friendship and intimacy reflect traditional stereotypes of men's and women's roles (Wood, 2003). Both women and men perceive women as more attentive, caring, and responsive, and a majority of both sexes report that friendships with women are more close and satisfying than those with men (Werking, 1997). One need only take a walk to a local grade school at recess time to note differences in the way that young children play and form friendship groups. From a very early age boys and girls form sex-segregated friendship groups, which differ in size and content of activities. Girls tend to engage in more affiliative, cooperative play in which a major activity is talk and the expression of feeling, whereas boys tend to interact in more instrumental ways forming into larger, more amorphous groups and engaging in competitive games (Leaper, 1996).

The fact that women use talk as a primary way to develop relationships and men generally do not underlies several gender-linked patterns in friendship. First, communication is central to women friends, whereas activities are the primary focus of men's friendships. Second, talk between women friends tends to be expressive and disclosive, focusing on details of personal lives, people, relationships, and feelings; talk in men's friendships generally revolves around less personal topics such as sports, events, money, music, and politics. Third, in general, men assume a friendship's value and seldom discuss it, whereas women are likely to talk about the dynamics of their relationship. Finally, women's friendships generally appear to be broader in scope than those of men; that is, women tend not to restrict their disclosures to specific areas but to invite each other into many aspects of their lives (Wood, 2003).

Traditional gender stereotypes suggest that men tend to disclose less than women due to sociocultural prohibitions against intimacy between men (Floyd, 1997) and because men are socialized to hide their emotions in order to avoid appearing weak or homosexual (Monroe, Baker, and Roll, 1997). Although not all studies have found gender differences in self-disclosure, some studies have shown differences in men's and women's perceptions of and experiences with intimacy (Hendrick, 1997), same-sex friendships (Parks and Floyd, 1996), and self-disclosure (Dolgin and Minowa, 1997). These studies suggest that women generally tend to self-disclose more frequently than men. A study by Wagner-Raphael, Seal, and Ehrhardt (2001) found that in relationships with women, men divulge personal feelings and express emotion, whereas men's same-sex relationships involve sharing personally relevant facts and shared activities. The reported ability of men to be emotionally expressive with women may reflect the impact of recent changes in gender roles on intimate cross-sex relationships.

The centering of attention on human relations learned by girls from a very early age sets the stage for the nature of male and female friendships and continues into adulthood. Married or single, employed or not, women make 10-20 percent more long-distance calls to family and friends than men, are responsible for nearly three times as many greeting cards and gifts, and write two to four times as many personal letters as men. Women spend more time visiting with friends, though full-time work blurs this gender difference by trimming friendship time for both sexes. "Keeping up with friends and relatives continues to be socially defined as women's work" (Putnam, 2000:95), or what Di Leonardo (1987) has referred to as "kin work." Even in adolescence women are more likely to express a sense of concern and responsibility for the welfare of others. And although American boys and girls in the 1990s used computers almost equally, boys were more likely to use them to play games, while girls were more likely to use them for e-mail (Putnam, 2000).

You might test the notion of kin work against your personal experiences. Who mails the birthday and holiday cards in your home? Who cooks the holiday dinners and telephones invitations to the relatives? If your family is at all typical of contemporary American families, the odds are that it is probably a woman (or women) doing these things. In most American families, women still consider it their duty to worry about family members and to take care of their everyday needs.

The gender patterns of activity established on kindergarten playgrounds sustain themselves throughout the life courses of men and women as such patterns are reinforced by cultural standards and structural arrangements. Together these factors result in women possessing more than men the social skills that foster greater intimacy within friendships. We might also presume that the differences we have been describing in this section help us to understand some of the communication difficulties men and women may have in their own intimate relationships. Women usually have to encourage men to talk about their deepest feelings, something they find very difficult to do. "Can we talk about us?" is the opening of innumerable conversations that end in misunderstanding and hurt (Wood, 2003). For most women, communication is a primary way to establish and maintain relationships with others. They engage in conversation to share themselves and to learn about others (Johnson, 1996). For women, talk *is* the essence of relationships, and women's speech tends to display identifiable features that foster connection, support, closeness, and understanding (Wood, 2003). Men, on the other hand, use communication to do things and solve problems. In general, men are inclined to think a relationship is going fine as long as there is no need to talk about it. They are interested in discussing the relationship only if there are particular problems to be addressed. Deborah Tannen's classics *That's Not What I Meant! How Conversational Style Makes or Breaks Relationships* (1986) and *You Just Don't Understand: Women and Men in Conversation* (1990) have helped shed light on the different conversational styles of women and men (and perhaps saved relationships). In her most recent book, *I Only Say This Because I Love You: How the Way We Talk Can Make or Break Family Relationships Throughout Our Lives* (2001), she revisits cross-cultural gender communication—women's "rapport-talk" and men's "report-talk." These underlying assumptions held by women and men about what constitutes communication explain why "lack of communication" is the most common complaint of women about their marriages, whereas men in the same marriages do not typically mention communication as a problem.

Gender roles have been changing, however, as women have entered the labor force in increasing numbers. In 1960, the rate for married women's labor force participation was about half that for single women, with 31.9 percent of married women and 58.6 percent of single women in the paid labor force. In 1980, the rate for married women was 77 percent that of single women, with 49.8 percent of married women and 64.4 percent of single women in the paid labor force. By 1999, the rates had almost converged, with 61.2 percent of married women in the paid labor force, compared to 68.7 percent of single women (U.S. Census Bureau, 2000b). Dual-earner couples have become the norm. The rates for mothers are even more striking. By 1999, 61.8 percent of married women with children under 6 were in the paid labor force, compared to 68 percent of single women with children under 6 and 54.4 percent of married women with no children under 18 (U.S. Census Bureau, 2000b). Despite the dramatic increase in women's labor force partic- ipation, gender inequity in the labor force continues (see chapter 6).

The growing social science literature focusing on the intersection of work and family (c.f., Hochschild and Machung, 1989, 1997), as well as the regu- lar appearance of articles in women's magazines ("You can have a 50/50 marriage: 4 happy couples tell how," *Redbook*, March 2001) testify to the importance of the issue of balancing the competing and often overwhelming demands of paid work and family commitments. In fact, this is perhaps the most central challenge in women's lives as we enter a new century. Much recent scholarship has concentrated on the experiences and consequences of the "second shift" (Hochschild and Machung, 1989) put in by employed women and the balancing act between work and family roles (Milkie and Pel- tola, 1999). When both marriage partners work outside the home, critical questions are raised about how to divide the everyday household tasks. These kinds of questions can lead to intense feelings of resentment on the part of the wife, who, despite the increased popularity of the image of an involved fam- ily man and societal espousal of egalitarian values, continues to shoulder most of the burden of household labor. Even the most recent studies reveal only slight changes from previous patterns of housework allocation. Gender segregation of tasks continues, with wives performing the "core," tradition- ally female tasks to a large degree and men concentrating their household labor on other, more episodic or discretionary tasks (Bianchi et al., 2000).

Intimate relations within the home are bound to be affected by wives' efforts to negotiate an equitable distribution of household chores, as well as their desire to be recognized as equal partners in the rights and responsibili- ties of the marriage. Wives' perceptions of unfairness have a tremendous impact on the marriage, resulting in negative associations such as depression, thoughts of divorce, and actual breakups (Greenstein, 1996; Rogers and Amato, 2000). This finding holds true across racial and ethnic groups (Stohs, 2000). When Stohs asked the African American, Asian American, Hispanic American, and Middle Eastern Americans in her sample about reasons for marital conflict, the issue of "unfair share" was cited more frequently than any other. Another study that included middle-class and working-class dual- earner couples found that for middle-class wives, perceptions of equity had the strongest effect on marital conflict (Perry-Jenkins and Folk, 1994).

Effects of Social Class

Social class position also influences the meanings attached to friendship. There is, for example, a strong relationship between **social mobility** and the maintenance of friendship ties. Some people maintain very strong allegiances to the same friends throughout their lives, while for others friendships are much more transitory and entail few obligations. Position in the occupa- tional structure has a lot to do with the processes of friendship choice and development, the social contexts in which friends are made, the influence of social mobility on friendship ties, and the significance of the workplace for friendship development.

Sociological studies have found that for lower- and working-class men, friendships require substantial commitments and the fulfillment of an extensive set of mutual obligations. Indeed, the requirements of friendships in these classes are said to be so extensive and morally binding that they can stand in the way of occupational and educational achievement.

In his classic study of a Boston slum community, *Street-Corner Society: The Social Structure of an Italian Slum* (1955), William Foote Whyte explained how the friendship loyalties of a group of "corner boys" (actually men in their twenties and thirties, mostly second-generation immigrants) restricted their social mobility. He described them as so tied to their group through a network of reciprocal obligations and so unwilling to sacrifice their friendships that they failed to get ahead. For example, friends were expected to share whatever money they had. Such a friendship norm prevented these young men from adopting the middle-class values of thrift, savings, and investment, and made the eventual financing of a college education or business career impossible. A leader of the corner gang—a man named Doc—expressed his feelings about his friends when he told Whyte:

> I suppose my boys have kept me from getting ahead. . . . But if I were to start over again—If God said to me, "Look here, Doc, you're going to start over again and you can pick out your friends in advance," still I would make sure that my boys were among them—even if I could pick Rockefeller and Carnegie. . . . Many times people . . . have said to me, "Why do you hang around these fellows?" I would tell them, "Why not, they're my friends." (1955:180)

This group distinguished different levels of friendship, ranging from an inner circle of individuals who were "uptight" with one another to others who remained at the periphery of a network of personal relationships. To be uptight with another person required trusting that person like kin, with the usual claims, obligations, expectations, and loyalties that such a status implies. The result was a contradiction between the requirements of friendship and the desire to get ahead. More recent interviews with working-class members suggest that this contradiction still exists and can be a source of acute strain or tension.

The friendship model of lower- and working-class men contrasts with the ways upper-middle-class men in managerial occupations construct and define their friendships. In another famous book, *The Organization Man* (1956), William H. Whyte described the friendships of career-oriented, rising young executives as short-lived and largely utilitarian. Friends were frequently *cultivated* for their potential value in career advancement. Such friendships were often dissolved or forgotten when the aspiring executive moved up the corporate ladder or left the area. Breaking off friendship ties when they posed an obstacle to mobility did not create moral dilemmas for these men. They clearly recognized the need for an extensive network of the "right" friends, and who these friends were could change at each point in their career development.

From Strangers to Intimates:
The Construction of Love Relationships

Despite the variability in the ways individuals construct, maintain, and change the quality of their relationships with family members, friends, and lovers, it is possible to identify an **intimacy process** with certain common elements. This section is concerned with one part of that process, the construction and development of love relationships. It explores the steps through which two strangers typically become intimates—meeting, dating, becoming committed to each other, falling in love, and usually marrying. While the specifics of the process through which strangers are transformed into lovers may vary widely, the socially prescribed benchmarks or stages of these relationships are much alike.

We share certain expectations about the appropriateness of intimate relationships. We expect to fall in love, have sex, and get married within well-recognized time frames. Adults typically define teenagers' first attempts at establishing intimate relationships as infatuation or "puppy love"; they are considered too young to experience the real thing. At the other extreme, people who remain unmarried past their late twenties may be considered "problems" by parents, relatives, and friends—the stigma associated with singlehood has not disappeared, particularly for women (Chasteen, 1994). Similarly, sexual relationships between teenagers could be considered improper if not immoral, but status as a virgin after the middle to late twenties could be a source of embarrassment.

In American society the completion of formal education seems to be a key point in intimacy time conceptions. High-school students who do not go on to college are more likely to marry soon after graduation. For others the college years are thought to be an appropriate time to fall in love. Indeed, because college students constitute a readily accessible sample of participants for research studies, most of the generalizations concerning the process through which individuals fall in love come from studies of college students. To understand this process, we must first appreciate the conception of love that guides the construction of our intimate relations.

The Romantic Love Ideal

Some years ago a Korean graduate student who was becoming visibly distressed as she neared the completion of her master's degree work confided she had been receiving letters from her parents indicating that she would be married upon her return to Korea. Throughout her education in the United States she had known that she would eventually be expected to marry the person her parents chose for her. Now, however, she did not want to return to Korea, and she certainly did not want to marry someone she had never met. She knew it would be a breach of cultural tradition to refuse her parents' wishes, but she had adopted American values that consider love to be the only reasonable basis for marriage. The standards of her society, we note, are more typical of what young men and women experience around the world than is the Western notion that love should be the basis for marriage. Here, as elsewhere, we should place cultural values in historical context.

The **romantic love ideal**, formulated in France and Germany during the twelfth century, filtered down from the nobility to the lower classes over the centuries. In its pure form the ideal of romantic love involves the notion that there is only one person in all the world that we are meant to love: Although "love is blind" we will recognize our "true love" at first sight. The role of *fate* in this process is a strong feature of the romantic ideal. We are expected to "fall in love" and to believe that "you were meant for me!" From adolescence on, we wait for that moment when "that old black magic has us in its spell" (see box).

The Ideal and the Real

While love ought to be the sole basis for marriage according to the romantic ideal, most of us recognize the discrepancy between ideal and real. We may generally subscribe to the romantic ideal, but we also know that life rarely corresponds to ideals, that people do not and ought not to marry *only* because they are in love. Most young people are socialized to believe that love is necessary for marriage, but not always a sufficient reason to marry. We have a negative view of anyone who would marry *exclusively* for money, status, prestige, or security. But we also consider anyone foolish who would marry a poor person rather than a wealthy one, other things being more or less equal.

Studies have found differences between men and women in the weight they give to love as a condition for marriage. In an early well-known study, Willard Waller (1938) analyzed the dating patterns among young people (particularly college students) and found that, contrary to popular belief, men are more likely than women to hold to the romantic ideal. In other words, women are *less* romantic than men. Because of women's traditional dependence on men, in Waller's view, the process of mate selection is of much greater consequence to them. Women, therefore, have been comparatively less idealistic and more rational and cautious in love relationships.

If only the romantic ideal were operating in mate selection, we should expect that Cupid's arrow would strike only where there was romantic electricity between two people. Were this the case, we should expect that marriages would easily cut across class, racial, ethnic, and religious lines. However, even a casual glance at the marriage announcements in the Sunday newspaper illustrates that the vast majority of people marry within strict social channels. Although we are theoretically free to marry anyone who catches our eye, selection is generally limited to those we meet and can confidently introduce to relatives and friends. These considerations automatically reduce the "pool of eligibles" to those who are not all that different from our-selves. The tendency to pick a partner who shares our ascribed characteris-tics—race, religion, ethnicity, social class—is called **homogamy**. Young people today are able to travel a lot farther from home, at an earlier age, and more frequently than in the past, so the chances of meeting someone different from yourself have increased. As a consequence, in terms of ethnicity and religion especially, an increasing number of marriages are heterogamous.

Love Makes the World Go Round: The Code of Romance

It is often asked whether art imitates life or vice versa. Although it is difficult to answer this question, one thing is certain. The romantic ideal is celebrated in music, art, cinema, and literature. One particularly thriving industry caters to the apparent unquenchable thirst for romance stories. Romance fiction has become a billion-dollar business; romance is the most popular mass-market category with 58.2 percent of the market in 1999. Approximately 2,523 romances were published in 1999, generating $1.35 billion in sales (Rosen, 2000). Harlequin, number one in romance publishing, sells about 160 million books annually in 24 languages and more than 100 countries. Sales were $525 million in 1998, with nearly $88 million in profit (Jenish, 1999).

Some 14 percent of Americans buy romance fiction each year; the overwhelming majority are female. Harlequin's surveys find that 68 percent have attended or graduated college; 55 percent work outside the home and have average annual household income of $45,300; 48 percent began reading romances when they were 17 or younger. Apparently, the image of the dissatisfied housewife devouring romance novels is not and has never been true of the majority of the genre's readers. The readership has become more diverse: more multi-degreed professionals, younger women, as well as stay-at-home moms (*Publishers Weekly*, 1998). One major change has been the tremendous growth in African-American readers. According to one African-American author, the mass-market paperback publishers weren't interested in her stories before 1994. It wasn't until Toni Morrison, Terry McMillan, and Alice Walker that they became aware of the possibility of a lucrative market (Woods, 1997).

Despite the popularity of romance fiction, it remains stigmatized as "trashy novels." Readers often find it necessary to employ face-saving strategies in social situations, such as concealing the reading and criticizing the books and other readers (Brackett, 2000).

Always hoping to broaden the audience, as well as boost the reputation of romance fiction, Romance Writers of America (RWA) has set new marketing campaigns in motion. There have been movie theater previews and TV spots with big-name authors aiming to knock down stereotypes associated with the category and emphasize its diversity (Kinsella, 1998). Their "Look Who's Reading Romance" program sent posters showing readers who break stereotypes (a telephone lineman, a woman judge) to libraries and bookstores. Web sites abound and there is a new category of romance novels only published online—the reader is charged to download the whole "book." Romance readers have built a huge online community, connected via bulletin boards, where they can have conversations about books they mutually love (*Publishers Weekly*, 1998). AOL's Book Central site is a favorite meeting place for romance fans and includes a weekly live chat show with authors, "The Romance Club" (Dyer and Dahlin, 1997). Cable television gave romance a boost with Romance Classics, a channel featuring movies and programs with a romantic theme (Dyer and Dahlin, 1997). The Romance Classics network increased its subscriber base to 5.9 million on direct broadcast satellite service launches (*Broadcasting & Cable*, 1997).

Publishers have successfully mined the young adult romance category for generations, although sales have sagged in recent years. The appeal is logical, according to one editor-in-chief quoted in *Publishers Weekly*. At a time in their lives when love is "fast, furious, and often fickle," if teenagers "see a book where somebody else has many of the same feelings they have, it's quite satisfying" (Frederick, 1997). The average age of young adult romance readers has dropped, which has brought a corresponding change of content. Several publishers have series aimed at 16-year-old girls, while other series target older teen readers. Then there are the trendy series—such as a hybrid romance/sci fi series set in alien-sighting capital Roswell, New Mexico—based on the premise that aliens left offspring behind who have grown up to young adulthood and are now mixing with students at the local high school (Frederick, 1997).

So what exactly is romance fiction? Today the genre encompasses a wide range of books from contemporary to historical, racy to gentle, realistic to paranormal (Saricks, 1999). According to one author, a romance is defined as "a love story in which the central focus is on the development and satisfactory resolution of the love relationship between the two main characters, written in such a way as to provide the reader with some degree of vicarious emotional participation in the courtship process" (Kristin Ramsdell, quoted in Saricks, 1999). Harlequin's standardized formula is instructive. The company publishes four books monthly under its steamy Harlequin Temptation label. The stories contain "conflict and sizzling sexual tension," according to promotional literature, and one or two acts of lovemaking. Conflicts are resolved within the prescribed 220 pages, because in Harlequin books, romance rules (Jenish, 1999). As one magazine headline put it, "Romance novels these days are sensitive, affirming and hotter than July" (Woods, 1997).

Characters fall into easily identifiable categories. Men are handsome, strong, and elusive; women are strong, bright, and independent. Moral and social issues are often significant themes (alcoholism, the role of women in society, post-traumatic stress disorder). The women are not always beautiful, but they are, without fail, bright, independent, interesting, and articulate (Saricks, 1999). According to one author, "Romance has changed with the times; heroines have become more independent. But the idea of a happy ending was popular ten years ago and continues to be the main reason for the appeal of the romance" (*Publishers Weekly*, 1998).

And then there's the advice from *Men's Fitness*: "Many women love to read romance novels. Men who want to learn more about the art of seduction should take time to read such novels. They contain interesting and fresh ideas about slow-paced seduction" (Perlof, 1997:81J).

Hmm . . . .

Although the importance of religion and ethnicity have diminished, race remains a powerful factor. For example, black/white marriages comprised only 3 of every 1,000 marriages in 1980 and only 6 in 1998—a 100 percent increase, but still not very many. Twenty-five percent of Asian-American women and 12 percent of Asian-American men are married to a person not of Asian descent. Marriage across ethnic lines is even greater among Hispanics; 28 percent of all married Hispanics have a non-Hispanic spouse. Nevertheless, **endogamy** is still the social norm in the United States (U.S. Census Bureau, 1999a).

The Process of Falling in Love

You probably have known people who claim to have fallen in love at first sight—perhaps you have yourself. For most people, however, the development of a love relationship is a gradual process. Although social scientists have offered more recent models of what the falling in love process is like (c.f., Sternberg, 1988), we still find most useful Ira Reiss's (1960) description of the **wheel theory of love** in which the four stages of a love relationship—rapport, self-revelation, mutual dependency, and need fulfillment—are represented by the spokes of a wheel (see figure 5.1). According to Reiss, we proceed through these stages one at a time and in order. Before we are willing to reveal significant identity information about ourselves to another person, we must first have achieved a certain level of rapport with that person. Self-revelation then sets the stage for a sense of mutual dependency. The final stage in this process is the belief that the other person fulfills our basic needs.

Research conducted on various aspects of mate selection and marriage suggests that there is indeed considerable regularity and rationality to the

Figure 5.1   The Wheel Theory of the Development of Love

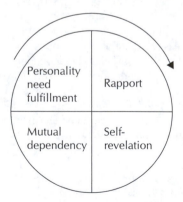

Source: Ira Reiss, "Toward a Sociology of the Heterosexual Love Relationship," *Marriage and Family Living 22* (May 1960): 143. Copyrighted 1960 by the National Council on Family Relations, 3989 Central Ave. NE, Minneapolis, Minnesota 55421. Reprinted by permission.

process. Using Reiss's wheel theory shown in figure 5.1 as a general guide, we can analyze the movement from rapport to self-revelation to commitment and marriage, as well as the factors that sometimes hinder such movement.

Rapport and Self-Revelation: "You Think You Know Me, but You Don't"

Meeting a stranger—at a party, through the introduction of mutual friends, in a class or church group—usually starts with casual conversation and the exchange of superficial biographical information. College students meeting at a party engage in fairly ritualistic conversation: "What year are you in? What is your major? Where are you from?" If one of the participants has no desire to continue the conversation, this incipient relationship is easily ended. If the individuals wish to pursue the relationship, the conversation becomes progressively less superficial and more far-reaching, as each person seeks to learn more about the other. The desire to continue a relationship, however, may be more related to assessments of physical attractiveness than to social or personality attributes, at least for men. Men continue to rate physical appearance more highly than women, whereas women consider financial status to be more important (Baize and Schroeder, 1995; Sprecher, Sullivan, and Hatfield, 1994). Among gay men physical appearance is of utmost importance (Hatala and Predhodka, 1996). We could say that women appear to emphasize the interpersonal dimension of romance, whereas men stress the physical aspects of attraction (Buss, 1994).

Personal ads have become an interesting source of information about interpersonal attraction, self-presentation strategies, relationship goals, desirable inner qualities, and gender stereotypes. People use personal ads as "meta-statements" about the kind of person they are (*Psychology Today*, 2000). When placing a personal ad, it is understandable that people will try to make themselves as desirable as possible in order to get a response. Gonzales and Meyers (1993) found that "to enhance the odds of initiating and maintaining a viable relationship, advertisers in personal ads are likely to offer those characteristics they believe a potential date or partner would find rewarding" (p. 131). And of course advertisers not only maximize their positive attributes but also seek to minimize their negative attributes. Goode (1996) found that most individuals rate themselves as above average compared to the norm on many dimensions, including attractiveness, intelligence, and ability as a lover.

There are factors other than appearance which influence whether two people will embark on a romantic relationship, such as similarity in lifestyle and psychological traits (Houts and Robins, 1996; Lamm, Wiesman, and Keller, 1998).

The impression management stage. Once two people have begun to interact, their primary goals typically are to determine the issues on which they agree and disagree and to assess the significance of their similarities and differences. While the **manifest function** of dating is to teach partners how to negotiate differences (e.g., which movie to rent or where to go to eat), the **latent function** is to prepare them for the skills necessary to maintain long-term relationships.

Complicating the information assessment during the initial stages of a relationship is the deliberate impression management engaged in by both parties. Individuals may be so intent on establishing a relationship that they systematically present attitudes and values they believe will be acceptable. Each will be careful to feel out the other person before expressing an opinion that might be disliked enough to bring an end to the relationship. Identity information is manipulated to present the proper first impression. Courtship is, then, a unique period in the love relationship in which each person typically offers an idealized image of herself or himself and is willing—even eager—to accept the idealized image the other person presents. When the couple learns more about one another, it may come as a surprise if the original presentation of self turns out to have been deliberately manipulated to create a favorable impression. In fact, relationships may end when one or both persons are forced eventually to conclude, "I thought I knew her (or him), but I didn't."

As we noted in chapter 3, people manage impressions of themselves by systematically concealing information they consider potentially damaging in the encounter, while at the same time they seek out information about the other person. It is relatively easy to manipulate information about attitudes and values. Other items of identity information, however, are difficult to hide or conceal, such as the ascribed attributes of ethnicity, race, religion, and social class. These social class attributes also serve as a **relationship filter.** If people discover that others' ethnic, religious, or class affiliations are very different from their own, they are likely to end the relationship at an early stage. The ability to garner resources may initially serve as a relationship filter (Ganong et al., 1996). For example, college-educated women may disregard males who are majoring in a field noted for low pay (e.g., education, social services).

Premarital romantic relationships consist primarily of the joint pursuit of leisure, and, to the extent that people "date" with the idea of selecting a mate, partners are likely to evaluate how congruent their ideas are about who will be responsible for what after marriage. This led one group of researchers to focus on couples' similarity in leisure interests and role preferences. They hypothesized that similar couples might be expected to fall more deeply in love, to be less ambivalent about the relationship, experience less conflict, and escalate their commitment to marriage more rapidly (Houts and Robins, 1996). Their findings support the idea that compatibility affects the developmental course of premarital relationships, especially for men. The more compatible couples were in their leisure preferences, the more men reported they loved their partner during courtship and engaged in communication designed to increase satisfaction. The more couples agreed on role performance preferences (food preparation and financial tasks), the less conflict/negativity was reportedly experienced by both men and women and the less ambivalence was reported by women.

Supplied with the information the participants have provided about themselves and the symbols defining their social worlds, the couple must then decide whether the worlds they respectively inhabit are close enough that they will eventually be able to produce and sustain a common reality. Social science studies have found that if two people have very dissimilar biographies, they will be unlikely to produce such a reality. It is the obvious disparity in biographies that forms the substance of such legends as Cinderella, for example. Cinderella is a fairy tale precisely because it relates the story of a successful love relationship despite vast differences in the individuals' biographies.

When a relationship endures beyond the point of self-disclosure and the participants are dating each other "seriously," they begin to try to interpret their level of commitment to the relationship. And in order to guarantee that their relationship will continue, they must make a commitment to each other.

Mutual Dependency and Commitment: "All I Ever Need Is You"

If the love relationship persists, eventually it reaches the point where the participants' everyday lives are much intertwined. At the stage of mutual dependency, the couple's relationship has ceased to be their private affair. The individuals have probably been publicly defined as a couple. Once this **public definition** has been applied, their relationship becomes more exclusive, and they are bound in a complex web of expectations. Not only do the participants have new expectations of each other, so do their friends and family. The couple is issued joint invitations; one is expected to accompany the other to social gatherings; and when they are apart, each partner is expected to be able to account for the other's ideas, attitudes, and whereabouts. The partners signal the seriousness of their relationship to each other, family, and friends by engaging in a variety of activities generally understood to indicate a growing level of commitment. Such symbolic gestures may include spending time together every day rather than just on weekends, introducing the partner to relatives, bringing the other person to such important family events as weddings and annual gatherings, and purchasing expensive gifts for each other.

The point of mutual dependency is a time when the relationship may undergo severe tensions and stresses. These difficulties are often related to the growing intensity of commitment demanded in the relationship. Their own and others' expectations for the couple may cause one or another to feel smothered by the pressure to make a permanent commitment. In the past, there often were gender differences in the meanings attached to commitment. Traditionally, males have been socialized to view the acceptance of a long-term relationship as a surrender of their freedom and independence, while females have been socialized to seek the security of a permanent commitment. Now women also are becoming wary of losing their identity in a relationship. Many women refuse to subordinate their interests to those of their male partners and would not hesitate to dissolve a relationship where they are treated as only an appendage to the male. In a study of late-adolescent romantic relationships, males and females did not report significantly different levels of commitment as measured by a "Commitment to Relationship Scale" and "Feelings of Entrapment Scale" (Galliher et al., 1999). In fact, in approximately half of the couples, girlfriends reported more commitment than boyfriends, while the opposite pattern emerged in the other half.

For some couples, graduation from college precipitates a **commitment crisis**:

> Everyone's asking when you're going to get married/move in/have that baby/buy a house. One of you is stalling because you're not entirely convinced you want to move the relationship onto a deeper level of intimacy and commitment. Sometimes, a nudge from others can make us push through silly fears and take the leap. But . . . outright pressure and nosy interference can send us in the opposite direction—flying over the edge to freedom. (Cox, 2000:324)

One frequent cause of breakups at this stage is that parents or friends dislike or disapprove of the dating partner. Your friends, for example, may demand to know what you see in your companion. In college, as in high school, students place a great deal of weight on the evaluations of their peers. Many students also form friendships with slightly older persons, such as seniors, graduate students, or young faculty members, who can offer guidance in the place of their parents. Conflicts with parents can easily threaten a developing relationship. If parents who have dreamed of sending their son or daughter to medical school perceive an intimate relationship as a potential threat to this plan, for example, they may demand: "Stop seeing this person or we will stop paying for your education." Parents' control over students' financial welfare can easily extend to control over their love lives.

In years past it was not unusual for a woman to subordinate her own career plans to those of a male in order to sustain a relationship. Today female and male college students do not differ in their desire for success or expectations to achieve (Ganong et al., 1996). Women in the United States are more likely to endorse egalitarian gender role attitudes than in previous decades (Harris and Firestone, 1998), including college women's marriage role expectations (Botkin, Weeks, and Morris, 2000). If college men do not share these attitudes, relationships may founder at this point unless arrangements can be made for both individuals to pursue their own career goals.

There is some evidence that college students—black and white, male and female—are generally egalitarian in their attitudes. Students believe, for the most part, that male and female romantic partners should be equivalent in education and occupational status, or that men should be superior to their partners in these areas. One difference between females and males that has the potential to strain relationships is the expectation on the part of men that they will do less parenting than their partners. The women expect equality in parenting (Ganong et al., 1996).

The popular stereotype of a love relationship that ends before marriage features poor pitiful Pearl pining away for a lost love. Such endings actually are harder on men, however, according to a classic study of breakups before marriage by Charles Hill, Zick Rubin, and Letitia Peplau (1977). This study distinguished between "his breakup" and "her breakup." His breakups are more devastating because men find it more difficult to believe that they are no longer loved. The difference might be explained by women's greater practicality in love relationships. As one of the female respondents in the survey for this study noted, "I don't think I ever felt romantic about David—I felt practical. I had the feeling that I'd better make the most of it." The partners in a lasting relationship are likely to share equal commitments to it, according to these researchers. Their data indicate that only 23 percent of equally involved couples broke up, compared to 54 percent of those in relationships where one person was more committed than the other.

Because the couples studied were college students, Hill, Rubin, and Peplau found that relationships tended to break up at clear demarcations in the school year: May–June, September, December–January. Understandably, the person interested in terminating the relationship found it easier to suggest just before vacation, "It might not be a bad idea for us to date others while we are apart." Also, as might be expected, each partner's conception of the terminated relationship differed according to whether he or she had acted in the role of "breaker-upper" or "broken-up-with." There is a tendency for each partner to claim to have initiated the breakup. It is obviously preferable to define a situation as one in which you have exercised power and controlled another person's behavior rather than the other way around.

Wanting to end a relationship is not unusual. Individuals may discover through frequent interaction that they no longer wish to be involved. In one study of 415 university students, 89 percent of males and 88 percent of females reported that they had been involved in at least one previously broken relationship (Laner, 1995). Many relationships end in the face of pressures, but many partners also develop a commitment to a relationship just because it has continued for a long time. Intimate relationships often develop a momentum of their own as a result of sheer endurance. Investing time and energy in their own relationship while foregoing them with others commits people; often they remain in the relationship even when it becomes a painful one.

Whatever the dynamics of a relationship that leads two people to declare their commitment to one another, the next step in their intimacy normally is plans for marriage. Today, however, it is not uncommon for individuals to decide to live together without marriage or to remain single. For some, living together represents a satisfactory alternative to marriage; for others, it is viewed as an additional opportunity to test out their relationship. To be sure, people have been marrying much later than in earlier decades and the numbers of men and women in their late twenties and early thirties who have never married has more than doubled since 1970 (U.S. Census Bureau, 1999a). Because of the magnitude of these changes, the meanings of commitment, intimacy, sexuality, and marriage have changed accordingly.

Alternatives to Marriage

In recent years there has been much discussion in both the popular press and academic literature about the perception that a sexual-moral revolution has occurred. Sociologists agree that there have been significant changes in sexual norms and behavior, but they disagree on the specific nature of these changes, just when they began, or whether they are tapering off. However, studies offer general support for the idea that a "sexual revolution" began during the turmoil of the 1960s. The same cultural atmosphere in which hippies and young political activists were challenging conventional standards about race relations, political authority, and structure of work was extended to changing norms about sexuality. The result was a striking increase in premarital sexuality that appeared to peak in the early 1980s.

According to Kinsey and his associates (1953), only about one-fifth of 19-year-old females had premarital intercourse during the 1940s and early 1950s. By the early 1980s the corresponding figure was between two-thirds and three-fourths (Hofferth, Kahn, and Baldwin, 1987). In the 1940s and 1950s about 45 percent of 19-year-old white males had experienced heterosexual intercourse. By the late 1970s the figure was about 80 percent (Gebhard, 1980). By the end of the twentieth century, the gap in sexual experience between girls and boys had closed completely. According to the Children's Defense Fund (CDF), four out of five young men and women have sexual intercourse before age 20, with average age of first intercourse for boys, 16; for girls, 17 (CDF, 1997). A study by the Kaiser Family Foundation (1998) found that age at first intercourse for both boys and girls was 15. Even teens who do not have intercourse do engage in other types of genital sexual activities, including oral sex and masturbation with a partner (Schuster, Bell, and Kanouse, 1996). Despite the liberalization of attitudes toward premarital sex, however, a considerable amount of research indicates that the sexual double standard continues—that is, the tradition of permitting young men to engage in sexual activity or at least ignoring their sexual escapades.

One analogue of these figures was a dramatic increase in teenage pregnancies through the 1980s, especially in the black and Hispanic communities (Williams, 1991). There was a change in the 1990s, however, with the teen pregnancy rate hitting a record low in 1997. The teen pregnancy rate fell by 4.4 percent from 1996 to 1997, continuing a trend that lasted through the 1990s. The rate of teen births in the U.S. declined steadily from 62.1 births per 1,000 girls 15–19 in 1991 to 54.7 births for every 1,000 girls 15–19 in 1996 (CDF, 1997). Experts credit long-lasting birth control, programs that encourage teens to postpone sex, and a strong economy that provides better opportunities.

Most of the teen pregnancies are among 18- and 19-year-olds. Teen pregnancy rates remain higher in low-income communities, and there are differences according to ethnicity, with African-American and Hispanic girls more than twice as likely to get pregnant as white girls. The disproportionately high birth rate of African-American and Latina teens has been linked to higher rates of poverty and lower levels of academic success (CDF, 1997). Still, the rates are falling among all races. According to the CDF (1997), teens who are least likely to get pregnant and give birth are those who: (1) live in financially stable or affluent families, (2) are academically successful, and (3) have high aspirations with opportunities available to fulfill those aspirations.

Another factor contributing to teen pregnancy is sexual coercion. Research indicates that as many as 50 to 70 percent of babies born to girls age 11–18 are fathered by males four to seven years older than the babies' mothers. According to the CDF, "The typical adolescent girl simply is not sufficiently empowered to negotiate sex and contraception with a male partner four or more years older" (CDF, 1997:85).

Living Together

The steady increase in the number of men and woman living together led to a new census category for the 1980 count of Americans. The category was "Persons of the Opposite Sex Sharing Living Quarters" or POSSLQs for short. By 1988, the number of POSSLQs stood at 2.6 million couples, four times the estimated number in 1970 (U.S. Census Bureau, 1988). The Census Bureau now uses the term "unmarried partners," defined as two unrelated people sharing living quarters and a "close personal relationship." They are distinguished from roommates who share space simply to save money. The number of unmarried partners was up almost 72 percent during the 1990s, from 3.2 million in 1990 to 5.5 million by 2000 (Roylance, 2001a). Although one tends to think of cohabitors as being college-aged, most are over age 25, with a high school education. It is estimated that close to one-half of American children will spend some part of their childhood living with one parent and her or his live-in partner (Smock, 2000). Most cohabitors will eventually marry (about 55 percent); however, 40 percent end the relationship within five years of the beginning of the cohabitation (Bumpass and Lu, 2000).

Although common sense suggests that premarital **cohabitation** should provide the opportunity for couples to learn about each other, strengthen their bonds, and increase their chances for a successful marriage, the evidence suggests just the opposite. Premarital cohabitation tends to be associated with lower marital quality and increased risk of divorce (Smock, 2000). Numerous studies have attempted to explain this; two explanations have received empirical support. The first, termed the *selection* explanation, refers to the idea that people who cohabit before marriage differ in important ways from those who do not, and these differences increase the likelihood of marital instability. The second explanation is that there is something about the *experience* of cohabitation that increases the likelihood of marital disruption (Smock, 2000).

Nock (1995), for example, describes cohabitation as an *incomplete institution*, "not yet governed by strong consensual norms or formal laws" (p. 74). The absence of these institutional norms is a plausible explanation for much of the poorer quality of cohabiting relationships. Nock compared national data on 499 cohabiting couples and 2,493 married couples and identified three major differences:

1. Less commitment. Cohabitants were more likely than marrieds to report that ending their relationship would have fewer negative consequences. This is supported by research by Forste and Tanfer (1996), who found that cohabitants are also less willing to be sexually monogamous than marrieds.

2. Poorer intergenerational relationships. Cohabitants were more likely than marrieds to report poorer relationships with both mothers and fathers, indicating a lack of emotional and financial support.

3. Lower relationship happiness. Cohabitants report that they are slightly less happy than spouses (Newport, 1996).

Perhaps cohabitants have lower-quality relationships, lower institutional commitment, and less hope for the future of their relationships because cohabitation draws people who are not ready to commit to each other or to the institution of marriage. Some research has found that men and women lacking economic stability are likely to cohabit, suggesting that cohabitation may provide an attractive alternative for those lacking the economic stability required for marriage (Clarkberg, 1999). Moving in together appears to be perceived more as an ambiguous commitment rather than a trial marriage (Lindsay, 2000). Perhaps most serious is the finding that domestic violence rates are higher in cohabitation relationships (Waite, 1999–2000).

As we noted earlier, during courtship individuals tend to selectively present their best self, emphasizing or exaggerating positive qualities and behaviors and minimizing or concealing negative ones. This tendency also applies to cohabiting couples who eventually marry. Cohabitants assume that because they are living with their partner this is the way the partner is and will behave in marriage. This is not necessarily true. After marriage, a new self may emerge and perhaps shock the partner.

Despite research showing a higher dissolution rate for marriages of couples who lived together prior to the marriage than those of noncohabitors (c.f., Smock, 2000; Waite, 1999-2000), many couples who live together contend that cohabitation leads to better marriages. Single people living together report satisfaction with some aspects of the situation and problems with other features, and generally recommend cohabitation. It can provide couples with the emotional security of an intimate relationship but at the same time allow them to maintain independence in many areas. Cohabitors enjoy the spontaneity of a relationship based on love, not law.

Cohabitation often encourages people to establish a meaningful relationship instead of playing superficial dating games. Long periods of intimate contact afford an opportunity for self-disclosure and may foster emotional growth and maturity. Living with someone can be annoying at times, but cohabitants may gain a deeper understanding of their partners' needs, expectations, and weaknesses.

As a group, cohabitors have less traditional views of sexuality compared to married couples in general. Cohabitors also have sex more frequently than either marrieds or singles who do not live together (Michael et al., 1994). This is related both to the availability of a partner and to being in a relationship for a shorter period of time (the longer a couple have been in a relationship, the less often they report having intercourse).

Domestic Partnerships

Census data indicate that about 2 percent of all households consist of same-sex couples. In half of these households, the respondents classify themselves as "married," despite state laws that preclude legal same-sex marriage (Fields and Clark, 1999).

In the 2000 Maryland census, about 90 percent of unmarried partner households were of the opposite sex; nearly 10 percent were same-sex partners. On the surface these numbers suggest a significant increase since 1990 in the number of same-sex partners (up from 3,028 in 1990 to 11,243 in 2000). Comparable jumps have been noted in other states (as of this date, national figures are not yet available). However, 1990 data cannot be compared directly with the 2000 figures, because in 1990 census officials invalidated responses from households who reported living with "spouses" of the same sex. In the 2000 census, officials routinely recorded same-sex "spouses" as "unmarried partners" as a result, according to a census official, of "a much more cognizant awareness on our part of changes in the living arrangements of people in the 1990s" (Roylance, 2001b).

Because homosexual couples tend to be very similar in educational and occupational statuses, these relationships are typically characterized by mutuality and equality (Sullivan, 1996). The educational and income levels of homosexual Americans tend to be higher than the American average, and high proportions have been in relatively long-term relationships, at least as long as many heterosexual unions (Black et al., 1999). Many gay and lesbian couples have children from an earlier heterosexual relationship, adoption, or *in vitro* fertilization. The research on lesbian and gay male parenting has found "no differences on any measures between the heterosexual and homosexual parents regarding parenting styles, emotional adjustment, and sexual orientation of the children" (Allen and Burrell, 1996).

Increasingly, businesses, local governments, and academic institutions are recognizing the rights of **domestic partners** (people who live together in a committed relationship) to be covered by the same benefits as married employees. However, in 1996, when it appeared that the Supreme Court of Hawaii might sanction same-sex unions, a majority of other state legislatures proposed laws to bar homosexual marriages and deny recognition to those performed in other states. Congress passed the Defense of Marriage Act of 1996 that releases states and other territories of the United States from an obligation to recognize same-sex marriages under the laws of another state (see Nock, 1999).

As of 2000, ten states, the District of Columbia, and more than 165 cities and counties in the United States had adopted civil rights laws protecting lesbians and gay men against discrimination in such areas as employment, housing, and public accommodations (American Civil Liberties Union, 2000).

Staying Single

Recent years have seen a sharp increase in the number of unmarried adults (never married, divorced, widowed) in our society. "Singlehood," not marriage, is now the most common lifestyle among people in their early 20s. By the end of the twentieth century, about 25 percent of U.S. women age 15 and above and 31 percent of men had never married (U.S. Census Bureau, 1999a). The never married comprise the largest and fastest-growing segment of the unmarried population. The biggest changes are among African Americans and Hispanics: in 1996, 39 percent of African-American adults over 18 had never been married, up from 21 percent in 1970; the number of never-married Hispanic adults over 18 increased from 19 percent to 30 percent during the same time period. (U.S. Census Bureau, 1997). The unmarried population in the United States constitutes a very diverse group of singles.

As of 1998, one out of every four households in the U.S. (accounting for over 26 million people) was a single-member household (U.S. Census Bureau, 1999b). As reported earlier in the chapter, these numbers partially result from the fact that, compared to earlier decades, people are delaying marriage until later in life. Many people are pursuing college educations, preparing for jobs or careers, and spending more time pursuing recreational or other activities before "settling down." Many people are living together, at least for awhile, rather than getting married. The median ages for first marriage—nearly 27 for men and 25 for women—are the oldest ever recorded by the Census Bureau (although men's median age at first marriage in 1990 "caught up" to what it had been in 1890—26.1!). Nevertheless, marriage is still the norm—nearly 95 percent of all Americans eventually marry (U.S. Census Bureau, 1999b).

The decision to marry (and its timing) differs for women and men. Males desire marriage more than do females (Frazier et al., 1996). Many women perceive that career advancement is slowed by marriage and the chances of one's future occupational success are improved by postponing marriage. Deferring marriage is not, however, useful for men's career advancement, so men lack that motivation for remaining single.

Research shows that economic well-being plays a role in choices about marriage and cohabitation versus staying single (c.f., Clarkberg, 1999). Single young adults were economically worse off in 1994–95 compared to their counterparts in either 1972–73 or 1984–85 (Paulin and Riordon, 1998), perhaps contributing to later marriage.

Pros and Cons

While there are many benefits in marriage, there are usually parallel incentives for being single, particularly independence and autonomy. One goal of marriage is companionship, or avoidance of being alone. According to a *Time* magazine/CNN Poll (Edwards, 2000), 75 percent of women said that companionship was what they missed most because of being single (only 4 percent said sex). Although companionship and having someone to talk to is important, one of the biggest advantages of remaining single is independence. Single adult women in the United States are more self-confident and selective than they have ever been, assuming many of the social, economic, and sexual freedoms previously reserved for single men (Edwards, 2000). Only 34 percent of single women said they would settle for less than a perfect mate if they couldn't find one, compared with 41 percent of men (Edwards, 2000).

Less social stigma is attached to remaining single today, with single people less likely to be perceived as socially inadequate or as failures. Nevertheless, some unmarried people still encounter stereotypes. Never-married men may be suspected of being gay; single women may worry that they are perceived as "loose." Single adults must contend with the inaccurate view that they are lonely, workaholics, and immature. These stereotypes help support the traditional assumption in America that to be truly happy and fulfilled, a person must get married and raise a family. To help counter these societal expectations, singles have formed numerous support groups, such as the Alternative to Marriage Project (www.unmarried.org). Although being single is more acceptable, many people still get married because it is expected of them.

Married people experience a consistently higher level of well-being across a number of dimensions, including financial well-being, happiness, health, and family/job satisfaction. Cohabitors fall between married and unmarried on the happiness scale (Waite, 2000; Waite and Gallagher, 2000). Married men and women feel that their lives have more meaning and purpose than unmarried individuals, and it is this sense of meaning and purpose that seems to be responsible for the better psychological health of husbands and wives (Burton, 1998). Single individuals have higher levels of loneliness compared to married individuals. Marriage lowers loneliness to a greater degree in men than in women (Stack, 1998). According to one well-known family sociologist, "Most social scientists who have studied the data believe that marriage itself accounts for a great deal of the difference in average well-being between married and unmarried persons. Indeed, loneliness is probably the negative feeling most likely to be alleviated simply by being married" (Glenn, 1997:11).

Many of the trends that we have been describing in this chapter about the cultural meaning of intimacy, including premarital and nonmarital sex, have felt the impact of the AIDS epidemic. The magnitude of the problem is presumably well known, but the facts bear repeating (see box).

Single-Parent Families

Single-parent families, in which there is only one parent present to care for the children, can hardly be viewed as a rarity in the United States. In 1998, a single parent headed about 19 percent of white families with children under 18, 34 percent of Hispanic families with children, and 54 percent of

Love in the Age of AIDS

University students are generally well-educated on the subject of HIV/AIDS; however, despite the increase in sexual activity among young people in recent years, condom-use rates are low, putting young people at high risk for AIDS/HIV (Svenson, Carmel, and Varnhagen, 1997). According to the CDC's National College Health Risk Behavior Survey (NCHRBS), nearly three-fourths of students who reported having sexual intercourse during the month prior to the survey did not use condoms consistently (Douglas, Collins, Warren et al., 1997), despite the fact that 49 percent of students reported having received information on preventing HIV infection and AIDS (Brener and Gowda, 2001). This suggests that college students are at some risk for contracting AIDS or other sexually transmitted diseases (Bon, Hittner, and Lawandales, 2001). One author has stated that college students have a rate of HIV infection 10 times higher than the general heterosexual population (Stine, 1998). As a result of the consistent finding that college students' awareness has not appreciably reduced their risk-specific sexual behaviors, researchers have begun to examine other factors that influence young people's sexual conduct (c.f., Lehr et al., 2000).

Think about your own knowledge about AIDS and other STDs. Do you and your peers "tune it out?" Why do you think college students do this?

African-American families with children (U.S. Census Bureau, 1999b). The number of children under 18 living in two-parent families has decreased from 77 percent in 1980 to 68 percent. Twenty-three percent live with mother, 4 percent with father, and another 4 percent with neither parent. While 75 percent of white children live with both parents, this is true for only 36 percent of black children. However, census data obscures the extent to which there may be a cohabiting adult in the household; it is estimated that 40 percent of children born to unmarried mothers are raised in homes with two adults, at least for part of the time (Bumpass and Lu, 2000).

Divorce

The media frequently report that one out of every two marriages ends in divorce. However, much that has been written about the American divorce rate is not accurate. The divorce rate has not risen for at least three decades. There was a sharp upturn in the late 1940s, most likely due to hasty wartime marriages or marriages that could not survive a long separation. Then came two decades of low divorce rates, with another upturn in the late 1970s, peaking in 1981 before leveling off, then dropping in the late 1990s (Paul, 2001). In an average year there are over 1.1 million divorces in the United States, a rate of almost 20 divorces per 1,000 existing marriages (U.S. Census Bureau, 2000b). The American divorce rate is somewhat higher than that for other modern societies, but so too is our marriage rate—the two tend to move together. Because divorces usually take place early in a marriage, most men and women will remarry, men sooner and at a higher rate than women. The older and better educated the divorced woman, the lower her chances of remarriage because the pool of eligibles—divorced, widowed, or never-married educated men—is not very large. Men seeking to remarry can dip into a larger pool, filled with younger and less-educated women.

Although the social stigma has largely disappeared, the economic consequences of divorce for women remain strongly negative (Smock, Manning, and Gupta, 1999). There also are negative outcomes of divorce for children, particularly loss of economic security. In terms of noneconomic consequences, women appear to fare better emotionally after separation and divorce than men (Arendell, 1995). This is attributed to the fact that women are more likely than men not only to have a stronger network of supportive relationships, but also to profit from divorce by developing a new sense of self-esteem and confidence since they are thrust into a more independent role. On the other hand, men are more likely to have been dependent on their wives for domestic and emotional support and have a weaker external emotional support system. As a result, divorced men are more likely than divorced women to date more partners sooner and to become remarried more quickly (Arendell, 1995).

Divorce often constitutes a dramatic transformation of a close, personal, and usually harmonious relationship into one that is deeply antagonistic and bitter. It is clearly a *process* rather than a single event, affected by the larger structure of meanings that define marriage in our culture, along with the interpretive logic that people use to make sense of their own experiences (Hopper, 2001) (see box).

Conclusion

This chapter began with the somewhat circular conception of intimate relationships as those which the participants define as intimate. Our goal has been to extend this idea by analyzing how people come to define their relationships as intimate. Relations of love and friendship are without intrinsic meaning and must be understood as symbolic constructions deeply rooted in social life. Individuals soon learn the values of the society and their immediate reference groups concerning the meanings of love, friendship, and family relationships.

Like any symbol whose meaning by definition is not fixed, the concept of intimacy is subject to substantial historical and contemporary variation in meanings. The meanings of sexual relations and relations of parents and children have changed over time, for example. The meanings given to love and friendship also vary with such social attributes as age, occupation, race, ethnicity, gender, and social class. The substantial differences in the definitions given friendships by males and females and by people in different social

The Symbolic Dimension of Divorce

The profound value attached to marriage engenders an important problem of meaning when couples go through divorce. That is, because most people get married with the belief that marriage is forever, they face a difficult interpretive problem in explaining why theirs is ending. To resolve the problem, they *undo* the previous meaning of their marriage.

Joseph Hopper was a participant/observer in an extensive four-year fieldwork and interview study focused on the experiences of divorcing people. Among those he interviewed, there was an important, socially meaningful way in which divorce was literally an *undoing* of marriage. As Hopper explains:

> In other words, it was not merely a transition from one kind of relationship to another or the end of one phase and the beginning of another; it was far more than the separation of two intimately related people. It was a retroactive nullification—a substantive and thoroughgoing reinterpretation—of what once existed. (2001:432)

For most of those interviewed, marriage was considered a sacred bond that was presumed to last forever. The ideal of marriage pervaded the reality of their daily lives; they knew divorce was common, but most said they had eliminated thoughts of divorce as a possibility for themselves: "I thought we'd stay together forever."

Dissolving marriage (even a "bad" marriage), then, involves substantial symbolic work, because it is essentially a process of "profaning the sacred."* To dissolve the sacred, in Durkheim's words, requires transformation *"totius substantiae*—of the whole being" such that the old object would "cease to exist, and . . . another [was] instantly substituted for it" (Durkheim, [1915]1965:54). The divorcing people Hopper interviewed were involved in "constructing deeply rooted and fundamental reinterpretations of their marriages that went to the core of what had constituted those marriages" (p. 435).

Hopper found that the distinction between *initiator* and *noninitiator* was important, because even though each had to explain the same circumstance of marriage being dissolved, "the interpretive burden was shaped differently depending on whether one had to justify the decision or respond to it; and this . . . set the stage for the intense conflict that followed" (p. 435).

Initiators of divorce come to see their marriage as not having been a true marriage from the start, so efforts to preserve it seem absurd. "With a negative chronology that went back to the beginnings of their marriages, most initiators subsequently argued that there was something fundamentally wrong with their marriages, something irrevocably flawed" (p. 436). This solved the interpretive problem they faced: "The sacred was not really violated, for there was nothing sacred to begin with" (p. 437).

The emerging interpretations of their marriages as false were not happily received by the noninitiating partners. "They were, in fact, being told that their marriages were phony, pretend, and untrue" (p. 440). As Hopper explains, "The fact that noninitiating partners did not conceptualize their marriages as irretrievably and fundamentally bad only exacerbated the interpretive difficulty they faced" (p. 440). The solution for noninitiators appeared to be a sense that "they and their marriages were evidently victims of initiators' deceit . . ." (p.

440). Some noninitiators came to believe that their partners were out-and-out liars; Hopper frequently heard the word "manipulative" used to describe initiating spouses.

"The Big Lie, then, emerged as the interpretive counterpart to The Marriage That Never Was" (p. 442). Although these interpretations may help individuals explain why their marriage is ending, they put partners dramatically at odds with each other. Hopper explains:

> Initiators saw their marriages as irrevocably, even originally, broken, a frame of reference that made noninitiators' reluctance to agree seem crazy and vengeful. Noninitiators reasserted a frame in which marriage was sacred and in which initiators' ending them seemed to be yet another maneuver in a nonobvious pattern of deceit. Some noninitiators reacted with threats, violence, or suicide attempts. This, of course, only confirmed the idea that they were dangerous and crazy. (p. 442)

Hopper concludes:

> Thus, initial hypotheses conjured to resolve certain dilemmas became self-fulfilling prophecies, and new problems and realities emerged. . . . Each partner provoked the other and confirmed negative images of themselves; a cycle of preemptory and protective moves—a dynamic of conflict through which most divorces subsequently unfolded—was begun. (p. 442)

Hopper has shown that the symbolic structure and logic of how divorce narratives get constructed can generate the conflict that typically characterizes divorce. His findings suggest that family researchers should look closely at "the symbolic dimension of family life to understand how interpretive processes may themselves be a source of important phenomena in families" (p. 443).

* Durkheim ([1915]1965) made a sharp distinction between the sacred and the profane. Marriages were sacred in the sense that the social collectivity brought them into being— they represent and embody the power, sentiments, and beliefs of society. Nearly every divorced person with whom Hopper spoke evidenced some conviction in the sacredness of marriage, "A sacredness or inviolability that set marriage apart from other kinds of relationships" (p. 433).

classes are particularly apparent in the connection between social mobility and the nature of friendships ties.

Intimate relationships are continually being interpreted and reevaluated by the participants in a regular, patterned process. The wheel theory of love describes the process through which strangers are transformed into intimates. The typical movement of such a relationship is from achievement of rapport to self-revelation to mutual commitment. The next step normally would be plans for marriage. In recent years, however, many young people have chosen to live together without marriage or to remain single. These efforts to refashion social ties have brought changes in the meanings given to intimacy and commitment.

Our treatment of intimate relations has been based on the assumption that individuals are joint participants in the construction of their social relationships. In most relationships, however, they are not equal participants. Some individuals have restricted choices about how they can respond to others and about the meanings conferred on objects, events, and situations. In the next chapter we will focus on the important issue of the distribution and application of power in everyday life.

DEFINITIONS

Cohabitation   A situation in which unmarried heterosexual couples live together and share the same household.

Commitment crisis   A situation in which a person must make a decision about how important a relationship is to him or her.

Domestic partners   Two unrelated adults who reside together; agree to be jointly responsible for their dependents, basic living expenses, and other common necessities; and share a mutually caring relationship.

Endogamy   The principle that people should marry within a certain group.

Extended family   A household made up of husband and wife plus other relatives, often including several generations. The extended family includes a kinship network of people related by birth or by marriage.

Gender roles   Societal and cultural expectations that regulate feminine and masculine behaviors.

Homogamy   The tendency to pick a partner who shares our ascribed characteristics—race, religion, ethnicity, social class.

Intimacy process   The ways individuals establish a relationship of emotional closeness with one another.

Latent functions   The unintended consequences of the ways in which an organization or institution actually operates.

Manifest functions   The explicit, or stated, purposes of an organization or institution.

Need for affiliation   The perceived need or desire for meaningful relationships with others.

Nuclear family   A family consisting only of a husband, wife, and their children.

Public definition   The ways in which others in an immediate social circle define an individual. Two individuals who have been publicly defined as a couple become bound in a web of societal expectations.

Relationship filter   Subtle devices by which individuals determine if they have anything in common with one another.

Romantic love ideal   The notion that the love of a man and woman for each other is the only basis for marriage.

Social construction   Meanings of things and situations which are created by people through their interactions with one another.

Social mobility   The process by which people make changes in their occupation or social class.

Wheel theory of love   A metaphor used by Ira Reiss to describe the circular process by which two people pass through phases of increasing intimacy with each other.

DISCUSSION QUESTIONS

1. Do you agree with the authors' point of view that intimacy is a social construction—that relationships of love and friendship are symbolic productions and have no intrinsic meaning?

2. How would you describe the distinguishing characteristics of a love relationship? What are the distinctive obligations and expectations defining love relationships? How do such obligations and expectations differ from those defining friendship relationships?

3. Describe a relationship that you have had with a boyfriend or girlfriend. Did the relationship pass through discernible stages as it developed? Do these stages conform to those named in the chapter? Are there similar stages to the "breaking up" process?

4. How would you characterize the attitudes of your friends toward premarital sex? How has the AIDS epidemic influenced the behaviors of college students?

5. Would you interpret the increase in the number of unmarried people choosing to live together as signaling basic shifts in the meanings people are giving to intimacy and commitment?

6. What do you think are the positive and the negative aspects of being single?

REFERENCES

Allen, M., and N. Burrell. 1996. "Comparing the impact of homosexual and heterosexual parents on children: Meta-analysis of existing research." *Journal of Homosexuality* 32:19–35.

American Civil Liberties Union. 2000. "State and local laws protecting lesbians and gay men against workplace discrimination." <http://www.aclu.org/issues/gay/gaylaws.html>. Accessed 10/05/02.

Anderson, A. 2001. "Surf here often?" *Christianity Today* 45(8):38.

Arendell, T. 1995. *Fathers and Divorce.* New York: Sage Publications.

Aries, P. 1962. *Centuries of Childhood: A Social History of Family Life.* New York: Vintage Books.

Baize, H., and J. Schroeder. 1995. "Personality and mate selection in personal ads: Evolutionary preferences in a public mate selection process." *Journal of Social Behavior and Personality* 10:517–36.

Bellah, R., R. Madsen, W. Sullivan, A. Swidler, and S. Tipton. [1985] 1996. *Habits of the Heart: Individualism and Commitment in American Life.* Berkeley: University of California Press.

Benedict, J. 1997. *Public Heroes, Private Felons: Athletes and Crimes against Women.* Boston: Northeastern University Press.

Bergen, R. 1996. *Wife Rape: Understanding the Response of Survivors and Service Providers.* Thousand Oaks, CA: Sage.

———.1998. *Issues in Intimate Violence.* Thousand Oaks, CA: Sage.

Bianchi, S., M. Milkie, L. Sayer, and J. Robinson. 2000. "Is anyone doing the housework? Trends in the gender division of household labor." *Social Forces* 79(1):191–228.

Black, D., G. Gates, S. Sanders, and L. Taylor. 1999. "Demographics of the gay and lesbian population in the United States." Paper presented at the Annual Meeting of the Population Association of America, March 25–27, New York.

Bon, R., J. Hittner, and J. Lawandales. 2001. "Normative perceptions in relation to substance use and HIV-risky sexual behaviors in college students." *Journal of Psychology* 135(2):165–78.

Boswell, A., and J. Spade. 1996. "Fraternities and collegiate rape culture: Why are some fraternities more dangerous places for women?" *Gender & Society* 19(2):133–47.

Botkin, D., M. Weeks, and J. Morris. 2000. "Changing marriage role expectations:1961–1996." *Sex Roles* (May):933–42.

Brackett, K. 2000. "Facework strategies among romance fiction readers." *The Social Science Journal* 37(3):347–60.

Brener, N., and V. Gowda. 2001. "U.S. college students' reports of receiving health information on college campuses." *Journal of American College Health* 495:223–28.

Broadcasting & Cable. 1997. "Romantic encounters." March 24, 127(12):66.

Brownlee, S. 1997. "Can't do without love: What science says about those tender feelings." *U.S. News & World Report* 122(6):58–60.

Bumpass, L., and H. Lu. 2000. "Trends in cohabitation and implications for children's family contexts in the U.S." *Population Studies* 54(1):29–41.

Burton, R. 1998. "Global integrative meaning as a mediating factor in the relationship between social roles and psychological distress." *Journal of Health and Social Behavior* 39:201–15.

Buss, D. 1994. *The Evolution of Desire: Strategies of Human Mating.* New York: Basic Books.

Chasteen, A. 1994. "The world around me: The environment and single women." *Sex Roles* 31:209–28.

Children's Defense Fund. 1997. *The State of America's Children—Yearbook 1997.* Washington, D.C.: Children's Defense Fund.

Choat, I. 2000. "Love at first site." *Computer Weekly,* February 10, p. 49.

Clark, M. 1996. "All penises are at least eight inches, and nobody is ever bald: Welcome to the gay men's on-line dating service." *New Statesman* 130(4538):24.

Clarkberg, M. 1999. "The price of partnering: The role of economic well-being in young adults' first union experiences." *Social Forces* 77(3):945–68.

Correll, S. 1995. "The ethnography of an electronic bar: The lesbian café." *Journal of Contemporary Ethnography* 24(3):270–98.

Cox, T. 2000. *Hot Relationships: How to Know What You Want, Get What You Want, and Keep It Red Hot!* New York: Bantam Books.

Cross, G. 1997. *Kids' Stuff: Toys and the Changing World of American Childhood.* Cambridge, MA: Harvard University Press.

Curtis, D. 1997. "Perspectives on acquaintance rape." The American Academy of Experts in Traumatic Stress. http://www.aaets.org/arts/art13.htm. Accessed 9/28/02.

Di Leonardo, M. 1987. "The female world of cards and holidays: Women, family and the work of kinship." *Signs* 12:40–53.

Dines, G., R. Jensen, and A. Russo. 1998. *Pornography: The Production and Consumption of Inequality.* New York: Routledge.

Dolgin, K., and N. Minowa. 1997. "Gender differences in self-presentation: A comparison of the roles of flatteringness and intimacy in self-disclosure to friends." *Sex Roles* 36:371–80.

Douglas, K., J. Collins, and E. Warren et al. 1997. "Results from the 1995 National College Health Risk Behavior Survey." *Journal of American College Health* 46:55–66.

Duin, J. 1999. "Intimacy isn't all about sex." *Insight on the News* 15(34):28.

Durkheim, E. [1915] 1965. *The Elementary Forms of Religious Life*. Glencoe, IL: The Free Press.

Dyer, L., and R. Dahlin. 1997. "Birds do it, bees do it: These days players on the Net do it." *Publishers Weekly* 244(46):40–45.

Edwards, T. 2000. "Single by choice." *Time* magazine online 156(9), August 28.

Farrell, B. 1999. *Family: The Making of an Idea, an Institution, and a Controversy in American Culture*. Boulder, CO: Westview Press.

Fields, J., and C. Clark. 1999. "Unbinding the ties: Edit effects of marital status on same gender groups." Paper presented at the Annual Meeting of the American Sociological Association, August, Chicago.

Floyd, K. 1997. "Brotherly love II: A developmental perspective on liking, love, and closeness in the fraternal dyad." *Journal of Family Psychology* 11:196–209.

Forste, R., and K. Tanfer. 1996. "Sexual exclusivity among dating, cohabiting, and married women." *Journal of Marriage and the Family* 58:33–47.

Francis, L., ed. 1996. *Date Rape: Feminism, Philosophy, and the Law*. University Park: Pennsylvania State University Press.

Frazier, P., N. Arikian, S. Benson, A. Losoff, and S. Maurer. 1996. "Desire for marriage and life satisfaction among unmarried heterosexual adults." *Journal of Social and Personal Relationships* 13(2):225–39.

Frederick, H. 1997. "The future looks bright for teen romance." *Publishers Weekly* 244(46):47.

Galliher, R., S. Rostosky, D. Welsh, and M. Kawaguchi. 1999. "Power and psychological well-being in late adolescent romantic relationships." *Sex Roles* (May):689–710.

Ganong L., M. Coleman, A. Thompson, and C. Goodwin-Watkins. 1996. "African American and European American college students' expectations for self and future." *Journal of Family Issues* 17(6):758–75.

Gebhard, P. 1980. "Sexuality in the Post-Kinsey Era." In *Changing Patterns in Sexual Relations*, edited by W. Armytage, R. Chester, and J. Peel. New York: Academic Press.

Glenn, N. 1997. *Closed Hearts, Closed Minds: The Textbook Story of Marriage*. New York: Institute for American Values.

Gonzales, M., and S. Meyers. 1993. "'Your mother would like me': Self-presentation in the personal ads of heterosexual and homosexual men and women." *Personality and Social Psychology Bulletin* 19(2):131–41.

Goode, E. 1996. "Placing/answering personal ads as a form of courtship." *Sex Roles* 34:141–69.

Greenstein, T. 1996. "Gender ideology and perceptions of the fairness of the division of household labor: Effects on marital quality." *Social Forces* 74:1029–42.

Harris, R., and J. Firestone. 1998. "Changes in predictors of gender role ideologies among women: A multivariate analysis." *Sex Roles* 38:239–52.

Hatala, M., and J. Predhodka. 1996. "Content analysis of gay male and lesbian personal advertisements." *Psychological Reports* 78:371–74.

Hatfield, E., and R. Rapson. 1996. *Love and Sex: Cross-Cultural Perspectives*. New York: Allyn & Bacon.

Hendrick, C. 1997. "Roles and gender in relationships." In *Handbook of Personal Relationships*, 2nd ed., edited by S. Duck, pp. 429–47. Chichester, England: Wiley.

Hill, C., Z. Rubin, and L. Peplau. 1977. "Breakups before marriage: The end of 103 affairs." In *Family in Transition*, edited by A. Skolnick and J. Skolnick. Boston: Little, Brown.

Hochschild, A., and A. Machung. 1989. *The Second Shift*. New York: Avon Books.

———. 1997. *The Time Bind*. New York: Metropolitan Books.

Hofferth, S., J. Kahn, and W. Baldwin. 1987. "Premarital sexual activity among U.S. teenage women over the past three decades." *Family Planning Perspectives* 19:46–53.

Hopper, J. 2001. "The symbolic origins of conflict." *Journal of Marriage and Family* 63:430–45.

Houts, R., and E. Robins. 1996. "Compatibility and the development of premarital relationships." *Journal of Marriage and the Family* 58(1):7–20.

Hyde, J., and J. DeLamater. 1997. *Understanding Human Sexuality*. 6th ed. Boston: McGraw Hill.

Institute of Medicine. 2000. *No time to lose: Getting more from HIV prevention*, edited by M. Ruiz et al. Washington, D.C.: National Academy Press.

Jenish, D. 1999. "Love and lucre." *Maclean's*, September 20:60.

Jensen, R. 1995. "Pornographic Lives." *Violence Against Women* 1:32–54.

Johnson, F. 1996. "Friendships among women: Closeness in dialogue." In *Gendered Relationships*, edited by J. Wood, pp. 79–94. Mountain View, CA: Mayfield.

Kaiser Family Foundation. 1998. *New KFF/YM Magazine survey of teens on dating, intimacy, and sexual experiences*. Menlo Park, CA: Kaiser Family Foundation.

Karp, D., G. Stone, and W. Yoels. 1991. *Being Urban: A Sociology of City Life*. New York: Praeger Publishers.

Kelly, D. 2001. *Sexuality Today*. 7th ed. New York: McGraw Hill.

Kinsella, B. 1998. "Love for sale: A new marketing push for romance." *Publishers Weekly*, November 9:16.

Kinsey, A., et al. 1953. *Sexual Behavior in the Human Female*. Philadelphia: Saunders.

Kirby, D. 1999. "Reducing adolescent pregnancy: Approaches that work." *Contemporary Pediatrics* 16:83–94.

———. 2001. *Emerging Answers: Research Findings on Program to Reduce Teen Pregnancy*. Washington, D.C.: National Campaign to Prevent Teen Pregnancy.

Kirschenbaum, M. 1999. *Women & Love*. New York: Avon Books.

Lamm, H., U. Wiesman, and K. Keller. 1998. "Subjective determinants of attraction: Self-perceived causes of the rise and decline of liking, love and being in love." *Personal Relationships* 5:91–104.

Laner, M. 1995. *Dating: Delights, Discontents and Dilemmas*. 2nd ed. Salem, MA: Sheffield Publishing.

Lanis, K., and K. Covell. 1995. "Images of women in advertisements: Effects on attitudes related to sexual aggression." *Sex Roles* 33:639–49.

Leaper, C. 1996. "The relationship of play activity and gender to parent and child sex-typed communication." *International Journal of Behavioral Development* 19:689–703.

Lehr, S., C. Dilorio, W. Dudley, and J. Lipana. 2000. "The relationship between parent-adolescent communication and safer sex behaviors in college students." *Journal of Family Nursing* 6(2):180–97.

Lindsay, J. 2000. "An ambiguous commitment: Moving to a cohabitating relationship." *Journal of Family Studies* 6(1):120–34.

Lynch, A. 1999. "On-line and in love." *Accent on Living* 44(1):52–55.

Michael, R., J. Gagnon, E. Laumann, and G. Kolata. 1994. *Sex in America: A Definitive Survey*. Boston: Little, Brown.

Milkie, M., and P. Peltola. 1999. "Playing all the roles: Gender and the work-family balancing act." *Journal of Marriage and the Family* 61(2):476–90.

Monroe, M., R. Baker, and S. Roll. 1997. "The relationship of homophobia to intimacy in heterosexual men." *Journal of Homosexuality* 33:23–37.

Newport, F. 1996. "Americans generally happy with their marriages." *Gallup Poll Monthly* (September):18–22.

Newsweek. 2001. "Love on-line: Millions are turning to the Internet to find romance. The pursuit can be fruitful—but chemistry is a tricky thing to transmit." February 19:46.

Nock, S. 1995. "A comparison of marriages and cohabiting relationships." *Journal of Family Issues* 16:53–76.

———. 1999. "The problem with marriage." *Society* 36(5):20–27.

Orenstein, P. 1994. *SchoolGirls: Young Women, Self-Esteem, and the Confidence Gap*. New York: Doubleday.

Pappano, L. 2001. *The Connection Gap: Why Americans Feel So Alone*. New Brunswick, NJ: Rutgers University Press.

Parks, M., and K. Floyd. 1996. "Meanings for closeness and intimacy in friendship." *Journal of Social and Personal Relationships* 13:85–107.

Paul, P. 2001. "Millennial myths: National Center for Health Statistics report on fertility, marriage, and divorce rates." *Forecast* 21(15):4.

Paulin, G., and B. Riordon. 1998. "Making it on their own: The baby boom meets Generation X." *Monthly Labor Review* 121(2):10–21.

Perlof, J. 1997. "Formula for love." *Men's Fitness* 13(2):81J.

Perry-Jenkins, M., and K. Folk. 1994. "Class, couples, and conflict: Effects of the division of labor on assessments of marriage in dual-earner families." *Journal of Marriage and the Family* 56:165–80.

Prager, K., and D. Buhrmester. 1998. "Intimacy and need fulfillment in couple relationships." *Journal of Social and Personal Relationships* 15:435–69.

Price, J. 1999. "Love Gets Lab Tests." *Insight on the News* 15(7):43.

Psychology Today. 2000. "Behind the personals." 33(2):Q.

Publishers Weekly. 1998. "What is this thing called love?" November 9:1.

Putnam, R. 2000. *Bowling Alone: The Collapse and Revival of American Community*. New York: Touchstone.

Reis, H., and P. Shaver. 1997. "Intimacy as an interpersonal process." In *Handbook of Personal Relationships: Theory, Research, and Intervention,* 2nd ed., edited by S. Duck, pp. 367–89. Chichester, England: Wiley.

Reiss, I. 1960. "Toward a sociology of the heterosexual love relationship." *Marriage and Family Living* 22:139–45.

Riesman, D. 1950. *The Lonely Crowd*. New Haven, CT: Yale University Press.

Robinson, J., and G. Godbey. 1997. *Time for Life: The Surprising Ways Americans Use Their Time*. University Park: Pennsylvania State University Press.

Rogers, S., and P. Amato. 2000. "Have changes in gender relations affected marital quality?" *Social Forces* 79(2):731–53.

Roiphe, K. 1993. *The Morning After*. Boston: Little, Brown.

Rosen, J. 2000. "And the sales keep climbing." *Publishers Weekly* 247(46):42.

Roylance, F. 2001a. "More women raising children without spouse." *The Baltimore Sun*, May 15:1A, 5A.

———. 2001b. "Count of same-sex couples jumps past 11,000 in state." *The Baltimore Sun*, July 3.

Sanday, P. 1990. *Fraternity Gang Rape.* New York: New York University Press.

————. 1996. "Rape-prone versus rape-free campus cultures." *Violence Against Women* 2:191–208.

Saricks, J. 1999. "Rules of the romance genre." *Booklist* 96(2):244.

Satcher, D. 2001. *The Surgeon General's Call to Action to Promote Sexual Health and Responsible Sexual Behavior.* U.S. Department of Health and Human Services, Office of the Surgeon General.

Schacter, S. 1959. *The Psychology of Affiliation.* Stanford, CA: Stanford University Press.

Schuster, M., R. Bell, and D. Kanouse. 1996. "The sexual practices of adolescent virgins: Genital sexual activities of high school students who have never had vaginal intercourse." *American Journal of Public Health* 86:1570–76.

Schwartz, M., and W. DeKeseredy. 1997. *Sexual Assault on the College Campus.* Thousand Oaks, CA: Sage.

Schwartz, P., and V. Rutter. 1998. *The Gender of Sexuality.* Thousand Oaks, CA: Pine Forge Press.

Sexuality Information and Education Council of the United States. 1995. *A Report on Adolescent Sexuality.* New York: SIECUS.

Smith, T. 2000. *Data from the General Social Survey.* National Opinion Research Center. University of Chicago.

Smock, P. 2000. "Cohabitation in the United States: An appraisal of research themes, findings and implications." *Annual Review of Sociology* 26:1–20.

Smock, P., W. Manning, and S. Gupta. 1999. "The effect of marriage and divorce on women's economic well-being." *American Sociological Review* 64:794–812.

Sprecher, S., Q. Sullivan, and E. Hatfield. 1994. "Mate-selection preferences: Gender differences examined in a national sample." *Journal of Personality and Social Psychology* 66:1074–80.

Sprout, A. 1997. "Looking for love in all the Web places." *Fortune* 135(4):186.

Stack, S. 1998. "Marriage, family and loneliness: A cross-national study." *Sociological Perspectives* 41(2):415–23.

Starling, K. 2000. "The joys and dangers of love on the Internet." *Ebony* 55(4):46.

Sternberg, R. 1988. *The Triangle of Love.* New York: Basic Books.

Stine, G. 1998. *AIDS Update 1998.* Englewood Cliffs, NJ: Prentice Hall.

Stohs, J. 2000. "Multicultural women's experience of household labor, conflicts, and equity." *Sex Roles* (March):339–61.

Sullivan, M. 1996. "Rozzi and Harriet? Gender and family pattern of lesbian coparents." *Gender & Society* 10:747–67.

Svenson, L., S. Carmel, and C. Varnhagen. 1997. "A review of the knowledge, attitudes and behaviours of university students concerning HIV/AIDS." *Health Promotion International* 12(1):61–68.

Tannen, D. 1986. *That's Not What I Meant! How Conversational Style Makes or Breaks Relationships.* New York: Ballantine.

————. 1990. *You Just Don't Understand: Women and Men in Conversation.* New York: Morrow.

————. 2001. *I Only Say This Because I Love You: How the Way We Talk Can Make or Break Family Relationships.* New York: Random House.

Thoits, P. 1989. "The sociology of emotions." *Annual Review of Sociology* 15:317–42.

Time. 2000. "The love machines: Valentines may now be wired, but on-line dating is also fostering some very 19th century courtship." February 14:73.

————. 1999. "Click here for love: A Foreign Affair offers lonely hearts an electronic emporium of brides on-line." March 29:10.

U.S. Census Bureau. 1989. *Statistical Abstracts of the United States: 1989.* 108th ed. Washington, D.C.: GPO.

———. 1997. *Statistical Abstracts of the United States: 1997.* 117th ed. Washington, D.C.: GPO.

———.1999a. "Marital Status of the population 15 years old and over, by sex and race: 1950 to present." (Internet release date: January 7, 1999).

———. 1999b. *Statistical Abstracts of the United States: 1999.* 119th ed. Washington, D.C.: GPO.

———. 2000a. Table DP-1. Profile of General Demographic Characteristics: 2000.

———. 2000b. *Statistical Abstracts of the United States: 2000.* 120th ed. Washington, D.C.: GPO.

U.S. Department of Justice, Bureau of Justice Statistics. 1997. *Criminal Victimization in the United States, 1994.* Washington, D.C.: Department of Justice.

Wagner-Raphael, L., D. Seal, and A. Ehrhardt. 2001. "Close emotional relationships with women versus men: A qualitative study of 56 heterosexual men living in an inner-city neighborhood." *The Journal of Men's Studies* 9(2):243–56.

Waite, L. 1999–2000. "The negative effects of cohabitation." *The Responsive Community* 10(1):31–38.

———. 2000. "Trends in men's and women's well-being in marriage." In *The Ties That Bind: Perspectives on Marriage and Cohabitation*, edited by L. Waite, C. Bachrach, M. Hindin, E. Thomson, and A. Thornton, pp. 368–92. New York: Aldine de Gruyter.

Waite, L., and M. Gallagher. 2000. *The Case for Marriage.* New York: Doubleday.

Waller, W. 1938. *The Family: A Dynamic Interpretation.* Hinsdale, IL: Dryden Press.

Werking, K. 1997. *We're Just Good Friends: Women and Men in Nonromantic Relationships.* New York: Guilford.

Whitehead, B. 1994. "The Failure of Sex Education." *Atlantic Monthly,* October:55–80.

Whyte, W. F. 1955. *Street-Corner Society: The Social Structure of an Italian Slum.* Chicago: University of Chicago Press.

Whyte, W. H. 1956. *The Organization Man.* New York: Simon & Schuster.

Williams, C. 1991. *Black Teenage Mothers.* Lexington, MA: Lexington Books.

Wood, J. 2003. *Gendered Lives: Communication, Gender, and Culture.* 5th ed. Belmont, CA: Wadsworth.

Woods, P. 1997. "Isn't it romantic? Romance novels these days are sensitive, affirming and hotter than July." *Essence* 28(3):75.

Zelizer, V. 1985. *Pricing the Priceless Child: The Changing Social Value of Children.* New York: Basic Books.

POWER AND STRATIFICATION
THE POLITICS OF INTERACTION

Karl Marx, a noted observer of human affairs, remarked long ago: "Human beings make history, but not under conditions of their own choosing." While symbolic interactionists would agree, they would put it that individuals jointly construct reality, both socially and symbolically (see chapter 2). However, everyone in a society does not participate equally in the construction of social worlds. People with various ascribed and achieved attributes and members of different social classes have varying opportunities to gain access to the decision-making processes in a society. These differences are reflected in the prevailing systems of social stratification.

We are born into a social world whose symbols have been prefabricated by the activities of previous generations (Schuman and Scott, 1989). Their actions have resulted in the construction of social realities whose existence we, as newcomers, must acknowledge if we are to operate as "sane" and "normal" members of society. We see here evidence of the social dialectic between freedom and constraint discussed in chapter 1. We are free to make choices and decisions in our everyday lives, but the range of alternatives from which we choose is the result of historical and institutional factors beyond our control.

For many social scientists, **social stratification** is simply a ranking of the people in a society from upper class to lower class, according to such measures as their income, education, or occupation. Symbolic interactionists believe it more appropriate to think of social stratification as a power phenomenon; that is, in discussing stratification we are really talking about how

181

opportunities, or **life chances**, are distributed in a certain society. People's access to such valued goals as well-paying jobs; positions of prestige and status; opportunities for a long, comfortable life; and even adequate health care are determined to a large extent by their *position* in the stratification system. It is in terms of these life chances that the importance of history, as Marx suggested, becomes evident.

Americans believe that rewards should be distributed by personal merit and by one's contributions to the social good. This belief legitimates the economic and class system of the United States. Once an idea is legitimated, it is taken for granted and becomes part of the cultural fabric of daily life. The deep, unconscious agreements that make up the structure of legitimacy can be expressed in the concept of *hegemonic culture*, the dominant culture.

The concept of **hegemony** is associated with the Italian sociologist Antonio Gramsci (1928–1971). According to Gramsci, the process of domination is a pervasive and enduring part of our entire experience—at home, at school, at work, in church, at leisure, as well as in politics and government. Ideas and practices become legitimate as the result of powerful groups' success in institutionalizing their definitions. Unfortunately, most Americans do not recognize that the economy and its class system are the historical creation of power groups. The work of sociologist C. Wright Mills in the 1950s and 1960s elaborated the concept of a hegemonic U.S. culture by pointing to economic concentration at the top of the stratification structure in the hands of a small **power elite**, and the control of the masses through ideology, fear, and consumerism.

Interactionists have focused their attention on understanding the ways in which social position affects individuals differently. Social position can have profound effects on self-development, for example. Regardless of what one thinks of oneself, certain characteristics denoting social status affect interaction in certain predictable ways, and these interactions affect one's sense of self.

The distinction between ascribed and achieved statuses is particularly important in this regard (see chapter 3). Ascribed statuses are those society confers on us at birth, such as gender and race, while achieved statuses are those acquired (achieved) during the course of our lives, such as our organizational and occupational statuses. In contemporary American society, despite a great deal of official rhetoric to the contrary, our ascribed-status characteristics have much to do with the nature of our life chances. One lesson of social science, alas, is that one must choose one's parents with great care!

Symbolic interaction is interested in the *processes* that produce and reproduce inequality. In order to study these processes, both **quantitative** and **qualitative** methods are used. Quantitative analyses provide information about how resources such as wealth, power, and prestige are distributed (*who has how much of what?*). Qualitative research can examine these processes directly; for example, what happens in face-to-face interaction so that a form of inequality is the result, or, how are symbols and meanings created and used to sustain the patterns of interaction that lead to inequality (Schwalbe et al., 2000)? A number of qualitative studies have looked at the reproduction of inequality (see Horowitz, 1997 for a review).

Power Relations in the Macro and Micro Worlds

Those who have comparatively greater access to scarce and highly valued resources such as jobs and money have a power advantage in everyday, face-to-face relations. Interactions between men and women, husbands and wives, even children and parents are inextricably bound up with the issue of power between **superiors** and subordinates, or **inferiors**. The process by which a dominant group defines into existence an inferior group has been referred to as *othering* (Fine, 1994). This process entails the invention of categories and ideas about what marks people as belonging to these categories; e.g., skin color as the basis for a racial group, African Americans (or blacks), that historically has been treated with prejudice and discrimination in this country.

Face-to-face relations between members of different social classes, racial and ethnic groups, and genders must be seen within the broader context of power relations. In this sense everyday interactions are political acts, and they can be studied within the frame of the *politics of interaction*, thereby taking into account these power differentials.

This interface between individuals' daily lives and the social organization of the society also shows clearly the manner in which personal biographies intersect with the larger arenas of history and social structure. As Peter and Brigitte Berger put it, we simultaneously inhabit different worlds, the **micro world** and the **macro world**:

> First of all, crucially and continuously, we inhabit the micro world of our immediate experience with others in face-to-face relations. Beyond that, with varying degrees of significance and continuity, we inhabit a macro world consisting of much larger structures and involving us in relations with others that are mostly abstract, anonymous and remote. Both worlds are essential to our experience of society, and . . . each world depends upon the other for its meaning to us. (1975:8)

The Bergers suggest that any analysis of face-to-face behavior must consider it within the context of broader institutional arrangements. Similarly, any analysis of an institution, such as religion or education, must take into account its origin in the daily communications among its members. To use the terms introduced in chapter 1, both macrosociological and microsociological investigation are necessary for the analysis of behavior.

The Broad Contours of Power: Money and Jobs

In contemporary American society, access to the means for the production and distribution of wealth is a crucial factor in one's ability to establish a dominant position in the stratification system. To begin our analysis, we will sketch the broad outlines of how certain resources are distributed in American society.

Family Income and Wealth

Table 6.1 presents data on the distribution of family income in the United States in the period 1950–1999, during which the concentration of income fluctuated slightly but remained virtually unchanged. The fifth of the population with the highest income, which accounted for 42.7 percent of the nation's total income in 1950, accounted for an even larger percentage (47.2)—in fact almost half of total income—in 1999. The percentage of income held by the lowest fifth changed hardly at all from 4.5 to 4.3 percent in this period. Those families in the highest fifth, however, increased their percentage by almost 5 points while everyone else lost ground.

The gap in income between the bottom fifth and top fifth is large, indicating significant income inequality. This becomes even more striking when we look at the top 5 percent, who held 20.3 percent of total income in 1999. In effect then, this 5 percent of families accounts for a larger share of total family income in the United States than that of the total income of the bottom two quintiles—40 percent of all families.

Membership in the upper class, at the top of the stratification system, is determined by wealth, or total assets, rather than just family income or earnings. Whereas income is monetary gain, wealth includes stocks, bonds, real estate, business equity, and so forth and is most often measured in terms of "net worth." In fact, wealth produces income in the form of dividends on investments or profits from business assets. Wealth more than income contributes to the perpetuation of the class hierarchy because wealth can be passed down from generation to generation. This enables the rich to stay rich, and does not lead to significant change in the distribution of wealth. Entrance into the ranks of the wealthy occurs mainly through inheritance or, for a few,

---

Table 6.1
Distribution of Family Income, United States, 1950–1999

| | Family Income Level | | | | |
Year	Lowest fifth	Second fifth	Middle fifth	Fourth fifth	Highest fifth
1950	4.5%	12.0%	17.4%	23.4%	42.7%
1960	4.8	12.2	17.8	24.0	41.3
1970	5.4	12.2	17.6	23.8	40.9
1980	5.1	11.6	17.5	24.3	41.6
1982	4.7	11.2	17.5	24.3	42.7
1989	4.6	10.6	16.5	23.7	44.6
1999	4.3	9.9	15.6	23.0	47.2

Source: U.S. Census Bureau, 2000a, *Historical Income Tables—Families*, Table F-2.

the ability to amass a fortune through extraordinary business success or achievement in professional sports or entertainment.

Wealth is even more unevenly distributed than income in the United States. Although there was a decline in the maldistribution of wealth (and income) from the mid-1960s through the 1970s, the trend reversed itself sharply in the 1980s. By 1998, the wealthiest 10 percent of the population owned more than 70 percent of all wealth (Mishel, Bernstein, and Schmitt, 2001).

Between 1900 and 1980, there was little change in the 20–25 percent of wealth owned by the top 1 percent of the U.S. population (Domhoff, 1983). It is this 1 percent at the top of the stratification system that may be considered the "upper class." The gap between the very wealthy and everyone else has grown enormously in the past several decades. In 1965 the richest 1 percent of Americans held 37 percent of the nation's wealth; by 1979 their share had dropped to 22 percent. After 1979, however, it rose sharply. By 1998, the top 1 percent—referred to as the "Super Rich" by economist Edward Wolff (1995)—owned almost 40 percent of total wealth.

Even looking only at the wealthiest 1 percent understates the concentration of wealth at the top. The majority of wealth at the top is actually owned by only a fraction of the families that make up the top 1 percent (Keister, 2000). Andrew Hacker, in his analysis of income and wealth in the United States, defines the rich as all individuals and households that have an annual income of at least $1 million (Hacker, 1997). This comprises about one-twentieth of 1 percent of households!

For the past three decades, political sociologist G. William Domhoff has studied the upper class. In his classic work, *The Higher Circles* (1970), Domhoff documented the exclusiveness and impermeability of upper-class social worlds. He also noted the gender distinctions in management of this wealth: "The American upper class is based upon large corporate wealth that is looked after by the male members of the intermarrying families that are its basis . . . [upper-class women] participate in a great many activities which sustain the upper class as a social class and help to maintain the stability of the social system as a whole" (p. 56). It is the men who "look after" the wealth, however.

Social changes, particularly the feminist movement, have affected the socialization of wealthy young women since Domhoff first wrote about this group. Many private schools are coeducational, and women graduates are encouraged to go to major four-year colleges rather than finishing schools. Women of the upper class are more likely to have careers—there are examples of women who have risen to the top of their family's business. Women are also more likely to serve on corporate boards. Despite these changes, Domhoff suggests that there may be even less gender equality in the upper class than there is in the professional stratum, and it is not clear how much more equality will be attained (1998).

Domhoff concludes that the upper class is essentially a ruling class (1998 and earlier works). He posits that there is a readily apparent relationship between those who own or control a disproportionate share of society's wealth, those who exercise control over major corporations, and those who greatly influence the governmental elite. He emphasizes the social nature of the dominant corporate ownership and managerial class. The cohesiveness of this ruling group is largely a product of their common upper-class ties. "They belong to the same exclusive social clubs, frequent the same summer and winter resorts, and send their children to a relative handful of private schools. Members of the corporate community thereby become a *corporate rich* who create a nationwide *social upper class* through their social interaction" (1998:2).

Effects of Ascribed-Status Characteristics

To a dramatic extent, ascribed-status characteristics such as gender and race are embedded in the institutions of American society. Differential access to positions of power and prestige is built into the organization of society, or the macro world. This macro world sets the stage for the daily dramas of the micro world as people engage in face-to-face contacts.

Women's occupational opportunities.   Women's access to better-paying jobs has been consistently restricted, though the earnings of women relative to those of men have increased slightly in recent years. The median wage for female workers with full-time jobs was 62.2 percent of that of full-time male workers in 1970, 73.2 percent in 1998, and 76 percent by 2000 (see table 6.2). The earnings difference between women and men varies by demographic group. Among blacks and Hispanics, for example, women's earnings are about 85 to 88 percent of men's; for whites, women's earnings are about 75 percent of men's. Young women and men (16–24 years old) had fairly similar earnings. For example, women aged 20–24 earned 91.9 percent as much as did men. Middle-aged and older female workers did not fare as well: among workers 55 to 64 years old, the women's-to-men's earnings ratio was just 68.5 percent (U.S. Department of Labor, 2001).

The male-female gap is wider in some occupations than in others. Census data indicate that in 1998 women professionals earned 71 percent of male professionals' earnings, women managers earned 67.7 percent of male managers' earnings, and women in sales earned 59.6 percent of male counterparts' earnings (U.S. Census Bureau, 2000b; U.S. Department of Labor, 2001). Women's employment in occupations with high earnings has grown. In 2000, 47 percent of full-time wage and salary workers in executive, administrative, and managerial occupations were women, up from 34.2 percent in 1983. Over the same period, women's employment in professional specialty occupations rose from 46.8 percent to 51.9 percent. Despite increased representation in the higher paying managerial and professional occupations, women remain a relatively small proportion of other high-paying occupations, such as protective service and precision production, craft, and repair. In both managerial and professional occupational categories, women and men tend to work in different specific occupations. In professional specialty occupations, where women earn the most, they are much less likely than men to

Table 6.2
The Male-Female Earnings Gap, United States, 1970–2000

Year	Women's median earnings as percent of men's (full-time positions)
1970	62.2%
1975	61.9
1977	61.9
1978	61.2
1979	62.4
1980	63.3
1981	64.5
1982	64.9
1989*	68.9
1998	73.2
2000	76.0

* In 1987 the Census Bureau changed its processing procedures; as a result, the 1989 figures are not directly comparable to those of prior years.

Source: U.S. Census Bureau, Statistical Abstract of the United States, various years: 1983, Table 716; 1991, Table 736; 2000, Table 697; U.S. Department of Labor, 2001.

be employed in some of the highest paying occupations, such as engineers and mathematical and computer scientists. Women are more likely to work in relatively lower paying professional occupations, such as teachers and registered nurses (U.S. Department of Labor, 2001). Most female professionals are employed in traditional occupations such as elementary and secondary teaching and nursing. Women are not well represented in such professions as college teaching, medicine, and law. Indeed, the greater the prestige of a profession, the smaller the proportion of women in it. In 2000, for example, women held 83 percent of the teaching positions in American elementary schools, 57 percent of high school positions, but only 38.5 percent of the teaching positions in colleges and universities. While women are making increasing inroads into professional fields, currently they constitute only 10.5 percent of all engineers, 31 percent of all physicians, and 29 percent of lawyers and judges. The male-female earnings gap ranges from 57.9 percent for physicians to 84.3 percent for engineers (U.S. Department of Labor, 2001).

Racial/ethnic income differences. There also are racial and ethnic differences in access to occupations, which largely determines family incomes. Table 6.3 compares median family income in the United States for whites, blacks, Hispanics, and Asian/Pacific Islanders between 1970 and 1998. During this period the gap between black and white median incomes was very slightly reduced. Black median family income went from 54.3 percent of white family income in 1950 to 61 percent by 1997. Despite such changes, the

Table 6.3
Median Family Income by Race and Hispanic Origin, 1970–1998*

Year	All Families[†]	White	Black	Hispanic	Asian/Pacific Islands
1970	$38,345	$39,779	$24,401	NA	NA
1980	40,999	42,717	24,717	28,699	NA
1985	41,371	43,484	25,039	28,381	NA
1990	43,414	45,332	26,308	28,773	51,878
1995	42,769	44,913	27,350	25,876	48,820
1996	43,271	45,783	27,131	26,780	50,232
1997	44,568	46,754	28,602	28,142	51,850
1998	46,737	49,023	29,404	29,608	52,826

* In 1998 dollars.
[†] Includes other races not shown separately.
Source: U.S. Census Bureau, *Statistical Abstract of the United States: 1999.* (Washington, D.C.: Government Printing Office, 1999) Table 750; 2000, Table 744.

income differences between white and black families have remained very large indeed. Interestingly, since 1990, median family income of Asians and Pacific Islanders has consistently surpassed that of white families.

The lingering economic gap between whites and blacks (and, to some extent, between whites and Latinos) has prompted debate among sociologists as to whether this gap is attributable to lingering racism, to something unique about the African-American experience that contributes to the group's continued plight, or to deeper structural forces that impede the attainment of economic equality (Marger, 2002). The black population is by no means homogeneous in terms of economic status. In fact, some have suggested that there are really "two black Americas"—one that has established itself solidly within the middle and working classes, and one that is isolated and not fully part of the mainstream workforce (Gates, 1998).

The aggregate difference in socioeconomic status between African Americans and Euro-Americans is readily apparent. African Americans experience much higher rates of poverty, unemployment, and low income. African Americans are also underrepresented in jobs at the top of the occupational hierarchy and overrepresented at the bottom.

The percentage of blacks below the poverty line remains three times greater than the percentage of whites. The substantially greater percentage of blacks below the poverty line accounts in large measure for the general differences between income patterns for blacks and whites. Another contributing factor is the increasing number of female-headed, single-parent families, who earn considerably less than two-parent families.

The low income and high poverty rates of Latinos, particularly Mexicans and Puerto Ricans, reflect their generally lower occupational levels. Except for Cubans, Latinos are underrepresented in the higher-status occupational categories and overrepresented in the lower ones. Hispanics also experience high unemployment rates. More than 20 percent of all Latino families fall below the poverty line, three times the percentage for non-Hispanic white families. Table 6.4 correlates percent in poverty with educational attainment, by race/ethnicity.

Table 6.4
Persons in Poverty, High School and College Graduates by Race/Ethnicity, 1999

	White	Black	Hispanic	A/PI	Total pop
Persons in poverty	7.7%	23.6%	22.8%	10.7%	11.8%
H.S. graduates	87.7	77.4	56.1	84.7	83.4
College graduates	27.7	15.5	10.9	42.4	25.2

Source: U.S. Census Bureau, 2000c, *Poverty in the United States: 1999*, CPR P60-210; U.S. Census Bureau, 2000d, *Educational Attainment in the United States: March 1999*, CPR P20-528.

One of the most striking features of tables 6.3 and 6.4 is the high ranking of Asian Americans compared to the other ethnic categories. That is, Asian Americans rank higher than most ethnic groups in family income, occupational prestige, and educational attainment. Some sociologists and psychologists point to cultural factors such as values that emphasize the importance of education as an explanation. Another possible explanation has to do with the fit between the opportunity structure of contemporary American society and the class background of the new Asian immigrants. A disproportionate number of highly skilled and educated individuals comprise the Asian immigrant population.

Social Class, Power, and Self-Concept

Perhaps no aspect of social position has a more fateful hand in individuals' control over their own lives than their membership in a particular **social class**. Social classes are largely distinguished from one another in terms of the resources and power their members possess. Social identities provide status and enhance (or not) self-esteem. The process of attaining a positive social identity is a challenge for members of stigmatized, negatively valued groups (Howard, 2000). Studies of working-class and lower-class members, for example, have demonstrated the effects of powerlessness on one's self-concept.

Men and Work

Sociologists have analyzed the connection between the dominant values of American society and the specific values of lower- and working-class males. In one well-known study of black "street-corner men" in Washington, D.C., Eliot Liebow (1967) contends that their behaviors can be understood in terms of a social class position that renders them powerless and virtually ensures their failure to succeed by middle-class standards.

To protect themselves from the assaults on their self-conceptions created by repeated failures in work and family settings, these men construct what Liebow terms a "shadow system of values." He maintains that they actually subscribe to middle-class achievement values, but are unable to realize them because of the constraints imposed by their ascribed class position. They therefore develop an alternative value system. Unable to sustain the breadwinner role, for example, the men respond by depreciating the value of family life. Reluctant to face unemployment or a demeaning job every day, they demean the value of work. Without the resources to raise their children as they would like, they limit their intimacy with them. In short, the street-corner man's behavior

> . . . appears not so much as a way of realizing the distinctive goals and values of his own subculture, or of conforming to its models, but rather as his way of trying to achieve many of the goals and values of the larger society, of failing to do this, and concealing his failure from others and from himself as best he can. (Liebow, 1967:222)

Liebow shows how the daily, face-to-face relationships of men with their wives, lovers, friends, and children relate to the broader configurations of power in the society. He also illustrates how the "hurts" of a powerless class position influence individuals' self-conceptions and their patterns of adaptive behavior.

In another book with much the same theme, *The Hidden Injuries of Class* (1973), Richard Sennett and Jonathon Cobb present interviews that describe how working-class men create their own interpretations of dominant American social values. The emphasis in American society on achievement is continually reaffirmed in education and the mass media. Americans are socialized to measure a person's worth, honor, and respect in terms of individual achievement. It follows that those who fail to achieve in the work world suffer from feelings of self-doubt and shame.

Working-class men, near the bottom of the occupational scale, must somehow adapt to a society that measures their value in terms of occupational achievement. There is a sort of "Catch 22" operating in this situation. Those who are born into a powerless, dependent, and subordinate social class position come to feel bad about themselves because they lack autonomy. A social sleight of hand occurs whereby the victims of a system of institutionalized inequality are socialized to blame themselves for that state of affairs. According to Sennett and Cobb, these men "know they are supposed to work hard, and do the best they can. They see that a few do 'make it,' but not, as far as can be seen, because of anything different about them. To keep going in the face of this riddle, a defense . . . is needed" (p. 201).

A respondent in Rubin's (1994) study of working-class families articulates the experience of many working-class individuals in the wake of changes in the economy:

> Used to be you worked hard, you figured you got someplace. Not anymore. . . . We did everything we were supposed to do—worked hard,

> saved some money, tried to raise our kids to be decent law-abiding peo-
> ple—and what do we get? . . . The #@*& company goes belly-up and
> look at me now. (p. 126)

According to Rubin, the hope that sustained working-class individuals
through bad times twenty years ago—the belief that if they worked hard and
played by the rules they would eventually grab a piece of the American
dream—has been shattered.

Changes in the macro, structural context of work, as demonstrated by
William Wilson (1987, 1996), John Kasarda (1989, 1995), and others, have
powerfully altered the living conditions of working- and lower-class males,
especially inner-city minority residents. Jobs that once served to secure the
lives and identities of many working-class people are swiftly becoming a
thing of the past. In the span of a few decades, foreign investment, corporate
flight, downsizing, and automation have left members of the working class
without a steady family wage, which, compounded with the dissipation of
labor unions, has left many white working-class men feeling emasculated and
angry (Weis, Proweller, and Centrie, 1996). In fact, the working-class white
men interviewed by Weis and her colleagues feel that they are under siege in
their jobs, their neighborhoods, their homes, and their schools, no longer
holding the position of privilege that they sense is rightfully theirs.

The stagnation of wages for most of the past twenty years among the
working class and part of the lower-middle class has created a growing fissure
between this class and the upper-middle class. Although the latter may also
depend on their salaries for income, they are ordinarily able to supplement
them with interest, dividends, capital gains, and other nonwage sources
(Kacapyr, 1996) that are not necessarily available to working-class individuals. Some of the gap between high- and low-wage workers is explained by
education. Workers at the high end of the occupational hierarchy, whose jobs
require higher education, have increased their income at the same time that
those with only a high-school diploma or less have suffered a sharp decline in
wages (Levy, 1998). By 1998, male college graduates were earning 68 percent
more than those with only high-school diplomas (Danziger and Reed, 1999).

The sharp decline in inner-city employment rates has been an instrumental factor in the creation of female-headed (i.e., male-absent) families. Wilson's (1996) research in Chicago found that only one-quarter of the black
families whose children lived with them in inner-city neighborhoods in Chicago were husband-wife families, compared with three-quarters of the inner-
city Mexican families, more than one-half of the white families, and nearly
one-half of the Puerto Rican families. In census tracts with poverty rates of at
least 40 percent, only 16.5 percent of the black families with children were
husband-wife families. Marriage rates have dropped much more sharply
among jobless black fathers than among employed black fathers, although
this drop applies only to younger men age 18–31 (Testa and Krough, 1995).
Wilson concludes:

In the inner-city ghetto community, not only have the norms in support of husband-wife families and against out-of-wedlock births become weaker as a result of the general trend in society, they have also gradually disintegrated because of worsening economic conditions in the inner city, including the sharp rise in joblessness and declining real incomes. . . . The decreasing marriage rates among inner-city black parents is a function not simply of increased economic marginality or of changing attitudes toward sex and marriage, but of, as Testa (1991) emphasizes, "the interaction between material and cultural constraints." (Wilson, 1996:97)

One reason for concern about the sharp decline in the marriage rate is that children living in one-parent families in the United States suffer from many more disadvantages than those in married parent families. The median income for single female-headed families ($23,732 in 1999) is considerably lower than for married-couple families ($56,676 in 1999) (U.S. Census Bureau, 2000e). The poverty rate for single female-headed households (27.8 percent) is much higher than for married couple households (4.8 percent), and is higher for blacks (26.5 percent) than for whites (11.0 percent) (U.S. Census Bureau, 2000c). See also table 6.5.

The position of inner-city black women in the labor market is also problematic. Their high degree of social isolation in impoverished neighborhoods reduces their employment prospects. Although they may be considered by some employers as more acceptable as workers than the inner-city black men, their social isolation is likely to provide few supports for moving into white-collar employment (Wilson, 1996).

Table 6.5
Persons in Poverty by Household Type, Children Under 18, Race and Hispanic Origin: 1999

Household type	White	Black	Hispanic	All Races
Married couple	5.9%	8.6%	16.8%	6.3%
Female householder, no husband present	30.1	46.1	46.6	35.7

Source: Dalaker and Proctor, 2000.

Women, Work, and Family Politics

Working-class women also suffer from the "hidden injuries of class." Like working-class men, they also feel trapped and demeaned by jobs that have little social worth and prestige in American society. Stuck in boring, routine jobs as clerical workers, sales personnel, or factory workers, it is not unusual to experience hidden injuries that are work-related. Gorman (2000) relates the following comments from a secretary: "One boss used to belittle us. He was a pig. He said, 'I only hired you because you graduated from high school—it doesn't take a brain surgeon to work in a job like this.' I was ashamed that all I had was my associate's degree" (p. 105).

Gorman notes that the injuries experienced at work may be carried over to other situations. Although the feelings of injury are hidden, they constantly shape daily interactions among members of different social classes. Among Gorman's working-class respondents, these interactions at times had the effect of increasing their contempt for the middle-class. Three things in particular emerged as sources of anger for the working-class respondents: middle-class language, middle-class clothing, and middle-class attitudes. Working-class individuals expressed resentment at attempts by middle-class college graduates to showcase their language skills, referred to middle-class people as "suits," and complained about the attitudes that college-educated, white-collar workers have toward those without a college education. According to Gorman, members of the working class struggle to find dignity in a society that is quick to judge one's worth on the basis of income, educational credentials, and occupational prestige. "There was a feeling among many working-class respondents that college-educated, white-collar workers look down on them or think they are better than them" (2000:102–3). In fact, many of the working-class respondents felt that middle-class college graduates are "perpetual students; they waste time and money in college just to get a piece of paper that does not guarantee a job" (p. 103).

As we noted in chapter 5, there has been a vast increase in the numbers of women in the labor force. The home itself often becomes a forum for family politics in which wives seek an equitable trade-off for the work they do outside the home. Questions of power become critical in such situations. Among working-class couples, the wife's decision to look for paid full-time work may be experienced by the husband as a threat to his masculinity and a challenge to his ability to perform in the role of family breadwinner. As one working-class male in Rubin's (1994) study of working-class families so eloquently put it:

> I know my wife works all day, just like I do . . . but it's not the same. She doesn't *have* to do it. I mean, she *has* to because we need the money, but it's different. It's not really her job to have to be working; it's mine. . . . Know what I mean? I'm not saying it right; I mean, it's the man who's supposed to support his family, so I've got to be responsible for that, not her. And that makes one damn big difference. (p. 85)

The white, working-class male respondents in Weis and colleagues' 1996 study of working-class men echo this; they were well aware that they could no longer support a family on their own, but needed their wives' income. Nevertheless, they continued to believe that the meaning of maleness is to go out, earn a living, support a family.

The macro-level industrial changes noted in the previous section have clearly altered the power arrangements in those working-class families in which previously only the husband worked full time. The 1980s and 1990s marked a time when jobs for working-class men became scarce, unions became weak, and the relatively privileged position of white working-class men was threatened. The women with whom working-class men associated became independent, and equal rights and affirmative action were seen as threats. Traditional bases of white male power—head of the family, productive worker, and access to "good" public sector and/or unionized jobs— eroded rapidly (Fine et al., 1997). According to Weis and associates (1996), because of the loss of real material space inside working-class culture (due to what these men perceive as privileging of racial/ethnic minorities—affirmative action), white working-class men turn to the family in an attempt to assert or re-assert dominance in that realm. While this may have always been the case, as Rubin's (1976) earlier work suggests, the move to sustain dominance in the white working-class home is particularly important at this time of economic loss for working-class men.

The Relationship of Power to Role-Taking

If you think of the world in dramaturgical terms (see chapter 3) as a Shakespearian stage on which everyone is a player of roles, then in real life as in any play some roles evoke much more respectful attention and applause than others. Some people are able to elicit far more consideration and respect for their wants, desires, and needs than are others. Indeed, in daily encounters with others, this is the most basic face that power presents. The powerful *demand* attention and interest. They do it overtly through the resources at their disposal to punish people who ignore them. And they do it covertly through the way people are socialized by society's institutions—family, school, church, and so on—to respect those whom society deems most worthy.

Role-taking has been described as the basic process by which people develop their selves (see chapter 2). By putting themselves in the role (i.e., the "place") of others, individuals are able to view themselves from the perspective of others, while anticipating how others are going to respond to them. This is certainly accurate as a general statement about interaction, but something is missing. That missing ingredient, we suggest, is the acquisition and use of power.

Many learned treatises have been presented on the nature of power, but for our purposes it is sufficient to conceive of **power** as the English scholar R. H. Tawney defined it years ago:

> Power may be defined as the capacity of an individual, or group of individuals, to modify the conduct of other individuals or groups in the manner which he desires, and to prevent his own conduct being modified in the manner in which he does not. (1931:229)

This definition indirectly acknowledges the necessity of taking the role of others in order to communicate with them meaningfully. But some people face much less pressure to engage in role-taking than do others. Their power allows them to demonstrate insensitivity, callousness, or indifference to the desires of others. Others must respond sensitively and, above all, accurately to the wishes of the powerful.

In the process of role-taking, the requirements for accuracy vary with the power of the position occupied by the role-taker. In Erving Goffman's terms (see chapter 3), some individuals "make" the roles and others are constrained to "take" them; that is, some people's symbols evoke a more deferential response than do others'. As an example of how the more powerful make the roles that the less powerful must take, consider the situation of women in the corporate world. Women who manage to rise above the glass ceiling emphasize the need to develop similarities with male peers in order to be successful. They use strategies such as altering appearance to fit the proper business attire (a suit) and changing speech and behaviors to conform to situations with other (male) elites *because they know that this is the way male elites expect them to look and behave* (Davies-Netzley, 1998; emphasis added).

The Less the Power, the Better the Role-Taking

Studies of the relationships between power and role-taking ability have generated an interesting body of findings. Generally, role-taking ability varies inversely with the degree of power ascribed to social positions. The possession of power, and especially authority, to some extent lessens the need to role-take with accuracy (Hewitt, 2003). Individuals in lesser positions of power are required to have more accurate perceptions of their superior's behaviors than vice-versa. Abused women, for example, develop keen role-taking abilities to anticipate, prevent, and minimize their partner's physical violence (Forte et al., 1996). Batterers, on the other hand, demonstrate less role-taking ability (Goodrum, Umberson, and Anderson, 2001); in fact, batterers' levels of empathy (a form of role-taking) appear to be inversely related to their levels of violence (Holtzworth-Munroe and Stuart, 1994). In the study of batterers cited above (Goodrum et al., 2001), almost 60 percent of the batterers expressed either no empathy or limited empathy when they described their partners' emotional pain following an abusive incident. Some of those with limited empathy seemed to exhibit simultaneous ability and inability to take the role of the other. For example, one subject explained that although he felt bad about an episode in which he pushed his partner to the ground, he needed to use violence to get his message across. Goodrum and colleagues explain this in terms of emotional versus viewpoint role-taking; that is, the batterer role-takes his partner's emotions but not her viewpoint. The difference is that emotional role-taking is less likely to challenge one's position in an argument (and perhaps a relationship) than viewpoint role-taking. Batterers, more than nonviolent men, feel threatened by challenges to their authority and views, and they often react to such threats with violence (Goodrum et al., 2001). This echoes Scully's (1990) earlier finding that convicted rapists were deficient in their ability to take the role of the other (i.e., their victims). She argues that people in power are not pressed to understand the "other," because their place of power in society allows them to set the terms of their interactions with others.

This suggests that the inability to see oneself from the perspectives of others makes it difficult for the person to experience emotions such as guilt, shame, or embarrassment—emotions which have the effect of making us control our own behaviors in light of the anticipated negative responses of others. So we see here how both self-control and social control are part of a mutually reinforcing network of self-other communications. Rapists and batterers often lack either the willingness or the ability to imagine the responses of others—the victim and the community—to their acts of physical aggression. The batterers in the Goodrum study, however, did express more tolerance for important others' (such as children or police) views of themselves than they did for their intimate others' views. The authors surmise that perhaps these parties represent less of a threat to the batterer's place in his intimate relationship and therefore may be able to exercise power over the batterer that his partner cannot.

The position the person occupies, not just within some organization but within society as a whole, is an important factor. The question of power is not simply a matter of individuals' personality characteristics. This is another demonstration of the importance of seeing the larger institutional order as the setting within which daily life occurs. One of the less obvious ways people exercise power in everyday life is through their control of the physical setting in which interaction occurs:

> Role-making and role-taking do not occur in a vacuum, but in the midst of props, physical objects, machines, locations, buildings, and habitats that have human meaning and usually are human creations. People do not merely interact in social spaces provided by roles, but in banks, stores, homes, physicians' offices, schools, parks, automobiles, beaches, factories, halls, and myriad other places, each with its objects, colors, sounds, and other physical attributes. . . . It follows that whoever has the power to control the physical elements of a situation also has considerable power to control how people in that situation will act (Hewitt, 2003:176–7).

The next time you are in a doctor's office (or a professor's!), notice how the setting influences the interaction.

Ascribed-Status Differences in Role-Taking

Studies such as those described above have raised a number of interesting questions about how differences in ascribed status affect role-taking ability. If, as they demonstrate, power and the ability to role-take are inversely related, we can hypothesize that women generally take the roles of men more accurately than men take the roles of women, since women continue to have less power than men in both the micro world of the family and the macro world of the society. Studies of nonverbal interaction lend support to this and similar propositions (see box).

Gender and Nonverbal Communication: The Role of Power

Research generally has found consistent gender differences in nonverbal communication. Women and men do different things with their eyes, faces, voices, and bodies. Women tend to be more expressive of emotions than men, which may be the result of socialization that encourages females to be sensitive to others. Women not only tend to display feelings more clearly, but also seem to be more skilled than men at interpreting others' emotions. A recurring question is whether this well-documented gender difference in nonverbal sensitivity is best understood as stemming from deep-seated differences between the sexes or whether it is due to structures that create power inequities between women and men (LaFrance and Henley, 1994).

Women's decoding skills probably result from a combination of socialization that emphasizes nurturing and pleasing, as well as the way power is distributed in society. Women are expected to respond expressively to others. Smiling sends the message that one is approachable, interested, friendly—part of the cultural definition of femininity. Gender socialization is so ingrained that women find it difficult not to smile, even when they deliberately try to refrain (Wood, 2003). However, the findings on gender and smiling are mixed. Although women may smile more than men overall, it may be that gender-related behavior depends on the nature of the context. Hecht and LaFrance (1998), for example, found a sex difference in smiling when women and men were in equal-power positions, but no sex differences between high-power men and women or low-power women and men.

The idea that women's nonverbal skills are linked to gender-differentiated power within our society was first suggested by Helen Hacker (1951), and was greatly expanded in the 1970s by work that documented other inequalities in the small stuff of everyday life. This research produced a considerable body of evidence in support of the idea that those who are oppressed learn to interpret others in order to survive. For example, classic research by Nancy Henley (1977) found consistent patterns in nonverbal behavior for minorities, women, and individuals in subservient roles.

The basic thesis of the unequal power explanation of women's greater ability to decode nonverbal behaviors of others is that it falls to people of lower power to be able to read the cues of someone possessing higher power, because their ability to respond appropriately, if not their very survival, may depend upon it (LaFrance and Henley, 1994). As in the case of women who have been battered by men, being able to anticipate and avoid the men's rage is important to survival (Tatum, 2000). However, a meta-analysis of studies examining "subordination" and nonverbal sensitivity found little overall support for the subordination hypothesis (Hall, Halberstadt, and O'Brien, 1997), leading these authors to conclude that nonverbal sensitivity may wax and wane as a function of particular roles and situations.

Gender differences in use of nonverbal behaviors to supplement verbal communication are found consistently. Since masculine socialization emphasizes self-assertion and dominance, we would expect men to use more nonverbal behaviors than women to complement, repeat, and highlight their verbal messages. This highlighting has the effect of increasing the visibility and force of male speech. Feminine socialization highlights relationships, deference, and expressiveness, so women learn to specialize in nonverbal functions such as complimenting and highlighting that add personal emphasis and feeling to their communication (Wood, 2003).

Another aspect of nonverbal communication used differently by men and women is eye contact. Whereas women frequently use nonverbal signals to invite others into conversation, men more frequently use them to sustain control of interaction. For example, women signal interest and involvement with others by sustaining eye contact, whereas men generally do not hold eye contact (Wood, 2003). This has an effect on the relationship messages communicated by nonverbal means, such as responsiveness (conveying interest and involvement). In one study, females showed responsiveness by maintaining more eye contact and direct body orientation, whereas males displayed responsiveness by leaning forward and adopting postures congruent with the person speaking (Guerrero, 1997).

And then there's the matter of perception of "nonverbal courtship signals" (Moore, 2002). Monica Moore's research on nonverbal courtship and rejection behaviors finds that not only do men rate invitational behaviors (licking lips, leaning forward, flipping hair) more positively than women, but men also see signals of rejection (looking at the ceiling, yawning, looking away) as sending a less potent message than that perceived by women.

You might want to keep this in mind for those "flirting" occasions. . . .

Role-taking ability also varies among racial groups—certainly an area in which there are substantial power differentials. A classic work by Judith Rollins (1985) explored the relationship between white elite women and the women of color who worked for them as domestics. The domestics engaged in acts of deference toward their employees: addressing the employer as "ma'am," accepting often useless gifts of used clothing (etc.) and acting grateful, and always appearing to be inferior to their employer. These women knew that if they appeared to be in a better position (i.e., more educated) than their employer expected them to be, they ran the risk of threatening the employer's belief in the innate inferiority of blacks. The domestics' stronger consciousness of the "other" functioned to both help them survive in the occupation as well as maintain their self. It was clear from Rollins' interviews that the domestics did not view themselves as inferior to their employers.

Collective identities generally provide social and emotional compensations for subordinate statuses that sustain systems of inequality. Wolf (1994) theorizes that people in subordinate social positions attempt through a reality-construction process to translate coercive relationships into dependency relationships, to maneuver oppressors into accepting obligations toward them. Her theory is based on analysis of responses of Japanese-Americans during the World War II Relocation, African-American slaves, and nineteenth-century European-American women.

Conning Strategies of the Powerless

Erving Goffman defined **deference** as a type of ceremonial activity "which functions as a symbolic means by which appreciation is regularly conveyed to a recipient," "something a subordinate owes to his superordinate" (1956). The inferior other must recognize the superior as such and must exhibit confirming behaviors. When the powerless are denied the opportunity to engage in overt confrontations with their superiors, they must resort to more subtle means.

Studies of race and ethnic relations have demonstrated that when members of the dominant group and members of subordinate groups engage in face-to-face relations, the latter often must resort to indirect **conning strategies** to maintain their self-esteem. As the book *Roots* by Alex Haley (1976) poignantly demonstrates, the **frontstage** performance of the slaves shuffling along saying "Yes, sir, massa," was a role brutally forced on them by the slaveholders. Behind the scenes, in what Goffman (1959) calls the **backstage** region, they could let their guards down and indicate their awareness of the roles they had been coerced into performing. Wolf (1994) describes black slaves who, "coolly calculating the situation, sometimes said they were 'puttin' ole massa on'"—clearly an attempt to shape interaction into channels less threatening and more advantageous to the slaves. She describes Jermain Loguen, a black slave who, "returning to his master after an absence of several months, wrote that he played his part of being so happy to see him with a calculated charade of feigned deference: '[I went] through the ceremony of servile bows and counterfeit smiles . . . and other false expressions of gladness'" (Loguen, 1859:226, in Wolf, 1994:376).

Qualitative studies of oppressive situations often highlight the strategies people use to cope with the deprivations of subordinate status. Some of the strategies may have positive consequences; others resist inequality or seek to abolish it. The modal adaptation to inequality is acquiescence: accepting one's place within existing hierarchies of status, power, and wealth, while trying to make that place reasonably comfortable. Other possibilities, however, include trading power for patronage, forming alternative subcultures, dropping out, and "hustling"—economic activity that is officially considered illegal or dishonest. Qualitative research shows, however, that most strategies of adaptation have dual consequences, challenging some inequalities while reproducing others (Schwalbe et al., 2000). For example, strippers are able to enhance their earnings by performing in ways that feed men's sexual fantasies—a conning strategy—but while this strategy may pay off for individual strippers, the larger consequence is reproduction of the sexist imagery that helps to sustain the subordination of women in general (c.f., Frank, 1998).

Adaptation to subordinate status can be collective, in effect creating alternative subcultures. For example, Bourgois (1995) shows how the urban drug trade offers a path to status and economic success for young men who have no chance for industrial work, nor the **cultural capital** to break into middle-class service jobs.

The Subtle Faces of Power in Everyday Interactions

The pervasiveness of power in our daily affairs can be demonstrated by numerous examples of verbal and nonverbal interactions. Deference behaviors, for example, are quite varied in character: they may be linguistic, gestural, spatial, task-embedded, or part of the communication structure (who initiates speech, speaks more frequently, receives more attention, and so on) (Goffman, 1956). A variety of nonverbal "gestures of dominance and submission," as the social psychologist Nancy Henley (1986) put it, mark the behavioral responses that acknowledge the power of others. These behaviors include staring, touching, interrupting, and crowding another's space, as well as the gestures of frowning, looking stern, and pointing.

Power Talks: The Names People Use

The ways in which we address one another may on the surface appear to be merely forms of etiquette. On a deeper level, however, they can be viewed as inextricably bound up with questions of power. Forms of address are powerful verbal symbols for affirming and reaffirming distinctions among people.

Have you ever, for example, called your boss by her or his first name without asking permission to do so? And has your boss ever asked your permission to use your first name? Quite probably you address your boss in some titular fashion such as Mr., Ms., Doctor, or Professor, while the boss calls you by your first name. You call your parents Mom and Dad or Mother and Father, while they address you with your first name or some endearment. You might say, what else should we call them and they us? But why is that so "natural"? We suggest that there is a power dimension to such common forms of address.

As creatures in a symbolic world, we use terms to refer to ourselves and others that convey a great deal about who and what we are. Our very conception of self is intimately related to the names we use to describe ourselves. Does a man refer to himself, for example, as Robert or Bob? Does a woman want others to call her Margaret or Peggy? We self-consciously fashion our names, within limits, to achieve some agreement with our beliefs about who we are and hope to be.

The use of first names rather than titles like Mr. or Ms. in relations with others represents a particular form of association. The exchange of first names is a way of quickly establishing intimate relationships. We must be careful here, however, since the use of first names is frequently decided by those who have the most power in a relationship. They have the prerogative of intruding into the intimate details of others' lives, though the others are denied similar access to details of theirs. Superiors easily become personal and familiar with subordinates, but the latter are not permitted to get personal. In public settings, boundaries of inclusion may be constructed through ploys such as recognizing by first name certain individuals. In a study of city commission proceedings (Futrell, 1999), commissioners were observed to manage interaction by recognizing by first name administrators, their assistants, and other participants linked to the commission. These expressions of familiarity served to assign an added degree of legitimacy and significance to these individuals during the meeting. On the other hand, commissioners' use of first names was sometimes used toward members or groups most likely to present argument. In this case, inclusion was used in an attempt to mollify these individuals (Futrell, 1999).

Staring

In American society, one of the privileges of power is the ability to intrude upon another's personal space by prolonged staring without suffering the consequences. Should those of lower status engage in similar behavior, they might be asked to explain their insubordination or lack of respect for their superior's position. The term *insubordination* means precisely failure to acknowledge one's subordinate status in the presence of a superior.

A large body of research on gaze indicates that, other factors being equal, men show more visual dominance in mixed sex interactions than women. Visual dominance is a pattern of looking at the other more while speaking than while listening, and is associated with perceived competence and influence (Ridgeway and Smith-Lovin, 1999). The relevance of gender to the setting affects gaze as well. Dovidio and colleagues (1998) found that when mixed sex dyads turned from a gender-neutral task to a masculine task, men's greater visual dominance and rate of gesturing became exaggerated. When the dyad shifted to discuss a feminine task, however, women displayed more visual dominance and gestured more than men. These shifts in gaze and gesture patterns reflect changes in the behavioral power and prestige orders of the dyads (Ridgeway and Smith-Lovin, 1999).

Touching

You have probably been in situations where a superior—a boss or teacher, for example—has approached and put his or her arm around you, perhaps to compliment you on something you had done. It is hard to imagine the positions reversed, however, with you putting an arm around a boss or teacher. The right to invade another's personal space through touching is another privilege of power and status. There is empirical evidence, for example, that men are more likely to invade others' spaces and to use touch to assert power, even when their interest is unwelcome. Women's training to be nice to others may make them reluctant to speak forcefully to a boss or coworker whose touches are unwanted. Socialization practices and the gendered identities they foster shed light on sexual harassment in workplaces and educational institutions (Wood, 2003).

Qualitative studies suggest that responses to sexual harassment are grounded in the organization of power relations at work. The deferential behavior of temporary workers, stemming from the feminized and powerless status of their job, increases workers' vulnerability and potential for experiencing sexual harassment. Female *and male* temporary workers have little recourse but to tolerate or ignore harassment (Rogers and Henson, 1997). Service workers are another powerless group of workers with little recourse. Subjected to constant sexual comments, leering, and touching from customers, these workers may be reluctant to complain about these behaviors to managers (c.f., Williams, Giuffre, and Dellinger, 1999). In one case study (Adkins, 1995), it was clear that reporting such behavior would not result in a complaint of sexual harassment, but more likely in loss of the job. (Personal note: When one of your authors complained to her boss at a popular pancake restaurant about a police officer who put his hand on her upper thigh, which was exposed as she leaned over a table because her skirt was short—a requirement of the job—she was told, basically, that if she wanted the job, shut up.)

Interrupting

Interrupting others' conversations is another behavior that has to do with the exercise of power in everyday affairs. Think about your own experiences in talking with someone of higher status than yourself. Who would be more likely to interrupt, you or the other person? One of the most widely contested areas of gender and language is whether men interrupt their conversation partners more often than do women. Although some investigations have replicated Zimmerman and West's (1975) often-cited finding that men tend to interrupt more often than women, there have also been contradictory results indicating either an absence of gender difference or even that women interrupted more than men (c.f., Aries, 1996). In order to address this, one study conducted a meta-analysis of 43 published studies comparing adult women's and men's interruptions during conversations (Anderson and Leaper, 1998). Because men have more often been associated with dominance in conversational interruptions, these authors hypothesized that men would be found to make more intrusive interruptions than women. (Intrusive interruptions were defined as those which suggest a dominating motivation on the part of the interrupter, as when the interrupting speaker successfully takes over the conversational floor.) Although the findings indicated that men were more likely than women to initiate interruptions, the magnitude of gender difference was not large.

These authors noted that the *type* of interruption made a difference. As Tannen (1994) has noted, some interruptions, which she describes as "overlaps," occur when a second speaker begins speaking at what could be a transitional place such as the end of a clause. According to Tannen, women and members of cultural communities she describes as "high involvement" often overlap with each other in speech as a way of demonstrating cooperation and enthusiasm. She proposes that cooperative overlapping is "supportive rather than obstructive, evidence not of domination but of participation, not power but . . . solidarity" (p. 62). She argues that by assuming that interruption is a monolithic conversational device "we are forced into a position that claims that high-involvement speakers, such as blacks and Jews and, in many circumstances, women, are pushy, aggressive, or inconsiderate or foolishly noisy" (p. 73). When interpreting interruption as a form of domineering behavior, the type Anderson and Leaper refer to as intrusive interruptions may be the most relevant. Intrusive interruptions function to usurp the speaker's turn at talk with the intent of demonstrating dominance. In contrast, interruptions that include back-channel listening responses (a conversational form such as uttering "uh-huh's" which communicates the listener's support for and encouragement of the speaker) or affiliative overlaps may demonstrate enthusiasm, agreement, or rapport.

Anderson and Leaper (1998) conclude that any tendency for gender differences in conversational interruptions may be more likely to be detected when the more narrowly defined intrusive interruption category is used. When they analyzed these interruptions separately, the effect size was larger. They found that men interrupted more than did women particularly in groups of three or more persons (versus dyads), suggesting that if interrupting is a demonstration of dominance, the need to display dominance is greater in a more public situation with witnesses than in one-to-one interactions in which pressure to act more stereotyped may be lessened.

Crowding Another's Space

One of the prerogatives of privilege and power is the freedom to restrict others' access to one's property and to circumvent the activities of inferiors. Most suburban communities in the United States have enacted housing standards and zoning ordinances which make it very difficult for low-income people to live in such communities, for example. These restrictions by local governments prohibit the construction of low-cost housing and the location of apartment houses and businesses in residential areas. The introduction of zoning ordinances was related to the desire of the emerging middle class, beginning in the nineteenth century, to establish barriers between itself and those considered inferior. By the 1920s, building restrictions and zoning ordinances bolstered divisions within metropolitan America:

> During the 1920s developers added to the list of protective restrictions in the deeds to subdivision lots, and among these restrictions were covenants forbidding sale or rental of the property to blacks, Jews, or others who might destroy the ethnic homogeneity of the suburban enclave. By 1923 there were 183 communities, containing 40 percent of the nation's urban population, that had enacted zoning ordinances, and the number of zoned municipalities was to increase rapidly during the remainder of the decade. (Teaford, 1986:70–71)

Places reflect and reinforce hierarchy by extending or denying life chances to groups located in detrimental spots. Segregated urban neighborhoods with physical, social, and cultural deterioration (whether due to the exodus of middle-class minorities or to racist real estate practices) have made it difficult for residents to better their conditions (Massey and Denton, 1993; Oliver and Shapiro, 1995; Wilson, 1996).

Gendered segregation via the geography and architecture of places contributes to the subordination and spatialized social control of women, either by denying access to knowledge and activities crucial for the reproduction of power and privilege or by limiting mobility more generally within places defined as unsafe, physically threatening, or inappropriate (McDowell, 1999; Spain, 1992). Gender-differentiated use of space is another indication of the asymmetry between females and males. From the playground to the boardroom, males are more likely to have space for themselves.

Places have power *sui generis*, apart from powerful people or organizations that occupy them. The capacity to dominate and control people or things comes through the geographic location, built-form, and symbolic meanings of a place (Gieryn, 2000). Police squad cars in Los Angeles maintain order in part by patrolling boundaries and restricting access—using place as a means to decide who and what properly belongs where (Herbert, 1997). As we noted in chapter 4, on-the-street harassment of women or racial minorities is one way to keep disadvantaged groups in their place (Duneier and Molotch, 1999; Gardner, 1995).

In 1968 Edward T. Hall coined the word **proxemics** to refer to space and our use of it (if you recall, we introduced this concept in chapter 1). Proxemics offers insight into the relative power and status accorded to various groups in society. Space is a primary means by which a culture designates who is important, who has privilege. Consider who gets space in our society (executives with large offices, wealthy families with large houses). Who gets space and how much space they get indicate power. Usage of private space illustrates the interplay between the organization of the institutional, macro world and the dynamics of face-to-face encounters in the micro world.

Henley (1986) notes:

> Our world is set up so that powerful humans own more territory, move through common areas and others' territory more freely, and take up more space with their bodies, possessions, and symbols. We yield space to them and they grab it from us, either openly or covertly as the occasion (and our acquiescence) allow. Even that corner of the world we call our own . . . will not gain us the resources, privileges, the pleasures, even the survival possibilities that come with the space of the powerful. This is what "position" means in life. (p. 42)

Frowning, Looking Stern, Pointing

Power and status give superiors license to express their anger, outrage, and displeasure with subordinates. Think of how you might have to handle your own anger if you were particularly upset with something your boss did. Could you tell your boss right out how angry YOU are? Probably not. More likely, you would have to express your real feelings very diplomatically to avoid provoking the boss's wrath. If you were in your boss's place, it would be much easier to express your resentment, disappointment, or other negative feelings. The gesture of pointing at another person may also be seen as a power play. Children may be told by adults that pointing, like staring, is not polite. But you never hear an adult admonish another adult not to point at children for the same reason. People in power can point at others and order them forward, backward, and, if need be, even sideways with a simple movement of their fingers. The classic example would be that of the traffic officer in the middle of the intersection, directing traffic by gesturing or pointing in various directions. Needless to say, we usually obey such pointers. In a broader sense, as William H. Whyte (1988) suggested, we must orient our actions to avoid continually colliding and bumping into others, both figuratively and literally. Society provides us with authority figures, analogous to traffic officers, who have the license to "point" us in the "proper" directions.

Conclusion

The idea that social life represents a balancing of freedom and constraint, which is an integral part of the interactionist perspective, is related to humans' capacity for acting upon their surroundings, exercising choice, injecting new meanings into social life, and changing the world through the process of interaction. In this chapter we have elaborated on the constraint side of the life equation. We have tried to show that opportunities for personal choice are not equally distributed throughout the social system. The plain fact is that some people are "freer" than others to control their personal destinies.

Whole categories of people can be distinguished in terms of the relative power they possess. Wealth is highly concentrated in the hands of a few, for example. Comparisons of men with women and whites with nonwhites along any power dimension reveal a patterned, institutionalized, culturally rigid system of superiors and subordinates. In each case, those with little power must pay deference to those with the resources to affect them directly. Studies illustrating the relationship between power and role-taking consistently have found that powerless people must be more accurate role-takers than the powerful.

The most comprehensive social groupings involving varying levels of power are called social classes. People who are born into social classes at the lower end of the stratification system have little opportunity for occupational success and then are devalued because they do not succeed. We briefly traced some of the adaptations lower- and working-class women and men make to this situation, pointing out that the poses such men adopt in their relationships with family and friends are a direct consequence of their social positions.

Power makes its presence felt throughout our daily lives. The way we look at people, what we call them, and where we travel all are instances in which we must be cognizant of our proper place in the social order. Staring, touching, interrupting, crowding another's space, frowning, and smiling are often political acts. Through such routine behaviors, power differences are expressed and maintained. Should we step out of line or forget our roles, the powerful will quickly respond. The politics of interaction operate in both the macro world of social structures and the micro world of face-to-face relations.

The general point made in this chapter is that people's daily interactions reflect the constraints of their particular social positions. It is possible to conceive of social positions in an even broader sense, however. We can consider a person's place in the organizations that characterize modern urban-industrial societies. In the following chapter we will examine the nature of life in bureaucracies, the organizational setting which most characterizes American society.

DEFINITIONS

Backstage   Private areas of social life that are off limits to those who are not members of a group.

Conning strategies   The subtle, indirect ways in which the powerless try to manipulate the powerful.

Cultural capital   The knowledge, skills, habits, values, and tastes that are acquired in the course of socialization and which can be turned to one's advantage in particular social settings (Bourdieu, 1977).

Deference   Behavior which functions as a symbolic means by which appreciation is regularly conveyed to a recipient; something a subordinate owes to his or her superordinate.

Frontstage   Public areas of social life in which those who are not group members can participate and affect the behavior of group members.

Hegemony   A term coined by sociologist Antonio Gramsci to refer to the power derived from controlling the construction of dominant ideologies in a society.

Inferiors   Those whose status makes them subordinate to the power of others. Another name for those in this position is *subordinates*.

Life chances   The ways in which people's opportunities in life are related to their place in society. Examples would include the likelihood of living a long life, staying healthy as opposed to being sick, attaining a high-paying job, and so on.

Macro world   The broader institutional and historical setting in which people's daily lives take place. Relations with others in this world are more abstract, anonymous, and remote, according to Peter and Brigitte Berger.

Micro world   The world of everyday, direct face-to-face relations between individuals.

Power   The ability to get others to do what one wants, while preventing them from changing one's own behaviors.

Power elite   Sociologist C. Wright Mills' term for the small group of power-holders at the top of the stratification structure consisting of members of the corporate world, the federal executive branch of government, and the military.

Qualitative methods   Research methods in which the qualities of objects, behavior, or relationships are evaluated in words rather than numbers.

Quantitative methods   Research methods in which objects, behavior, or relationships are evaluated in numbers.

Social class   Groupings of people based on their common standing on rankings of education, occupational prestige, and income.

Social stratification   The hierarchical ordering of a society in terms of the income, education, or occupation of people in it.

Superiors   Those whose status gives them power over others.

DISCUSSION QUESTIONS

1. Which of your ascribed attributes do you think have been or possibly will be important in determining your life chances positively or negatively? From among those you name, which seem most influential?

   What do your answers to these questions suggest about the ideology that America is a land of equal opportunity?

2. Think about an occasion when you felt powerless and oppressed. In that situation, who do you feel was doing the most accurate role-taking, yourself or the more powerful person? Which of your own or the other person's behaviors illustrate this differential role-taking sensitivity? What strategies did you employ to cope with your powerlessness?

3. Elaborate on the idea that such behaviors as staring, touching, interrupting, smiling, and frowning are often *political* acts.

4. How would you respond to the arguments that lower-class individuals who are unemployed are simply lazy and do not want to work, or that such people just do not hold middle-class achievement values?

REFERENCES

Adkins, L. 1995. *Gendered Work: Sexuality, Family, and the Labour Market*. Bristol: Open University Press.

Anderson, K. J., and C. Leaper. 1998. "Meta-analyses of gender effects on conversational interruption: Who, what, when, where, and how." *Sex Roles* 39(3/4):225–52.

Aries, E. 1996. *Men and Women in Interaction: Reconsidering the Difference*. New York: Oxford University Press.

Berger, P., and B. Berger. 1975. *Sociology: A Biographical Approach*. New York: Basic Books.

Bourdieu, P. 1977. "Cultural reproduction and social reproduction." In *Power and Ideology in Education*, edited by J. Karabel and A. Halsey, pp. 487–511. New York: Oxford University Press.

Bourgois, P. 1995. *In Search of Respect: Selling Crack in El Barrio*. New York: Cambridge University Press.

Dalaker, J., and B. Proctor. 2000. "Poverty in the United States: 1999." *Current Population Reports* (September) P60–210. Washington, D.C.: U.S. Census Bureau.

Danziger, S., and D. Reed. 1999. "Winners and losers: The era of inequality continues." *Brookings Review* (Fall):14–17.

Davies-Netzley, S. 1998. "Women above the glass ceiling." *Gender & Society* 12:339–55.

Domhoff, G. W. 1970. *The Higher Circles*. New York: Vintage Books.

———. 1983. *Who Rules America Now?* New York: Simon & Schuster.

Domhoff, G. W. 1998. *Who Rules America? Power and Politics in the year 2000.* 3rd ed. Mountain View, CA: Mayfield.

Dovidio, J., C. Brown, K. Heltman, S. Ellyson, and C. Keating. 1998. "Power displays between women and men in discussions of gender linked tasks: A multichannel study." *Journal of Personality and Social Psychology* 55:580–87.

Duneier, M., and H. Molotch. 1999. "Talking city trouble: Interactional vandalism, social inequality, and the 'urban interaction problem.'" *American Journal of Sociology* 104:1263–95.

Fine, M. 1994. "Working the hyphens: Reinventing self and other in qualitative research." In *Handbook of Qualitative Research*, edited by N. Denzin and Y. Lincoln, pp. 70–82. Thousand Oaks, CA: Sage.

Fine, M., L. Weis, J. Addelston, and J. Marusza. 1997. "(In)secure times: Constructing white working-class masculinities in the late 20th century." *Gender & Society* 11:52–68.

Forte, J., D. Franks, J. A. Forte, and D. Rigsby. 1996. "Asymmetrical role-taking: Comparing battered and non-battered women." *Social Work* 41:59–73.

Frank, K. 1998. "The production of identity and the negotiation of intimacy in a 'Gentleman's Club.'" *Sexualities* 1:175–201.

Futrell, R. 1999. "Performative governance: Impression management, teamwork, and conflict containment in city commission proceedings." *Journal of Contemporary Ethnography* 27(4):494–529.

Gardner, C. 1995. *Passing By: Gender and Public Harassment.* Berkeley: University of California Press.

Gates, H., Jr. 1998. "The two nations of black America." *Brookings Review* (Spring):4–7.

Gieryn, T. 2000. "A space for place in sociology." *Annual Review of Sociology* 26:463–96.

Goffman, E. 1956. "The nature of deference and demeanor." *American Anthropologist* 58:473–502.

———. 1959. *The Presentation of Self in Everyday Life.* New York: Doubleday Anchor Books.

Goodrum, S., D. Umberson, and K. Anderson. 2001. "The batterer's view of the self and others in domestic violence." *Sociological Inquiry* 71(2):221–40.

Gorman, T. 2000. "Cross-class perceptions of social class." *Sociological Spectrum* 20(1):93–120.

Guerrero, L. 1997. "Nonverbal involvement across interactions with same-sex friends, opposite-sex friends, and romantic partners: Consistency or change?" *Journal of Social and Personal Relationships* 14:31–58.

Hacker, A. 1997. *Money: Who Has How Much and Why.* New York: Scribner.

Hacker, H. 1951. "Women as a minority group." *Social Forces* 30:60–69.

Haley, A. 1976. *Roots.* New York: Doubleday.

Hall, J., A. Halberstadt, and C. O'Brien. 1997. "Subordination and nonverbal sensitivity: A study and synthesis of findings based on trait measures." *Sex Roles* 37(5/6):295–317.

Hecht, M., and M. LaFrance. 1998. "License or obligation to smile: The effect of power and sex on amount and type of smiling." *Personality and Social Psychology Bulletin* 24(12):1332–42.

Henley, N. [1977] 1986. *Body Politics.* Englewood Cliffs, NJ: Prentice Hall.

Herbert, S. 1997. *Policing Space: Territoriality and the Los Angeles Police Department.* Minneapolis: University of Minnesota Press.

Hewitt, J. 2003. *Self and Society: A Symbolic Interactionist Social Psychology.* 9th ed. Needham Heights, MA: Allyn & Bacon.

Holtzworth-Munroe, A., and G. Stuart. 1994. "Typologies of male batterers: Three subtypes and the differences among them." *Psychological Bulletin* 116:476–97.

Horowitz, R. 1997. "Barriers and bridges to class mobility and formation: Ethnographies of stratification." *Sociological Methods and Research* 25:495–538.

Howard, J. 2000. "Social psychology of identities." *Annual Review of Sociology* 26:367–93.

Kacapyr, E. 1996. "Are you middle class?" *American Demographics* (October):30–5.

Kasarda, J. 1989. "Urban industrial transition and the underclass." In *The Ghetto Underclass*, edited by W. Wilson. Beverly Hills, CA: Sage Publications.

———.1995. "Industrial restructuring and the changing location of jobs." In *State of the Union: America in the 1990s*, Vol. 1, edited by R. Farley. New York: Russell Sage Foundation.

Keister, L. 2000. *Wealth in America: Trends in Wealth Inequality*. New York: Cambridge University Press.

LaFrance, M., and N. Henley. 1994. "On oppressing hypotheses: Or differences in nonverbal sensitivity revisited." In *Power/Gender: Social Relations in Theory and Practice*, edited by H. Radtke and H. Stam, pp. 287–311. Thousand Oaks, CA: Sage Publications.

Levy, F. 1998. *The New Dollars and Dreams: American Incomes and Economic Change*. New York: Russell Sage Foundation.

Liebow, E. 1967. *Tally's Corner: A Study of Negro Street-Corner Men*. Boston: Little Brown.

Loguen, J. 1859. *The Rev. J. W. Loguen, As a Slave and As a Freedman*. Syracuse, NY: n.p.

Marger, M. 2002. *Social Inequality: Patterns and Processes*. 2nd ed. New York: McGraw-Hill.

Massey, D., and N. Denton. 1993. *American Apartheid: Segregation and the Making of the Underclass*. Cambridge, MA: Harvard University Press.

McDowell, L. 1999. *Gender, Identity and Place*. Minneapolis: University of Minnesota Press.

Mishel, L., J. Bernstein, and J. Schmitt. 2001. *The State of Working America, 2000–01*. Ithaca, NY: Cornell University Press.

Moore, M. 2002. "Courtship communication and perception." *Perceptual and Motor Skills* 94:97–105.

Oliver, M., and T. Shapiro. 1995. *Black Wealth/White Wealth*. New York: Routledge.

Ridgeway, C., and L. Smith-Lovin. 1999. "The gender system and interaction." *Annual Review of Sociology* 25:191–216.

Rogers, J., and K. Henson. 1997. " 'Hey, why don't you wear a shorter skirt?' Structural vulnerability and the organization of sexual harassment in temporary clerical employment." *Gender & Society* 11(2):215–37.

Rollins, J. 1985. *Between Women: Domestics and Their Employers*. Philadelphia: Temple University Press.

Rubin, L. 1976. *Worlds of Pain*. New York: Harper & Row.

———. 1994. *Families on the Faultline: America's Working Class Speaks About the Family, the Economy, Race, and Ethnicity*. New York: HarperCollins.

Schuman, H., and J. Scott. 1989. "Generations and collective memory." *American Sociological Review* 54:359–81.

Schwalbe, M., S. Godwin, D. Holden, D. Schrock, S. Thompson, and M. Wolkomir. 2000. "Generic processes in the reproduction of inequality: An interactionist analysis." *Social Forces* 79(2):419–52.

Scully, D. 1990. *Understanding Sexual Violence: A Study of Convicted Rapists*. Boston: Unwin Hyman.

Sennett, R., and J. Cobb. 1973. *The Hidden Injuries of Class*. New York: Random House.

Spain, D. 1992. *Gendered Spaces*. Chapel Hill: University of North Carolina Press.

Tannen, D. 1994. "Interpreting interruption in conversation." In *Gender and Discourse*, edited by D. Tannen. New York: Oxford University Press.

Tatum, B. 2000. "The complexity of identity: 'Who am I?'" In *Readings for Diversity and Social Justice*, edited by M. Adams, W. Blumenfeld, R. Casteñeda, H. Hackman, M. Peters, and X. Zúñiga, pp. 9–14. New York: Routledge.

Tawney, R. 1931. *Equality*. London: Allen & Unwin.

Teaford, J. 1986. *The Twentieth-Century American City*. Baltimore, MD: Johns Hopkins University Press.

Testa, M. 1991. "Male joblessness, nonmarital parenthood and marriage." Paper presented at the Chicago Urban Poverty and Family Life Conference, October 10–12.

Testa, M., and M. Krough. 1995. "The effect of employment on marriage among black males in inner-city Chicago." In *The Decline in Marriage Among African Americans: Causes, Consequences and Policy Implications*, edited by M. Tucker and C. Mitchell-Kernan, pp. 59–95. New York: Russell Sage Foundation.

U.S. Census Bureau. 1999. *Statistical Abstract of the United States: 1999*. Washington, D.C.: Government Printing Office.

———. 2000a. *Historical Income Tables*. Table F-2.

———. 2000b. *Statistical Abstract of the United States: 2000*. Washington, D.C.: Government Printing Office.

———. 2000c. "Poverty in the United States: 1999." *Current Population Reports*, P60-210. Washington, D.C.: Government Printing Office.

———. 2000d. "Educational attainment in the United States: March 1999." *Current Population Reports*, P20-528. Washington, D.C.: Government Printing Office.

———. 2000e. "Money income in the United States: 1999." *Current Population Reports*, P60-209. Washington, D.C.: Government Printing Office.

U.S. Department of Labor, Bureau of Labor Statistics. 2001. *Highlights of Women's Earnings in 2000*. Report 952.

Weis, L., A. Proweller, and C. Centrie. 1996. "Re-examining a moment in history: Loss of privilege inside white, working-class masculinity in the 1990s." In *Off White*, edited by M. Fine, L. Powell, L. Weis, and M. Wong. New York: Routledge.

Whyte, W. H. 1988. *City*. New York: Anchor Books.

Williams, C., P. Giuffre, and K. Dellinger. 1999. "Sexuality in the workplace: Organizational control, sexual harassment, and the pursuit of pleasure." *Annual Review of Sociology* 25:73–93.

Wilson, W. 1987. *The Truly Disadvantaged*. Chicago: University of Chicago Press.

———. 1996. *When Work Disappears: The World of the New Urban Poor*. New York: Vintage Books.

Wolf, C. 1994. "Dependency-bond as construct." *Symbolic Interaction* 17:367–93.

Wolff, E. 1995. *Top Heavy: A Study of the Increasing Inequality of Wealth in America*. New York: The Twentieth Century Fund Press.

Wood, J. 2003. *Gendered Lives: Communication, Gender, and Culture*. 5th ed. Belmont, CA: Wadsworth.

Zimmerman, D., and C. West. 1975. "Sex roles, interruptions and silences in conversations." In *Language and Sex: Differences and Dominance*, edited by B. Thorne and N. Henley. Rowley, MA: Newbury House.

CHAPTER OUTLINE

SOCIAL ORGANIZATION
LIFE IN BUREAUCRACIES

The power individuals can exercise is not simply a matter of personality characteristics. Rather, as we argued in chapter 6, it is dependent on the positions people occupy in society, as determined by their achieved and ascribed statuses. In this chapter we will extend this argument to include people's positions in bureaucratic organizations, such as those in the institutions of education and work, which exert a large influence on daily interactions.

In calling attention to the organizational nature of social life we are focusing on one of the central dimensions of modern existence, the extent to which behaviors are shaped by **bureaucracy** and the bureaucratic form of organization. You were probably born in a bureaucratically organized medical setting called a hospital, for example. Your parents paid for your arrival into the world with medical charge cards from bureaucracies like Blue Cross/Blue Shield. As a child you entered society through bureaucratic institutions such as the public schools, which grouped you into grades composed of children of a similar age. You moved through this organization in steps, passing from the lowest grades up to the final year of high school. Because you have chosen to continue your schooling in a college or university, you again are experiencing the progression from new student to senior.

The Pervasive Effects of Bureaucracy

For most American adults, even the smallest daily experiences are shaped by large-scale bureaucratic organizations. Waking up in the morning, we turn on the radio or television and listen to the news presented by a local station owned by a national corporation such as NBC. The network gets its information from a worldwide news source such as the Associated Press. More importantly, the national corporation has a great deal of control in deciding what local affiliates present—the leading corporations control about 90 percent of all technology, including what goes into the mass media, information systems, and popular culture (Boggs, 2000).

Our breakfast foods are provided by multinational corporations such as General Foods. Then we get into our mass-produced cars and drive to work on highways built and maintained with funds allocated by state and federal agencies. We are likely to work for a bureaucratically organized firm, which employs large numbers of people with officially designated job titles. We encounter bureaucracies if we pay taxes or purchase licenses, seek medical services at a hospital or clinic, have a question about a bill at a department store, try to make a change in a utility service, and in numerous everyday activities.

Arriving home at the end of the day, we read our mail, which has been delivered by another government bureaucracy, the U.S. Postal Service. At certain times of the month, the mail includes a large number of computerized bills from utility companies, banks, credit card agencies, and department stores—organizations that maintain a keen interest in our prospects and locations as long as we occupy a numbered niche in their computer systems. Corporate organizations dominate the state apparatus, own and control the mass media, profoundly shape education and medicine, and penetrate into even the most intimate realms of social life (Boggs, 2000).

In modern American society people are continually confronted with problems that cannot be resolved informally and must be referred to government agencies, business organizations, insurance companies, or the courts. Because our society is composed of hundreds of millions of people of diverse backgrounds, it is almost impossible to establish policies that would be sensitive to all the subtle meanings of individual behaviors. The bureaucratic solution is to set standardized procedures and rely on elaborate systems of rules and regulations for interactions between individuals in specific situations. Society seems to have reached a point where individual behaviors are increasingly controlled and directed by the policies of large-scale public and private organizations.

There are costs to this. According to Robert Bellah and colleagues (1996), "We spend much of our time navigating through immense bureaucratic structures—multiuniversities, corporations, government agencies—manipulating and being manipulated by others" (p. 150). Individualism has been transformed into a "bureaucratic individualism" where "freedom to make private decisions is bought at the cost of turning over most public decisions to bureaucratic managers and experts" (Bellah et al., 1996:150).

Charles Edgley and Dennis Brissett have written a book decrying the fact that we have become *A Nation of Meddlers* (1999):

> Meddling in the lives of others is now the republic's most visible obsession. Examples are everywhere—from national crusades against bad habits such as drinking, smoking, and gambling to the efforts . . . to cre-

ate a "fragrance-free" work environment. . . . In Phoenix, Arizona, the city council passes a law requiring that the installation of a swimming pool be accompanied by the child-proofing of any access from the house to the pool, even if no children reside in the house. (p. 1)

The list goes on and on. These authors are particularly critical of the "meddling" done by workers and bureaucrats in the helping professions, although this meddling is described in euphemistic terms: "Social workers, for instance, never meddle; they engage in 'professional intervention strategies' " (p. 3).

The Bureaucratization of Modern Life

Noted sociologists such as Émile Durkheim and Max Weber traced the origins of modern society to the processes of urbanization and industrialization that began in the late eighteenth century. The rise of the industrial city was accompanied by such developments as the capitalist economy, technological advances, and new social categories like the working class (or **proletariat**, in Karl Marx's term), which arose to meet the factory system's demand for workers.

From Mass Society to Organizational Society

The development of industrial technology and the factory system of production attracted newcomers of varied social origins to the cities. Peasants prevented from farming by agricultural reforms or "enclosure acts" were forced to seek their livelihoods in the urban factories. The most dramatic effect of these processes on social life was the separation of work from the home, however. As Peter Laslett put it, the result was a **mass society**:

> The factory won its victory by out-producing the working family, taking away the market for products of hand-labour and cutting prices to the point where the craftsman had either to starve or take a job under factory discipline himself. . . . [W]e can say that the removal of the economic functions from the patriarchal family at the point of industrialization created a mass society. It turned the people who worked into a mass of undifferentiated equals, working in a factory or scattered between the factories and mines, bereft forever of the feeling that work was a family affair, done within the family. (1971:18–19)

The factory system brought the introduction of labor for wages and mechanized methods of production marked by repetition and standardization. During the early phases of industrialization in both Europe and the United States, some women—especially unmarried women, women from the lower classes, and minority women—worked in the factories. A sex-based division of labor developed, with women working with smaller equipment and machinery on average, concentrated in jobs in the textile industry. The jobs women performed paid lower wages than those performed by men, who were viewed as the primary breadwinners. Women employed in factories continued to be responsible for domestic work at home, creating for the first time a "double shift" for women consisting of eight or more hours of paid work followed by another shift of work at home (Dunn, 1997). The effects of industrialization on the lives of workers led to various reform movements, often headed by women, which attempted to improve working conditions. The union activist Mary Harris ("Mother") Jones reported the horrendous plight of women and children in industry, "condemned to slave daily in the washroom (of breweries) in wet shoes and wet clothes . . . in the vile smell of sour beer, lifting cases . . . weighing from 100 to 150 pounds" (Woloch, 1994:238).

Efforts to make workers as efficient as machines led in the early twentieth century to the development of administrative techniques called **scientific management**. An industrial engineer, Frederick Taylor, developed ideas for a factory workplace in which the division of labor was highly specialized and individual work tasks were minutely scrutinized and reduced to their most basic elements. Managers sought to take over control of the production process from the hands of the workers, in line with a distinctive characteristic of bureaucratic functioning—**control from the top down**. Between the period of rapid westward expansion and industrial growth that followed the Civil War and the entry of the U.S. onto the world scene in World War I, American society passed through the most rapid and profound transformation in its history. New technologies, particularly in transport, communications, and manufacturing, pulled the many semi-autonomous local societies into a vast national market. The new economically integrated society emerging at the turn of the century developed its own forms of social organization, political control, and culture. The new social form, capable of extending the control of a group of investors over vast resources, huge numbers of employees, and often great distances, was the business corporation (Bellah et al., 1996). Beginning about 1875, social, economic, and political trends in the United States prepared the way for what Robert Presthus (1978) called the **organizational society**, characterized by large-scale bureaucratic institutions in virtually every area of social life.

The Rise of the Service Economy

According to Bellah and coauthors (1996), the most distinctive aspect of twentieth-century American society was the division of life into a number of separate functional sectors: home and workplace, work and leisure, white collar and blue collar, public and private. This division suited the needs of the bureaucratic industrial corporations. One of the most significant changes has been in the types of work done by the majority of adults in American society. The data in table 7.1 on major occupational groups in the United States show a substantial increase in the proportion of the workforce in **white-collar occupations**, which includes clerical and sales positions, from 18 percent in 1900 to 59 percent in 1989, but then almost no change between 1989 and 2000. The percentage of workers employed in all **blue-collar** occupations declined through the twentieth century, dropping from 37 percent in 1900 to

27 percent in 1989 and to 24.5 percent by 2000. Employment in farm occupations has remained small and fairly constant during the past 20 years—ranging between 3 and 4 percent.

Skilled blue-collar craft workers and operatives, who make up the membership of the large national labor unions such as the United Automobile Workers and United Steelworkers, more-or-less held their share of the labor force until the early 1980s recession. Recent years, however, have witnessed a steady decline in the percentage of workers in the labor force who are unionized, falling from 20 percent in 1983 to 13.5 percent in 2000 (U.S. Department of Labor, 2001). Government workers have a substantially higher unionization rate (37.5 percent) than workers in the private sector (9.0 percent). Blacks continued to have higher unionization rates (17.1 percent) than whites (13.0 percent) and Hispanics (11.4 percent). White and Hispanic women had the lowest rates (10.9 and 10.2 percent) in 2000. Union members' median weekly earnings were higher than those of workers not represented by unions, although this reflects a variety of influences in addition to coverage by a collective bargaining agreement.

One author (Troy, 2001) refers to the situation of unionism in the private sector as the "twilight of organized labor," meaning that he does not expect it to recover either the membership or the market share it had in the recent or historical past. The United States is not unique in the decline of private sector unions; the International Labour Office has reported that "[i]n a large number of countries around the globe, trade unions have experienced a considerable drop in membership over the past decade" (International Labour Office, 1997:2). The United States led the way, however, and its descent has been deeper than in other countries (Troy, 2001).

One of the most notable transformations in the U.S. labor market since World War II has been the rising share of employment in the services industry and the declining share in manufacturing. In 1945, at the end of the war, the services industry accounted for 10 percent of nonfarm employment, compared with 38 percent for manufacturing. In 1982, services surpassed manufacturing as the largest employer among major industry groups. By 1996, the services industry accounted for 29 percent of nonfarm employment, and manufacturing, at 15 percent, was somewhat smaller than retail trade (Meisenheimer, 1998). This industry is part of a larger category called service-producing industries, and has the largest share of employees in the service-producing group. Included in this category are a broad variety of **service occupations**, such as health care, advertising, computer and data processing services, personnel supply, private education, social services, legal services, and so on (Meisenheimer, 1998). There is a wide variety of average hourly earnings among these jobs. Some have earnings below the average for retail trade, the lowest paying major industry group. These include videotape rental; child day care; detective and armored car services; automotive services (except repair); services to buildings; and laundry, cleaning, and garment services. Other service industries have average hourly earnings above the average for mining, the highest paying major industry; for example, computer and data processing, legal services, and engineering and management services. Most service industries pay somewhere in between. In health services, the largest services industry, average hourly earnings are about a dollar higher than the average for all services (Meisenheimer, 1998).

The shift of employment away from manufacturing and toward services has caused considerable consternation among some labor market observers, policymakers, business leaders, and workers. Because average wages are higher in manufacturing than in services, some observers view the employment shifts as generally representing a shift from "good" to "bad" jobs. However, because of the diversity of job quality in the services industry—many industries within services equal or exceed manufacturing and other industries on measures of job quality—employment shifts away from manufacturing and toward services do not necessarily signal a deterioration in overall job quality in the United States (Meisenheimer, 1998). More than just average pay must be examined when assessing the quality of jobs in each industry. "The quality of services industry

---

Table 7.1

Percentage of Labor Force in Types of Occupations, United States, 1900–2000

Type of occupation	Years						
	1900	1920	1940	1970	1982	1989	2000
White-collar occupations	18%	25%	32%	48%	55%	59%*	60%
Professional and technical	4	5	8	14	17		19
Managers, officials,							
and proprietors	6	7	7	11	12		15
Clerical	3	8	10	17	19		14
Sales	5	5	7	6	7		12
Blue-collar occupations	37%	41%	39%	36%	30%	27%	25%
Craft and kindred workers	11	13	12	13	12		11
Operatives	13	16	18	18	13		10
Nonfarm laborers	13	12	9	5	5		4
Service occupations	10%	8%	12%	12%	14%	12%	14%
Service workers, except							
private households	4	5	7				11
Farm occupations	38%	27%	17%	4%	3%	3%	2.5%
Farmers and farm							
managers	20	15	10				
Farm workers	18	12	7				

* Total percentage of workers in the category.

Sources: U.S. Census Bureau, *Historical Statistics of the United States: Colonial Times to 1957* (Washington, D.C.: U.S. Government Printing Office, 1960), Table Series D 72–12; *Statistical Abstract of the United States, 1984* (Washington, D.C.: U.S. Government Printing Office, 1983), Table 693; 1991, Table 656; U.S. Department of Labor, Bureau of Labor Statistics, *Household Data Annual Averages, Table 10: Employed Persons by Occupation, Race, and Sex* (www.bls.gov/cps/home.htm, accessed 12/29/01).

jobs is especially diverse, encompassing many of the 'best' jobs in the economy and a substantial share of the 'worst'" (Meisenheimer, 1998:45).

Effects on Society

By 1970, white-collar workers were employed in large-scale organizations where the conditions of work included standardization, impersonality, specialization, a hierarchy of authority, and dependence. Such organizations, moreover, could provide the research and management skills which intensified these conditions. The growth of white-collar work was the force behind the emergence of a new social category: the **new middle class** of corporate managers, salaried white-collar professionals, salespeople, and office workers. By contrast, the old middle class that had dominated American society was composed of farmers, self-employed businessmen, and independent professionals (Mills, 1956).

Thinking about Bureaucracy

Nineteenth-century social scientists, living through the monumental social changes that accompanied industrialization and urbanization, sought to comprehend their effects on both individual behaviors and society. Max Weber (1922) was among the first to identify the characteristics of bureaucratic organizations, which he considered to be the most efficient means of managing or controlling large groups of people. Numerous social scientists have advanced different ideas on the nature and consequences of this organizational form and have debated the issue of its dehumanizing effects. The symbolic interaction perspective is that bureaucratic organizations are not separate entities with a life of their own, but are created and sustained by the daily interactions of their members (see Strauss, 1978).

Weber's Model of Bureaucratic Organizations

A bureaucracy, according to Weber, has certain readily identifiable characteristics, such as a clear-cut and specialized **division of labor**, a **hierarchy of authority**, and an elaborate system of rules and regulations. Bureaucracies are organized in a pyramidal fashion, with power concentrated in the hands of a few officials in the higher positions. Employees at one level are responsible to those immediately above them and exercise authority over those immediately below them. The division of labor is carefully specified by formal descriptions of job content and the range of authority entailed in the various positions. In the name of efficiency and to eliminate needless motion and time from the production process, tasks are divided into their most basic operations. In working situations, however, as many observers have pointed out, bureaucracies can generate a good deal of excess paperwork and encourage buck-passing and other procedures that actually are counterproductive. In the words of one author:

> Bureaucratic organizations live by, maintain, and modify an autonomous world of their own creation. This world deserves to be called papereality,

not because it may misrepresent reality but because it functions as a binding representation. As soon as something (e.g., a word, a document, or a bill) is allowed to stand for something else (e.g., agreements, decisions, or purchase power), then, as every thief and counterfeiter knows, the representation becomes as valuable as the thing represented. (Dery, 1998:686)

Think about the last time you needed an "official" transcript!

In most bureaucracies employees are listed by job title in a personnel department, which has an administrative staff to perform the necessary specialized record keeping. The emphasis on files and record keeping is not simply an internal personnel matter but rather reflects a much deeper quality of organizational life—the tendency to reduce relationships with customers and clients to definable categories of behavior. Individuals are dealt with in terms of the category into which they fall. Universities, to choose an example close to home, have separate files for students in good standing, students on probation, students who lack the necessary courses for admission, and so on.

Weber's model of bureaucracy emphasizes the **meritocracy** inherent in such organizations. Employees are supposed to be hired on the basis of their personal merit or individual abilities, independent of political considerations, family ties, or personal favoritism. Career movements within the organizations also are supposed to reflect meritocratic principles, with the most competent employees rising to the highest positions. In practice, however, the system often fails to work this way. The well-known *Peter Principle* describes the idea that employees in a hierarchy tend to rise to their individual levels of incompetence—and remain there. It suggests that individuals who are doing their work competently are singled out for promotion until they are given a job in which their incompetence becomes apparent. Then the promotions stop and the employees remain in their highest positions, where they continue to perform incompetently. Scott Adams, creator of the popular comic strip, *Dilbert*, has developed a typology of "boss types" that includes the categories "incompetent-harmless" and "incompetent-evil" (Adams, 1998). The popularity of *Dilbert* highlights the cynicism felt by many employees about the effectiveness of management (Feldman, 2000).

For Weber, bureaucratic organizations exemplified a principle that he termed **rationalization**: the systematic and logical application of formal rules and procedures to every aspect of modern life. In his writings, Weber demonstrated how this principle came to permeate all spheres of life, ranging from economic activities to even art and classical music. In the final analysis, Weber remained deeply pessimistic about the prospects for a fully human life in a world in which bureaucratic policies continually reduce people to files in anonymous record-keeping systems. An example of the extremes such policies can produce can be seen in the experiences of the character Joseph K. in Franz Kafka's haunting novel, *The Trial*.

The "McDonaldization" of Society

George Ritzer builds on Weber's idea of rationalization with his theory of the "McDonaldization" of society, "The process by which the principles of the fast-food restaurant are coming to dominate more and more sectors of American society as well as the rest of the world" (2000:1). His work is premised on the idea that whereas the processes of rationalization and bureaucratization described by Weber have continued, if not accelerated, the bureaucracy has been supplanted by the fast-food restaurant as the best exemplification of this process. That is, the characteristics Weber identified as being advantages of bureaucracy—efficiency, predictability, quantification, control over people through the replacement of human judgment with the dictates of rules, regulations, and structures—exemplify the fast-food industry as well as many other modern organizations. McDonaldization affects education, work, health care, travel, leisure, dieting, politics, the family, and virtually every other aspect of society. Just think about the many fast-food businesses which have adopted the McDonald's model: Burger King, Wendy's, Pizza Hut, Kentucky Fried Chicken, Taco Bell, Subway. It should come as no surprise that the model (which is extremely successful) has been extended to "casual dining"—more upscale, higher-priced restaurants with fuller menus, e.g., Outback Steakhouse, Fuddrucker's, Chili's, The Olive Garden, Red Lobster. According to a *New York Times* article about one such chain: "Despite the fawning service and the huge wine list, a meal at Morton's conforms to the same dictates of uniformity, cost control and portion regulation that have enabled American fast-food chains to rule the world" (Collins, 1996). And then, of course, there's Starbucks. Other types of business are increasingly adapting the principles of the fast-food industry to their needs: Toys R Us, Kidsports Fun and Fitness Club, Jiffy Lube, AAMCO Transmissions, Midas Muffler & Brake Shops, Hair Plus, H&R Block, Pearle Vision Centers, Kampgrounds of America (KOA), Kinder Care, Jenny Craig, Home Depot, Barnes & Noble, Petstuff, and Wal-Mart (Ritzer, 2000:3).

Moreover, the rational principles that underlie the fast-food restaurant not only are spreading throughout American society, but through the rest of the world as well. Just about half of McDonald's restaurants are outside the United States (compared to 25 percent in the mid-1980s). Other nations have developed their own variants, such as Canada's chain of coffee shops, Tim Hortons (which has merged with Wendy's); Paris has a large number of fast-food croissanteries; India has a chain of fast-food restaurants that sells mutton burgers; and so on. According to Ritzer, "McDonaldization has shown every sign of being an inexorable process, sweeping through seemingly impervious institutions and regions of the world" (2000:2).

One of the hallmarks of McDonaldization is the incorporation of scientific management, leading Ritzer to write about "McJobs"—jobs specifically connected to the McDonaldization of society. He notes that it is not just that these are "simply the deskilled jobs of our industrial past in new settings"; rather, McJobs have a number of new characteristics including "many distinctive aspects of the control of these workers" (1998:63). These jobs not only reach new depths in **deskilling**, but they also entail control of the self through emotional labor. That is, a number of service organizations insist that workers exhibit cheerfulness and friendliness toward customers as part of the service encounter. Perhaps the best example of this is exemplified in the Disney theme parks (see box).

The Disneyization of Society

Alan Bryman proposes that a case similar to McDonaldization can be made for what he calls "Disneyization"—"the process by which the principles of the Disney theme parks are coming to dominate more and more sectors of American society as well as the rest of the world" (1999:26). Bryman identifies four dimensions of Disneyization that are discernible in and have implications for (late) modernity: (1) theming, (2) dedifferentiation of consumption,* (3) merchandising, and (4) emotional labor. It is emotional labor that is at issue here.

The behavior of Disney theme park employees is controlled through scripted interactions, and encouraging **emotional labor** is one of the key elements (Bryman, 1995). The ever-smiling Disney employee has become a stereotype of modern culture. Their demeanor is designed, among other things, to convey the impression that the employees are having fun too and therefore not engaging in real work. However, it was not quite that way at the beginning. In Disneyland's very early days, Walt Disney was appalled by the behavior of some of the park's staff toward visitors. They lacked training and were gruff and unhelpful towards visitors. The only employees who exhibited the kind of behavior Walt wanted were the attraction operators who had been trained by the company itself. The Disney University was created precisely in order to inculcate the necessary training, and introduced a new vocabulary of "friendly phrases" (France, 1991:22). Since then, Disney has developed seminars that introduce executives from all types of organizations to this distinctive approach to human resource management (c.f., Eisman, 1993). A number of management texts have emphasized this ingredient in the success of Disney theme parks (c.f., Connellan, 1996).

Sometimes the emotional requirements of the job (Smile!) are resented by Disney employees (Project on Disney, 1995). This is a reflection of the demands of emotional labor, just as it was for Hochschild's (1983) flight attendants. Most Disney staff, however, accept the emotional requirements of the job. Even among some former Disney employees who had adverse employment experiences, there seems to be a certain ambivalence that combines a degree of admiration with a recognition that the job was not for them (Zibart, 1997).

Bryman ties Disneyization into theories of consumerism. The emotional labor of Disney employees "serves to convey a sense that the employee is not engaged in work, so that the consumer is not reminded of the world of work and can get on with the happy task of buying, eating, gambling and so on. The smiling, helpful demeanor may also encourage spending in its own right" (Bryman, 1999:43). It's a small world, after all!

* This term refers to the general trend where forms of consumption associated with different institutional spheres become interlocked with each other and increasingly difficult to distinguish; e.g., shopping at theme parks. Walt Disney realized early on that Disneyland had great potential as a vehicle for selling food and various goods (Bryman, 1999).

Weber's "Iron Cage"

Although Weber recognized bureaucracy's fundamental rationality, he had serious reservations about it. Believing that bureaucracy's influence on every aspect of life could erode individual freedom and responsibility, and that its structuring of behavior could suppress human feelings and values, Weber referred to bureaucracy as an "iron cage."

Contemporary analysts of bureaucratic life have suggested a number of changes in Weber's model that would allow a less jaundiced view of such organizations. Jay Klagge (1997), for example, visualizes the iron cage as a playground structure. That is, the bureaucratic structure of organizations is similar to the monkey bars or jungle gyms found on the typical playground. Rather than being imprisoning:

> These structures, although rigid, cold, and sterile, provide the framework upon which and within which organization members act, reflect, imagine, and create. In this metaphor, work is recognized as the creative playground of adults. Life is given to the lifeless structure through the creativity and energy of those who engage it. Organizational life is played out in daily dramas as members give meaning, life, and ethics to the sterile structure. In sum, the iron cage of bureaucracy, being a neutral structure, calls for the creative, ethical, energetic play of adults that most of us know by the name of "work." (Klagge, 1997:67)

Viewing bureaucracy as a playground structure offers a more positive view than Weber's iron cage. In Klagge's view, bureaucracy is a neutral apparatus upon which either positive or negative acts may occur. The outcome depends on how the apparatus is used. Klagge explains:

> Softening the rigidity of the iron bars, warming the coldness of the cage, and breathing life into the sterile structure can result in positive outcomes. Our childhood memories of the iron cage ought to be the most powerful, positive, and important referents provided by this metaphor . . . everyone has a rich childhood playground experience base from which to draw. Granted this experience base provides positive and negative memories, friendly and unfriendly encounters, and exciting and boring scenes, but these experiences that require energy, imagination, creativity, and commitment also correspond to life in a public bureaucracy. (1997:76)

Klagge's rosy view is that playful action on the iron cage can become a daily experience.

H. George Frederickson takes a different approach, arguing that bureaucracy is a form of beauty and that organization and the work of organizations, including what is described as administration or management, can be beautiful (2000). Although hierarchy is still the norm, modern-day hierarchy "hardly resembles the rigid boxes and lines associated with the early era of scientific management" (p. 49).

According to Frederickson:

When hierarchy is out of balance, often in the direction of too great an emphasis on order, it becomes static and out of touch with its changing context. When hierarchy is in balance—combining enough order to engender trust and predictability, enough fairness to include workers in important decisions and to give them the required security to ensure their loyalty, enough fixing of responsibility to satisfy political leaders, and enough leadership to imagine the future—could it not be said that all of those who are part of that hierarchy have created something beautiful? (p. 52)

He continues:

Because beauty is subjective, one has at least some choice of the occupation or organization that holds the prospects for beauty. When there is extensive self-identity with an organization, it can be said that these positive human feelings approximate beauty. And when there is alienation—negative human feelings—between individuals and their organizations, it is the opposite of beauty. Beauty in the organizational sense, then, is based on experience. (p. 53)

This idea certainly fits with the symbolic interactionist perspective on bureaucracy.

The Symbolic Interaction Perspective on Organizations

The symbolic interaction perspective stresses that organizations are humanly created phenomena. They owe their origin, maintenance, and eventual change to the daily interactions and communications taking place among their members. According to this view, people transform their social organizations as well as themselves through their interactions with one another. Organizational life, therefore, is not preordained, but is shaped by fluid processes. Humans live in a world of socially constructed meanings which can always be changed through dialogues like those the civil rights activists of the 1960s engaged in to redefine the meaning of the word *black* (McAdam, 1989). In the face of life's uncertainties, individuals create social organizations such as bureaucracies to serve both as tools to achieve various goals and, in the broadest sense, as avenues to make the world meaningful and thereby manageable. By imposing some sense of social structure, organizations make the terrors occasioned by life's imponderable mysteries more bearable and predictable.

We live in a world of increasing complexity, characterized by the growing influence of multinational corporations whose business operations cut across the boundaries of individual nation-states. The deep structural impacts of a highly globalized and interconnected market system still need to be fully demarcated. As Benjamin Barber has beautifully put it:

McWorld is a product above all of all of popular culture driven by expansionist commerce. Its template is American, its form is style, its goods are images. It is a new world of global franchises where, in place of the old cry, "Workers of the world unite! You have nothing to lose but your chains!" is heard the new cry, *"Consumers of the world unite! We have every-thing you need in our chains!"* (1996:78; emphasis added)

While bureaucracies embody the formal characteristics Weber identified, such as a hierarchy of authority and the division of labor, there is also a great deal of leeway in any organizational environment. To use Karl Weick's (1976) felicitous phrase, in all organizations there are enough "loose cou-plings" or situations marked by uncertainty or ambiguity, so that individuals must supply their own definitions of reality.

The Construction of Organizations by Their Members

The way an organization is structured, how its set of occupations are organized, and the way it connects with the outside world affect the specific behaviors and cultures in the workplace (Fine, 1996). As organizational members respond to and redefine the formal rules of bureaucratic settings, they construct **informal subcultures** within the organization, which play important roles. In his study of restaurant kitchens, Gary Fine (1996) found that each restaurant he observed had cultural traditions known by the kitchen staff, which they used as points of reference. For example, nicknames were common, argot (slang) developed, and often this culture was connected to humor. In particular, horseplay, teasing, and pranks served to provide inter-personal closeness and create shared memories among the restaurant workers he studied. Much of the horseplay was centered on food (playing catch with a steak or a cauliflower) and tools (dueling with knives), sometimes transform-ing "work space into a playground" and "generating satisfaction within a structure that does not have worker satisfaction as an explicit goal" (p. 120). Teasing—a marker of community in that its existence shows that there is enough looseness in relationships that one person can make a joke at another's expense without the belief that those sentiments are real—was used to bring new workers into the group. Pranks also are central to the establish-ment of interpersonal closeness in restaurant kitchens. Although major pranks (as opposed to minor ones) were rare, they were vividly described in interviews. As Fine explains, "Memories and reports of memory are shared by workers; this sharing connects them in a powerful web. They have a humor culture" (p. 123).

Fine concludes: "All workplaces, but small workplaces in particular, have cultures that emerge from the doing of work and cannot easily be con-structed by management. The culture becomes a reality for all those who are a party to it" (p. 137).

Subcultures provide different experiences to organizational members, according to their positions in the hierarchy. In effect, organizations are thickly populated by multiple realities (see chapter 2). The meanings that constitute these realities define what the organization is in terms of human behaviors.

The interactionist approach to the study of bureaucracy emphasizes the ongoing, interpretive communication process by which members construct their own organizational realities. It suggests that organizations should be viewed as the result of a process of **negotiated order,** rather than as fixed in granite or completely regulated by an organizational chart of official positions. Researchers such as Anselm Strauss (1978, 1993) argue that the social order reflects ongoing negotiations between participants as they deal with each other in order to get things done. In this view, negotiation is not just a specific human activity or process that appears in particular relationships such as diplomacy and labor relations. Rather, it is "of such major importance in human affairs that its study brings us to the heart of studying social orders. . . . A given social order, even the most repressive, would be inconceivable without some forms of negotiation" (Strauss, 1978:234–35).

In thinking about bureaucracies, the interactionist perspective is principally concerned with how people respond to formal rules and procedures. New meanings are created by those at the top and the bottom of the hierarchy, despite official patterns of authority and control. Efforts at spontaneity and innovation continually occur, even though the "higher-ups" attempt to mold the behaviors of the "lower-downs" into highly predictable forms. Life in a bureaucracy, then, is determined more by the informal interactions of individuals than by the formal rules and procedures of the organization.

Work in Bureaucracies

From the interactionist view that bureaucracies have no life of their own but are constructed by the interactions of their members, it follows that the way to study life in bureaucracies is to examine the experiences of the members. In contemporary American society, the need or desire to work leads most adults to become involved in corporate organizations.

Social scientists have studied the conditions of corporate life by identifying a new social ethic and examining leadership in relation to the employee's position in the organizational hierarchy. They have explored the multiple realities of corporate life, including the psychological isolation of top-level executives, the frustrating status of secretaries, and the routine, predictable, powerless jobs of unskilled blue-collar workers.

The Protestant Ethic (Work) versus the Social Ethic (Managing)

William H. Whyte's controversial study, *The Organization Man* (1956), called attention to a fundamental change in the nature of American society: the transformation of the **Protestant work ethic** into the **social ethic.** Earlier generations of Americans had believed that work is service to God and respectability goes hand in hand with the accumulation of wealth through hard work, competition, and individual effort. In the 1950s, Whyte argued, a new ethic oriented to cooperation and managing others' work was emerging. This social ethic was ideally suited for life in a world of large, bureaucratically administered corporations.

The social ethic was based on three major premises: "A belief in the group as the source of creativity; a belief in 'belongingness' as the ultimate need of the individual; and a belief in the application of science [to human relations] to achieve the belongingness" (Whyte, 1956:7). Such beliefs encouraged loyalty and total commitment to the organization. A person's private life and innermost desires were considered secondary to smooth organizational functioning.

Whyte concluded his study with a plea for the accommodation of individualism within the corporate social ethic. He was not pining for a nostalgic return to the wide-open frontier of the nineteenth century or the rugged individualism of "robber barons" like John D. Rockefeller and Andrew Carnegie. Rather, he was urging corporate leaders to act more flexibly in the creation of job tasks and to pay more respect to the unique differences in individuals' skills and talents. In short, he was arguing that "the individual is more creative than the group" (p. 445), and that corporate policies should not obscure this fact by their unquestioning standardization and compartmentalization of behaviors.

The title of his study, *The Organization Man* (1956), reflected a corporate ideology which regarded man (literally; women were only peripherally involved in the corporate world) as existing as a unit of society: "Of himself, he is isolated, meaningless; only as he collaborates with others does he become worthwhile, for by sublimating himself in the group, he helps produce a whole that is greater than the sum of its parts" (pp. 7–8).

Organization Man Meets Organization Woman

Under the original auspices of Organization Man, gender was not an issue (Coates, 1997). However, it has become crucial to understanding contemporary corporate culture. The traditional image (one gaining resurgence now with employers) was that employees put in extra effort beyond the paid cycle. Organization Man was a workaholic; this, however, is not compatible with the other responsibilities in women's lives (see chapter 5). There is a need to make a distinction between women and men concerning their perceptions of their organizations and their roles within.

A study by Coates (1997) was designed to uncover the similarities between men and women in relation to those aspects of corporate culture that are prominent in the literature: training, commitment, and values. Coates surveyed 220 managers in the U.K.; 60 men and women from the original survey were interviewed about their experience of work. The study sought to uncover the motives and meanings individuals have in relation to work and organizations and whether women and men are interpreting the messages of corporate culture similarly. One important point is that while women represented one-third of overall managers in the study, they represented only 4.3 percent of executive positions compared to 9.9 percent of men. By far the largest single group overall was middle managers (47 percent), and even in this case only 35 percent of the women had attained this level. The vast majority (60 percent) of women were junior managers.

Corporate success for women in the study meant learning male-type behaviors and male emotional expression. According to one of Coates' interviewees, "It's like a man wearing a skirt to work and expecting to be taken seriously. I have to look like a woman and act like a man. I guess it's what schizophrenics must feel like" (p. 11).

Coates explains: "Organizations thus assert in subtle ways what employees feel and how they can express those feelings" (p. 11). Subtle sexual stereotyping defines who has control of the presentation of self and the images to which individuals must perform (Coates, 1994).

Interviewees were asked if they felt themselves to be "team players." Women interviewees overwhelmingly answered that they were. Women also expressed levels of commitment to their organization similar to those of male interviewees. If women were not committed, it was due to the bureaucratic management style of their organization. Many women interviewees indicated that they shared the values of their organization. However, this was not generally reflected in the particular position of women. While many women felt committed to their organization, they also felt their job did not give them self-respect/esteem within the organization. This was also true for status. Women continue to be marginalized from the organizational benefits that men apparently receive. Coates concludes:

> [I]n gender terms the data illustrated that women were as likely to be drawn under the umbrella of organizational ethos; that they were as likely and more so to feel committed to the organization. This in general supports the claim that the OM (Organization Man) analysis could not be applied to contemporary organizations as they now encompass women much more fully. Under CC [Corporate Culture] women express themselves in similar terms to men. This has not necessarily been the wholesale eradication of female attributes, but a meeting of paths, on women's part. For example, men now see the family as increasingly important in their career decisions, whereas women do so less. However, women now compare favorably with men in terms of commitment, loyalty and trust, and are, in some cases, better bets for long term future employees, as they are less likely to leave for other jobs or self-employment. They are also as likely to relocate to wherever the organization decides. This however, has encompassed a loss of femininity. (Coates, 1997:21–22)

Corporate culture has yet to figure out how to deal adequately with gender (women) in the organizational setting. Coates' analysis suggests that Organization Man has met Organization Woman; OW has adopted OM's masculine attributes and thus lost some degree of femininity; however, OW continues to be marginalized.

"The End of Employment as We Knew It"

The subheading above is the title of a chapter in Robert Reich's *The Future of Success: Working and Living in the New Economy* (2000/2002). Reich's premise is that:

> Organizations used to be recognizable: they were shaped like pyramids, with top executives, layers of middle-level managers and staff, and a

large number of people doing relatively simple and repetitive tasks at the bottom. . . . Now bureaucratic controls are no longer necessary for coordinating large numbers of people. People can coordinate themselves through the Internet. . . . In a few years, a "company" will be best defined by who has access to what data, and gets what portion of a particular stream of revenues, over what period of time. (p. 84)

Reich describes how the logic of the new economy—which is founded on quick innovations and on surges in demand—is changing the employment relationship. Fewer working people are "employees," as the term traditionally has been used, and this will continue into the future. Reich explains: "You won't be an utterly free agent selling your individual services in the open market to the highest bidder, nor will you be an 'organization' man or woman" (p. 89). But, "Even if you're *called* a full-time employee, you're becoming less of an employee of an organization than you are a seller of your services to particular customers and clients, under the organization's brand name" (p. 89).

Steady work (a predictable level of pay from year to year) has disappeared for all but a handful of working people—although as Reich notes, tenured professors who write about employment are among the rare holdouts! There is a new precariousness, as it is almost impossible for any organization to guarantee a consistent stream of income to its workers. Many organizations are dependent on "soft money," in that earnings vary with contracts, grants, or sales. "Much has been said about the rising tide of temporary workers, part-timers, freelancers, e-lancers, independent contractors, and free agents" (p. 98).

In the old economy, people got ahead by being well liked. The successful "organization man" was accepted by all. David Reisman's (1950) "other-directed" personality sought above all else to be approved of by his peers. According to Reich, in the new economy you get ahead not by being well liked but by being well marketed. "The goal is no longer to fit in or to gain the approval of one's peers. It's to stand out among one's peers, to dazzle and inspire potential customers, or people who will connect you to them" (p. 154). Personal worthiness is measured by one's net worth: "By making your personality into a marketable commodity and selling it successfully, you can increase your worth and thus gain worthiness in the divine eyes of the market" (Reich, 2000/2002:154).

The sale of the self makes relentless demands on one's life and encroaches on one's personal relationships, in that all relationships turn into potential business deals. Unlike Reisman's "other-directed" man who wished only to be liked, "the new market-directed man or woman wants only to make a deal. Yet when friends, relatives, and casual acquaintances become vehicles for selling oneself, all relationships can become tainted with ulterior motive" (p. 156). Reich's analysis is disquieting:

Reisman's other-directed person of mid-century America was in danger of losing his identity to the group. The market-directed person at the start of the new century is in danger of selling it. Which is the greater danger? Once, the worst thing that could be said of someone was that he had sold out. Now the worst thing that can be said is that he's not selling. (p. 157)

The necessity of selling one's self to the corporation was one of the most lamentable aspects of white-collar work for postwar sociologists, who decried the rise of the "personality market" in which people are required to sell themselves by marketing attractive images of themselves. **Alienation** from the products of one's labor was far less alarming than the alienation of the laborer from him or herself (Jurca, 1999). In today's image-conscious society, the demands of running a successful organization make what people do with their emotions a central issue for employer direction and control. Because of the shift from the industrial production of goods to the post-industrial production of services, for many, job success depends on one's ability to produce speech, action, and emotion that symbolize a willingness to "do for" the customer or client (Bulan, Erickson, and Wharton, 1997).

Although interactive work usually is characterized by formal affective requirements, it also can include the informal mastery of people skills that workers require of themselves and which may affect all work-related interactions, not just those involving customers or clients. For example, paralegals interviewed by Lively (2001) created a set of norms for professional behavior—appear competent, maintain a credible front—which they not only employed at work, but also in their presentation of themselves to the community. "Whether in or out of the firm, with coworkers, clients, or employers, these paralegals linked their ability to monitor and control any of their behaviors that might be construed as unprofessional or interfering with their ability to be, or appear, competent" (p. 355).

Bulan and colleagues (1997) conceptualize these formal and informal expectations as a set of *affective requirements* that potentially govern all workplace interactions. They use the term "affective" because they assume that workers must be able to manage their emotional self-presentations to support the emotional culture of the workplace and to fulfill the emotional expectations of other interactants. They distinguish this from Hochschild's (1983) concepts of emotional labor and feeling rules. "While emotional labor refers to the actual 'management of feeling' to create the appropriate facial and bodily display, 'affective requirements' refers to the *organizationally imposed rules* requiring such facial and bodily display" (p. 237). Recall the box on Disney earlier in the chapter.

Women in the New Economy

Although women have made progress in entering the world of executives, they continue to face difficulties in trying to pierce the seemingly impenetrable "glass ceiling"—the set of subtle barriers that seem to inhibit women and minorities from reaching the upper echelons of corporate America, government, and academia (Blau, Ferber, and Winkler, 2002). Women have increased their share of executive, administrative, and managerial positions from 4.6 percent of the female labor force employed in such jobs in 1972 to 14.2 percent in 2000, while the percentage of the male labor force in such positions increased from 13 percent in 1987 to 15 percent in 2000 (U.S. Department of Labor, 2001). By 1999, women held almost one-half (45.1 percent) of these positions (U.S. Census Bureau, 2000). However, there is an extremely low representation of women in the senior ranks of management. According to a report on Fortune 500 companies (Catalyst, 1999a), only 11.9 percent of all corporate officers and 5.1 percent of top-level executives were women in 1999. Women held just 3.3 percent of the top five most highly paid executive positions. Women also were very sparsely represented on corporate boards of directors in these firms, holding 11.2 percent of board seats, up from 8.3 percent in 1993 (Catalyst, 1999b).

The reality for most women is that they are not at the top of the bureaucratic workplace. In her classic *Men and Women of the Corporation* (1977), Rosabeth Kanter described what life is like at the bottom of the bureaucratic white-collar world by examining the secretary-boss relationship. A more recent study by Lynda Ames (1996) provides a good illustration of the symbolic interaction perspective on bureaucracy (see box).

The work experiences of secretaries reflect both gender domination and bureaucratic domination (Ames, 1996). Ames finds that the structures of domination are seen and resisted by the secretaries, yet taken for granted and consented to—even constructed—by them. The social realities that the more powerful members construct—in this case the professionals in the organization—are different from the realities perceived by the secretaries. Within their own subculture secretaries develop negotiating skills to reconcile their realities with those of the bosses and to accommodate to the rules and regulations of the organization, both formal and informal. Their autonomy, or ability to control the bureaucratic world in which they work, depends upon their ability to negotiate within an arena where the rules are set by those who have official power and authority.

Glenn and Feldberg (1989) called attention to the deskilling of clerical workers, where both the *variety* of skills required in a job and the skill *levels* required for the job are reduced. The combined effect of these aspects is to place further limits on the already quite limited levels of autonomy experienced by contemporary clerical workers. Kovacik's (2001) study of waitresses and clerical workers describes how some workers are able to experience a degree of autonomy through their "poetic resistance" to the confining gender scripts of pink-collar work. This type of work, with its depressed wages (tips excluded) and relatively low status, requires "performing some caricature of femininity on the job" (p. 22). The poetry written by these workers "resists such scripts by offering counter-performances, alternative rhetorics, in which secretaries and waitresses emphatically call attention to their presence as individuals and as members of a collective" (p. 23). For example, a secretary-poet imagines working-class women in control of the technology that currently controls them; a waitress-poet shows the disdain that servers often feel for customers:

"Women's Work" in a Bureaucracy

For women, two of the most salient features of the modern world of paid labor are bureaucratized workplaces and a sex-segregated labor market. Most women work in jobs predominantly held by women, most of which are near the bottom of hierarchical and compartmentalized organizations (Ames, 1996).

Jobs at the bottom of bureaucratic hierarchies give incumbents little or no power or **autonomy** over their work, nor much opportunity to move up in the organization or change the conditions of the work. As *women's* work, too, jobs are organizationally and culturally defined as relatively unskilled and are consequently demeaned in terms of both pay and respect. Women working in these female-dominated, low-level jobs experience the weight of bureaucratic power and the devaluation of their work on a daily basis.

Given the lack of power and autonomy and lack of reward in terms of respect and wages, it is not surprising that workers exhibit resistance to the demeaned character and to the demeaning treatment such work receives from other workers (Ames, 1996). Workers' day-to-day activities, in response to those conditions, may be both accommodating *and* contrary to those conditions.

As you may have guessed, we are talking about secretaries. Lynda Ames conducted a participant observation of secretaries in a large, public bureaucracy. For a year, she worked as one of seven secretaries in a regional office of a state department of social services. As a result, she was part of some of the situations and events she observed. Although subject to compartmentalization (workers separated by department, which may have the effect of isolating them), the women's day-to-day working habits resisted its negative effects. The women reduced the effects of status distinctions among themselves by sharing and helping arrangements that circumvented the formal organizational status hierarchy and compartmentalization. For example, secretaries shared their word-processing machine skills, allowing those who normally would not have received training to gain skills and leveling status differences among the women.

The relations between secretaries and professionals in the organization were not collegial. According to Ames, "These women working at the bottom of an organization clearly perceived *class* distinctions. The support staff went to a great deal of trouble to reduce the effects of individual status distinctions among themselves but were quite unwilling to ignore group distinctions between themselves and their bosses" (p. 49).

Although the activities Ames observed still exhibited much attention to the formal hierarchy, she describes them as being essentially nonbureaucratic, even antibureaucratic (p. 44). Ames describes such responses as "contrarieties" in that "the contrary character of their actions was clear in their attempt to determine *themselves* how to do their work rather than execute predefined tasks. Thus isolation was reduced and the support staff could operate with a somewhat greater degree of autonomy than bureaucratic structure normally allowed" (p. 45).

However, in the end, what mattered most was the power and authority of the bureaucracy. Although Ames concludes that there is no doubt that women at the bottom of organizational charts fight back, "ultimately there seems little chance that such attempts at resistance will topple any organization or revise the expectations of any bureaucracy. Secretaries, as women and as low-status workers, remain demeaned and discounted" (p. 57).

We write down on a pad
what it is they want,
but we don't let them see it.
They think we remember,
So we let them.
They watch what moves
under the black swing of skirt,
how the candles underlight
the faces that lean to clear
their plates. (Balliro, 1995)

The poet observes the patrons sexualizing the waitresses, romanticizing them as they do their job. But instead of feeling demeaned, the waitresses engage in subtle power plays of their own (Kovacik, 2001:30).

Autonomy and Job Satisfaction

The issue of autonomy in the workplace also is central to the lives of blue-collar workers, whose daily activities are likely to be as unchallenging and unrewarding as those of female white-collar workers. Many working-class males experience drudgery or heavy exertion (or both) in their work, compounded by the knowledge that they have little chance of improving their economic status (Rossides, 1997). Industrial plants in the United States are typically still organized in terms of ideas formulated in the early 1900s by Frederick Taylor. Work tasks are bureaucratized and structured to provide management with maximum control over workers' jobs. By the process of deskilling, as noted above, the skilled components of production jobs are replaced by tasks that require repetitive actions rather than talents developed on the job by experienced craftworkers. Workers, in general, are more satisfied with jobs that allow variety rather than repetition (Lambert, Hogan, and Barton, 2001). Unskilled blue-collar workers can exert very little control over their work, so it comes as no surprise that assembly-line work is associated with low levels of **job satisfaction**. Craftworkers, however, show the highest levels of job satisfaction and pride (Hodson, 1996).

The relationship between income and job satisfaction is not straightforward. According to some surveys, higher-income workers experience more job satisfaction (Ireland, 1999). However, a 1998 survey by *R & D* magazine found financial rewards ranked sixth in job satisfaction criteria, below factors such as the opportunity to solve challenging problems, work with the right people, do what you're good at, and work independently. For the second year in a row, "too much bureaucracy" was named the least satisfying aspect by respondents to the survey (Merrick, 1998).

Jobs lower down in the prestige pecking order require different kinds of extrinsic motivations in order to sustain worker interest. Research in the service sector has found that service-based employees who understand the standards for service in their organization and who feel that management supports these standards are more satisfied with their jobs (Susskind et al.,

2000). In service-based organizations employee feedback about job performance—sometimes immediately from the customer, or through weekly
meetings with team members and supervisors—leads to increased job satisfaction (Andrews and Kacmar, 2001). In a survey of bank and hospital workers, positive feelings about work were higher for both women and men when
they felt effective in their work with people, spent more time interacting with
employees, had greater control over work, and had higher levels of job
involvement. In addition, positive feelings about work were associated with
being older and having a higher income (Bulan et al., 1997).

Getting around Top-Down Control

Since the working conditions of unskilled workers are largely dictated by
management, they face the constant problem of trying to achieve some degree
of control over their own jobs without being reprimanded, laid off, or fired by
management. Workers develop strategies for protecting and maximizing their
dignity in the workplace, which Hodson (1996) describes as "attempts to
defend or regain dignity in the face of work organizations that violate workers' interests, limit their prerogatives, or otherwise undermine their autonomy" (p. 722). Studying workers' autonomous strategies for defending and
maximizing their dignity on the job poses some difficult challenges because
these "strategies are subtle and at times cloaked in duplicity" (p. 723).

The lower one's position in the organization, the more one's behavior is
channeled in the service of goals established by the decision-making activities
of higher management. Those whose positions are relatively less powerful
cannot bargain to influence agency outcomes in any substantial way. They
can, however, engage in what Brower and Abolafia (1997) call "politics from
below," defined as "actions or intentional inaction that defies, opposes, or
sidesteps the rules, roles, or routines of the organization. . . . It is not merely
an annoyance or anomaly; it is a frequent and purposeful everyday mode of
organizational activity" (p. 308). "Lower participants" invariably socially
construct "local rationalities" (Abolafia, 1996) from which they make sense
of their everyday routines and make decisions for resolving dilemmas.

For an organization to function efficiently and to reduce alienation in its
workers, participants must feel that they belong. One effective strategy of
connecting workers to work is for management to put forth the metaphor that
the organization is a family, "a primary group providing personal self-image,
community, and local culture" (Fine, 1996:113). The metaphor may be
claimed explicitly by the organization in a "self-serving or sincere attempt to
increase worker loyalty; on other occasions workers will make this point
themselves" (p. 113). A quote from an interview with a restaurant employee
illustrates Fine's point: "I like the closeness that you have in the kitchen. I
love people in kitchens. . . . It's like a family" (p. 113).

Given their opposite positions in the corporation's hierarchy of authority, it is not at all surprising that workers at the bottom and management
have different conceptions of the reality of the work situation. In fact, multi-

ple realities exist within an organizational setting. Donald Roy's (1959) classic study of machine operators found that the workers divided their workday with break times that they heavily invested with their own meanings. While management saw the workday as composed of distinct units of clock time marked by check-in, lunch, and checkout, the workers created intermediate periods which they referred to with such terms as coffee time, peach time, banana time, and fish time. Other planned interruptions were called window time and pickup time, and the staggered hours of two coworkers were called "quitting time for Sammy and Ike." The workers in Roy's study endowed these interruptions with a variety of meanings that made a boring day endurable and, at times, enjoyable for them. The breaks were events that stood out from the rest of the day and could be looked forward to as times when joking, socializing, and good-humored heckling might reaffirm the humanity and personal identity of the workers. In banana time, for example, Ike would "steal" a banana from Sammy's lunchbox every day, while crying out "Banana time!" In response, Sammy would appear to make a fuss. All the actors played their parts in this little scenario with such skill and verve that it became an event that all eagerly awaited. These created "times" had the effect of stimulating group interactions that "not only marked off the time . . . but gave it content and hurried it along" (p. 246).

The twenty-first-century version of "banana time" may lie in the Internet, which ". . . has supplied new dimensions to workplace recreation. It infuses opportunities for diversion into everyday work contexts—although the individuals with whom one enjoys banana time can be many miles distant" (Oravec, 2002). Although concern has been voiced about the potential for abuse, constructive use of online recreation may perhaps ultimately make workers more productive (see box).

Negotiating a More Satisfactory Order

Interactionists note that the relationship between management and labor is not fixed. In fact, it is always negotiated in practice. "The precise amount of time workers have off, their opportunities for conversation, their personal autonomy results from local situational conditions" (Fine, 1997:186). Organizational interaction is embedded within a complex set of structural and cultural relations (Fine, 1996). The structure of the organization is mediated by interactional relations and cultural images. Fine's analysis of restaurant kitchens suggests that the decisions and social organization in an organization (in his case, the kitchen) are channeled by the needs of actors to create pleasant and smooth workdays, and equally by the needs of the organizations to operate in a highly competitive market environment. The relations of power and authority that operate within organizations have real consequences if these relationships are breached; they do not stand apart from interaction systems. Both actors and external forces set constraints in which interaction is played out (Fine, 1996).

The symbolic interactionist perspective underlines the centrality of the interactional domain for accomplishing work. The workplace becomes a

Playing at Work

Workplace realities have changed in a tightening economy. For many employees, the social and recreational activities they need to function at their best have to be obtained during breaks and unoccupied moments in the workplace rather than after work. Online recreation helps to make long and demanding working hours more tolerable. According to Jo Ann Oravec, associate professor in the College of Business and Economics at the University of Wisconsin at Whitewater, allowing for reasonable amounts of online recreation can have considerable advantages, both for the individuals involved and the organization as a whole. Not only can it serve to open blocked creative channels, but is may provide stress relief as well.

Oravec points out that managers have often used organizationally sanctioned recreation as a perquisite—a bonus for acceptable conduct—and although softball and bowling leagues, picnics and celebrations may be viewed in cynical terms, these can help provide "part of the glue that holds the at-work community together" (p. 62). As employees telecommute or put in long and irregular hours, the adhesive that binds organizations has been increasingly conveyed through electronic channels. "Whether organization-approved fantasy football, discussion group and collaborative filtering forums, joke-of-the-day contests, or other recreations are ultimately successful will depend on how they fit into everyday working experiences" (p. 62).

Although the importance of recreation and play is widely recognized for children, it is only slowly being understood in adult terms. Author and musician Pat Kane has proposed that a "play ethic" be fostered, which accommodates the adult requirement for play (see www.theplayethic.com). Oravec suggests that a "work/play ethic" is more appropriate, "fostering a balance between effort that is immediately productive and other forms of human expression" (p. 63).

And it probably does make for more contented workers. According to Normal Behar, president and CEO of Xylo, a market research firm for businesses which surveyed workers on Internet usage in the workplace, it's just an electronic extension of flexible work policies to meet employees' general needs. Behar continues:

> When companies allow employees to spend a few moments online each day to handle personal issues, such as making dinner reservations, planning a trip or selecting a last-minute gift, these employees are able to better balance the demands of their work and home lives. . . . When employees feel their employers are supportive of a balanced work and home life, they tend to become more productive, loyal, and committed to their company. (quoted in Rabbit, 2000)

Forms of online diversion are already becoming an integral part of everyday workplace life. With effort on everyone's part—managers become more flexible and employees learn self-discipline and skills of balancing work and play—constructive use of recreation can help the entire organization work harder and play harder. Solitaire anyone?

staging area in which meanings are generated, often through talk, which have effects on relationships and on patterns of action. According to Fine, "Talk and action come to constitute the workplace" (p. 222). The way that an organization has been structured, with its set of occupations, the way that an organization connects with clients and suppliers, and the way that an occupation organizes itself in its domain of expertise affects the specific behaviors and cultures in the workplace (p. 111). Fine continues:

> The effects of organization on interaction patterns are equally real . . . interaction patterns are altered by forces over which individual actors have little control. For instance, the pace of work, which generates patterns of interaction, is constrained by forces derived from management or externally imposed: the availability of resources provided by management (material and personnel), the work assignments . . . and the customer flow. (p. 222–23)

Fine's point is that in restaurants, as in other organizational environments, interaction is not an autonomous realm but is contingent on structural forces.

Conclusion

The emergence of large-scale bureaucratic organizations can be linked to the process of urbanization, industrialization, and the development of capitalism and technology. Factories and corporations were organized to ensure maximum managerial control over workers' activities. Bureaucracies also were organized to control government functions. Now bureaucracy is shaping a wide variety of everyday behaviors. Contacts between intimates and strangers are mediated by the intervention of third-party agencies such as insurance companies, government bureaus, and the courts.

Scholars, beginning with Max Weber, have used various approaches in thinking about bureaucracy. Interactionists view organizations as created, maintained, and changed through the daily interactions of their members, using the process of negotiated order. Complex organizations therefore include multiple realities which people experience in varying ways depending on their positions in the organization's hierarchy of authority. Informal subcultures define the organization in terms of human behaviors rather than rules and regulations.

In the world of work, people's locations in the hierarchy—executives, secretaries, and blue-collar workers, for example—shape their conceptions of the job and the organization. Workers with little autonomy in their jobs strive to achieve some degree of control over their work lives through collective arrangements with their peers in similar situations.

In the following chapter we will explore another sphere of life—that of health and illness—where people often find themselves dealing with bureaucratic rules and regulations concerning eligibility for treatment, as well as encountering medical personnel in settings having bureaucratic features. Let us, then, turn to this issue.

Definitions

Alienation　Marx's term for the sense of being cut off from one's labor. People create the world through their labors but then become constrained by the very things they have created.

Autonomy　The ability to control one's own daily activities. Autonomy is particularly sought in the workplace.

Blue-collar occupations　Work in which people use their hands as well as their minds to make a product or supply a service.

Bureaucracy　A principle of organization utilizing a hierarchical structure of authority, the clear specification of work tasks, and an elaborate system of rules and regulations. The goal of a bureaucratic organization is to maximize efficiency.

Control from the top down　A system of authority that is characteristic of bureaucracies. The orders are issued by upper management, and those lower down in the hierarchy of authority are expected to comply without resistance.

Deskilling　The process by which the skilled components of production jobs are replaced by tasks requiring little skill or talent.

Division of labor　The assignment of different functions as tasks in the workplace to accomplish a group goal.

Emotional Labor　Hochschild's (1983) term for effort required of workers to produce, suppress, or alter their feelings to evoke the appropriate emotion.

Hierarchy of authority　The chain of command in an organization which specifies who can issue orders to whom.

Informal subcultures　The unique ways of doing things developed by members of various subgroups in an organization. These subcultures, which often have no formal structure, form an *informal organization* that sets the norms for behaviors within the formal organization.

Job satisfaction　The extent to which people find their work enjoyable and meaningful.

Mass society　A large-scale society in which the status distinctions between various groups have been blurred.

Meritocracy　A principle of organizational functioning that would allocate rewards on the basis of the quality of a person's performance. Hiring and promotion are supposed to be done solely on the basis of personal merit or ability.

Negotiated order　The process by which members construct organizations. Negotiation by individuals also is the process by which social order is constructed.

New middle class　A social category composed of corporate managers, salaried white-collar professionals, salespeople, and office workers.

Organizational society　An urban-industrial society characterized by the presence of large-scale bureaucratic organizations.

Proletariat　The working class. Karl Marx applied the term to industrial workers who were prevented from owning the means of production, that is, the factories where they worked.

Protestant work ethic　The notion that the ultimate value and meaning of life are to be found in hard work and industrious labor. Work is regarded as service to God and a mark of respectability.

Rationalization   The systematic and logical application of formal rules and procedures to every aspect of modern life. According to Max Weber, bureaucracy exemplifies this principle.

Scientific management   An effort to organize work, particularly in the factory, in terms of the principles of scientific efficiency. The idea was developed by Frederick Taylor to promote task specialization and control of workers' activities by management.

Service occupations   Work in which people perform various services for others rather than producing a product.

Social ethic   The notion that the ultimate value and meaning in life are to be found in one's acceptance by others.

White-collar occupations   Work that is primarily mental in character. White-collar workers provide the support services needed for industrial production.

DISCUSSION QUESTIONS

1. Have you ever had a dispute concerning a bill with a bureaucratic organization—a credit union, hospital, or department store, for example? What kinds of frustrations, if any, did you experience in trying to rectify the situation?

2. How have your experiences in college supported the notion of the university as a bureaucratic organization? What strategies have you developed to "get around" the official bureaucratic rules? Which ones have been the most successful?

3. Fifty years ago your grandmother probably would never have imagined suing her neighbor because she fell on ice in front of the neighbor's house. Nowadays such actions are commonplace. What kinds of situations do you think might be brought into the courts in the future as bases for suing another person?

4. Think of an incident in which you had an argument or disagreement with a stranger. Is there anything about that incident that led you to think about going to court to settle the issue? What does such an incident reveal about everyday life in a bureaucratic society?

5. In the past workers formed labor unions as a collective response to the alienating conditions in bureaucratic factory settings. Do you think white-collar workers will form organizations to make their jobs more meaningful in the face of increasing bureaucratization? What kinds of organizations would these be?

6. If you have ever worked in a bureaucratic setting—an office or factory, for example—describe how your place in the organization's hierarchy influenced your view of how the organization functioned. How do you think your boss and colleagues viewed the organization?

7. Numerous critics have noted how bureaucracies make individuals "faceless" by reducing them to particles in a mass of particles. This allows individuals to blend into the mass and not have to take personal responsibility for their actions. What might be the political consequences of this process?

REFERENCES

Abolafia, M. 1996. "Hyper-rational gaming." *Journal of Contemporary Ethnography* 25:226–50.

Adams, S. 1998. *The Joy of Work: Dilbert's Guide to Finding Happiness at the Expense of Your Co-workers*. New York: HarperCollins.

Ames, L. 1996. "Contrarieties at work: Women's resistance to bureaucracy." *NWSA Journal* 8(2):37–59.

Andrews, M., and K. Kacmar. 2001. "Confirmation and extension of the sources of feedback scale in service-based organizations." *The Journal of Business Communication* 38(2):206–26.

Balliro, L. 1995. "French Restaurant, 1982." In *For a Living*, edited by P. Oresick and N. Coles. Champaign-Urbana: University of Illinois Press.

Barber, B. 1996. *Jihad vs. McWorld: How Globalism and Tribalism are Reshaping the World*. New York: Ballantine Books.

Bellah, R., R. Madsen, W. Sullivan, A. Swidler, and S. Tipton. 1996. *Habits of the Heart: Individualism and Commitment in American Life*. Berkeley and Los Angeles: University of California Press.

Blau, F., M. Ferber, and A. Winkler. 2002. *The Economics of Women, Men, and Work*. 4th ed. Upper Saddle River, NJ: Prentice Hall.

Boggs, C. 2000. *The End of Politics: Corporate Power and the Decline of the Public Sphere*. New York: The Guilford Press.

Brower, R., and M. Abolafia. 1997. "Bureaucratic politics: The view from below." *Journal of Public Administration Research and Theory* 7(2):305–31.

Bryman, A. 1995. *Disney and His Worlds*. London: Routledge.

———. 1999. "The Disneyization of society." *Sociological Review* 47(1):25–47.

Bulan, H., R. Erickson, and A. Wharton. 1997. "Doing for others on the job: The affective requirements of service work, gender, and emotional well-being." *Social Problems* 44(2):235–56.

Catalyst. 1999a. *Fact Sheet: 1999. Catalyst Census of Women Corporate Officers and Top Earners*.

———. 1999b. *Catalyst Census of Women Board Directors of the Fortune 1000*.

Coates, G. 1994. "Performance appraisal as icon: Oscar-winning performance or dressing to impress?" *International Journal of Human Resource Management* 5(1):167–92.

———. 1997. "Organization man: Women and organizational culture." *Sociological Research Online* 2(3):1–31. <http://www.socresonline.org.uk/socresonline/2/3/7.html>

Collins, G. 1996. "A Big Mac strategy at porterhouse prices." *New York Times*, August 13:D1.

Connellan, T. 1996. *Inside the Magic Kingdom: Seven Keys to Disney's Success*. Austin, TX: Bard.

Dery, D. 1998. " 'Papereality' and learning in bureaucratic organizations." *Administration & Society* 29(6):677–89.

Dunn, D. 1997. *Workplace/Women's Place*. Los Angeles: Roxbury.

Edgley, C., and D. Brissett. 1999. *A Nation of Meddlers*. Boulder, CO: Westview Press.

Eisman, R. 1993. "Disney magic." *Incentive* (September):45–56.

Feldman, D. 2000. "The Dilbert syndrome. How employee cynicism about ineffective management is changing the nature of careers in organizations." *American Behavioral Scientist* 43(8):1286–1300.

Fine, G. 1996. *Kitchens: The Culture of Restaurant Work*. Berkeley: University of California Press.

———. 1997. *Talking Sociology*. 4th ed. Boston: Allyn & Bacon.

France, V. 1991. *Window on Main Street*. Nashua, NH: Laughter Publications.

Frederickson, H. 2000. "Can bureaucracy be beautiful?" *Public Administration Review* 60(1):47–53.

Glenn, E., and R. Feldberg. 1989. "Clerical work: The female occupation." In *Women: A Feminist Perspective,* edited by J. Freeman. Mountain View, CA: Mayfield.

Hochschild, A. 1983. *The Managed Heart.* Berkeley: University of California Press.

Hodson, R. 1996. "Dignity in the workplace under participative management: Alienation and freedom revisited." *American Sociological Review* 61(October):719–38.

International Labour Office. 1997. "Industrial relations, democracy and social stability, 1997–98." *World Labour Report.* Geneva: ILO.

Ireland, B. 1999. "Working for the fun of it." *The New York Times,* July 18:BU9.

Jurca, C. 1999. "The sanctimonious suburbanite: Sloan Wilson's *The Man in the Gray Flannel Suit." American Literary History* 11(1):82–106.

Kanter, R. 1977. *Men and Women of the Corporation.* New York: Harper & Row.

Kovacik, K. 2001. "Between L=A=N=G=U=A=G=E and lyric: The poetry of pink-collar resistance." *NWSA Journal* 13(1):22–39.

Klagge, J. 1997. "Approaches to the iron cage: Reconstructing the bars of Weber's metaphor." *Administration & Society* 29(1):63–77.

Lambert, E., N. Hogan, and S. Barton. 2001. "The impact of job satisfaction on turnover intent: A test of a structural measurement using a national sample of workers." *The Social Science Journal* 38(2):233–50.

Laslett, P. 1971. *The World We Have Lost.* New York: Charles Scribner's Sons.

Lively, K. 2001. "Occupational claims to professionalism: The case of paralegals." *Symbolic Interaction* 24(3):343–66.

McAdam, D. 1989. "The biographical consequences of activism." *American Sociological Review* 54(October): 744–60.

Meisenheimer, J. III. 1998. "The services industry in the 'good' versus 'bad' jobs debate." *Monthly Labor Review* (February):22–47.

Merrick, A. 1998. "Companies keep employees happy by targeting their personal needs." *R & D* 40(10):S3–6.

Mills, C. W. 1956. *White Collar.* New York: Oxford University Press.

Oravec, J. 2002. "Constructive approaches to Internet recreation in the workplace." *Communications of the ACM* 45(1):60–3.

Presthus, R. 1978. *The Organizational Society.* New York: St. Martin's Press.

Project on Disney. 1995. *Inside the Mouse: Work and Play at Disney World.* Durham, NC: Duke University Press.

Rabbit, T. 2000. "Surf and be happy: Web access at work makes workers feel more productive, less stressed, says survey." *Network World* (September 25): pNA.

Reich, R. 2000/2002. *The Future of Success.* New York: Vintage Books.

Reisman, D. 1950. *The Lonely Crowd.* New Haven: Yale University Press.

Ritzer, G. 1998. *The McDonaldization Thesis.* London: Sage.

———. 2000. *The McDonaldization of Society.* Thousand Oaks, CA: Pine Forge Press.

Rossides, D. 1997. *Social Stratification.* 2nd ed. Upper Saddle River, NJ: Prentice Hall.

Roy, D. [1959]1982. "Banana time: Job satisfaction and informal interaction." In *The Sociological Outlook,* edited by R. Luhman. Belmont, CA: Wadsworth. Originally published in *Human Organization* 18 (Winter 1959–60): 158–64.

Strauss, A. 1978. *Negotiations.* San Francisco: Jossey-Bass.

———. 1993. *Continual Permutations of Action.* New York: De Gruyter.

Susskind, A., C. Borchgrevink, K. Kacmar, and R. Brymer. 2000. "Customer service employees' behavioral intentions and attitudes: An examination of construct validity and a path model." *International Journal of Hospitality Management* 19:53–77.

Troy, L. 2001. "Twilight for organized labor." *Journal of Labor Research* 22(2):245–59.

U.S. Census Bureau. *Statistical Abstract of the United States: 2000.* Table 669. "Employed civilians by occupation, sex, race, and Hispanic origin: 1983 and 1999."

U.S. Department of Labor, Bureau of Labor Statistics. 2001. *Current Population Survey.* "Employed persons by occupation, race, and sex." Table 10, p. 177.

Weber, M. [1922]1946. "Bureaucracy." In *From Max Weber: Essays in Sociology,* edited by H. Gerth and C. W. Mills. New York: Oxford University Press. Originally published in 1922.

Weick, K. 1976. "Educational organizations as loosely coupled systems." *Administrative Science Quarterly* 21(March): 1–19.

Whyte, W. H. 1956. *The Organization Man.* New York: Simon & Schuster (Doubleday Anchor).

Woloch, N. 1994. *Women and the American Experience.* New York: McGraw-Hill.

Zibart, E. 1997. *The Unofficial Disney Companion.* New York: Macmillan.

HEALTH AND ILLNESS

It would be impossible to reflect on contemporary America without being continually reminded of our concern with and preoccupation about matters pertaining to "health." You woke up early this morning to be sure you had enough time for a run before class (need those endorphins!). In today's mail you received a special offer on a one-year membership at the local health club, and this month's *Shape* or *Men's Health* has the latest "expert advice" on how many minutes of aerobic activity are needed for optimal cardiovascular functioning.

You've agreed to try a new French restaurant tonight, and probably the first thing you'll do on perusing the menu is to engage in a mental calculation of saturated fat grams and cholesterol contained in the various food items. Having figured out the "costs" and "benefits" to your health of the various choices, you've now settled in to enjoy dinner. Maybe you've splurged a little on a hard-to-resist dessert, and so perhaps an after-dinner walk is in order, maybe over to the nearby mall to look over the recent best-sellers.

In the mall, bookstores feature sections with headings like "Health, Fitness, and Diet." You encounter dozens of books on the latest low-fat diets. Perhaps you'll try the fruit only or the pasta only diets. Maybe the Atkins diet is what you've really been looking for but just didn't know it. That will surely get those pounds off, the ones which have grown so "attached," so to speak, to your body. On the other hand, that book about turning fat into muscle looks appealing as well. Maybe the solution is "fitness walking," or Pilates, or yoga—sure enough there are books to instruct you on that.

Of course, the extent to which people engage in such behaviors is something that will vary by age, gender, and social class. We would expect that middle-aged, middle-class Americans would be the most likely to exhibit such concerns, although the research on eating disorders presents alarming and disturbing statistics on how our cultural obsession with beauty and thinness seriously disadvantages young women (see Hesse-Biber, 1996). The Protestant ethic so powerfully enunciated by Max Weber many years ago may find its new focus in the body as something to be worked at with the same kind of discipline and diligence formerly reserved for one's job. The body is molded and shaped with the concerned attention one used to pay to the product one was manufacturing. In short, the body and its healthful functioning have become a project for huge numbers of Americans.

In the broadest sense we want to argue in this chapter that the term *health,* like any other concept created by human beings, is fundamentally *symbolic* in character; that is to say, it has no inherent or intrinsic *meaning.* Whatever meanings it has derive from those conferred on it by people acting in concert, through communication with other human beings. Recalling the central propositions of symbolic interaction discussed earlier, we must seriously consider that (1) the term *health,* like any other symbol, submits to a multiplicity of meanings; (2) those meanings attached to health emerge out of our interactions with others; (3) the meanings of health are likely to be modified and reinterpreted, depending upon the definitions of the situations in which we act; and (4) the meanings of health will vary *cross-culturally.*

In the sections to follow we will briefly explore how health can be seen as a **cultural construction**. After discussing such issues we will then focus on what happens when patients bring a health problem to a doctor. We will conclude the chapter with a discussion of how patients make sense of and learn to live with a very pervasive contemporary problem—clinical depression.

Health as a Cultural Construction

From a purely commonsensical point of view, health seems to be a pretty clear-cut issue; either you are sick or you aren't. Sickness, we tend to think, is a category comprised of physically based phenomena. When the body exhibits certain *symptoms,* we "know" that we are ill or that we ought to see a doctor for a diagnosis. Once we begin to see health and illness, however, as terms whose meanings vary across different societies, we can begin to appreciate how the interpretive process involves socially based judgments about the human body and its functioning.

In a classic article written more than fifty years ago, the medical historian Erwin H. Ackerknecht (1947) eloquently argued against the view that disease was a strictly physical phenomenon by noting the important role that social factors play in the definition and treatment of what is considered a disease. According to Ackerknecht, "Medicine's practical goal is not primarily a biological one, but that of *social adjustment* in a given society . . . even the notion of disease depends rather on the *decisions of society* than on objective facts" (1947:142–43; italics added). As the following examples illustrate, societies differ dramatically in their response to the *same* bodily, physical symptoms:

Pinto (dyschromic spirochetosis), a skin disease, is so common among many South American tribes that the few *healthy* men that *are not* suffering from pinto are regarded as *pathological* to the point of being excluded from marriage. . . . Intestinal worms among the African Thongas are not at all regarded as pathological. They are thought to be necessary for digestion. (Ackerknecht, 1947:143; italics added)

Not only is the definition of what constitutes an illness or pathological condition subject to cultural variations, but in an even more far-reaching sense one's *experience* of bodily symptoms is shaped by social processes and expectations as well. In one of the earliest social science treatments of this issue, Mark Zborowski (1953) illustrated how responses to pain for hospitalized males in a Veterans Administration Hospital varied by the respondent's ethnicity. Jewish-American patients, for example, evidenced a great deal of philosophical concern and anxiety about their condition while displaying a pessimistic orientation toward the future course of their illness. White, Protestant patients tended to respond optimistically toward their prospects for recovery while viewing doctors as experts to whom one went when needing "mending," much like bringing a car to an auto mechanic for repairs. Italian-American respondents, by contrast, were very interested in getting the pain stopped immediately; unlike the Jewish respondents, Italian Americans had little concern about the larger "meanings" of the pain. Although Zborowski's work has been criticized for its limited sample, broad and overly stereotypic generalizations about ethnic groups, and the fact that subjects were studied only in a medical setting, it pointed the way to understanding cultural variations in the expression and possibly also the experience of pain (Freund and McGuire, 1999).

Pain researchers are increasingly exploring the effects of demographic and cultural factors on pain. The *biopsychosocial* model of pain maintains that the experience of pain is sculpted by interactions among biological, psychological, and social factors. To date, pain researchers have mainly focused on documenting racial and ethnic differences in pain (c.f., Edwards, Fillingim, and Keefe, 2001), as well as gender differences (see box).

Another illustration of cultural differences in the health arena can be seen in the different effects of *collectivism* and *individualism* on patient-physician interaction. Individualists tend to be more concerned about the consequences of their own behavior and their own needs, interests, and goals, whereas collectivists tend to focus on the impact their behavior has on others and are more willing to sacrifice personal interests in order to save face and maintain harmony (Young and Storm Klingle, 1996). Although people in every culture have both collectivist and individualist tendencies, there is an emphasis on individualism in the West (particularly the U.S.) and collectivism in the East. Collectivist societies are more likely to practice holistic medicine (e.g., traditional Chinese medicine), whereas individualistic societies tend to use a **biomedical model**. The individualistic-collectivistic distinction, including the distinction between focus on the self versus the other, has implications for

The Influence of Social Processes and Expectations on the Experience of Pain—Gender Matters

Pain is a multidimensional experience involving biological, psychological, and social processes. Pain is unique as a medical phenomenon because its measurement relies on individuals' accounts of what they are feeling as well as doctors' observations of pain-related behavior. Pain generally involves more than simply a physical sensation, because it is imbued with meaning. Pain expression—how a person shows and behaviorally responds to pain—is clearly influenced by sociocultural factors. The ability to control the social presentation of pain even under conditions that inflict a great deal of pain may be interpreted as a sign of one's moral status. The expression "big boys don't cry," for example, reveals a U.S. cultural expectation that males should repress the expression of pain (Freund and McGuire, 1999).

Are there differences in the prevalence of specific common pain conditions for men and women? If differences exist, what might be the reasons for them? Most of the epidemiologic data on sex differences in chronic pain are in the form of prevalence differences. Women report more temporary and persistent pains, more severe pain, more frequent pain, and pain of longer duration than do men (Unruh, 1996). The most common chronic pain conditions in women include migraine headaches; oral facial pain, including TMD; musculoskeletal pain; abdominal pain; and a variety of pelvic pains, including endometrial pain, menstrual pain, postpartum pain, and pelvic floor disorders (Meisler et al., 1999).

What is it about being female or male that can influence these differences in prevalence? Perhaps there are anatomic or physiologic or genetic differences between women and men that affect transmission of pain signals. Or, differences may exist in the ways men and women perceive pain, or in the ways people think about pain. That is, perhaps there are differences in people's emotional experiences in relation to pain and how they cope with it. For example, willingness to report pain is an important issue, one that is probably influenced by differential socialization of women and men. A number of authors have suggested various social learning influences on sex differences in pain behavior. Koutanji, Pearce, and Oakley (1998) posit that social roles for women are more supportive of pain expression and pain awareness, making them more cognizant of their own and others' pain. Klonoff, Landrine, and Brown (1993) found that males were less likely to disclose pain to others and associated feelings of embarrassment with having to admit pain.

Generalizations about different groups' responses to pain must be used cautiously and not become the basis of stereotyping. Although we may have typical ways of expressing ourselves, social situational factors can affect how we will express ourselves. *Expressing* pain is not the same as *feeling* pain; for example, acting stoic does not mean that one feels no pain. Even if people from various social categories (social classes, gender, or cultures) do present pain differently, social and cultural factors also influence how observers interpret their pain expressions (Freund and McGuire, 1999).

beliefs about health and illness, expectations for the health care provider-patient relationship, and health communication preferences (Armstrong and Swartzman, 2001). Specifically, the Asian value on harmonious relationships results in an indirect, nonassertive communication style (Kim and Wilson, 1994). This value suggests that Asian Americans would have a difficult time asserting themselves with physicians and that this might cause them to shy away from patient participation and collaborative medical decision-making. For example, in a study in Hawaii of Mainland-American and Asian-American patients (Young and Storm Klingle, 1996), Asian-American patients perceived themselves as participating less in the medical interview than did patients from Mainland-American culture, possibly due to cultural differences in beliefs about the appropriateness of patient participation. This has important implications in that patient participation increases patient commitment to medical decisions and patient satisfaction, and decreases misunderstandings and unrealistic expectations associated with prescribed treatments.

> Thus, patients who participate are more likely to choose treatments that they are able to follow. Throughout the decision-making process, patients have a chance to clarify information and weigh the advantages against the disadvantages. At the end of this process, the patient should have picked the "best" option. . . . (Young and Storm Klingle, 1996: 34)

As we have seen, cultural definitions and expectations play a crucial role in what comes to be seen as sickness and how that sickness will be experienced. In contemporary America, access to health care is perhaps the most critical determinant of how sickness and health are experienced. Let us turn to this issue.

Health Care Access

Who Goes to the Doctor?

Access to health care is important for prevention and for prompt treatment of illness and injuries. Use of preventive health services helps reduce morbidity and mortality from disease. While use of some preventive services has been increasing, disparities continue in use of preventive health care by race and ethnicity and by family income. For example: between 1990 and 1999 the percent of mothers receiving prenatal care in the first trimester of pregnancy increased from 78 to 83 percent, with the largest increases occurring for racial and ethnic groups with the lowest levels of use; between 1987 and 1998 the percentage of women 40 years of age and over with mammography screening in the previous two-year period more than doubled, from 29 to 67 percent, with the gap between poor and nonpoor women narrowing (National Center for Health Statistics, 2001).

Coverage by health insurance, either private or public (e.g., Medicare or Medicaid), is a key indicator of access to medical care. According to data from the 2001 National Health Interview Survey (NHIS), 39.9 million Americans (14.2 percent) were without health insurance in 2001, down from 15.4 percent in 1997 (National Center for Health Statistics, 2002). Especially among men, Hispanics and blacks are less likely to have health insurance than non-Hispanic whites. Health insurance is highly correlated with income, however, and the difference in insurance coverage between white and black men can be explained almost entirely by differences in income (Council of Economic Advisors, 1998). Those most likely to be uninsured are single men, people between ages 18 and 24, Hispanic Americans, immigrants, and full-time workers whose incomes still fall below the poverty line (Pear, 2000).

Having a usual source of health care, having a recent health care contact, use of the emergency department, and treatment of health problems such as dental caries also vary according to income. As you can see in the following examples, income clearly has an impact on access to health care. In 1999:

- Sixteen percent of children 6–7 years of age had no health care visits to an office or clinic within the past year, with poor children nearly twice as likely as nonpoor children to have had no visit (23 versus 12 percent).

- Poor and near-poor children were less likely to have a recent dental visit than those with family incomes at least twice the poverty level (58 and 62 percent versus 80 percent).

- Fifteen percent of school-age children and 17 percent of adults age 18 and over had an emergency department visit within the last 12 months. Having two or more visits was three times as common among poor adults as among those with family incomes at least twice the poverty level (12 versus 4 percent) (National Center for Health Statistics, 2001).

The U.S. health care system has changed from a *fee-for-service* system, where doctors set the fee and patients pay only for what is done on each visit, to one dominated by **health maintenance organizations** (HMOs) and other forms of **managed care**. As physician fees and the costs of hospital stays escalated, many people with private health insurance could no longer afford the premiums. Employers began to cut back on what they could offer. The combination of high costs and shrinking coverage created a "health care crisis" that was met in part by the emergence of HMOs and other managed care. Enrollment in HMOs, the dominant form of managed care, increased from 9 million in 1980 to almost 77 million in 1998 (National Center for Health Statistics, 2000). The majority of insured workers are in some form of managed care; however, not all workers are insured. Sizable numbers of working-class and middle-class people possess insurance that is inadequate for handling major medical problems. We can see, then, that the decision to present an illness to a doctor is the result of an interpretive process taking place within the **structural constraints** of the distribution of available medical services.

Minorities and Health Care

How individuals experience the health care system differs according to social factors. Given what we have learned about the gender-, race-, and class-based organization of society, it should come as no surprise that these play a significant role in health and health care.

Members of minority groups—e.g., African Americans, Hispanics, gays, lesbians, bisexuals, HIV-infected individuals, and the mentally ill—experience difficulties in accessing adequate medical care. Individuals who belong to more than one of these groups may experience difficulties exponentially greater than those faced by members of only one group (Wainberg, 1999). Health care providers are not immune to labeling, preconceptions, fears, and beliefs that may interfere with provision of adequate health care. Cultural barriers may make it difficult for doctors to gain patients' cooperation or to understand patients' beliefs or wishes.

A review of more than 100 studies by the Institute of Medicine found that racial minorities in the United States receive worse health care than whites, even when the minorities had the same income and health insurance as whites. Racial stereotyping by doctors under increasing time pressure to see as many patients as possible may contribute to the inferior treatment of minorities, according to the report. Some minorities have a mistrust of doctors that can worsen the problem. Among the study's findings:

- Whites are nearly four times more likely than blacks to receive coronary bypass surgery when they need it.
- Nearly twice as many black prostate cancer patients as whites received no treatment for the disease.
- Black and Hispanic patients with HIV or AIDS were 24 percent less likely than whites to receive protease inhibitors.
- Among people who sought care in an urban emergency room, blacks were more likely to be denied authorization by managed-care providers.

Among the solutions suggested are cultural education programs for doctors, increased awareness of bias, better education for patients, and more federal money for the civil rights office of the U.S. Department of Health and Human Services. In addition, there is a need for more minority doctors. There has been little progress made in opening the medical field to blacks and Hispanics since 1968, when 3.5 percent of physicians in the U.S. were minorities. Now, 3.9 percent of doctors are minorities (Pelton, 2002).

Gays, lesbians, and bisexuals may receive inadequate care because of homophobia. The HIV/AIDS epidemic in particular reflects the issues of access and allocation of health care. Fear of contagion may hinder the care of HIV-positive individuals (see box). Unfortunately, already stigmatized minorities are affected to the greatest extent by HIV.

HIV Discrimination Continues

Gay & Lesbian Advocates & Defenders (GLAD) strongly criticized a May 22, 2001 decision by the United States Court of Appeals in Boston which ruled that a Leominster, Massachusetts, obstetrician did not violate disability antidiscrimination laws when he refused to continue care in 1995 for a pregnant woman after she tested HIV-positive. The doctor claimed that he did not feel comfortable treating an HIV-positive pregnant woman. Despite the evidence presented by both GLAD and the Massachusetts Department of Public Health that there was no medical justification for termination of care simply on the basis of HIV-positive status, the Court of Appeals ruled in the doctor's favor, refusing to second-guess his ultimate decision to terminate the patient's care.

GLAD brought the case in order to overcome the courts' traditional reluctance in these types of scenarios to determine whether a doctor's medical justification is in actuality driven by discrimination—that is, in "situations where doctors don't want to deal with HIV, but cloak their refusal to provide services in language which makes it look like they are just making a medical judgement in the best interests of the patient."

The good news is that the physician stated he would not make the same decision today that he made in 1995. Despite the court's decision, the case had the effect of educating health care providers about HIV, many of whom believed in 1995 that HIV simply did not exist in their communities.

Source: http://www.biresource.org/news/GLAD05_23_01.html (accessed 3/14/02).

Gender and Health Care

According to a report released by the National Women's Law Center, the Oregon Health & Science University, and the University of Pennsylvania School of Medicine entitled *Making the Grade on Women's Health: A National and State Report Card* (2001), women are second-class citizens when it comes to health care in America. More than one in eight women lack health insurance; for those with insurance coverage, it is often inadequate to meet women's needs. Because women are often excluded from medical research, doctors know less about how to recognize and treat diseases among women. There are substantial disparities in women's health care by state and by race, ethnicity, socioeconomic status, and other factors (National Women's Law Center, 2001).

There were improvements compared to the previous year, such as increased efforts to screen for life-threatening illnesses such as cervical and colorectal cancer. There was little progress in reducing the number of uninsured women, however. Only five states and the District of Columbia improved Medicaid coverage for pregnant women. Only four states improved Medicaid coverage for single parents. "Poverty, unhealthy lifestyles, poor mental health, violence, lack of education, and low income continue to interfere with women's ability to achieve good health in every part of the country" (National Women's Law Center, 2001).

The *Report Card* includes a special chapter on cardiovascular health, an issue that has long been ignored in women. The report finds that heart disease is the leading killer of women in the United States. Research on diseases such as cardiovascular disease (CVD) based on a male model led to the assumption that CVD was a "men's problem." However, in 1998 over 500,000 women died of the disease—60,000 more than the number of men. When women's experience with CVD was studied, a number of differences between women and men were revealed. Not only are women *more* likely than men to have CVD risk factors such as high blood pressure, suffer a severely damaging heart attack, delay seeking care after the onset of heart attack symptoms, and suffer a second heart attack within six years, but women are *less* likely to receive preventive counseling from physicians on CVD risk factors, have their heart attack symptoms recognized by a health care provider, and be enrolled in rehabilitation programs after a heart attack or receive a referral for such services from their physician (National Women's Law Center, 2001).

There are significant gaps not only in health research relating to conditions that primarily affect women, but also regarding racial, ethnic, and socioeconomic disparities in disease prevalence and treatment. We know now, for example, that African-American women are disproportionately at risk of dying from heart disease.

The 2001 *Report Card* gives the nation an overall grade of "Unsatisfactory." Although there was improvement, in that only Louisiana received a failing grade compared to eight states and the District of Columbia the previous year, not a single state received a grade of "Satisfactory" in the 2001 *Report Card*.

When Doctors and Patients Meet

Interaction between physicians and patients does not always follow a preset course in which all parties work together under the same set of mutual understandings. There is potential for misunderstanding, uncertainty, even noncompliance. Various social factors affect doctor-patient interaction.

Presenting an Illness

The patient presents an **illness** to the doctor, a lived experience of discomfort, disease, or response to pain. That lived, subjective experience is transformed by the doctor using a biomedical explanatory model into a less ambiguous, more controllable entity called a **disease**, which is amenable to medical monitoring. Illness, then, is a *social construction*. That is, it does not exist in the world as an objective condition; rather, it exists *because we have defined it as existing* (Weitz, 2001).

In presenting an illness experience to a doctor, what does a typical patient desire from the doctor? Such a question calls our attention to the importance of the ongoing interpretive process that all human beings engage in as we continually assess and reassess our life experiences.

What Patients Want and Get

According to participants in one study in which subjects were asked to describe their "ideal doctor," 60 percent mentioned the doctor's personality, with the majority saying that doctors should be easy to talk to, friendly, and sympathetic (Finlay and Jones, 1998). Participants in another study described a bad doctor as "someone who treats patients as if they were on a 'production line,' who 'doesn't spend time with you,' who hurries and does not listen to the patient's concerns or questions" (Lupton, 1996:160).

Patient satisfaction is recognized by many health care providers as a legitimate measure of health care quality. The major determinants of patient satisfaction are the physician's interest in patient **psychosocial concerns** and the quality of communication between physician and patient. Patients' conceptions of the types of clinician behavior that lead to trust and communication include terms like "listening," "friendly," "respectful," "nonjudgmental," "eye contact," "reassuring" (Mechanic and Meyer, 2000). Many of the behaviors referred to are skills that can be taught. Despite the fact that contemporary health researchers increasingly advocate a patient-centered, holistic approach encompassing the patient's lifeworld and subjective experiences as essential aspects of medical practice, this is not the focus of most medical school training. According to one group of authors:

> Through classroom, laboratory, and ward experiences students quickly learn that "real" medicine applies a biomedical model to physically based diseases while ignoring the extraneous psychosocial "wrapping" in which the diseased body presents itself. (Baker, Yoels, and Clair, 1996:174)

By the time U.S. medical students have graduated and completed residencies, they will have been exposed to almost seven years of socialization that powerfully communicates to them that "listening to patients' stories may be a nice thing to do, but is really an 'extra,' to be indulged in only after the real work of medicine is accomplished" (Baker et al., 1996:178).

Despite some physicians' reluctance to delve into such areas, patients want these matters discussed and are more satisfied with the care received when they are (Schauffler, Rodriguez, and Milstein, 1996). High levels of socioemotional behavior of physicians increase patient self-disclosure, trust, satisfaction, and likelihood of recommending the physician (Roberts and Aruguete, 1999). Patients who trust their providers are more likely to cooperate in treatment in ways that facilitate outcomes (Kao et al., 1998; Mechanic, 1998). Patients who are more dissatisfied with physicians' socioemotional behavior are more likely to change physicians (Gandhi et al., 1997; Kaplan et al., 1996).

Part of the reluctance of physicians to engage in "patient-centered" visits, particularly visits in which psychosocial concerns are addressed, is the perception that these visits are more time consuming than biomedical exchanges and more likely to overwhelm a tight schedule. However, in a study examining physicians' communication patterns, this was not found to be the case (Roter et al., 1997). In fact, psychosocial visits averaged only a few minutes longer (22.9 minutes) than the narrowly biomedical visits (20.5 minutes). Patients gave the highest satisfaction ratings to visits marked by a psychosocial pattern of communication, particularly regarding a sense of partnership and support. However, the frequency of these visits was quite low (less than 10 percent). The narrowly biomedical pattern was associated with the lowest levels of both patient and physician satisfaction; 66 percent of these visits were characterized as physician-dominated and narrowly focused on biomedical concerns (Roter et al., 1997).

We should note that visits in the Roter study are longer than those in many managed care organizations, where face-to-face time is reduced to 10 to 12 minutes. Managed care is having a tremendous impact on patient-physician relationships. Modern managed care is:

> more than ever before characterized by contractual relationships specifying services . . . to which an enrollee is entitled. . . . Thus, as with the purchase of other commodities and services, managed care may be characterized by the old buyer-beware approach used in the general marketplace rather than by the more trusting, respectful relationship of the doctor and patient in the past. (Kronenfeld, 2001:301)

Patients are aware of physicians' new roles and responsibilities, as well as restrictions imposed by HMOs and other managed care organizations. In this environment, patients experience a loss of individualized and personalized care, partly due to restrictions on whom a patient can see and how the patient must move through the health care delivery system, resulting in a barrage of criticism. Americans give choice high priority and are not accustomed to some of the restrictions on access and choice of specialists. In response, managed care organizations are placing growing importance on both physician and patient satisfaction studies (Kronenfeld, 2001).

Although a great deal of the discussion of the importance of patient satisfaction deals with its importance for private sector managed care, it also has relevance for assessing the delivery of care in systems for low-income individuals. Although a variety of public and private programs provide care for low-income individuals, little is known about patient satisfaction (see box).

Managed care plans cannot afford to ignore physician satisfaction—it affects both quality of care and patient satisfaction. Under managed care, physicians' clinical autonomy may be compromised, as they often must obtain approval before beginning care, prescribe only authorized drugs, or follow specified treatment plans for given ailments. In addition, managed care has pressed physicians to abandon entrepreneurial solo practices and their own fee-for-service schedules and to accept working in ever-larger group practices and receiving payment via capitation, salary, or third parties' fee schedules. Another impact of managed care is that physicians have considerably less control over their patient pool, as patients enter and leave practices based on their employers' contracts with managed care firms. All of these have the potential to contribute to physician dissatisfaction. However, participation in managed care does not have to lead to physician dissatisfaction (c.f., Schultz et al., 1997). A study by Warren, Weitz, and Kulis (1998) found that "whereas physicians 20 years ago may have been horrified at the prospect of managed care, physicians now accept it as the rules of the game . . . and recognize that the price of refusing to play by those rules is bankruptcy" (p. 364). It is not clear from this study, however, whether

---

Patient Satisfaction and Income: Insurance Matters

The University of Kentucky Survey Research Center conducted a statewide telephone survey to examine patient satisfaction across a variety of health insurance programs (Mainous, Griffith, and Love, 1999). The sample consisted of three groups: (1) individuals with private insurance; (2) individuals with Medicaid, public insurance for the low-income and underserved; and (3) individuals served by a charity program for uninsured indigents (below 100 percent of Federal Poverty income, ineligible for Medicaid). In general, private insurance individuals were more educated, had higher incomes, better health status, and were less likely to be minority. The low-income groups are relatively similar except that Medicaid recipients are more likely to be female and younger.

Satisfaction was measured by the patient's assessment of their most recent outpatient visit in the past 12 months, and included questions about satisfaction with the personal manner of the person seen, length of time spent waiting at the office, time spent with the person seen, explanation of what was done.

Those with private insurance were significantly more satisfied than individuals in the low-income programs. There was no difference in satisfaction among the low-income individuals, regardless of health financing program. The authors conclude that these results seem to indicate the importance of patient socioeconomic status in patient satisfaction with care. That is, regardless of insurance, the lower the patient's income, the less satisfied the patient is with the care they received. This suggests the possibility of a system of care where private insurance patients receive one type of care and low-income individuals receive another.

Although the study did not assess the interaction between patient and physician except through the patient's perspective, the authors suggest that a possible explanation for the difference in patient satisfaction may stem from differences in physician attitudes toward their patients and their problems. Personal interactions have been shown to be particularly important in patient satisfaction. Particularly significant is the respect shown by the physician to the patient in this interaction. Individuals in the low-income groups in this study had significantly lower ratings than their private insurance counterparts on the item assessing satisfaction with the personal manner (courtesy, respect, sensitivity, friendliness) of the caregiver they saw.

changes in patient/physician relationships have had much effect on physician satisfaction because physicians have learned to manage such patients
without spending much time or giving up clinical autonomy or because physicians have concluded that educated patients are easier to work with and
have better outcomes.

Alternative Medicine

A countertrend, perhaps, to the rise of managed care is alternative medicine, which involves use of a wide variety of folk practices to promote health
and potentially cure diseases. Alternative interventions include acupuncture,
use of traditional herbs as medicine, massage, meditation, and so on. Alternative medicine is attractive because it is "relatively inexpensive, incorpo-
rates a high degree of choice, involves accessible practitioners of lower status
than physicians, and produces few negative side effects" (Vandenburgh,
2001:287). Although measurable health outcomes from alternative medicine
are not always established, patients often choose it because it provides a
degree of control they feel they lack with conventional health care.

Interest in alternative therapies has grown rapidly in the United States
among those with chronic or acute illnesses as well as healthy people interested in avoiding illness. Millions of people use alternative healers. The most
widely cited data on use of alternative therapies comes from two national,
random surveys conducted in 1990 and again in 1997 (Eisenberg et al.,
1998). This research looked at use of 16 alternative therapies, including chi-
ropractic, acupuncture, megavitamins, "folk" remedies, and biofeedback.
According to these surveys, 42 percent of American adults used some form of
alternative care in 1997, compared with 34 percent in 1990. Respondents
made more visits in 1997 to alternative health care providers than to general
and family practitioners combined.

Women are more likely than men to use alternative therapies, especially
those who are upper-income, middle-aged, college-educated, not African-
American, and suffering from chronic health problems (Astin, 1998; Eisenberg
et al., 1998; Fairfield et al., 1998; Krauss et al., 1998). Alternative therapies are
generally used to complement rather than replace traditional medicine. Many
HMOs have begun to include coverage for alternative practices.

Some authors argue that the rise of alternative healing reflects dissatisfaction with the mismatch between doctors' concerns and patients' concerns
(Schneirov and Geczik, 1996). That is, doctors typically are concerned with
diagnosis and treatment, whereas patients are primarily concerned with the
impact of illness on their lives (Mechanic, 1995). Patients can be left feeling
like depersonalized objects, dissatisfied with the care they receive. Schneirov
and Geczik argue that alternative healing offers patients the opportunity to
work as collaborators with health care providers. Their research indicated
that alternative health care users shared several beliefs, including the belief
that modern medicine focuses too much on surgery and medication to treat
symptoms rather than lifestyle changes to prevent illness. They conclude:

The alternative health movement may be seen as part of a larger wave of discontent with the bureaucratic-administrative state, its reliance on expert systems, and the way it coordinates people's health care practices "behind their backs"—without their knowledge and participation. (1996:642)

The Internet as a Source of Health Care Information

The Internet is another factor with the potential to affect interaction between patients and health care providers. Goldsmith (2000) suggests that use of the Internet to obtain health information "will enable patients to begin their dialogue with physicians at a much higher level and provide them with leverage to influence the health care process" (p. 151). Traditionally, physicians have been the purveyors and integrators of health care information. Increased access to this information via the Internet means that the doctor is no longer necessarily the "distributor, interpreter, and filter of information in the health care setting," resulting in a "shifting paradigm of practitioners as information provider to information broker" (Bischoff and Kelley, 1999:42).

Surveys of online health care consumers have found that the majority (57 percent) think it is somewhat likely that the Internet will help reduce or eliminate frustrations associated with visits to their doctors, the most widely noted frustration being "forgetting to ask all my questions when I'm with my doctor" (Pastore, 2001a).

Although the Internet provides vast amounts of information to guide people in their health care decision-making processes, one cannot ignore the fact that there is a great division in American society between those who use and have access to the Internet and those who do not (Cotten, 2001). Income is the strongest predictor of online access, and there is a racial gap in Internet access (U.S. Department of Commerce, 1999). The utility of the Internet to improve medical care remains poorly characterized, especially for those living in economically depressed urban areas (Robinson et al., 1999). There is evidence to suggest that individuals who have preventable health problems and lack health insurance coverage are less likely to have access to and use Internet-related technologies (Eng et al., 1998). Inequitable distribution of Internet technology may widen social disparities already existent in health care and health outcomes (Mandl, Kohane, and Brandt, 1998).

On the positive side, the Internet may be a potential alternative health care resource. Some research suggests that individuals who use the Internet frequently are more likely than infrequent users to take action that affects their diagnosis and treatment. For example, the information that patients find online results in asking physicians more questions and in greater detail (Pastore, 2001b). Most physicians now go online on a daily basis, although privacy concerns have kept physicians from exploring many clinical uses of the Internet. More than half (55 percent) of practicing physicians use e-mail to communicate with professional colleagues; 34 percent use e-mail to communicate with their support staff. However, only 13 percent communicate with patients via e-mail (Pastore, 2001c).

The Internet has become a significant source of health information for teens and young adults. A survey by the Kaiser Family Foundation found that 68 percent have used the Internet to search for health information, and a significant proportion (39 percent) said they have changed their own behavior because of information they found on the Web. What is surprising is that the study found that the percentage of young adults who have searched for health information is higher than the percentage playing games online, downloading music, chatting, shopping, or checking sports scores (*CyberAtlas* Staff, 2001)!

Online support programs may lead to reduced economic costs associated with particular health problems. Moreover, access to support groups through the Internet, particularly for individuals who are physically challenged or who are not mobile, may be key to decreasing loneliness, anxiety, and depression (Cotten, 2001).

The Health Care Crisis

We have seen that the rise of managed care has raised concerns about the quality of health care now available in the United States. A more serious problem is that the increased cost of health care and the resulting decrease in access to it challenges the very basis of the U.S. health care system. Given the growing rate of both uninsured and underinsured people in this country, it is not hard to envision access to health care services becoming one of the major political issues of the coming decade.

The final issue we want to discuss in this section concerns the phenomenon of illness and the self.

Illness and the Self

When someone gets ill, not only are finances, mobility, and independence lost, but also the familiar sense of self (Frank, 2000). "The self is disrupted; the community through which one knows oneself disappears" (Richardson, 2000:333). What Frank refers to as the "illness story" begins when life suffers a *disruption* (Becker, 1997) that renders its previous "point" either forgotten or no longer viable. Not only are one's plans disrupted but also the basis of the interactionist notion of the self—a self grounded in the need for others' recognition. The ill and disabled are typically denied this recognition. Frank uses Ritzer's (2000) notion of "McDonaldization" to show how medicine alienates one from one's self, "because commodified medicine incarnates a person as a blip on a monitor, numbers on a chart, specimens in a tube, computerized printouts, research data, money" (Richardson, 2000:334).

When Americans enter typical U.S. hospitals, for example, they are usually required to don a standardized hospital gown of some sort; there is little space in their room for placing large numbers of personal mementos. They will often encounter medical specialists of various kinds for the first time while in the hospital—doctors with whom they have had no prior contact.

Various kinds of hospital **identity markers** such as wristbands are usually worn and one begins to be treated by others—doctors, nurses, and other patients—as a "patient." The hospital and its routines are organized in such a way as to continually remind the patient that one's identity as a *body in need of repair* is far more salient than one's personal life history and subjective experiences. The ultimate effect of such processes is to make the person feel less like an "individual" and more like a member of an undifferentiated aggregate called *patients*. It appears, then, that being ill in an American hospital is to be in a place where one's sense of oneself as a unique person is sadly diminished.

This is a reflection of the shift in American medicine that occurred during the twentieth century, from "the more intimate setting of the hearth and bedside to the more impersonal, bureaucratic world of clinics, large-scale hospitals, and health maintenance organizations" (Baker et al., 1996:191). What was an "often home-based, person-centered, emotionally laden form of practice" became transformed into "a technical, procedurally driven activity; an activity in which only such procedures (not time spent talking to patients) are paid for by health care insurers" (p.192).

The typically brief actual doctor-patient encounter launches the patient toward experiencing herself or himself as simply a body. According to one author, an essential feature of contemporary medical practice is "the dislocation of the case from the patient's bedside and indeed from the patient's physical presence" (Atkinson, 1995:149). Patients resent doctors who do not treat them as "real people" with feelings. Patients want to be viewed as individuals rather than "part of a mass of anonymous patients" (Lupton, 1996:161).

Interestingly, humor can play a central role in allowing both doctors and patients "to navigate the ambiguous boundaries of *body and self* intrinsic to medical encounters, while simultaneously maintaining the traditional doctor/patient status order" (Baker et al., 1997:181). That is, "When examining patients, doctors may subtly invoke their power to cross at will from the physical into the social by joking with patients while raising possibly intrusive questions about personal lifestyle matters such as smoking, drinking, and sexual practices" (pp. 181–82). Patients, by responding in a "nervously humorous" manner to such medically legitimate intrusions by doctors, "tacitly acknowledge physicians' control over the agenda, while also distancing and protecting the self 'in' the body" (p. 182). Such probing, however, also puts physicians in the role of **moral entrepreneurs** who are "custodians and enforcers of mainstream societal moralities" (Baker et al., 1996:192). Patients (especially lower-income minority patients) may experience the "powerful medical gaze of high-status professionals as morally judgmental as well as therapeutically curative" (p. 193).

We need much more research on what patients are experiencing and the meanings they are constructing in response to the different encounters taking place in the broader medical setting. In the last decades of the twentieth century, medicine has undergone extensive scientific and technological rationalization. According to one prominent medical sociologist:

Nevertheless, the treatment of disease remains substantially a humanistic endeavor that must take account of the fact that the ills of patients are in important ways a product of the larger environment, the socio-cultural context, and the ways people live their lives. Medical care has deep significance for those who are sick and their loved ones and it is inevitably tied to the values and meanings that shape their actions and associations. (Mechanic, 2002)

The ultimate question, of course, is how such experiences play out in terms of patient health outcomes and the quality of medical care.

Having examined a broad range of issues pertaining to the diagnosis of an illness, we now want to focus on how people deal with a very pervasive current life problem—clinical depression.

The Social Construction of Illness Identities*

As we have argued throughout this book, we are constantly in the business of **negotiating social reality**. While negotiating the reality of social life is, therefore, an inevitable and generic human task, some statuses and social conditions create an unusual degree of uncertainty or ambiguity and thereby require more intensive efforts at sense-making. In fact, according to one of your authors, "Social reality is a very messy thing" (Karp, 1996:20). Ambiguous situations are especially useful for analysis because they illustrate in high relief how people cope with situations demanding particularly extensive interpretive work. Depression is a particularly good example, not only because of the large number of people who are affected by it, but also because it provides a case study for considering how individuals arrive at illness definitions and then reconstruct their identities accordingly.

To study how people deal with such conditions, David Karp interviewed 50 people "officially" diagnosed as depressed. In his book, *Speaking of Sadness* (1996), people describe how their lives, feelings, attitudes, and perspectives have been influenced by depression. This approach differs from much of the research on depression (and there is a lot of it), which generally focuses on causation and treatment, presented from the vantage point of "experts." Although these studies are valuable, what is missing is the point of view of the people experiencing it. In Karp's words, "Research about a feeling disorder that does not get at people's feelings seems, to put it kindly, incomplete" (p. 12).

Karp found it remarkable how candidly most of those interviewed spoke about their experiences, which provided a depth of insight not generally attainable through clinical studies. In particular, the acquisition of an identity as a "depressed person" is "often the product of a long journey aimed at discovering the kind of self one is" (Karp, 1996:48). Given that depression is a health problem that dominates lives and often seems fundamentally intracta-

*This section borrows from David Karp (1996) *Speaking of Sadness: Depression, Disconnection, and the Meanings of Illness*. New York: Oxford University Press.

ble, how, we might ask, do depressed individuals create explanations, understandings, agreements, and common **illness ideologies** in order to impose some order onto such a hazy and ill-understood life condition?

Depressed individuals face a number of interpretive tasks as they endeavor to make sense of their situation. They go through a process of defining what is wrong with them and attaching a label to their experience; that is, a process of **achieving a diagnosis**. Once a label has been attached to moods and behaviors, everyone seeks to understand the causes of their condition. Efforts to appreciate whether depression is explained by biology (nature) or environment (nurture) are an ongoing puzzle.

The experiences of Karp's respondents suggest regularities in the depression experience. A depression consciousness arises in an extraordinarily patterned way, making it possible to analyze the depression experience as a "career" sequence characterized by distinctive identity transformations, or "turning points" in identity. That is, each juncture in the career requires a redefinition of self. Although there was considerable variation in the timing of events, all the respondents in Karp's study described a process of moving through particular identity turning points in their view of themselves and their problem with depression:

1. a period of *inchoate feelings* during which they lacked the vocabulary to label their experience of depression;

2. a phase during which they conclude that *something is really wrong with me*;

3. a *crisis stage* that thrusts them into a world of therapeutic experts; and

4. a stage of *coming to grips with an illness identity* during which they theorize about the cause(s) of their difficulty and evaluate the prospects for getting beyond depression (Karp, 1996: 57).

The Career Path of Depression

All of Karp's respondents described a period of time during which they had no vocabulary for naming their problem, sometimes going back to ages as young as three or four. Respondents typically went for long periods of time feeling different, uncomfortable, marginal, ill-at-ease, scared, and in pain without labeling this as depression. In the words of one respondent:

> Well, I knew I was different from other children. I should say that from a very early age it felt like I had this darkness about me. Sort of shadow of myself. And I always had the sense that it wasn't going to go away so easily. And it was like my battle. And so, from a very early age I felt, okay, "There's something going on here, [but] don't ask me for a word [for it]." It hurts me. I feel sad. (Karp, p. 57)

Even when ill feelings did not emerge until later in life, individuals initially chalked up their difficulty to immediate life circumstances—a failed relationship, job problems, etc.—and believed that as soon as the situation changed their discomfort would disappear. However, when circumstances change and mood problems persist, the explanation for what is wrong must be redefined. A major cognitive shift occurs when people come to see that the problem may be internal, not situational. That is, something is wrong with *them*. The rejection of situational theories for bad feelings is a critical identity turning point. Full acceptance that one has a damaged self requires acknowledgement that "I am not the same as I was, as I used to be" (Karp, 1996:62). So the second phase of the illness career involved the recognition that they possessed a self that was working badly in every situation.

At some point everyone interviewed experienced a crisis of some sort, in particular, hospitalization. At this point they could not prevent their situation from becoming public knowledge. And whether they were hospitalized or not, everyone reached a point where they had to rely on psychiatric experts. Once an individual received an "official" diagnosis of depression and consequent treatment with medication, the need to redefine their past, present, and future in illness terms was greatly accelerated.

Achieving a Diagnosis

At the point of crisis, people fully enter a therapeutic world of hospitals, mental health experts, and medications, and for many, this occurs simultaneously with first receiving the "official" diagnosis of depression. Official diagnoses and labeling are critically important in the illness career. Knowing that you "have" something that doctors regard as a specific illness imposes definitional boundaries onto an array of behaviors and feelings that previously had no name. Being diagnosed suggests the possibility that the condition can be treated. As one respondent describes:

> It [getting a diagnosis] was a great relief. I said, "You mean there is something wrong with me. It's not some sort of weird complex mental thing." I was like tying myself up in knots trying to figure out what strange mechanism in my mind was producing unhappiness from this set of circumstances. . . . It's like, "No, you're sick!" (sigh) There was an enormous relief. (Karp, 1996:66)

Achieving a diagnosis is a critical stage in helping people to identify and interpret the meaning of their experiences. The good news associated with achieving a diagnosis is that one finally has a name and category to attach to a whole history of troubles, and thereby a partial explanation for those troubles. The bad news, however, is that the diagnosis puts one into the devalued category of those with a "mental illness." The **interpretive dilemma** for individuals is to highlight the positive features of the diagnosis while avoiding those that are potentially stigmatizing or personally unacceptable. The response of one of Karp's respondents to being asked if she thought of herself as having a disease reflects the ambivalence and confusion heard in the answers of many others:

> I think of it less as an illness and more something that society defines. That's part of it, but then, it *is* physical. Doesn't that make it an illness?

> That's a question I ask myself a lot. Depression is a special case because everyone gets depressed. . . . I think that I define it as not an illness. It's a condition. When I hear the term illness I think of sickness . . . [but] the term mental illness seems to me to be very negative, maybe because I connect it with hospitalization. . . . I connect it with how people define people who have been hospitalized. . . . It's something that I can deal with. It's something that I can live with. I don't have to define it as a problem. But the thing about mental illness is that it lasts. . . . Once a diagnosis always a diagnosis. (Karp, 1996:53)

However, having a diagnosis still leaves unanswered the ultimate causes(s) of one's problem. Achieving a diagnosis, in other words, is the starting point for further interpretive work about causation and personal responsibility.

Anyone who has taken a basic course in sociology or psychology learns about the **nature/nurture debate**. For most people the debate remains at an abstract level, removed from the stuff of daily life. For those suffering from depression, however, efforts to appreciate whether their condition is explained by biology or environment is an ongoing puzzle. Although a few respondents were willing to define their condition as a mental illness, most wanted simultaneously to embrace the definition of their problem as biochemical in nature while rejecting the notion that they suffer from a "mental" illness.

> If you say illness, that means there's something wrong with you . . . especially a psychiatric label. That means I'm defective. If you told me I was diabetic I wouldn't think of it as bad. (Karp, 1996:73)

Adopting the view that one has a biochemically sick self constitutes a comfortable *account* for a history of difficulties and failures and absolves one of responsibility. The interpretive dilemma for Karp's respondents was to navigate between rhetorics of biochemical determinism and a sense of personal efficacy.

> There was a sense of relief when I started finding out that the medication was helpful, because then I could say it was a chemical problem and that I'm not looney tunes and that, you know, it's not a mental illness which sounds real bad to me. . . . So, in a sense it was very comforting to be able to use the word chemical imbalance as opposed to mental illness. (Karp, 1996:73)

Because all of the individuals included in Karp's study had at some point been diagnosed and treated for depression by doctors, there is a built-in bias in the sample toward acceptance of a medical definition of depression's cause and the proper response to it.

Looking for Dr. Right

As several cultural observers (c.f., Edgley and Brissett, 1999) have noted, the behaviors of people in today's society are dominated by "experts." Experts advise us on virtually every aspect of our lives; they follow us through the life course. They are there when we are born and follow us each step along the way, eventually to our graves. Many have come to feel reliant on experts to tell them how to maintain their health, how to become educated, and how to raise their children. Most critical to the present discussion, however, is the fact that medical experts now tell us when our bodies and our "selves" need repair and the proper procedures for doing it. The medical profession has played a key role in the rise of what might be termed a **therapeutic culture** (Rieff, 1966; Polsky, 1991) with its focus on finding a "cure" for whatever ails you. In fact, the term *therapeutic* suggests a life focused on the need for cure (Bellah et al., 1996). Medical control over more and more areas of life is legitimated, typically by asserting and establishing the primacy of a medical interpretation of that area. This process has been referred to as **medicalization** (see Conrad and Schneider, 1992). According to some critics, especially of psychiatry, the medical model is used to support an essentially political reality. These writers point out that the term *healthy,* as used in the medical model, can be replaced by the word conforming, and that in societies where it predominates, the medical model is often used in lieu of the law or religious sanctions to legislate behavior. According to Peter Berger and Thomas Luckmann (1967), teachers, judges, physicians, and other health professions constitute a coalition of **universe maintenance specialists** who set norms defining proper and improper behavior, deviant and conforming behavior, sick and healthy behavior. Speaking specifically about the social-control role of psychotherapy, Berger and Luckmann write the following:

> Therapy entails the application of conceptual machinery to ensure the actual or potential deviants stay within the institutionalized definitions of reality. . . . Since therapy must concern itself with deviation from the "official" definition of reality, it must develop a conceptual machinery to account for such deviations and to maintain the realities thus challenged. This requires a body of knowledge that includes a theory of deviance, a diagnostic apparatus, and a conceptual system for the "cure of souls." (1967:112)

Those who have long histories as patients are uncertain about the proper role of psychiatrists in defining reality and the adequacy of their conceptual knowledge for curing the soul. On the one hand, these individuals see psychiatrists as the professional experts who hold out the possibility of helping them. However, for every person who talks of having found a warm, sensitive, and sensible psychiatrist, there are those who tell psychiatric horror stories involving, as they see it, insensitivity and incompetence. Karp was surprised at the virulence of the animosity expressed toward psychiatrists by those he interviewed. Although many of those interviewed eventually found psychiatrists whom they trusted and from whom they benefited, early in their treatment individuals saw psychiatrists as "oppressively evangelistic 'true believers' in biochemical causes of depression," a view that they did not at that time hold (Karp, 1996:89). This negative evaluation can be seen in the frequency and regularity with which respondents angrily labeled their doctors "pill pushers." As one respondent put it:

> This particular doctor was such an asshole. He sounded like a used car salesman for antidepressants. He was just like so gung-ho. "Oh yeah, you're the typical depressed [person], here's the drug that will cure you. Let me know if you go home and just want to kill yourself or something. We'll try something different for you." And I hated him. I just really hated him. (Karp, 1996:89–90)

Karp surmises that perhaps the relationship between extremely depressed, vulnerable patients and powerful psychiatrists intrinsically generates friction, discomfort, and anger. Because the gap between the expectations that patients bring to psychiatric professionals and what their doctors can actually deliver may be great, disillusionment may be inevitable. That is, perhaps patients and doctors have very different versions of therapy's "reality." Where patients want warmth, understanding, even love, they encounter detached professionals who often do not even inquire about their feelings, only their symptoms. This mutual misunderstanding can be heard in the way that patients talk about searching for the "right" doctor:

> It is really hard with depression. It's like you've got to get to the right doctor who's going to understand it. (Karp, 1996:117)

> The woman who became my analyst completely misunderstood the problems. She kept criticizing me. I mean, it turns out that [it] was just wrong. She wasn't right for me anyway. (p. 117)

> I was seeing one therapist for awhile, and that didn't work out, and I started seeing another one. . . . I think he's the best doctor I've ever had. He just knows what the hell I'm talking about. He's empathetic but he's not, you know, coddling. (p. 117)

Repetition of the theme of finding the therapist who is "right for you" reminded Karp of stories about soured romances. The respondents' accounts parallel comments often heard in everyday conversation about falling in and out of love. People's relations with a series of therapists might be seen as similar to a pattern of "serial monogamy": finding someone you believe is right for you, becoming dependent on that person for meeting certain needs, making a commitment, eventually realizing that you may have made the wrong choice, leaving the relationship, and searching once more for the person who is *really* right for you.

While some people seem to have found the right psychiatrist for themselves, the more typical pattern appears to be one of disillusionment about the efficacy of psychiatry. And if some are disillusioned with psychiatrists, others are downright angry. Predictably, the most profound expressions of anger toward psychiatrists Karp heard were reserved for those who exercised complete control over respondents in hospitals when they had little choice about their treatment. For example:

> I remember I saw this doctor who looked like a frog. I hated him. No, he looked like a pig. I didn't like his personality and he kept asking me ques-

tions about sex and stuff. It made me uncomfortable and I just didn't like him as a person. He was a shrink. And then comes that whole power thing. Psychiatrists and mental health workers, but particularly psychiatrists, have the power to decide when you are going to leave, if you are going to leave, if you can go out on a pass, when you can go out on a pass, if you're good, if you're not good, that sort of thing. (p. 120)*

This guy was just a supercilious, superior, arrogant prick. . . . I had the feeling that he was just looking down on me as a semi-vegetable, and did me absolutely no good at all. (p. 120)

The doctor I had [in the hospital] was an idiot. (p. 120)

In the end, the biggest disappointment for patients may be the eventual realization that doctors can't easily fix them. Despite the magic of Prozac (see box) and other drugs that are part of the new generation of antidepressants that certainly help those with depression to feel measurably better, a "cure" remains elusive. Among the 50 people in Karp's study there were a *few* who said that as a result of medical treatment (primarily drug treatment), their depression had vanished. For the others, depression comes and goes, with medication only modestly alleviating problems (or doing nothing at all). "Belief that this treatment, this new therapist, this new form of therapy, or this drug that you haven't tried yet might be the thing to finally cure you generates for many a frustrating cycle of high hope followed by varying degrees of disillusionment" (p. 123).

Despite physicians' best efforts, most of the patients with whom Karp talked came to realize that their therapists will not clear away their confusion about depression. "In a more fundamentally existential way, many conclude that their depression is likely never to be fixed once and for all" (p. 123). As one respondent so eloquently put it:

I have a feeling of unpredictability and lack of control over something that has a life of its own [and] that contradicts my feeling of mastery. And I know that now. I've had this experience for so long that I'm going to be up and that I'm going to be down and I suppose it makes it a little bit easier. (p. 124)

Recognition that the pain of depression is unlikely to disappear eventually provokes a redefinition of its meaning, of its place in one's life. As we have seen over and over again in this text, human beings confer meaning onto *everything* in their worlds. In the case of depression, the meaning of its pain can be refashioned. Most of Karp's respondents were not stumped when he asked, "Is there anything *good* about having depression?" Several felt that they had a deeper and more accurate picture of human nature and social life than happy people, even expressing disdain toward family and friends whose happiness they saw as built on a distortion of what the world is "really" like.

*A film that illustrates this well is *Girl, Interrupted*, from Susanna Kaysen's book of the same title, based on her experiences in a mental institution.

Prozac and the Self

Since its introduction in 1987, more than 35 million people worldwide have taken the antidepressant Prozac. Almost as soon as it hit the market, it was hailed as a miracle drug. By 1990 Prozac had become the top-selling antidepressant in the world; it continues to bring in around $3 billion in annual revenues (Zuckoff, 2000). In Peter Kramer's influential book, *Listening to Prozac* (first published in 1993), he puts forth the view that Prozac transforms the self. Perhaps most controversial was the claim (based on patients' experiences) that the new selves created were the "real" selves. The so-called "Prozac debates" have frequently been cast in terms of a search for the foundations of the "modern self," and whether these are located in chemical or in socio-psychological phenomena (Lyon, 1996). Kramer describes his patients as feeling "better than well" on Prozac, reporting noticeable improvement in their popularity, business sense, self-image, energy, and sexual appeal. He argues that Prozac can (and perhaps should) also be used to remove aspects of our personality we find objectionable, likening the use of Prozac to overcome undesirable psychological traits to the use of cosmetic surgery in overcoming undesirable physical ones (Kramer, 1997).

But if Prozac does make people "better than well," how might its popularity affect social life? Critics fear that Prozac (as well as other drugs that may modify character) is aimed not so much at "sick patients" as at people who already function at a high level and want enriched memory, enhanced intelligence, heightened concentration, and a transformation of bad moods into good ones (Begley,1994). In our fast-paced, achievement-oriented society, motivations for gaining a competitive edge are obvious. Those who earn higher grades, sell more cars, or come across as more charming and attractive can reap enormous financial and social benefits (Newman, 2002). But what about those who do not use the drug, either for reasons of principle or because they can't afford it? Do they risk losing out and becoming the less rewarded and less valuable members of the community (Rothman, 1994)?

The technological possibilities of Prozac raise important issues about the role of medicine in defining deviance, controlling behavior, constructing personality, and ultimately determining social life and the culture that guides it (Newman, 2002).

Others viewed depression as the price paid for insights that were inaccessible to others (Sylvia Plath comes to mind). The word "sensitivity" came up most frequently when the values of depression were cited, with people indicating that depression had given them a more profound appreciation for others' difficulties. In the words of one respondent:

> I think depression has made me a stronger person somehow. I mean in learning to handle this kind of thing. I think that I've had to develop skills and abilities that I wouldn't otherwise. And sensitivities too. I think it's made me more compassionate. I think, because of it, I know what it's like to go through something like that and I'm more curious about other

people and what they're going through. [I'm also] more intent in trying
to make some meaning out of the whole thing [life]. . . . (p. 130)

Along with the problems associated with managing their daily lives, individuals with affective disorders must cope with a "mental illness" status.
They must deal with the fact that to suffer from depression is not only debilitating but also casts one into a deviant, disvalued, and sometimes stigmatized
status. Beginning with Goffman's (1963) groundbreaking formulation of the
problem of **stigma**, social scientists have studied how groups as diverse as
overweight individuals, wheelchair users, and people with HIV/AIDS manage information and adopt behavioral strategies that serve to protect tainted
identities (see chapter 9). Despite the increased awareness of depression,
those diagnosed as depressed know they have a condition that is convention-
ally defined as a mental illness. That is, they fall into a category with a range
of "others" who have what Goffman terms "blemishes of individual character." It is not surprising, then, that depressed people may adopt "passing"
strategies similar to others whose stigmatized conditions are not immediately
visible. Self-management may simply take the form of keeping one's unacceptable identity secret.

> Of course, you could never tell anybody, because [of] the stigma. . . .

> Depression is a mental illness, Sssssh! Don't talk. Don't tell any-
> body. . . . Nobody talked because of the stigma attached, depression
> being a mental illness.

> All I know is that I could never run for political office.

> I'm still afraid of people. I feel if I don't tell them [about my depression] I
> can never really become close to them. . . . I can't even make just fun
> friends because I need so much to talk to people and let everyone know
> about it, but I can't because it's just too damaging. (Karp, 1996:46)

Sociological literature contains many examples of how stigmatized individuals attempt to foster more positive definitions of their situation. Subcultures, for example, not only provide support for alternative, nonstigmatizing
definitions of a common circumstance, but may have a larger agenda of
responding to negative definitions with the aim of changing them. Although
those with a range of mental illnesses have begun to enter the arena of "identity politics," depression is a unique case because the most critical assaults on
the self come from within. Although those with depression may want a
greater public understanding of their "illness," when they are in the middle
of an episode of depression they feel a self-hatred far greater than could possibly be expressed by others toward them. As people cycle through depression, "the dialectical intersection of self and society" can be plainly seen. In
Karp's words:

> The process begins with a range of bad feelings. Chief among them is
> that one possesses a deeply problematic self, a self that feels socially
> uncomfortable. At a point, it becomes a self deemed wholly unworthy of

public presentation. Such feelings lead, as we have seen, to social withdrawal. Withdrawal, in turn, makes the performance of social functions difficult and sometimes impossible. The inability to meet social obligations expands the disdain and hatred people feel toward themselves, thus sustaining and extending the felt need to withdraw. In this way, depression is characterized by an ongoing and mutually reinforcing double stigmatization—by self and society. (1996:47)

Individuals with depression learn to navigate between rhetorics of "victimization" and "positive thinking" in a way that accounts for their situation while empowering them to do something about it. Also, since those with diagnosed affective disorders are thrust into a world of therapeutic experts, much discussion is designed to affirm that, despite their dependence on physicians, they are the ultimate experts on the value of therapeutic interventions. Such a posture also helps them to realize a sense of competence in a situation where their competence is dangerously undermined. In this regard, while the individuals discussed in this section have a distinctive life problem with which to contend, they are quite like every human being. At one time or another we all face life circumstances that are difficult to fathom and where our competence is actually or potentially called into question. How we rely on each other to negotiate such situations in ways allowing us to preserve a positive self-image is, therefore, a problem of general sociological interest.

Conclusion

This chapter has examined several issues pertaining to definitions of health. We have seen that the term *health* like any other symbolic construct displays considerable variation in meanings across cultures. Based on such definitions, people's experiences of illness will differ as well. For example, how a person responds to pain is influenced by sociocultural factors, such as gender expectations. How individuals experience the health care system also differs according to social factors, in particular income and race/ethnicity. Having health insurance coverage is a key indicator of access to medical care. The growing rates of uninsured and underinsured people constitute a looming health care crisis. Since interactions between patients and doctors constitute a prime arena in which health definitions are established, we devoted considerable attention to what happens when doctors and patients meet. We called attention to several features of medical practice, such as the briefness of typical office visits and the emphasis on biomedical rather than psychosocial issues—factors which play a role in the diagnostic process. Managed care is having a tremendous impact on patient-physician relationships, and the use of alternative medicine may reflect a countertrend to the rise of managed care. The Internet is another factor with the potential to affect interaction between patients and health care providers.

We are particularly interested in the effect of illness on the self. In the last part of the chapter we examined the social construction of illness identities, focusing on clinical depression. The ambiguous nature of this ailment, its lack of clear "location" in either the body or the mind, makes the question of its meaning especially problematic. As we have argued throughout this book, people construct the meanings of their lives through ongoing conversations with others; in this sense, then, individuals experiencing depression are illustrating as well some of the generic features of how meanings are created.

In the final part of this book, we will devote our attention to the larger social contexts in which meanings are created. In the last three chapters we will deal with the themes of deviance, personal change, and social change. We will consider how everyday deviances upset the fragile order of everyday life. In addition, our treatment of the humanly constructed life cycle and the ongoing transformations of personal identity will locate changing social selves within the broad sweep of history.

DEFINITIONS

Achieving a diagnosis A process, often taking many years, during which people seek to acquire a clear definition of the illness from which they suffer. Being given an "official" diagnosis by medical experts is a critical benchmark in the process of defining oneself in terms of a particular illness.

Biomedical model The dominant therapeutic orientation in the United States, essentially disease-oriented or illness-oriented rather than patient-oriented. The key to effective medical care is believed to be correct diagnosis of some physiological aberration followed by proper application of the curative agent.

Cultural construction Social meanings created by people, which vary from one culture to another.

Disease A biological problem within an organism.

Health maintenance organizations (HMOs) A form of managed care based on prepayment for health care by patients who agree to use member physicians and hospitals.

Identity markers Symbolic creations that serve to represent one's identity to others.

Illness Refers to the social experience and consequences of having a disease.

Illness ideologies Explanatory schemes used to interpret and justify a particular diagnosis of what is "causing" an illness.

Interpretive dilemma All life situations require human interpretation to endow them with meaning. However, some situations, such as illness, are so intrinsically unclear that they may pose interpretive dilemmas or problems of meaning.

Managed care A medical system in which physicians and hospitals contract with employers to cover the health care needs of employees for a fee agreed upon in advance.

Medicalization The process of legitimating medical control over an area of life, typically by asserting and establishing the primacy of a medical interpretation of that area.

Moral entrepreneurs   Howard Becker's term for people who are constantly on crusades to establish rules, implement them, and then label those who do not follow them as offenders.

Morbidity   Refers to the amount of disease, impairment, and accident in a population.

Mortality   Refers to the number of deaths in a population.

Nature/nurture debate   A fundamental debate regarding explanation of virtually all human behaviors. The debate is whether human behavior is a product of nature (biology and genetic structure) or the result of nurture (cultural learning). The relative influences of nature and nurture in explaining psychiatric disorders are especially difficult to decipher.

Negotiating social reality   The social process by which people communicate to one another a sense of what is "real."

Psychosocial concerns   Problems of daily living, issues regarding social relations, feelings, and emotions.

Stigma   An attribute that has a deeply discrediting effect on the individual who possesses it, reducing the individual from a whole and usual person to a tainted, discounted one. Goffman identifies three types: abominations of the body—the various physical deformities; blemishes of individual character; and "tribal" stigmas of race, nation, religion.

Structural constraints   The ways in which the social organizational features of a setting or environment constrain and set limits on possible modes of behavior.

Therapeutic culture   The term therapeutic culture was first used by Philip Rieff to describe American society's disposition to think of an increasing range of human behaviors as expressing underlying psychological pathologies that should be treated by growing numbers of psychiatric experts.

Universe maintenance specialists   Those societal roles which allow the occupants to set norms defining what is to be considered proper, normal, and "healthy," as opposed to deviant, immoral, or "sick."

DISCUSSION QUESTIONS

1. Do you think Americans are more, or less, concerned about their health than Europeans, for example? How would go about studying such an issue? What kinds of data sources would you look for?

2. What seems to be the key determinant of access to health care? Who is most likely to lack adequate access to health care?

3. Have you ever been hospitalized? If so, how were you treated and how did it make you feel? Specifically, what impact did it have on your *self*?

4. When being examined by a doctor, have you ever felt that there were communication problems during the examination? How did you deal with such problems? Are there things you would have liked to have said or done that you didn't do for some reason or another?

5. If you could design the "ideal" medical system in which patients would get the best health care possible, what would such a system look like?

6. Everyone feels "blue" from time to time. What, in your view, distinguishes those who simply feel badly because of some situation in their life and those who suffer

from clinical depression? Have you ever felt badly enough to seek out the help of a psychiatric expert? If you did, how did that experience shape your definition of self? If you have never seen a psychiatrist or psychologist, do you have an image of people who are regularly involved in therapy?

REFERENCES

Ackerknecht, E. 1947. "The role of medical history in medical education." *Bulletin of the History of Medicine* 21:135–45.

Armstrong, T., and L. Swartzman. 2001. "Cross-cultural differences in illness models and expectations for the health care provider-client/patient interaction." In *Handbook of Cultural Health Psychology*, pp. 63–84. San Diego, CA: Academic Press.

Astin, J. 1998. "Why patients use alternative medicine: Results of a national study." *Journal of the American Medical Association* 279:1548–53.

Atkinson, P. 1995. *Medical Talk and Medical Work*. London: Sage.

Baker, P., W. Yoels, and J. Clair. 1996. "Emotional expression during medical encounters: Social dis-ease and the medical gaze." In *Health and the Sociology of Emotions*, edited by V. James and J. Gabe, pp. 173–99. Oxford: Blackwell Publishers Ltd.

Baker, P., W. Yoels, J. Clair, and R. Allman. 1997. "Laughter in triadic geriatric medical encounters: A transcript-based analysis." *Social Perspectives on Emotion* 4:179–207.

Becker, G. 1997. *Disrupted Lives: How People Create Meaning in a Chaotic World*. Berkeley: University of California Press.

Begley, S. 1994. "One pill makes you larger, and one pill makes you small . . ." *Newsweek*, February 7.

Bellah, R., R. Madsen, W. Sullivan, A. Swidler, and S. Tipton. 1996. *Habits of the Heart: Individualism and Commitment in American Life*. Berkeley and Los Angeles: University of California Press.

Berger, P., and T. Luckmann. 1967. *The Social Construction of Reality*. Garden City, NY: Doubleday.

Bischoff, W., and S. Kelley. 1999. "21st century house call: The Internet and the World Wide Web." *Holistic Nursing Practice* 13(4):42–50.

Conrad, P., and J. Schneider. 1992. *Deviance and Medicalization: From Badness to Sickness*. Philadelphia: Temple University Press.

Cotten, S. 2001. "Implications of Internet technology." *Sociological Spectrum* 21(3):319–40.

Council of Economic Advisors for the President's Initiative on Race. 1998. *Changing America: Indicators of Social and Economic Well-Being by Race and Hispanic Origin*. Washington, D.C.: U.S. Government Printing Office.

CyberAtlas Staff. 2001. "Young adults use Net as health information source." (December 11, 2001). Copyright 2002 INT Media Group, Inc.
http://cyberatlas.internet.com/big_pictur. Accessed 3/29/02.

Edgley, C., and D. Brissett. 1999. *A Nation of Meddlers*. Boulder, CO: Westview Press.

Edwards, C., R. Fillingim, and F. Keefe. 2001. "Race, ethnicity and pain." *Pain* 94:133–37.

Eisenberg, D., R. Davis, S. Ettner, S. Appel, S. Wilkey, M. Van Rompay, and R. Kessler. 1998. "Trends in alternative medicine use in the United States, 1990–

1997: Results of a follow-up national survey." *Journal of the American Medical Association* 280:507–13.

Eng, T., A. Maxfield, K. Patrick, M. Deering, S. Ratzan, and D. Gustafson. 1998. "Access to health information and support: A public highway or a private road?" *Journal of the American Medical Association* 280(15):1371–75.

Fairfield, K., D. Eisenberg, R. Davis, H. Libman, and R. Phillips. 1998. "Patterns of use, expenditures and perceived efficacy of complementary and alternative therapies in HIV-infected patients." *Archives of Internal Medicine* 158:2257–64.

Finlay, F., and R. Jones. 1998. "Doctors' dress." *British Journal of Psychiatry* 172:188b.

Frank, A. 2000. "Illness and the interactionist vocation." *Symbolic Interaction* 23(4):321–32.

Freund, P., and M. McGuire. 1999. *Health, Illness, and the Social Body.* Upper Saddle River, NJ: Prentice Hall.

Gandhi, I., J. Parle, S. Greenfield, and S. Gould. 1997. "A qualitative investigation into why patients change their GPs." *Family Practice* 14:49–57.

Goffman, E. 1963. *Stigma: Notes on the Management of Spoiled Identity.* New York: Simon & Schuster.

Goldsmith, J. 2000. "How will the Internet change our health system?" *Health Affairs* 19(1):148–56.

Hesse-Biber, S. 1996. *Am I Thin Enough Yet?: The Cult of Thinness and the Commercialization of Identity.* New York: Oxford University Press.

Kao, A., D. Green, N. Davis, J. Koplan, and P. Cleary. 1998. "Patients trust in their physicians: Effects of choice, continuity and payment method." *Journal of General Internal Medicine* 13:681–86.

Kaplan, S., L. Sullivan, D. Spetter, K. Dukes, A. Kahn, and S. Greenfield. 1996. "Gender and patterns of physician-patient communication." In *Women's Health: The Commonwealth Fund Survey,* pp. 29–76. Baltimore, MD: Johns Hopkins University Press.

Karp, D. 1996. *Speaking of Sadness: Depression, Disconnection, and the Meanings of Illness.* New York: Oxford University Press.

Kim, M., and S. Wilson. 1994. "A cross-cultural comparison of implicit theories of requesting." *Communication Monographs* 61:210–35.

Klonoff, E., H. Landrine, and M. Brown. 1993. "Appraisal and response to pain may be a function of its bodily location." *Journal of Psychosomatic Research* 37(6):661–70.

Koutanji, M., S. Pearce, and D. Oakley. 1998. "The relationship between gender and family history of pain with current pain experience and awareness of pain in others." *Pain* 77:25–31.

Kramer, P. 1993/1997. *Listening to Prozac.* New York: Penguin.

Krauss, H., C. Godfrey, J. Kirk, and D. Eisenberg. 1998. "Alternative health care: Its use by individuals with physical disabilities." *Archives of Physical Medicine and Rehabilitation* 79:1440–47.

Kronenfeld, J. 2001. "New trends in the doctor-patient relationship: Impacts of managed care on the growth of a consumer protections model." *Sociological Spectrum* 21(3):293–317.

Lupton, D. 1996. "Your life in their hands: Trust in the medical encounter." In *Health and the Sociology of Emotions,* edited by V. James and J. Gabe, pp. 157–72. Oxford: Blackwell Publishers, Ltd.

Lyon, M. 1996. "C. Wright Mills meets Prozac: The relevance of 'social emotion' to the sociology of health and illness." In *Health and the Sociology of Emotions,* edited by V. James and J. Gabe, pp. 55–78. Oxford: Blackwell Publishers Ltd.

Mainous, A., C. Griffith, and M. Love. 1999. "Patient satisfaction with care in programs for low-income individuals." *Journal of Community Health* 24(5):381–91.

Mandl, K., I. Kohane, and A. Brandt. 1998. "Electronic patient-physician communication: Problems and promise." *Annals of Internal Medicine* 129(6):495–500.

Mechanic, D. 1995. "Sociological dimensions of illness behavior." *Social Science & Medicine* 41(9):1207–16.

———. 1998. "The functions and limitations of trust in the provision of medical care." *Journal of Health Politics, Policy and Law* 23:661–86.

———. 2002. "Socio-cultural implications of changing organizational technologies in the provision of care." *Social Science & Medicine* 54(3):459–67.

Mechanic, D., and S. Meyer. 2000. "Concepts of trust among patients with serious illness." *Social Science & Medicine* 51:657–68.

Meisler, J., V. Pinn, C. Kitt, L. LeResche, C. Stohler, and J. Levine. 1999. "Chronic pain conditions in women." *Journal of Women's Health* 8(3):313–20.

National Center for Health Statistics. 2000. "Health Insurance Coverage." NCHS FASTATS. http://www.cdc.gov/hchs.

———. 2001. *Health, United States, 2001 with Urban and Rural Health Chartbook.* Hyattsville, MD: NCHS.

———. 2002. "Early release of health insurance coverage estimates: New data from Quarter 3 of the 2001 National Health Interview Survey (NHIS)." http://www.cdc.gov/nchs. Accessed 3/16/02.

National Women's Law Center. News Release: December 11, 2001. "Despite limited advances, America's health policies are failing women, comprehensive new study concludes." http://www.nwlc.org.

National Women's Law Center, University of Pennsylvania School of Medicine, and Oregon Health & Science University. 2001. *Making the Grade on Women's Health: A National and State-by-State Report Card.*

Newman, D. 2002. *Sociology: Exploring the Architecture of Everyday Life.* 4th ed. Thousand Oaks, CA: Pine Forge Press.

Pastore, M. 2001a. "Patients look to Net to help with medical care." *CyberAtlas* (January 19, 2001). Copyright 2002 INT Media Group, Inc. http://cyberatlas.internet.com/markets. Accessed 3/29/02.

———. 2001b. "Online health consumers more proactive about healthcare." *CyberAtlas* (April 30, 2001). Copyright 2002 INT Media Group, Inc. http://cyberatlas.internet.com/markets. Accessed 3/29/02.

———. 2001c. "Physicians' Internet use excludes clinical applications." *CyberAtlas* (March 8, 2001). Copyright 2002 INT Media Group, Inc. http://cyberatlas.internet.com/markets. Accessed 3/29/02.

Pear, R. 2000. "Still uninsured, and still a campaign issue." *New York Times*, June 25.

Pelton, T. 2002. "Minorities in U.S. get worse medical care than whites, study says." *The Sun*, March 21: 8A.

Polsky, A. 1991. *The Rise of the Therapeutic State.* Princeton, NJ: Princeton University Press.

Richardson, L. 2000. "The metaphor is the message: Commentary on Arthur Frank's 'Illness and the interactionist vocation.'" *Symbolic Interaction* 23(4):333–36.

Rieff, P. 1966. *Triumph of the Therapeutic.* New York: Harper & Row.

Ritzer, G. 2000. *The McDonaldization of Society.* Thousand Oaks, CA: Pine Forge Press.

Robert, S. 1999. "Socioeconomic position and health: The independent contribution of community socioeconomic context." *Annual Review of Sociology* 25:489–516.

Roberts, C., and M. Aruguete. 1999. "Task and socioemotional behaviors of physicians: A test of reciprocity and social interaction theories in analogue physician-patient encounters." *Social Science & Medicine* 50(3):309–15.

Robinson, C., C. Flowers, B. Alperson, and K. Norris. 1999. "Internet access and use among disadvantaged inner-city patients." *Journal of the American Medical Association* 281(11):988–89.

Roter, D., M. Stewart, S. Putnam, M. Lipkin, W. Stiles, and T. Inui. 1997. "Communication patterns of primary care physicians." *Journal of the American Medical Association* 277(4):350–56.

Rothman, D. 1994. "Shiny happy people." *New Republic*, February 14.

Schauffler, H., T. Rodriguez, and A. Milstein. 1996. "Health education and patient satisfaction." *The Journal of Family Practice* 42:62–68.

Schneirov, M., and J. Geczik. 1996. "A diagnosis for our times: Alternative health's submerged networks and the transformation of identities." *Sociological Quarterly* 37:627–44.

Schultz, R., W. Scheckler, D. Moberg, and P. Johnson. 1997. "Changing nature of physician satisfaction and dissatisfaction of family physicians." *Journal of Family Practice* 45:321–30.

Unruh, A. 1996. "Gender variations in clinical pain experience." *Pain* 65(2–3):123.

U.S. Department of Commerce. 1999. *Falling Through the Net III*. Washington, D.C.: GPO.

Vandenburgh, H. 2001. "Emerging trends in health services." *Sociological Spectrum* 21(3):279–91.

Wainberg, M. 1999. "The Hispanic, gay, lesbian, bisexual and HIV-infected experience in health care." *The Mount Sinai Journal of Medicine* 66(4):263–66.

Warren, M., R. Weitz, and S. Kulis. 1998. "Physician satisfaction in a changing health care environment: The impact of challenges to professional autonomy, authority, and dominance." *Journal of Health and Social Behavior* 39:356–67.

Weitz, R. 2001. *The Sociology of Health, Illness, and Health Care*. 2nd ed. Belmont, CA: Wadsworth.

Young, M., and R. Storm Klingle. 1996. "Silent partners in medical care: A cross-cultural study of patient participation." *Health Communication* 8(1):29–53.

Zborowski, M. 1953. "Cultural components in responses to pain." *Journal of Social Issues* 8:16–31.

Zuckoff, M. 2000. "Lawsuit accuses drug maker Eli Lilly of concealing Prozac data from trial." *Boston Globe*, June 8.

Part Three

Disorder and Change in Everyday Life

Perhaps the most fundamental sociological question is how order is possible in society—how society hangs together as an ongoing concern. So far in this book, we have focused on those features of social life that give it stability, predictability, and order. We would be theoretically shortsighted if we neglected the study of change and disorder in social life, however. While we have stressed the idea that human beings are symbolic animals who collectively give meaning to their worlds, it is also true that everyone does not abide by the same set of social rules or share the same significant symbols and social realities. Moreover, human beings and society are constantly changing. In part three it will become clear to you that the symbols and meanings which make a life coherent in certain circumstances may not "work" in others.

One source of disorder in social life is the fact that people break rules. Individuals who accidentally fail to follow social norms may experience embarrassment as the structure of social interaction is momentarily threatened, and their identities are called into question. As a result, they are likely to experience discomfort, dis-ease, and personal dis-order. In chapter 9 we will analyze how social encounters sometimes go awry and how people try to fix such fractured interactions.

Transgressions of cultural expectations also can have more serious consequences for individuals and society. Some people so consistently break the conventional rules of society that they are labeled as criminals or mentally ill, for example, and may seem to threaten social order to the extent that they are removed from society altogether. Chapter 9 will give you an understanding of how both everyday deviances and those that envelop a person's whole life can threaten the social order.

The social order is also continually subject to change, which is characteristic of the entire life cycle from birth to death. Each significant point in the life cycle, such as childhood, adolescence, middle age, and old age, requires the adoption of new roles, statuses, and identities. Chapter 10 will explore the meanings people confer on the process of aging throughout the course of their lives.

In the analysis of aging, we will examine processes of change at two levels. Not only do people change as they move from one age status to another, but aging must also be understood within the context of broader cultural, structural, and historical changes. For example, the meanings given to different age categories (such as middle or old age) certainly are not the same now as they were at the turn of the twentieth century. Purely from a statistical point of view, the significance attached to age categories varies with such demographic factors as the number of people falling into each age category and changes in life expectancy. Structural changes such as these result in changing interpretations of specific phases of the life cycle. The theoretical perspective of symbolic interaction also emphasizes how people occupying different locations in society experience aging differently. Chapter 10 will help you see, for example, how occupational careers structure the way people think about aging, and how the power positions of women compared to men influence the social process of aging.

Discussions of both deviance and aging should lead you to think about how individuals deal with disorder and change in their lives. Both involve the analysis of identity change. The most powerful kind of personal dislocation, however, results when people become uncertain of their identities, when they have trouble answering the question "Who am I?".

Questions of personal identity are linked to broad historical changes in society. In simpler preurban societies, the question of identity raised no problems. People had little difficulty knowing who they were, and battalions of psychiatric experts and talk-show hosts did not exist to help them "find themselves." Numerous social scientists have observed that one of the most dramatic consequences of industrialization has been the rapid, widespread increase in geographical and social mobility for large segments of the population. The sense of rootlessness which often accompanies industrialization has led to enormous concern with questions of identity, self-worth, alienation, and the larger significance of life. In the final chapter of this book, you will learn how the issue of personal identity has been brought to the forefront of contemporary consciousness in the Western world.

DEVIANCE

Imagine that you have made an appointment with your sociology teacher to discuss a term paper. Because your meeting extends through the lunch hour, the professor takes out a brown-bag lunch and, shortly after, a smear of ketchup adorns the professor's cheek. Now you have a bit of a problem on your hands. How should you deal with this situation? A little thought suggests that all of the choices open to you pose difficulties. You could immediately interrupt the conversation and inform the professor of the smear, but such communications are typically reserved for intimates, such as a wife or husband. Your second alternative is to pretend that there is nothing wrong about the situation and hope that the professor will wipe off the smear in the normal course of things. This strategy also involves some risk, however. The situation might be punctured by the appearance of a colleague who would immediately remark on the professor's social blunder. Then the professor would realize that you had known about it for some time and had pretended not to see it. The professor's discovery of the smear under this circumstance could heighten the discomfort felt by everyone in the room.

Social life abounds with similar situations in which people's behaviors or presentations of self somehow harm or compromise the identities they are trying to present. These situations may make them appear to be wrong, incorrect, improper, or possibly even immoral, and they may feel awkward, uneasy, or embarrassed as a result. In some situations a person's presented self or identity becomes so compromised or tainted that the result is a fractured interaction. The social situation may even completely break down. In this sense everyday life is risky because of the ever-present possibility that events will make a person "look bad." Even in the most routine encounters we may be defined by others as improper, nonsocial, or deviant.

Everyday Deviances and Deviant Careers

In this chapter we are departing momentarily from conventional discussions of deviance, which typically address such issues as various kinds of criminal behavior, delinquency, drug use, prostitution, and mental illness. These are broad, **lifestyle deviances** that effectively involve people in lifelong deviant careers. The causes and solutions of many of these types of behavior, the extent of the harm they do, and what can be done about them are controversial (c.f., Curra, 2000). Individuals who behave in these ways are considered deviant when they are labeled as such by those in positions of power in the society. In the second part of this chapter we will consider how and why people become involved in deviant subcultures. Before that, however, we will analyze the **everyday deviances**—the occasional improprieties that temporarily mark certain individuals as somehow nonconforming, awkward, or improper.

The interactionist perspective on deviance differs from the traditional sociological definition of deviance as violation of the social order, in that the focus is on the *meaning* of an act as deviant or not—that is, deviance is a matter of *negotiation* and social definition, not something inherent in a particular act or behavior. Circumstances clearly affect the meanings of various acts in the eyes of those involved, both offenders and observers. A classic definition by Edwin Schur illustrates that deviance is a matter of degree, not an all-or-none classification. Behavior is deviant to the extent that it comes to be viewed as involving a personally discreditable departure from a group's normative expectations, and it elicits interpersonal or collective reactions that serve to "isolate," "treat," "correct," or "punish" individuals engaged in such behavior (1971:24).

The interactionist perspective on deviance is based on the premise that the meaning of an act as deviant or not is contained in the social response it produces rather than merely in the act itself. This reflects the symbolic interactionist view we have used throughout the book that objects take on meaning according to how people act toward them.

Deviant acts reflect negatively on the identities of those who engage in them, thus the term "deviants." The response of others to an individual's perceived deviance often has tremendous impact on how these individuals see themselves. Responses set the "deviant" individual apart from others and subject them to differential treatment, often negative.

It is individuals who are held responsible for their acts and who are targeted for correction, rehabilitation, punishment, isolation from society, and other such responses intended to root out the causes of the behavior from the individual and to protect the society from him or her. This social treatment establishes and sometimes controls the identities of those who are labeled deviant (Hewitt, 2003:245).

The principal characteristic of most everyday deviances is that they may be unsettling or embarrassing, but they mar a person's identity only momentarily. Embarrassment may cause only limited discomfort or be so intense it disrupts an interaction, however. Later in the chapter we will discuss the process of labeling and deviant careers.

Everyday Deviances in the Social Order

Everyday deviances are far less dramatic than those that envelop a person's whole life. After all, we are not thrown in jail for embarrassing ourselves. Nevertheless, it is important to study everyday deviances in order to understand how society hangs together. While in a statistical sense very few people are involved in lifelong deviant careers, everyone must continually create, sustain, and repair the social interactions that comprise everyday life. A key assumption of this book is that any theoretical conception of how a society operates must begin with an understanding of how the everyday, face-to-face encounters of its members are ordered.

Our interactions are inherently fragile things, easily disrupted by inappropriate remarks, improper displays of emotionalism, lack of bodily control, and the like. Further, there is a deep morality in everyday life which requires efforts to protect both our own and others' identities in our interactions. In those instances where our selves—and thus our social situations—are somehow tarnished, we are charged with the responsibility of setting things right. People who have been properly socialized know how to improve situations when there is the perception that they have done something embarrassing or somehow wrong. To shed some light on how and why encounters sometimes go awry and how people try to fix fractured interactions, we will consider the nature of embarrassment and its relation to roles, identities, and social organization.

Embarrassment and Social Organization

If a social scientist wants to know what normally keeps a social system in balance, or in **social equilibrium**, it is a good strategy to examine what happens when that equilibrium is disturbed. **Embarrassment**, one such disturbance, arises out of individuals' knowledge that others are evaluating them negatively. This knowledge can produce feelings of social discomfort great enough to impede a person's thought, speech, and action, making it difficult or impossible to continue an interaction. By showing what happens in these circumstances, studies of embarrassment can reveal a good deal about the social order and the basic requirements of successful role performance.

While we all know from experience what constitutes an embarrassing situation, those social scientists who have written on the subject recognize that there are a cluster of emotions and experiences that overlap each other. Once you begin to think deeply about the meaning of embarrassment, it becomes necessary to consider just how embarrassment is to be distinguished from shyness, shame, or generalized social anxiety, for example. Analysis of each of these social and emotional states is not simply an exercise in semantics, but is necessary as part of the process of thinking through just what precipitates each of them and how people remedy the problems each creates.

It seems immediately clear that the distinguishing characteristic of embarrassment in contrast to shyness, for example, is that the latter characterizes a person whereas the former is the product of social interaction (Crozier, 1990). People are shy; awkward social situations create embarrassment. Shyness is most closely associated with a lack of social self-confidence, expressed in low self-esteem in social situations and concern about lack of social skills. "Shy people lack confidence about their ability to know what to say to people or how to manage a social situation. This is much more important for their shyness than fear of being negatively evaluated by others" (Crozier, 2001:175).

A common observation in almost all shyness research is that the consequences of shyness are deeply troubling (see box). Shy individuals don't take advantage of social situations, date less, are less expressive verbally and nonverbally, and experience more loneliness than do non-shy people. Extreme shyness that continues into later years can result in chronic social isolation that leads to increasingly severe loneliness and related psychopathology, even to chronic illness and a shorter lifespan (Henderson, Zimbardo, and Carducci, 1999).

The linkage between embarrassment and shame seems somewhat closer in that both states eventuate from an individual's recognition that he or she has

---

The Shyness Institute

The Shyness Institute is a nonprofit research corporation (founded in 1994) dedicated to research on shyness, social phobia, and related anxiety disorders. Its co-director (with Lynne Henderson) is Philip Zimbardo, perhaps best known for the infamous Stanford Prison Experiment (Zimbardo, 1986). Designed to examine the effects of social roles on the person, the mock-prison study revealed sadistic behavior on the part of the "guards," while "prisoners" relinquished basic human rights and demonstrated anxiety, depression, and sleep disturbances (Henderson, 1999). Or in Zimbardo's words, "good boys" were transformed into "evil guards" and "healthy boys into pathological prisoners" (Zimbardo, 1999). One of Zimbardo's students noted the similarity between these dynamics and those experienced by the problematically shy; that is, the problematically shy person submits to critical and authoritarian aspects of the self and others, and becomes unduly compliant or avoidant (Henderson, 1999).

This led Zimbardo to conduct research on shyness, a topic with which he has been heavily involved for the past 30 years and which he continues to pursue. He is currently interested in explaining the apparent increase in shyness. (His research at a half dozen colleges found that over 50 percent of individuals were willing to label themselves as currently shy, compared to 40 percent a decade ago.) Zimbardo attributes this increase to two factors: (1) the negative impact of all the new technology on social behavior (yes, he's talking about the Internet), and (2) changes in the social structure of families, in part influenced by the undermining of family life by the intrusion of work into private time. In terms of technology, Zimbardo says:

> As technology insidiously invades every aspect of our lives, it makes us passive reactors to virtual reality, eliminating human face-to-face reality wherever possible. Technology and the affluence associated with it generally isolates people from other people. . . . It replaces service personnel with computer chips that are cheaper and more efficient. . . . It replaces shopping in book stores and retail stores with web buying. It replaces playing in the streets with friends with watching kids play on TV or with video game characters or with chat room conversations. It replaces conversations and schmoozing with friends and colleagues with efficient information exchanges via e-mail. . . . There is the illusion of interaction with electronic mail exchanges, but it is an illusion. (1999:15–16)

Zimbardo argues that the increasing amount of time spent in social isolation engaging in technological activities decreases social opportunities, taking time away from people contact. As a result, young people are not doing the things necessary to learn the basic and complex skills involved in social interaction. The lack of these basic social skills promotes feelings of shyness. Older people who may not have been shy are now beginning to feel awkward in face-to-face conversations because they are becoming acclimated to the ease and comfort of electronic communication. (Admit it—don't you sometimes prefer e-mail and voice mail to talking with an actual person?)

In addition, smaller families, single-parent families, dual-earner families, mobile families, lack of nearby extended family, taking work home, working longer hours, commuting longer distances, fear of crime in the streets—all combine to reduce opportunities to practice being a social animal, for both kids and grown-ups. Perhaps that's why Zimbardo now regards shyness as an index of social pathology; that is, the extent of shyness in society may be an index of the degree to which there is a disruption in the bonds that form the human connection. Zimbardo is concerned:

> If shyness has increased by 10 percent in the last decade so that at least half of our population are willing to label themselves as shy, that is cause for alarm. It is an epidemic in the making, a silent one, which makes it all the more terrifying to me. The social forces and technological takeover of our lives will grow greater in the coming years. What does that tell us about the spread of shyness and the loss of the human connection? (p. 17)

Visit The Shyness Institute's website at www.shyness.com.

visibly broken social rules that cast doubt on the adequacy of his or her identity. Until fairly recently, the view was that embarrassment is a less intense degradation of self than shame (embarrassment as a mild form of shame). According to this view, embarrassment normally involves relatively trivial breaches of social rules and the person breaking the rules is not seen as having done it purposely.

Shame results when the rules broken are seen as more serious and when the actor is viewed as having had control over the rule-breaking behavior. (We are thought less personally responsible for dropping a bowl of soup in our lap than for having knowingly cheated on a college examination.) There is intuitive appeal to the idea that embarrassment is weak, whereas shame is strong; however, more recent data suggest, contrary to the traditional view, that shame and embarrassment are distinct emotions (see box), and do not differ simply in intensity (c.f., Keltner and Buswell, 1997; Tangney et al., 1996).

Embarrassed? Or Ashamed?

People do not seem to have much difficulty recalling events which caused them to experience shame and embarrassment. In a study in which participants were asked to produce events that made them feel shame, embarrassment, or guilt, the 51 participants came up with 757 events (Keltner and Buswell, 1997). Social life is very precarious! The most common triggers of embarrassment were: (1) physical pratfalls, e.g., slipping in mud, (2) cognitive shortcomings, e.g., forgetting someone's name, (3) loss of control over the body, e.g., burping out loud, (4) shortcomings in physical appearance, e.g., walking around with toilet paper stuck to one's shoe, and (5) failure at privacy regulation, e.g., accidentally walking in on others having sex. Shame, on the other hand, was most commonly caused by (1) poor performance, (2) hurting others emotionally, (3) failing to meet others' expectations, (4) disappointment in oneself, and (5) role-inappropriate behavior. It seems that people are able to distinguish between the two emotions, and the appraisals involved in embarrassment and shame are of different kinds of failings.

In other studies (Sabini, Garvey, and Hall, 2001), students were asked to imagine scenarios and indicate whether they would feel shame or embarrassment (and to what degree). Try some of these yourself:

1. You are attending a formal party at your boss's house. Everyone present is very prominent in your workplace as well as your community. After getting punch, you head for the patio. As you stride toward the group outside, you slam into the sliding glass door that you thought was open, spilling the drink all over you. You hear the muted laughter and a few people ask you if you are all right.

2. Your professor has agreed to give the class a take-home essay exam, provided you won't discuss the exam with anyone. Your roommate is in the same class and has already written the test by Sunday afternoon. You start Sunday evening and cannot come up with anything intelligent to say. You glance over at your roommate's desk and see the completed paper. Because you are suffering from a block, you look at the answers and copy some of them, rewording them as best you can. You hand in the exam the next day. A few days later, the professor calls you into his/her office and tells you that he/she knows you have cheated and that you may be expelled for this.

Think about the most recent event in your life when you experienced shame or embarrassment. When it happened, you probably didn't analyze it in these terms, but think about it now—did you feel shame, or was it embarrassment?

In general, Tangney and colleagues' (1996) findings were that embarrassing events were lighthearted, things at which the participants wanted to laugh and at which they thought others would laugh. Shameful events were very different in that participants expected no one to laugh at those events. Shamed individuals felt more responsibility and regret, more anger and disgust with themselves, and believed that others, too, felt anger toward them. Keltner and Buswell (1997) concluded that although embarrassment and shame are similar in important ways, they differ in that embarrassment follows from violations of conventions, whereas shame follows from the violation of moral rules. However, a study designed to test these ideas did not find support for the moral-conventional distinction (Sabini et al., 2001). Rather, these authors suggest that embarrassment involves an *apparent flaw of character*—of the self—rather than a mild, real flaw. Slipping in the mud, for example, is not a violation of convention, but a failure of a different sort, of motor control. In fact, these sorts of events are often funny in retrospect in part because they typically do not in fact reveal serious flaws of the self. The implications of the event depend not on the behavior per se but on what the behavior says, or seems to say, about the self. In other words, "Although being drunk once does not necessarily reveal a serious flaw of character, being discovered to be an alcoholic is a serious matter. Accidentally walking in on someone having sexual intercourse is embarrassing, whereas being caught at being a peeping Tom cannot be laughed off" (Sabini et al., 2001:112).

Although embarrassing acts do not usually reveal seriously flawed selves, they *could* do so. Sabini and colleagues suggest that a person experiencing intense embarrassment is "at the moment of pain oriented toward the implication for his or herself that might be drawn from the infelicitous act; it is this serious flaw of self that accounts for the intensity of the affect" (p. 112). They take seriously the notion that people laugh at their embarrassments— people do tell funny stories about how they were embarrassed. An important point is that *telling* the story allows one to show the audience "that you are an okay person, despite this incident" (p. 112).

Generally, the type of embarrassment discussed thus far is triggered by some *faux pas*. A fuller account of embarrassment would be as follows:

> Embarrassment always involves a dramaturgic failing, an inability to continue to present oneself to an audience as the person one has been taken to be. It always involves flustering and inhibition. This dramaturgic trouble can be provoked by several things: *faux pas*, sticky situations, or simply being the center of attention, for example. When the embarrassment involves a flaw of some sort, then the person experiencing the flustered, painful state also may describe himself or herself as experiencing shame. In so doing, the subject of the painful experience concedes that the apparent flaw revealed is real; characterizing the experience as embarrassment, on the other hand, does not concede the presence of a real flaw. (Sabini et al., 2001:113)

These authors believe that the emotional state that underlies both embarrassment and shame fundamentally has to do with self-presentation. We need to refrain from doing things that make us look bad regardless of whether the appearance is real or illusory. It's all about breakdowns in self-presentation. It doesn't matter "whether the breakdown is the consequence of a real flaw or an apparent flaw or somebody else's flaw" (p. 113).

Whereas embarrassment is a response to a self-presentational failure (real or imagined), social anxiety is anticipatory in nature, arising out of concern that one may not make a desired impression on others (Leary and Kowalski, 1995). People have many good reasons to be concerned with how others perceive them, and it is not unreasonable to sometimes become worried about others' reactions. People become socially anxious not only when they are currently being evaluated, but also when the possibility or prospect of interpersonal evaluation exists. In fact, people may become anxious about social interactions that are entirely imagined rather than real. "We may become as distressed about an encounter that we imagine *might* happen as a real social situation. . . . Other people need not actually be present, except in the person's mind" (Leary and Kowalski, 1995:6).

While we could continue to analyze the subtle ways in which the related concepts of embarrassment, shame, shyness, and social anxiety differ from each other, we do better at this point to consider that all suggest in common a potential or actual social performance failure. In this regard, we should recognize that the dramaturgical perspective on interaction outlined in chapter 3 provides a useful framework for viewing the nature of embarrassment and the measures required to prevent it and then deal with it once it occurs. You should recall that according to Erving Goffman's model of impression management, we all feel obliged to put on performances that will gain the approval of the audience in front of whom we are behaving. Goffman himself notes in one of the earliest and still most important analyses of embarrassment:

> Whatever else, embarrassment has to do with the figure the individual cuts before others felt to be there at the time. The crucial concern is the impression one makes on others in the present—whatever the long range or unconscious basis of this concern may be. (1956:265)

At the heart of the matter of embarrassment is that we care deeply about the images we present to other people and the opinions they have of those images. Central to the symbolic interactionist view of the self is the idea that self-feelings, including embarrassment, come from the way we believe our performances are being evaluated by some audience. Embarrassment arises when there is a discrepancy between the nature and quality of performance we believe some audience expects of us and the actual quality of the performance we have put on. Of course, embarrassment arises when we feel (often incorrectly) that our actual performance falls short of the standard we believe some audience expects. We might note in this regard that shyness may be understood as reflecting a person's belief that he or she is likely to fail to meet an audience's expectations even before that person enters a social situation. The person who is shy expects to fail at meeting approved standards and responds by avoiding many social situations altogether, or, once in them, by interacting as little as possible with others. As the **self-fulfilling prophecy** suggests, the belief that one will put on a faulty performance magnifies the likelihood that this will actually occur. "A perceived inability to socialize by shy individuals, along with a pessimistic outlook for social interactions, becomes an excuse for anticipated failure and a self-handicapping strategy (e.g., 'I can't do it because I am shy')" (Henderson et al., 1999:3).

Drawing inspiration from the idea that embarrassment arises out of problems of impression management, Robert Edelman suggests that five factors are critical in the emergence of feelings of embarrassment (1987:119):

1. An ability to understand that one is a social object with an outward appearance to others.

2. An ability to see from someone else's viewpoint that impression-management styles influence the way in which the individual is perceived.

3. Knowledge of what constitutes acceptable behavior within a given culture or setting.

4. An ability to understand that changes in appearance can be conveyed by various impression-management strategies.

5. An ability to understand that one can make inferences about others on the basis of appearance.

These ideas conform to another principle of symbolic interaction theory that we have proposed over and again in this volume. It is that the meanings of behavior are bound to particular contexts and situations. In the context of the present discussion, this means that the perception of a behavior as causing embarrassment may differ from setting to setting. A wonderful example of this principle is afforded by an early study by Martin Weinberg (1965) on the nature of sexual modesty in nudist camps. He provides persuasive evidence that nudists behave in accordance with social norms that sustain modesty despite their total disregard for body covering, a situation where modesty might seem highly unlikely. The embarrassment that ordinarily accompanies such exposure is prevented by rules that desexualize the body. There are taboos against staring or otherwise showing over-involvement with another person's body, any form of bodily contact, attempts to cover areas of the body, and unnecessary accentuation of the body. The strictly enforced rules of the nudist camp prevented rampant sexual interest, promiscuity, embarrassment, jealousy, and shame and sustained a nudist morality. Of particular interest here is Weinberg's observation that inadvertently *leaving on* an article of clothing becomes a source of embarrassment in this context. He describes one woman who reported being embarrassed when she took all of her clothes off but forgot to take off her bra and people laughed at her.

The situational character of embarrassment extends to the idea that people are more or less susceptible to that emotion at different points in the life cycle. It comes as no surprise that adolescence is a time during which even the slightest sense that one might appear "incorrect" in front of one's peers engenders powerful feelings of embarrassment. This is understandable in light of the fact that adolescence is a moment in the life cycle during which an answer to the question "Who am I?" is far from certain. Adolescence is a time during which boys and girls are for the first time trying out a number of new social roles and statuses such as dating, which may not feel totally comfortable to them. At just the moment that their bodies are undergoing substantial changes, physical appearance becomes precisely the central criterion against which they evaluate their own and others' social value. The point is that uncertainty about self engendered by bewildering social and physical change in a context of high social risk makes the task of putting on acceptable social performances highly problematic. "Altogether, huge new predicaments must be mastered just as social acceptance and approval become especially consequential. If God wanted to create a perfect recipe for embarrassment, the teen years might be it" (Miller, 1996:87).

Very young children, on the other hand, do not appear to experience embarrassment. Although the precise time at which embarrassment emerges continues to be a matter of debate (some say it appears as early as 18 months; others argue that children are 10 before they are likely to experience mature embarrassment), "it seems clear that there are no signs whatsoever of embarrassment in young children until they become self-conscious" (Miller, 1996:78). As we learned in an earlier chapter, self-consciousness emerges during the second or third year. However, there may be more than self-consciousness involved in order for embarrassment to occur. Embarrassment requires recognition of what *others* are thinking of us. Since young children have difficulty putting themselves into others' shoes, children are "unlikely to be embarrassed by the possibility of negative evaluations from others unless the audience makes its disapproval plain" (p. 89). This suggests that "the development of embarrassment is a single continuous process that gradually results in increasingly sophisticated emotion as perspective-taking ability improves" (Miller, 1996:86). By the time you reach college, you are embarrassed, on average, more than once a week! (Stonehouse and Miller, 1994).

Other situational factors that influence the likelihood that people will have greater anxiety over the adequacy of their social performance include the size and status of the audience. Any of you who have had to make public presentations of one sort or another probably can attest to the truth of the hypothesis that nervousness increases as the audience grows in size and expertise concerning the subject matter of the presentation. We feel safe in saying, for example, that college professors worry more about being embarrassed when presenting a paper at a professional meeting in contrast to their day-to-day teaching performances in front of undergraduate students.

In the study by Tangney and associates (1996), participants (undergrads) reported that embarrassment occurred in front of larger audiences than did shame and guilt (on average, 6.8 people, compared with about 2 people), and that they experienced embarrassment more frequently around strangers and acquaintances rather than friends. They also reported that embarrassment was less likely to occur when they were alone, compared with shame and guilt. The authors, following Goffman, conclude that embarrassment, more so than shame and guilt, occurs during public, impersonal interactions and seems to implicate the "outer" or public self rather than the "inner" or private self.

Earlier we observed that embarrassment is lodged in social situations rather than in individuals. In this regard embarrassment is not only costly to the individual whose identity, honor, or coolness has been compromised. It also is contagious and has the potential of enveloping the whole situation in which it occurs. All interactions are joint ventures, joint actions. People become embarrassed within some social context that involves other people who recognize the embarrassment and must somehow deal with it. Embarrassment thus not only affects the person who is embarrassed; it is shared by all of those who are parties to the encounter.

We share the embarrassment felt by others; we blush at their blushing and we feel embarrassed for their embarrassment. When the self of any one person in a situation is threatened or discredited, the selves of all those involved become implicated. Further, if others who observe an embarrassing act do not handle it well—in a tactful fashion—they may increase the discomfort felt by all. According to Goffman, each participant in an interaction must honor the selves presented by all the other participants. If a participant is discredited, he says:

> By the standards of the wider society, perhaps only the discredited individual ought to feel ashamed; but, by the standards of the little social system maintained through interaction, the discreditor is just as guilty as the person he discredits. . . . This is why embarrassment seems to be contagious, spreading, once started, in ever-widening circles of discomfiture. (1967:106)

Thus far we have emphasized the negative consequences of embarrassment. However, embarrassment also can have positive functions as a form of **social control**. To be sure, we need only consider what a society would look like in which people were "beyond embarrassment." It would likely be a society where the only source of social order would be the threat of force. A more powerful source of social control is that which comes from within a person who has internalized social rules.

Casual observation indicates that people may be deliberately embarrassed in order to socialize or train them to put on a poised performance. One form of this training is the practical jokes children play on one another and their other attempts to cause their friends to "lose face." Teenagers, too, frequently engage in competitive testing encounters designed to assert their own superiority and skillfulness in maintaining personal honor. Deliberate embarrassment also can keep group members in line. For adolescents especially, any deviation from what is "cool" provokes enough teasing and joking to insure a return to accepted standards (Geraghty, 1997).

This type of embarrassment, called *strategic embarrassment*, occurs when a person intentionally makes a comment or points out a flaw for the sole purpose of embarrassing someone else. It acts as a form of social control and is often used to encourage conformity, according to Sandra Petronio, who has studied this topic extensively (Geraghty, 1997). Another example of strategic embarrassment occurs when newspapers publish names of "deadbeat dads" (fathers who have fallen behind in their child-support payments). This puts them on the spot in the community and indicates they have done something the community feels is inappropriate.

Petronio found that people are constantly embarrassing one another in various situations, without always thinking about the effect their actions will have on the person who is embarrassed. If you are unaccustomed to playful chiding and enter a conversation in which this occurs, it can seem like a personal attack. If others who are watching the interaction feel the embarrasser is out of line, then the embarrasser becomes the embarrassed one. According to Petronio, this makes strategic embarrassment tricky, best used "among equals, among friends—people who understand the game" (quoted in Geraghty, 1997:A8).

If, as we maintain, the loss of personal honor and a valued identity is a source of great dis-ease for individuals, we should expect that people will routinely organize their lives in order to reduce the likelihood of being embarrassed. Just as we are expected to engage in preventive measures to avoid physical disease, we should not be surprised that people are normally careful to control features of the social environment that pose the greatest threats to failed role performances. In one of the first studies of embarrassment and the social requirements of successful role performances, Edward Gross and Gregory Stone tried to clarify "the structure of transactions where identities have been misplaced or forgotten, where poise has been lost or destroyed, or where, for any reason, confidence that identities and poise will be maintained has been undermined" (1964: 2). Their analysis suggests that prevention of embarrassment and smooth role performances require control over the space surrounding interactions, the props we use in self presentations, and our bodies.

Efforts to Avoid Embarrassment: Controlling Space, Props, and Bodies

One source of embarrassment involves people's errors in occupying spaces or territories where they do not belong. An obvious example would be a man accidentally entering a women's restroom, or vice versa. In American society there are clear norms governing who should be doing what and *where*. The where is critical, since roles performed properly in one context may injure a person's identity when performed in a different one. The boundaries of space or areas within which interactions take place may be more or less sharply defined. When the bounds are overstepped, embarrassment, signaling a loss of poise, is likely to result.

The meaning and significance of role performances are defined by the context in which they take place, as we already noted. It is impossible to know the meaning of behavior or acts apart from the situations in which they occur. Some actions are restricted to particular settings. People are expected to act on their sexuality in private spaces, for example. Onlookers may feel discomforted by lovers who kiss passionately in a public place. Indeed, the bedroom has symbolic significance in American society because it is recognized as a place where people put on performances that reveal "deep" aspects of themselves. The bathroom, similarly, has been institutionalized as a "back region." Bedrooms and bathrooms are among the few places in American society where you can legitimately lock yourself in. In these two contexts people engage in behaviors which, if they could be seen, might not be in accord with the impressions of themselves they normally try to present.

The adequacy of a role performance may be determined by who controls the space or the situation. Because teachers control classroom spaces, students often experience a heightened sense of self-awareness in this context. Those who are late coming to class may be profusely apologetic about the impropriety they think they have committed. They feel embarrassed even though the teacher may attach little significance to the event. People may lose their poise when they act out of place or accidentally invade spaces where they feel they do not belong.

The props used in carrying off interactions are a second component of self and situation that must be controlled in order to protect identity and maintain poise. Spaces are filled with objects that frame interactions. Rooms are filled with furniture, rugs, paintings, mirrors, room dividers, stairways, and the like. Normally, these props stand unobtrusively in the shadows of interactions, but they can affect the chances that an interaction will be successful. Furniture may be rearranged to improve communication at a party, for example, and grocery store displays are artfully constructed to prompt impulse buying.

While most props facilitate transactions, a prop failure can also stop an interaction in its tracks, casting doubt on the intentions, motives, or capacities of the participants. The lights, pillows, and soft music props in a single's place may be so overdone that they provoke a date to laughter rather than inspiring the intended mood of sensuality. Props cause embarrassment most often when people lose control over them, as when someone stumbles over a rug or trips on a flight of steps. Often, through no fault of our own, objects or pieces of equipment cause disruptions that prove embarrassing. Bowling balls are unceremoniously dropped, cars become stalled in dense traffic, food accidentally spills in laps, teachers lose their grip on erasers so that they fly across the room and land on a student's desk! Much slapstick humor, like that in the Marx Brothers, Charlie Chaplin, or Three Stooges movies, is built around the awkwardness created by prop failures. The humor works because it exaggerates the misadventures that could befall anyone, as the following incident illustrates:

[A]t a formal dinner, a speaker was discovered with his fly zipper undone. On being informed of this embarrassing oversight after he was reseated, he proceeded to make the requisite adjustment, unknowingly catching the tablecloth in his trousers. When obliged to rise again at the close of the proceeding, he took the stage props with him and, of course, scattered the dinner tools about the setting in such a way that others were forced to doubt his control. His poise was lost in the situation. (Gross and Stone, 1964:10)

Clothing, another prop, was described in chapter 3 as a significant feature of the selves we present. This prop must be carefully maintained, controlled, and arranged. As a prop, clothing is a direct extension of a person's body. Sometimes our clothes fail us, spoiling the presentation we intend to give. Miller (1996) describes the predicament of a woman waiting to cross a wide, busy street:

She was running a bit late, and in her haste to get dressed she had donned an old maternity slip that was now too big for her. When the traffic finally came to a stop and she started across, the top of the slip slid down to her thighs. After a few more steps, it was around her knees, and moments later, around her ankles. Rather than stop in front of five lanes of traffic to adjust the slip, or even gather it up, she decided, in the heat of embarrassment, to just step out of the slip and keep going. She shook her feet free, pulled her umbrella down around her face, picked up her pace, and left the slip lying in the street, a wasted garment and a sodden symbol of embarrassment. (p. 3)

Finally, whether or not we will be regarded as proper people depends in large measure on the appearance of our bodies and the control we can exercise over them. Our bodies are monitored by others as a check on our internal feelings. Trembling hands, profuse sweating, dilated pupils, blushing, stuttering, turning pale, and involuntary breaks in the voice are among the body gestures that may belie our efforts to appear in charge of ourselves and situations. In extreme cases, complete loss of body control incapacitates further interaction, as when a person gives way to emotionalism, "floods out," or expresses violent anger or fear. Flatulence, drooling, involuntary urination, and other losses of visceral control can cause deep embarrassment. People who are physically handicapped or who have permanent disfigurements or disabilities face unique contingencies in interaction with "normals" (Goffman's [1963] term). Unlike others whose settings, props, and bodies might only infrequently fail them and cause embarrassment, those with permanent body impairments must adopt strategies to convince others they should not be defined as deviant in every social encounter. Disfigurement causes one to be discredited as a fully functioning individual. There is an assumption that something is wrong with you based on your body image (Goffman, 1963). People with disabilities present an image that differs from the perceived norm, defined in terms of being "able-bodied" (Oliver, 1996).

A central task of the person who has a physical handicap and who is widely regarded as disabled is dealing with the nondisabled. In most cases, people with disabilities see themselves as being fundamentally no different from others. However, this raises conflict when the social meaning of disability as a symbol dominates, with its view that disabilities are related to dependency, deficiency, and inability (Oliver, 1996).

Restoring Identities Damaged by Deviance

We have seen that every interaction is inherently risky because everyday deviances can threaten a person's identity and poise and can paralyze role performance efforts. The embarrassment that results—often producing a fractured interaction—is hardly a trivial outcome. In order to maintain the integrity and order of society there is a moral imperative that calls for efforts to salvage identities under assault and to save situations threatening to break apart. These efforts are part of the unwritten social contract underlying social life. All social life may be viewed as a kind of social bargain in which we agree to protect each other so that social life will proceed smoothly.

The protection of identities is a major concern in everyday encounters. Participants maneuver to achieve a valued identity for themselves but also try to conduct themselves so that others' identities are protected. Goffman (1955) introduced the concept of *face-work*, defined in terms of the strategies used to cope with interactional difficulties. Two broad categories may be distinguished: *preventive practices*, where the actor takes some action to avert threats to identity; and *corrective practices*, where remedial action is taken after a disruption. When events occur that openly damage the identity of one or more of the people involved in an interaction, it signals the need for what might be termed **face games**. The purpose of such transactions is to save face, or repair identities that have gone wrong. A face game can restore a situation to what it was before the intrusion of an unwelcome event or normalize a situation that has become abnormal.

Sometimes the events disrupting a situation are relatively slight, and the situation can be normalized easily and quickly. As an example, suppose you inadvertently belch loudly at a lecture. The process of identity restoration begins when others acknowledge the impropriety, perhaps by glancing at you momentarily. You then try to remedy the situation immediately by offering an apology, bowing your head slightly, covering your mouth with a hand, and uttering a quick "Excuse me." With these gestures you are in effect communicating: "I know that I did something wrong and I am acknowledging it. I am trying to show you that I am, in fact, a proper person who wishes to abide by the rules. Having done this I expect that you will readmit me to this situation as person with an identity that is once more intact." It is necessary to go through this brief social ritual in order to restore equilibrium to the situation. Goffman referred to "the sequence of acts set in motion by an acknowledged threat to face, and terminating in the reestablishment of ritual equilibrium," (1967:19) as an *interchange*.

Identity restoration efforts involve communication and a display of motives. Efforts to "clear" identities that are temporarily under a cloud call for satisfactory answers to such actual or implied questions as: "Why did you do that? What motivated you to behave as you did? Explain what was in your head that made you break the rules." Unless individuals can offer satisfactory reasons for their behavior when others have defined it as improper, their identities remain suspect, and their status in good standing remains in doubt.

Assessing Motives and Offering Accounts

Ascertaining others' motives and explaining our own are necessary parts of all ongoing interactions. In the broadest sense, human conduct is grounded in a continuous assessment of motives. We feel compelled to explain our own behavior, and we cannot formulate our behavior toward others without also assessing the motives underlying theirs.

C. Wright Mills says such assessments constitute a **vocabulary of motives**. Using Max Weber's definition of *motive* as "a complex of meaning, which appears to the actor himself or to the observer to be an adequate ground for his conduct," Mills defines a satisfactory or adequate motive as "one that satisfies the questioners of the act . . ." (1940:906–7). To Mills, "motive talk" is a central feature of everyday experience. It provides one of the organizing techniques of social interaction, determining how acts are interpreted, including the moral evaluations attached to them. To explain our motives when our actions are seen as deviant or damaging to our identity, we use linguistic devices called *accounts*. In their original formulation of the idea, Stanford Lyman and Marvin Scott define an account as a verbal statement made to explain "unanticipated or untoward behavior" (1968:33). Accounts can take the form of excuses or justifications.

Excuses and Justifications

Excuses are verbal accounts people offer to acknowledge that their behaviors have been undesirable or wrong, but also to indicate why they should not be held accountable for those behaviors. They are intended to indicate why admittedly incorrect behaviors could not have been avoided. Everyday deviances may be explained away as resulting from:

> *An accident:* "We had a flat tire and couldn't get home on time."

> *Events outside a person's will:* "I have family troubles and have been feeling depressed."

> *Factors rooted in biology:* "If only I could control my drinking, it wouldn't have happened."

> *The behaviors of others:* "I am doing poorly because he doesn't give me enough encouragement."

Such excuses offer an appeal to the charge of deviance by citing events beyond the person's control.

Like excuses, **justifications** also are accounts people offer to acknowledge that they have committed acts that are being questioned. These accounts, however, are also designed to indicate why the acts should not be interpreted as deviant. Justifying an act asserts its positive value, despite claims to the contrary. Justifications are used to attempt to neutralize possible definitions of acts as illegitimate by providing nondeviant interpretations of them. Techniques of neutralization include efforts to:

> *Deny that any real harm has come from an act:* "I know that I took your car out for a joy ride, but I was only borrowing it and did not hurt it."

> *Suggest that those who were injured deserved what they got:* "It's true we harassed them but, after all, they were being unpatriotic."

> *Argue that in the large scheme of things an act is not too awful:* "The amount of income I withheld from the IRS is nothing compared to the rip-offs of big business."

> *Indicate that an act is permissible and even proper because it was done out of loyalty.* "After all the times he's saved my skin, I just couldn't refuse to do what the lieutenant asked."

Both excuses and justifications lubricate interactions by explaining personal motives in such a way that charges of deviance are quickly defused. In this way, momentarily troubled encounters are allowed to resume a smooth course quickly. Sometimes, however, accounts are not honored, and efforts to restore identities fail. For a variety of reasons, motive explanations may be deemed unacceptable.

Some accounts have been so overused they may not be accepted even when true ("The dog ate my homework," or, more recently, "The computer ate my disk!"). Others will succeed with some people and not others. For example, explanations for recreational drug use may be accepted by other drug users but are likely to be rejected by nonusers. Accounts also may be deemed unreasonable if they do not conform to commonly held cultural expectations. Suppose you go home and find your roommate with his head in the oven. You would probably ask, "What are you doing?" If he responds, "I'm cleaning the oven" that would probably be a satisfactory explanation. But if he claims that he heard voices telling him to put his head in the oven, you would make quite a different interpretation of his action. People who continually offer culturally unacceptable motives for their behaviors run the risk of being labeled mentally ill.

Humor also can be effective in managing an awkward situation. Smiling and laughter are frequent reactions of onlookers; the embarrassed individual can take advantage of the potential for humor to cope with the predicament. Empirical studies show use of a variety of face-work practices. A survey of students' responses to predicaments (Miller, 1996) indicated that the most common were evasion (28 percent), making amends (17 percent), humor (17 percent), and apology (14 percent). Escapes, excuses, aggressive acts, and justifications comprised fewer than 10 percent of accounts (Crozier, 2001:149).

Making Disclaimers

Accounts are a form of motive talk which *follows* a questionable action. Other verbal strategies are used in *advance* to counter doubts and negative evaluations which could result from intended conduct. We rehearse our future acts in our minds, trying to anticipate the responses others will make to them. When we determine that what we plan to do could be interpreted negatively, we preface our actions with **disclaimers** to provide a nondeviant frame of reference within which our behavior can be interpreted (Hewitt and Stokes, 1975). Everyday talk is filled with disclaimers, including expressions of the following sort:

"I'm no expert, of course, but . . ."

"Don't get me wrong, I like your work, but . . ."

"I know this is against the rules, but . . ."

"This may seem strange to you, but . . ."

"I'm not a racist, but . . ."

Such disclaimers protect individuals by indicating that despite the way their present behaviors might appear, they really are people who abide by prevailing norms and cultural constraints (or want to appear as such).

Perhaps one of the most common situations in which people feel obliged to remediate encounters are those instances where they have said something improper. All who read this book have at some time or another made a comment that they wish they could take back. Such regrettable messages become a matter of public record, so to speak, and sometimes deeply damage relationships. Everyone knows of instances where people have not spoken for months or even years because of a comment made during an argument. Long-term friendships and even marriages have broken apart because someone has said something that is interpreted as unforgivable. In other instances, of course, the consequences of a face-damaging remark are much slighter and the relationship can be quickly repaired.

Being Different: Managing Social Stigma

Everyday deviances usually cause individuals' selves or identities to fall into disrepute only momentarily. In most instances they are not ruined beyond repair, and the situation can be saved. Some people, however, have attributes so stigmatized by others that their behavior is considered "wrong" in virtually every situation. Highly visible attributes such as physical handicaps, disfigurements, and mental retardation immediately tag people who have them as different. Others, such as HIV-positive individuals or those with a history of mental illness, may be able to hide their negative attributes, but discovery of them would complicate their everyday interactions and could cause them great social harm. Goffman (1963) describes those with disorders that are stigmatizing and cannot be hidden or disguised as *discredited*, and those with conditions that allow people to "pass as normal" as *discreditable*. Whereas the discredited may be confronted with problems of "impression management," the discreditable may face difficulties of "information management" (Scambler, 1998). Still others are marked by attributes that characterize them as members of devalued groups in a society, including certain racial, ethnic, religious, and occupational groups.

As he did in so many areas of everyday life analysis, Erving Goffman (1963) wrote the pioneering study of social stigma. His book, entitled *Stigma: Notes on the Management of Spoiled Identity,* provided the first comprehensive analysis of the distinctive problems faced by those with especially tainted identities and the kinds of strategies required to normalize their daily interactions. Stigmatized people may possess an attribute so deeply discrediting that they are viewed by "normals" as less than fully human because of it. At the outset of his classic work on the subject Goffman identified three types of stigma:

> First there are abominations of the body—the various physical deformities. Next there are blemishes of individual character . . . these being inferred from a known record of, for example, homosexuality, unemployment, suicide attempts, and radical political behavior. Finally, there are the tribal stigmas of race, nation, and religion, these being stigma that can be transmitted through lineage. (1963:4)

Beginning with Goffman's path-breaking formulation of the problem, social scientists have elaborated theoretically on the idea of stigma (see, for example, Lemert and Branaman, 1997) and have studied how groups as diverse as wheelchair users (Cahill and Eggleston, 1995) and those with other physical disabilities (Livingston, 2000); people with speech problems (Jezer, 1997; Richardson, 1996), hearing impairment (Perry, 1996), or minor bodily stigmas (Ellis, 1998); people with HIV/AIDS (Siegel, Lune, and Meyer, 1998); straight parents of adult gay and lesbian children (Fields, 2001); mentally retarded individuals (Angrosino, 1997); stripteasers (Ronai and Cross, 1998); divorced individuals (Kim and Kim, 2002); people with genital herpes (Lee and Craft, 2002); members of Debtors Anonymous (Hayes, 2000); and people with red hair (!!) (Heckert and Best, 1997) manage information and adopt behavioral strategies that afford maximum protection against the consequences of others' definition of them as deviant. Aside from shedding light on groups that are "different," these studies reveal a great deal about the processes that generate categories of stigma and the efforts of groups, sometimes political, to renegotiate the meanings attached to the attributes they possess.

In our everyday interactions we willingly provide some pieces of identity information about ourselves, while we conceal others (see chapter 3). We play information games, with stakes that are higher for those whose identities have been negatively evaluated. To participate in interactions comfortably, such people must give a great deal of attention to information management and control. The mode of information management used by those with damaged identities varies with the visibility and stigma of the status being questioned. In some cases, negative identities are highly visible and cannot be hidden. Physical handicaps, for example, are obvious attributes which cannot be missed. For those with such disabilities, information is less important than minimizing the inevitable problems and discomforts that are part of nearly every encounter (see box).

In some cases there may be attempts to disavow troublesome identities, as when criminals assume aliases, or nicknames are used in deviant subcultures to conceal participants' identities from outsiders. People who know that their attributes will be discrediting in particular situations may try to conceal them temporarily. In such situations, control and management of identity information can become quite complex.

Goffman argues that people with stigmatizing conditions usually have some sense that others are evaluating them negatively. As a result, people with stigmatizing conditions often use coping strategies (sometimes drastic) to establish the most favorable identity possible. Some stigmatized individuals, especially those with conditions that are not immediately observable, may conceal the condition, or practice selective disclosure.

Passing is a strategy which can be employed by those with negatively evaluated attributes that are not immediately apparent. Being able to conceal a socially devalued aspect of the self may be highly advantageous in social interactions, enabling the individual with the stigma to minimize the impact of their stigma on others' judgments of them and be accepted as "normal." However, having to continually contend with possible detection is stressful and demands a great deal of mental control. In the effort to hide something important about themselves, individuals who have concealable stigmas may face an internal struggle that can have serious costs. Perhaps in some cases, harboring a concealed stigma is more costly to an individual than suffering the social consequences of stigma visibility (Smart and Wegner, 1999). For example, in one study (of Harvard students), those with concealable stigmas

---

Disability or Tragedy?

The *Oregonian* (newspaper) won the 2001 Pulitzer Prize for best feature writing for its series on Sam Lightner, a teen with a facial deformity. The article gives a graphic description of Sam's deformity: "A huge mass of flesh balloons out from the left side of his face. . . . It looks as though someone has slapped three pounds of wet clay onto his face, where it clings, burying the boy inside" (quoted in Haller, 2001:4C). When he goes out in public, people assume he is either mentally retarded or his mother abused drugs while pregnant (neither is true). Others "give him their prayers or just look away" (p. 4C). The story is described as "poignant and gripping, as it draws the reader into his life and his decisions about trying to 'fix' his face surgically" (p. 1C).

Beth Haller, an assistant professor of journalism at Towson University in Maryland, is concerned about the messages these "coping with adversity" stories send to society about people who are physically different. She hopes they promote acceptance, but fears they sometimes promote pity. A few years ago Haller conducted a study of national journalism award winners from 1984 to 1999 that dealt with disability or illness. In the 56 stories she found, Haller looked for the cultural messages about disability and illness hidden with the stories. According to Haller, prestigious journalism awards not only signal "validation" of excellence, but they also "forcefully put information about disability or illness onto the public agenda and put images of people with disabilities into the news" (p. 1C). The stories remain in the public's consciousness much longer and provide models for younger journalists. "Put succinctly, these stories have staying power."

Haller's concern is about the impact of these award-winning stories on attitudes toward people with disabilities. What she finds is that many of the stories are "awash in inspiration." What's wrong with that—isn't inspiration uplifting, something that makes readers feel good? To Haller, the trouble with inspiration is that the flip side of its message is tragedy. Haller quotes a wheelchair user, who, in *Mainstream* magazine, says: "Being told that you're inspirational when you're doing something ordinary is an assault on your self-concept. Suddenly you're reminded once again of the traditional attitudes about disabilities, that no matter who you are, what you do, how you feel, to some people you'll always be a tragic figure" (Haller, 2001:1C). She goes on to explain what nondisabled people don't understand: "That a life with a disability is still a life after all, to be enjoyed and lived to the fullest" (p. 4C).

The problem, according to Haller, is that the notion of disability and chronic illness as tragedy "fits squarely with journalistic news values that focus on the unusual or the dramatic." That is, deviations from the normal are more newsworthy than the commonplace. Haller wants to challenge journalism's continuing use of the value of "unusualness," fearing that it may cause negative stereotypes in the news, especially of people who are physically different. "When journalists focus on how someone deviates from the norm and when they 'pull on heart strings' to add drama to content, they may send a message of pity and tragedy to their audience" (pp. 1C, 4C). Journalists could promote better acceptance of disabled people by focusing coverage on societal barriers, rather than on inspirational (and one-dimensional) stories of a person's life with a disability. For example, depicting people with disabilities doing something symbolically empowering or confronting barriers would send positive cultural messages of people with disabilities as equal citizens in society.

Frank Bowe, in his book *Handicapping America*, explains that one very incorrect assumption affects attitudes toward disability: "That disabled people are different from us more than they are like us, [and] that their disabilities somehow set them apart from the rest of us" (quoted in Haller, 2001:4C). It is this myth that Haller feels award-winning journalism should address.

(being gay/lesbian/bisexual, bulimic, or whose families earned less than $20,000 per year) reported lower self-esteem and were more anxious and depressed than both those whose stigmas were visible and those without stigmatizing characteristics (Frable, Platt, and Hoey, 1998). In a study of women who had had an abortion, almost half reported that they felt others would look down on them because of their abortion and said that they felt a need to keep their abortion a secret from their family and friends two years later. The effort of keeping this secret had the effect of exacerbating psychological distress (Major and Gramzow, 1999).

Stigma concealment also has been linked to poorer physical health. HIV infection, for example, progresses more rapidly among HIV-positive gay men who conceal their homosexual identity than it does among those who are "out" (Cole et al., 1996). Women attempting to manage the stigma of STDs by passing as healthy (because they have temporarily convinced themselves that they did not have a contagious infection) risk exposing sexual partners to infection (Nack, 2000).

Passing can be a dangerous strategy because once begun it is difficult to stop. Harold Garfinkel (1968) gives the example of a transsexual who, as she acted out her new status as a woman, felt that she knew something others did not, and the disclosure of her secret would ruin her: "Punishment, degradation, loss of reputation, and loss of material advantages were the matters at risk should the change be detected" (p.136). Garfinkel says it would be more accurate to say that she was continually engaged in the work of passing, rather than to say that she had passed.

Not all stigmas can be hidden. Some individuals can only minimize the degree to which their stigmas intrude on and disrupt their interactions with others. "Covering" is another of Goffman's (1963) means of stigma management. In this case, possession of a stigma is acknowledged, but great effort is made to keep the stigma from looming large. "The individual's object is to reduce tension, that is, to make it easier for himself and the others to withdraw covert attention from the stigma, and to sustain spontaneous involvement in the official content of the interaction (Goffman, 1963:102). For example, some of the gay or bisexual men with HIV/AIDS interviewed by Siegel and colleagues (1998) chose to conceal or misrepresent the true nature of their illness, usually preferring to report they had cancer. "This subterfuge seemed to convey the seriousness of their illness, while avoiding strong censure" (p. 12).

Some people with stigmas intentionally call attention to their condition, however, either as an individual or as part of a group effort. Other respondents in Siegel's study used proactive strategies to manage stigma such as taking active, socially valued roles as HIV educators. Speaking on behalf of PWA/HIV helped them to make proactive identity claims in opposition to the notion of a "spoiled identity" (p. 19).

Sociological analysis of those with stigmas as well as those participating in other forms of deviance is based on the fundamental assumption that no human behavior is intrinsically wrong. Since the early 1960s, many social scientists have emphasized the idea that conceptions of morality, respectability, and deviance are social constructions, reflecting the symbolic meanings which have been adopted by individuals or groups. In this view morality is a relative notion, and the behavior of an individual or group can be identified as wrong, evil, immoral, or threateningly different only in terms of the current, commonly held construction of reality adopted by a dominant group in a given setting. Immoral behavior is immoral only because it has been so defined in terms of some prevailing notion of social reality. Deviance does not float down from the skies, automatically attaching to deviants and automatically missing nondeviants. For deviance and deviants to exist as meaningful categories, somebody has to judge, to portray, to stigmatize, to insult, to abuse, to exclude, or to reject (Sumner, 1994:223).

This relativistic view of deviance is most fully expressed in what has been termed **labeling theory**. The central idea is that powerful people and groups are able to impose their definitions of morality on others by labeling certain activities and the individuals who engage in them as deviant. These labels are very "sticky." Once they have been applied by powerful individuals, they have tremendous, long-lasting consequences for those who are so labeled. In the following section we will consider the contributions of labeling theory in helping to explain how some individuals come to acquire a deviant identity and to embark on a lifestyle that centers on their deviance.

Labeling Theory and Lifestyle Deviance

Labeling theory is only one of several social science theories expressing ways to think about deviance. Other theorists attempt to explain it in terms of a learning process based on association with established deviants or the blockage of legitimate avenues of success for certain groups. Deviance may also be related to social class values or the inequities created within capitalist societies. These theories diverge on certain points, but they need not be viewed as in competition with one another. Because of the complex and varied nature of deviance, each has explanatory power. We have chosen to emphasize labeling theory in this chapter because it fits the interactionist perspective and because of the special capacities it provides for thinking about deviance in everyday life.

An important conceptual shift from earlier thinking on deviance is reflected in labeling theory. Theorizing about the causes of deviant behavior formerly focused on the type of person committing the behavior. Labeling theory suggests that such an emphasis is misplaced. Rather than putting the spotlight on rule breakers, as do most theories of deviance, it focuses on the activities of rule makers. Howard Becker, an early formulator and proponent of labeling theory, makes this point clearly: "Whether a given act is deviant or not depends in part on the nature of the act (that is, whether or not it violates some rule) and in part on what other people do about it" (1963:14). Labeling theory thus shifts attention from the individual actor to the audience that evaluates the act. Becker voices the argument this way:

> Social groups create deviance by making the rules whose infraction constitutes deviance, and by applying those rules to particular people and labeling them as outsiders. From this point of view, deviance is not a quality of the act the person commits, but rather a consequence of the application by others of rules and sanctions to an offender. (1963:9)

Just who makes the rules? On one level, we all have investments in our own version of reality, and to some degree we force our private rules onto others. The rules that govern our personal lives are the product of prior negotiations, however. Becker suggests that some individuals, whom he terms **moral entrepreneurs,** are on crusades to establish rules, to implement them, and then to label others who do not accept the rules as offenders. Members of certain religious groups, for example, may battle fiercely to control definitions of deviance, as the pro-choice and right-to-life arguments about abortion illustrate. Over time some groups become especially powerful in a society and particularly influential in creating the rules. The role of the institution of medicine in defining deviance is a case in point. It provides a compelling example of how a powerful group controls the fate of individuals through labeling—in this case, by being able to define certain behaviors as illnesses.

The Medicalization of Deviance

In the history of medicine, the number of behaviors that fit the medical model explanation has steadily increased (Conrad and Schneider, 1992). Under the medical model, behavioral problems that used to be regarded as misbehavior subject to punishment are considered instead as medical problems subject to medical intervention, often with the use of drugs. Acceptance of the medical model has led to the **medicalization of deviance,** or reliance on medical professionals to define conditions considered both normal and healthy. The medical model is based on the easily accepted assertions that normalcy is preferable to abnormalcy, and normalcy can be considered a synonym for health and abnormalcy a synonym for pathology. Health and pathology are defined in terms of experience and laboratory research, which are presumed to be based on scientific, objective, unbiased standards.

Because it is better to be healthy than to be sick, the medical model insists that physicians' decisions, whether they are requested or not, are necessary to ensure health and determine what is healthy. No other profession provides for the extensive access to a person's body and self that physical and psychiatric medicine do. By defining certain aspects of the human condition as illnesses to be cured, physicians give themselves the right to explore every part of the human anatomy, to prescribe myriad curative agents, and even to compel treatment.

The term *healthy,* as used in the medical model, also can be equated with the term *conforming.* In societies where this model predominates, it is often used instead of the law or religious commandments to regulate behavior. "Peculiar" individuals who were once viewed as "possessed" or as agents of the devil are classified as emotionally ill under the medical model. In the name of science, the advice of medical experts is used in the courts to determine whether certain actions should be defined as crimes. Medicine is used to "treat" those whose behaviors do not conform to the expectations of others or impinge on their moral sensitivities.

The medical model is supported by the political reality created by a coalition of physicians, teachers, judges, and other health professionals. Peter Berger and Thomas Luckmann (1967) refer to the members of this coalition as *universe maintenance specialists* from different disciplines who set the norms defining the behaviors that are proper or improper, deviant or conforming, normal or pathological, and sick or healthy. The social control role of psychiatry is especially powerful in ensuring that actual or potential deviants stay within the official, institutionalized definitions of reality (see box).

Moral and scientific judgments become entangled in the medical model, which not only defines behaviors as troublesome but also attempts to explain their causes. The redefinition of a behavior as sick rather than bad is not merely a semantic issue. These labels have critical implications for the treatment accorded those who have been so labeled. For example, Gamblers Anonymous is based on the view that compulsive gambling is a chronic illness. As with other twelve-step programs, emphasis is on members' identifying, recognizing, and admitting their affliction. The twelve steps are required to "treat" the illness from which all members of the group suffer. The result is a shared community of individuals "suffering" from the illness of compulsive gambling (Rossol, 2001). This medicalized view reduces stigmatization and shame with which compulsive gambling might otherwise be associated. The labeling of behavior as illness is very much a political process with policy and moral implications.

Deviant Careers

Labeling theorists are concerned with the politics of deviance, or how powerful groups create rules and then oversee their enforcement. The labels employed by groups such as physicians influence how the society responds to those to whom the labels are applied. But labels have an even deeper impact on individuals, because ultimately they influence how those who have been labeled *respond to themselves.* Labels can, in fact, alter people's identities, affecting not only what they do but who they become.

Those labeled as deviants face the task of constructing meaning under sometimes daunting circumstances; for example, in **total institutions** such as mental hospitals or nursing homes, where individuals are "stripped of their prior nondeviant conceptions of self and proffered a new definition of self . . . a deviant identity that not only is incompatible with prior self-images and

On Being Sane in Insane Places

A dramatic experiment which speaks directly to the matter of labeling in psychiatric hospitals is D. L. Rosenhan's study entitled "On being sane in insane places" (1973/2001). To find out whether the sane can be distinguished from the insane, he had eight colleagues pose as "pseudopatients" and apply for admission to twelve different mental hospitals. None of the eight had any history of mental illness, but they were told to present themselves at the hospital admission offices complaining that they had been hearing voices. With the exception of that one lie, they were to tell the truth about all other aspects of their lives. Once admitted, they were to say they were feeling fine and no longer experiencing the symptoms. They were to arrange their own releases by convincing the staff, through their behaviors, that they were sane.

The experimenters were easily and immediately admitted, all but one with the diagnosis of schizophrenia. Their subsequent show of sanity could not convince the staff that these "patients" were fakes, however. The only ones who ever questioned their status as real patients were the other patients on the ward. Once they had been officially diagnosed as schizophrenic, there was nothing the experimenters could do to shake the label. In fact, the staff interpreted everything they did in terms of the label. The social scientists made written notes on what they were seeing and experiencing, for example. After they were discharged, they learned from the nurses' records that their note taking was considered "obsessive," and "engaging in writing behavior" had been interpreted as evidence of their illness.

After hospitalization periods ranging from 7 to 52 days, the pseudopatients were discharged with a diagnosis of schizophrenia "in remission," but in the institution's view they were not sane and had not been since they applied for admission. Rosenhan concluded that "once a person is designated abnormal, all of his other behaviors and characteristics are colored by that label" (2001:438). He offers this conclusion about "the stickiness of psychodiagnostic labels":

> A psychiatric label has a life and an influence of its own. Once the impression has been formed that the patient is schizophrenic, the expectation is that he will continue to be schizophrenic. . . . Such labels, conferred by mental health professionals, are as influential on the patient as they are on his relatives and friends, and it should not surprise anyone that the diagnosis acts on all of them as a self-fulfilling prophecy. Eventually, the patient himself accepts the diagnosis, with all its surplus meanings and expectations, and behaves accordingly. (2001:439–40)

identities but also carries with it corresponding negative social statuses and roles" (Herman and Musolf, 1998:433). Individuals in such settings may attempt to renegotiate meaningful identities in order to counter labels imposed by those in power. In one case, residents of a long-term facility for the aged and mentally ill used narratives to create definitions of self that distinguished them from definitions imposed by staff and their work (Paterniti,

2000). By claiming a "noninstitutional" self-identity in "the otherwise regimented, mundane, and sometimes inhumane circumstance" (p. 109), residents attempted to establish an alternative definition for interaction. One resident told stories about her experiences running a general store with her husband. Another talked about his life as a country and western musician. These alternatives are what Goffman (1961) referred to as *secondary adjustments*—"personal ways of negotiating organizational categories and institutional careers that provide evidence of identity apart from institutional parameters and definitions" (Paterniti, 2000:111). These secondary adjustments permit individuals some control in a situation in which they have little.

Deviant identity labels acquired in total institutions "stick" long after the termination of the labeled individual's institutional career. Herman and Musolf (1998) found that a deviant subculture developed among ex-psychiatric patients "in response to their negative post-hospital situations: the effects of negative labeling, the stigma of mental illness, oppressive psychiatric and post-psychiatric treatment, and the mental health system in general" (p. 430). Through participation in this deviant subculture, members came to internalize a deviant ideology:

> ... a set of perspectives about themselves against the larger perceived hostile society; moreover, they learned and transmitted to one another strategies on how to manage their spoiled identities and sets of justifications for engaging in deviant activities, and generally taught one another how to "make it on the outside." (p. 430)

In order to retaliate against mental health agents and the community at large when they had "experienced the stigma of their 'failing' "(Herman and Musolf, 1998:439), members of this subculture engaged in *rituals of resistance* which ranged from *antideferential rituals* (e.g., "mooning" those defined as the "enemy"—police, neighbors, mental health officials), to instrumental action such as "organized sit-downs during programs in community mental health centers, walk-outs from sheltered workshops, protest marches, distribution of protest leaflets and newsletters, and the like" (p. 441). Both strategies are ones in which the powerless confront the powerful. These rituals of resistance, however, can serve to promote social solidarity and distort power relations, allowing ex-psychiatric clients to transform a negative identity into a positive one.

Charles Horton Cooley, a turn-of-the-century sociologist, coined the term the **looking-glass self** to convey the idea that others serve as mirrors in which we see ourselves reflected. Through these reflections, we adopt subjective definitions of ourselves. Labels applied by powerful people or **significant others** in our lives (for example, parents, teachers, and peers) are profoundly influential because they fashion images of self that we may maintain for a lifetime. The proposition that individuals who are consistently responded to as deviant eventually come to define themselves that way is a central idea in labeling theory. Labeling theorists, however, qualify this idea by arguing that deviant identities arise from a *process over time,* and deviant identities lead to deviant careers.

Development of a Deviant Identity

All acts of deviance, even those considered to be lifestyle deviances, do not produce deviant identities. Many people commit acts which could land them in jail if they were caught, but most people do not routinely think of themselves as deviant. To understand the differences between acts of deviance that remain isolated and those that lead to a deviant career, labeling theorists distinguish between primary and secondary deviances.

Primary deviances are the initial, usually isolated breaches of rules that nearly everyone has engaged in. Rule violations resulting from accident, peer pressure, or experimentation may elicit negative responses from others, but they remain primary as long as the individuals involved define them as incidental to "who they really are." The violations become **secondary deviances** when, *as a result of consistent responses* from the society to their actions, individuals begin to think of themselves as deviant and to behave accordingly. That is, the deviant label becomes a *self-fulfilling prophecy.* The distinction between primary and secondary deviances was first made by the sociologist Edwin Lemert. His description of the process whereby secondary deviances are produced is as follows:

> (1) primary deviation; (2) social penalties; (3) further primary deviation; (4) stronger penalties and rejections; (5) further deviation, perhaps with hostilities and resentment beginning to focus on those doing the penalizing; (6) crisis reached in the tolerance quotient, expressed in formal action by the community stigmatizing of the deviant; (7) strengthening of the deviant conduct as a reaction to the stigmatizing and penalties; (8) ultimate acceptance of deviant social status and efforts at adjustment on the basis of the associated role. (1951:77)

Studies of deviant subcultures have confirmed the movement from primary to secondary deviance described by Lemert. The process does not apply to every group which supports deviant acts, however. Young people who engage in truancy and vandalism may be perceived by the public, the schools, and the police as good students who are merely sowing a few wild oats or as hooligans and delinquents, depending on the social groups to which they belong. The truth of this assertion is evidenced in a well-known and often-cited study by the criminologist William Chambliss (1973/2002) (see box).

While we believe that labeling powerfully explains how some people become committed to deviant lifestyles, the theory does not adequately explain why people engage in deviant acts in the first place. When we begin the discussion of deviance in our undergraduate classes we often take a poll, asking students how many have done something against the law. Always, virtually every hand is raised. Such an informal poll accords with the material presented by Stuart Henry (1990) in a book which contains students' own

The Saints and the Roughnecks

Almost every high school has gangs or groups of youths like those studied by Chambliss. One group, which he calls the Saints, were the sons of "good, stable, white upper-middle-class families." They were active in school affairs, were popular, and bound for college. In their relations with police and school authorities they were polite and respectful. The group Chambliss called the Roughnecks, on the other hand, were lower-class white boys who received average grades in school and were constantly in trouble with the police and the community. A high level of mutual distrust and dislike characterized their relations with authorities. In the public's perception, Chambliss says,

> The Saints were good boys who just went in for an occasional prank. After all, they were well dressed, well mannered, and had nice cars. The Roughnecks were a different story. Although the two gangs of boys were the same age, and both groups engaged in an equal amount of wild-oat sowing, everyone agreed that the not-so-well-dressed, not-so-well-mannered, not-so-rich boys were heading for trouble. (2002:196)

In fact, however, Chambliss found that the Saints were almost constantly occupied with truancy, drinking, reckless driving, petty theft, and vandalism. They cheated in class and contrived elaborate schemes to get out of class and off the campus. On weekends they went to a nearby city, where they drank heavily, drove dangerously, and committed acts of vandalism which damaged property and had the potential of seriously injuring others. A favorite prank was to steal lanterns and barricades around construction sites or road repairs, enjoy the plight of those who fell into the traps, and then erect the warning signals where they could cause more confusion.

The Roughnecks' behavior in school was not particularly disruptive, and they generally regarded it as a necessary burden to be borne with the least possible conflict. Their delinquency took three forms: theft, drinking, and fighting. Of these, petty stealing of both small and expensive items was the most regular and frequent activity. Their drinking was limited because they lacked the cars and the cash required for ready access to liquor. There were frequent fights between members and others, but they seldom involved the whole group.

After observing the two groups for about two years, Chambliss looked for answers to two questions: Why did the community, the school, and the police consider the Saints to be "good boys" with bright futures, but regard the Roughnecks as delinquents and potential criminals? Why did the careers of the Roughnecks and the Saints after high school generally live up to these expectations? Chambliss concluded that the reasons for the different reactions to the behaviors of the groups' members related to the differences in the visibility of their activities, their demeanor, and the bias of the community, the schools, and the police. Primarily because of their social class position, the members of the two groups received widely different labels, and eventually they came to see themselves in terms of these labels. The Saints never thought of themselves as deviant, while the Roughnecks responded to the community's definition by becoming more involved in deviant activities. Chambliss describes the Roughnecks' progression from primary to secondary deviance this way:

> The community responded to the Roughnecks as boys in trouble, and the boys agreed with that perception. Their pattern of deviancy was reinforced, and breaking away from it became increasingly unlikely. Once the boys acquired an image of themselves as deviants, they selected new friends who affirmed that self-image. As that self-conception became more firmly entrenched, they also became willing to try new and more extreme deviances. With their growing alienation came freer expression of disrespect and hostility for representatives of the legitimate society. This disrespect increased the community's negativism, perpetuating the entire process of commitment to deviance. (2002:202)

accounts of their deviant behavior. The focus of the essays is on how students rationalize such diverse behaviors as visiting prostitutes, smoking marijuana, using cocaine, stealing from the workplace, and concealing handguns. To the list of behaviors covered in Henry's book we would add cheating as a practice that appears to be condoned by large numbers of college students. According to the Center for Academic Integrity at Duke University, 75 percent of all college students "confess to cheating at least once" (Kleiner and Lord, 1999). Some of the students' accounts were: "I realize that it's wrong but I don't feel bad about it, either, partly because I know everyone else is doing it"; ". . . there are times that you cheat because there aren't enough hours in the day . . . I understood how to do it; I just didn't have the time" (Kleiner and Lord, 1999). As suggested by our earlier discussion in this chapter, students are able to invoke a range of accounts explaining why their behavior either shouldn't be called deviant or, if deviant, should be excused. Students' justifications for a number of behaviors generally considered deviant is eloquent evidence of human beings' ability to reject widespread social definitions about what is right or wrong.

The interactionist perspective on deviance increases our understanding of the kinds of choices actors make and the kinds of social organizational factors that both constrain and facilitate those choices. Actors confront large social organizational arrangements in everyday life and make choices that are variously facilitated and constrained by these arrangements (Ulmer and Spencer, 1999). To truly understand behaviors we must try to see them from the point of view of the people who engage in them.

Conclusion

When the word *deviant* is used to describe a person, it normally conjures up an image of someone whose behaviors are against the law or, at the very least, unmistakably different and "odd." In this chapter we have adopted a broader view of deviant behavior to include any act that compromises the perception that a person's identity is proper or socially correct. Everyday deviances are occasional improprieties that *everyone* engages in from time to time. They may result only in discomfort or embarrassment.

When individuals somehow "lose face," remedial interactions are necessary to restore the identities of self and others and remedy the situation. Our discussion of the contours of embarrassment and the vocabulary of motives that accounts for untoward behaviors pointed out that analysis of everyday deviances is part of a larger theoretical agenda. A close look at circumstances in which interaction is threatened by deviance can shed light on how an ordered daily life is produced, sustained, and protected.

Lifestyle deviances are related to the labeling of individuals and actions as deviant by powerful groups. Labeling theory fits the symbolic interactionist perspective because it conceives of deviance as a matter of arbitrary human definition. According to this view, no act is inherently deviant. As the discussion of the medicalization of deviance showed, definitions of deviance are connected to matters of power. The position of people and groups in the society determines their ability to have their views of deviance become "official" definitions.

Labeling theory thus shifts the focus in deviance from rule breakers to rule makers. Labeling also influences the ways individuals think of themselves. Movement from primary to secondary deviance occurs when people accept the negative labels that others put on them. As their own identities shift, they seek out others who have been similarly labeled. Membership in a deviant subculture is a step in embarking upon a deviant career. At the same time we should acknowledge that people are sometimes capable of rejecting deviant labels and redefining their behaviors as thoroughly legitimate. We also put forth the idea that part of understanding deviance from the point of view of the individual requires us to learn about the emotions people feel when they break rules.

Fundamentally, deviance is concerned with the breaking of rules or violations of the social norms that direct behaviors. In the next chapter we will consider how the meaning of the life cycle and people's movement through it are guided by clear age norms. What people do and feel at different ages cannot be interpreted apart from the social context in which they are living. Such age categories as childhood, adolescence, middle age, and old age are social constructions, in the same way deviance is.

DEFINITIONS

Disclaimers Statements meant to provide a nondeviant frame of reference within which forthcoming behaviors can be interpreted.

Embarrassment The feeling of self-shame following the commission of an impropriety which arises out of individuals' knowledge that others have negatively evaluated something they have done. Embarrassment may vary in intensity from very mild to so severe that an individual must withdraw entirely from a situation.

Everyday deviances   Acts of deviance which occur during the normal course of everyday interaction and temporarily mark individuals as nonconforming or improper.

Excuses   A type of verbal *account* offered for behaviors that have been deemed unacceptable or deviant by some audience. Those who offer excuses admit that their behavior has been undesirable or wrong, but they also indicate the extenuating circumstances that required them to behave as they did.

Face games   Ritualized behaviors designed to help individuals "save face" when events occur during interactions which openly damage the identity of participants.

Justifications   Accounts that people offer to acknowledge they have committed acts being questioned but which are designed to indicate why the acts should not be interpreted as deviant.

Labeling theory   The idea that powerful people and groups are able to impose their definitions of morality on others by labeling certain activities and the individuals who engage in them as deviant. People who are repeatedly labeled as deviant are said to accept the label eventually and then define themselves as deviant.

Lifestyle deviances   Acts of deviance which an individual engages in repeatedly and over a long time. People who engage in lifestyle deviances such as crime or drug addiction can be described as following a deviant career. They usually are members of a deviant subculture composed of people who engage in the same deviance.

Looking-glass self   The idea, suggested by Charles Horton Cooley, that others serve as mirrors in which we see ourselves reflected, and through those reflections we adopt subjective definitions of ourselves.

Medicalization of deviance   The process through which medical professionals have been allowed to define various deviant behaviors as states of illness requiring treatment. Increasingly, medicine is being used to "treat" those whose behaviors do not conform to societal expectations.

Moral entrepreneurs   People who are constantly on crusades to establish rules, to implement them, and then to label those who do not follow them as offenders. The term was coined by Howard Becker.

Passing   Presenting oneself as having attributes that are different from one's real status to avoid being evaluated negatively by others. People who change distinctive ethnic names may try to pass as members of an entirely different ethnic group, for example.

Primary deviances   The initial, usually isolated breaches of rules that nearly everyone has engaged in. Rule violations remain primary as long as the individuals involved define them as incidental to "who they really are."

Secondary deviances   Norm violations that result from individuals' self-definitions as deviant. Violations become secondary deviances when, as a result of consistent negative responses from others, individuals begin to think of themselves as deviant and to behave accordingly.

Self-fulfilling prophecy   Howard Becker's notion that labeling may encourage an individual to become what they have been labeled, even though the original accusation (e.g., of deviant behavior) may have been false. Labeling sets in motion a chain of actions and reactions that make the original expectations come true.

Significant others   Those other people with whom we have strong emotional attachments and whose judgments are most important in determining our behaviors.

Social control   The various techniques and strategies for regulating human behavior in a society and ensuring that individuals conform to social norms. Techniques of social control can range from expressions of dissatisfaction with another's behavior, to ridicule, to outright force.

Social equilibrium   The state which exists when a social system is operating free of conflict or disruption. Sociologists are interested in the conditions that allow social systems to operate trouble-free, as well as the forces that create *disequilibrium.*

Total institutions   Goffman's term for closed environments in which the time and space of inmates can be controlled (e.g., mental hospitals, prisons, chronic care facilities), in which inmates experience "civil death" and "mortification of self" upon entry.

Vocabulary of motives   C. Wright Mills' term for the broad explanatory schemas used to explain different categories of behavior. *Motives* are the "whys" of behaviors, the intentions or purposes which explain their direction and persistence. Basic physiological needs such as hunger or thirst, as well as complicated motives such as the needs for love, achievement, belonging, and esteem, can all motivate behavior.

DISCUSSION QUESTIONS

1. Think about three instances in which you have felt embarrassed. For each one analyze the aspects of role performance that were disrupted. What did you do to "correct" your identity in each case? What did others do to decrease or increase your embarrassment?

2. What is "coolness"? How do you recognize coolness when you see it? What do you lose when you lose your cool?

3. Think of a time when you have interacted with a person who has a visible physical handicap. Did the person's handicapped status alter the interaction? If so, was there a point when it ceased to influence the encounter? When did this happen, and why?

4. Throughout a one-day period take note of every instance in which you or others explain motives for behaviors. How would you categorize these specimens of motive talk—as excuses, justifications, or disclaimers? Were there any cases when the audience did not honor the motive explanation? If not, why not?

5. Describe a time when you were labeled by some authority figure or person significant to you. (Labels, of course, can be positive as well as negative.) How powerful was the label? Did it significantly affect the ways others responded to you? Did the label influence your view of yourself?

6. Have you ever committed an act which would have landed you in a courtroom were you caught? Was this a case of primary deviance? If so, did it lead to any secondary deviances? Why or why not?

REFERENCES

Angrosino, M. 1997. *Opportunity House: Ethnographic Studies of Mental Retardation.* Walnut Creek, CA: AltaMira Press.

Becker, H. 1963. *Outsiders.* New York: Free Press.

Berger, P., and T. Luckmann. 1967. *The Social Construction of Reality*. New York: Doubleday Anchor Books.

Cahill, S., and R. Eggleston. 1995. "Reconsidering the stigma of physical disability: Wheelchair use and public kindness." *Sociological Quarterly* 36:681–98.

Chambliss, W. [1973]2002. "The saints and the roughnecks." *Society* 11 (November-December): 24–31. Reprinted in *Deviance: The Interactionist Perspective*, edited by E. Rubington and M. Weinberg. Boston: Allyn & Bacon.

Cole, S., M. Kemeny, S. Taylor, B. Visscher, and J. Fahey. 1996. "Accelerated course of human immunodeficiency virus infection in gay men who conceal their homosexual identity." *Psychosomatic Medicine* 58:219–31.

Conrad, P., and J. Schneider, 1992. *Deviance and Medicalization: From Badness to Sickness*. Philadelphia: Temple University Press.

Crozier, W. 1990. "Social psychological perspectives on shyness, embarrassment, and shame." In *Shyness and Embarrassment: Perspectives from Social Psychology*, edited by W. Crozier. New York: Cambridge University Press.

———. 2001. "Shyness and embarrassment." In *Understanding Shyness: Psychological Perspective*, edited by W. Crozier, pp. 140–177. New York: Palgrove.

Curra, J. 2000. *The Relativity of Deviance*. Thousand Oaks, CA: Sage Publications.

Edelman, R. 1987. *The Psychology of Embarrassment*. New York: John Wiley & Sons.

Ellis, C. 1998. "'I hate my voice': Coming to terms with minor bodily stigmas." *Sociological Quarterly* 39(4):517–37.

Fields, J. 2001. "Normal queers: Straight parents respond to their children's 'coming out.'" *Symbolic Interaction* 24(2):165–87.

Frable, D., L. Platt, and S. Hoey. 1998. "Concealable stigmas and positive self-perceptions: Feeling better around similar others." *Journal of Personality and Social Psychology* 74(4):909–22.

Geraghty, M. 1997. "The art and science of public humiliation." *Chronicle of Higher Education* 43(30):A8.

Garfinkel, H. 1968. *Studies in Ethnomethodology*. Englewood Cliffs, NJ: Prentice Hall.

Goffman, E. 1955. "On face-work: An analysis of ritual elements in social interaction." *Psychiatry: Journal for the Study of Interpersonal Processes* 18(3):213–31.

———. 1956. "Embarrassment and social organization." *American Journal of Sociology* 62: 264–71.

———. 1961. *Asylums: Essays on the Social Situation of Mental Patients and Other Inmates*. Garden City, NY: Anchor.

———. 1963. *Stigma: Notes on the Management of Spoiled Identity*. Englewood Cliffs, NJ: Prentice Hall. (1986 Touchstone Edition. New York: Simon & Schuster.)

———. 1967. *Interaction Ritual*. New York: Pantheon Books.

Gross, E., and G. Stone. 1964. "Embarrassment and the analysis of role requirements." *American Journal of Sociology* 70 (July): 1–15.

Haller, B. A. 2001. "Confusing disability and tragedy." *The Sun*, April 29:1C, 4C.

Hayes, T. 2000. "Stigmatizing indebtedness: Implications for labeling theory." *Symbolic Interaction* 23(1):29–46.

Heckert, D., and A. Best. 1997. "Ugly duckling to swan: Labeling theory and the stigmatization of red hair." *Symbolic Interaction* 20(4):365–84.

Henderson, L. 1999. "Social Fitness Training: Integrated short-term treatment for chronic shyness." *The California Psychologist*. (Accessed via Internet 6/8/02). http://www.shyness.com/shyness-research.html

Henderson, L., P. Zimbardo, and B. Carducci. 1999. "Shyness." *Encyclopedia of Psychology*. (Accessed via Internet 6/8/02). http://www.shyness.com/shyness-research.html

Henry, S. 1990. *Degrees of Deviance: Student Accounts of their Deviant Behavior.* Salem, WI: Sheffield Publishing.

Herman, N., and G. Musolf. 1998. "Resistance among ex-psychiatric patients: Expressive and instrumental rituals." *Journal of Contemporary Ethnography* 26(4):426–49.

Hewitt, J. 2003. *Self and Society.* 9th ed. Boston: Allyn & Bacon.

Hewitt, J., and R. Stokes. 1975. "Disclaimers." *American Sociological Review* 40: 1–11.

Jezer, M. 1997. *Stuttering: A Life Bound Up in Words.* New York: Basic Books.

Keltner, D., and B. Buswell. 1997. "Embarrassment: Its distinct form and appeasement functions." *Psychological Bulletin* 122:250–70.

Kim, J-Y., and H. Kim. 2002. "Stigma in divorces and its deterrence effect." *Journal of Socio-Economics* 203:1–15.

Kleiner, C., and M. Lord. 1999. "The cheating game: 'Everyone's doing it,' from grade school to graduate school." *U.S. News & World Report*, November 2:55–66.

Leary, M., and R. Kowalski. 1995. *Social Anxiety.* New York: The Guilford Press.

Lee, J., and E. Craft. 2002. "Protecting one's self from a stigmatized disease . . . once one has it." *Deviant Behavior: An Interdisciplinary Journal* 23:267–99.

Lemert, E. 1951. *Social Pathology.* New York: McGraw-Hill.

Lemert, C., and A. Branaman, eds. 1997. *The Goffman Reader.* Malden, MA: Blackwell Publishers Ltd.

Livingston, K. 2000. "When architecture disables: Teaching undergraduates to perceive ableism in the built environment." *Teaching Sociology* 28:182–91.

Lyman, S., and M. Scott. 1968. "Accounts." *American Sociological Review* 33 (December): 46–62.

Major, B., and R. Gramzow. 1999. "Abortion as stigma: Cognitive and emotional implications of concealment." *Journal of Personality and Social Psychology* 77(4):735–45.

Miller, R. 1996. *Embarrassment: Poise and Peril in Everyday Life.* New York: The Guilford Press.

Mills, C. W. 1940. "Situated actions and vocabularies of motive." *American Sociological Review* 5:904–13.

Nack, A. 2000. "Damaged goods: Women managing the stigma of STDs." *Deviant Behavior: An Interdisciplinary Journal* 21:95–121.

Oliver, M. 1996. *Understanding Disability: From Theory to Practice.* New York: Macmillan Press.

Paterniti, D. 2000. "The micropolitics of identity in adverse circumstance: A study of identity making in a total institution." *Journal of Contemporary Ethnography* 29(1):93–119.

Perry, J. 1996. "Writing the self: Exploring the stigma of hearing impairment." *Sociological Spectrum* 16:239–61.

Richardson, L. 1996. "Speech lessons." In *Composing Ethnography*, edited by C. Ellis and A. Bochner, pp. 231–39. Walnut Creek, CA: AltaMira Press.

Ronai, C., and R. Cross. 1998. "Dancing with identity: Narrative resistance strategies of male and female stripteasers." *Deviant Behavior: An Interdisciplinary Journal* 19:99–119.

Rosenhan, D. [1973]2001. "On being sane in insane places." *Science* 179:250–58. Reprinted in *The Production of Reality*, 3rd ed., edited by J. O'Brien and P. Kollock, pp. 434–42. Thousand Oaks, CA: Pine Forge Press.

Rossol, J. 2001. "The medicalization of deviance as an interactive achievement: The construction of compulsive gambling." *Symbolic Interaction* 24(3):315–41.

Sabini, J., B. Garvey, and A. Hall. 2001. "Shame and embarrassment revisited." *PSPB* 27(1):104–17.

Scambler, G. 1998. "Stigma and disease: Changing paradigms. *The Lancet* 352(9133):1054.

Schur, E. 1971. *Labeling Deviant Behavior: Its Sociological Implications.* New York: Harper & Row.

Siegel, K., H. Lune, and I. Meyer. 1998. "Stigma management among gay/bisexual men with HIV/AIDS." *Qualitative Sociology* 21(1):3–24.

Smart, L., and D. Wegner. 1999. "Covering up what can't be seen: Concealable stigma and mental control." *Journal of Personality and Social Psychology* 77(3):474–86.

Stonehouse, C., and R. Miller. 1994. "Embarrassing circumstances, week by week." Poster presented at the annual meeting of the American Psychological Society, Washington, D.C. (July).

Sumner, C. 1994. *The Sociology of Deviance: An Obituary.* New York: Continuum.

Tangney, J., R. Miller, L. Flicker, and D. Barlow. 1996. "Are shame, guilt, and embarrassment distinct emotions?" *Journal of Personality and Social Psychology* 70:1256–69.

Ulmer, J., and J. Spencer. 1999. "The contributions of an interactionist approach to research and theory on criminal careers." *Theoretical Criminology* 3(1):95–124.

Weinberg, M. 1965. "Sexual modesty, social meanings, and the nudist camp." *Social Problems* 12: 311–18.

Zimbardo, P. 1986. "The Stanford Shyness Project." In *Shyness: Perspectives on Research and Treatment*, edited by W. Jones, J. Cheek, and S. Briggs, pp. 17–25. New York: Plenum.

———. 1999. "Recollections of a social psychologist's career: An interview with Dr. Philip Zimbardo." *Journal of Social Behavior & Personality* 14(1):1–22.

AGING AND THE LIFE CYCLE

At age 88, Colonel Sanders, the original fried chicken fast food expert, told a reporter: "I'm real interested in old folks because I guess maybe someday I'll be old myself." Satchell Paige, probably the oldest man ever to play professional baseball (although he would never reveal his age), recognized old age as a social construct when he asked, "How old would you be if you didn't know how old you was?" (Stoller and Gibson, 2000). There is a clear connection between general cultural values, the values particular to specific social contexts, and the meanings attached to chronological age.

The **meanings of age** are contextual; that is, they are tied to the societies and situations in which people find themselves. As we move from situation to situation in our daily lives, we are defined differently by those around us at various times and are required to behave in accordance with quite different age conventions. Your classmates may consider you one age, your professors another, and the members of your family a quite different one. Within each of these contexts you have to be responsive to a number of age definitions. Your parents may define you throughout your life as their little boy or girl, a definition you may seek to avoid. Your children may eventually define you as too old to understand their problems, while your brothers, sisters, friends, and cousins will think of one another as still "the boys" or "the girls." In some contexts a person's age requires adopting a subordinate position, in other situations the same age merits a dominant position. Different situations call forth varying expectations about age-appropriate behaviors. What you can say, the attitudes you can safely express, the respect you believe is due you, and the responses you predict others will make to you, all relate to their expectations of someone your age. In short, age is a critical factor in determining how others define us and how we define ourselves. In dramaturgical terms, age helps determine the performances we put on in front of a given audience.

In this chapter we take the position that age, as such, has no intrinsic meaning. In every society meanings which often are quite arbitrary are assigned to different ages in the life cycle. In this view there are many definitions of the aging process, and aging is a social construction built on age norms. The age structure of a society, however, is produced by demographic changes and historical processes. Before we examine the meanings attached to age, we will describe the present age structure in American society and consider how various age categories have developed over time.

Age Categories in American Society

There has been a widespread tendency in the social and biological sciences to search for the *naturalized life course*; that is, to chart the innate development and decline of human capacities, tendencies, proclivities, and so on, over the lifespan (Gergen and Gergen, 2000). Erik Erikson's (1968) notion of the **life cycle**, conceived as regular stages of development, has been particularly influential. As interactionists we find such theories of adult development intriguing, but we suggest that theories which claim to identify *universal* stages of human development should be approached with caution. Although people may well move through regular stages in their lives, we question whether such movement applies equally to all segments of society. For example, we are hard-pressed to imagine that people from upper-class social circles in the United States move through the same life stages as those whose income is below the poverty level.

A complex web of social and cultural factors shapes our concepts of age. Old age is just one of the life stages that societies create—the number and timing of such stages vary. For example, prior to the twentieth century there was no term for adolescence. People arrived at adulthood at much earlier ages than in today's Western industrial societies. Today, entire markets (e.g., clothing, entertainment) cater exclusively to teenagers. People construct different meanings that they associate with various stages of the life course. Age serves to distinguish acceptable behavior for different groups. Voting rights, the legal right to consume alcohol, and the age at which one can collect Social Security benefits as a retired worker are all examples of specific, formal age norms in the United States.

The Aging of the U.S. Population

One's **age status** in a society is determined by social and cultural as well as biological factors. The meanings attached to different age categories are influenced, for example, by the **age structure** of a society, or the number of people in different age categories. The age structure of a society is one of the key factors determining the need for various social resources. Perhaps the most important—and potentially problematic—demographic trend in the United States today involves the increasing average age of the population, or the "graying" of America.

In thinking about the age structure of a population, demographers usually focus on the rate of birth and rate of death. Two hundred years ago, the median age for U.S. residents was 16, so in 1800 the United States was a very "young" nation in terms of its age structure. In the past decades, however, both the mortality rate (which had been declining since 1800) and the birth rate have simultaneously declined. Currently, we are witnessing significant increases in the number of people surviving into old age. The median age of the population, which was 30 in 1980, rose to about 35.8 in 2000, and is expected to be over 38 by mid-century, as the baby boom cohort reaches old age (U.S. Census Bureau, 2000). For the first time in our history, the population over age 65 is increasing in size while the population under 35 is decreasing. Life expectancy has risen from 67.1 for males and 74.0 for females in 1970 to 74.2 for males and 79.9 for females in 1997. Between 1960 and 1980, the proportion of people over 65 grew by 54 percent (U.S. Census Bureau, 2000). By 2030, the United States will have more old people than children. The number of people over 85 will grow fastest, doubling to 6.5 million by 2020. By 2050, more than 1 million people will be over the age of 100 (Rimer, 1998).

One of the consequences of this changing age structure is that as an age category increases in size, its political importance as a voting bloc whose collective interests must be considered also increases. Table 10.1, which shows actual and projected changes in the age distribution of the population from 1960 to 2000, indicates the shifting balance of political power held by different age groups in the United States. The number of children under 18 continues to drop, decreasing from 35.7 percent in 1960 to a projected 24.9 percent in 2005 (table 10.2). While the 18 to 44 age group remains the largest category of the voting-age population, the percentage of the population in this group is declining.

The percentage of the population between 45 and 64 remained fairly stable between 1960 and 2000. At the same time, the over-65 age group, which represented only 9.2 percent of the population in 1960, has been rising steadily. It is this age group that is most likely to vote. Sixty-seven percent of those over 65 voted in the 2000 presidential election, compared to only 28 percent of those between 18 and 20 (U.S. Census Bureau, 2001).

The potential power generated by the large numbers of elderly people in American society could stimulate major changes in governmental health and economic policies. The likelihood of such changes, of course, depends on whether the elderly can achieve a unity of purpose through effective political organization. The political clout of the elderly could also improve younger people's conceptions of the aged, thereby lessening discrimination and prejudice.

Robert Butler (1969:243) first coined the term **ageism** to describe the "systematic stereotyping of and discrimination against people because they are

Table 10.1
Percentage of Population in Age Groups, United States, 1960–2000

Age group	1960	1970	1980	1990	2000*
Under 18	35.7	34.1	27.7	26.4	24.5
18–44	35.0	35.7	41.2	42.7	39.6
45–64	20.0	20.5	19.6	18.3	22.9
65+	9.2	9.8	11.3	12.6	13.0

*Percentages for 2000 are projections.

Sources: U.S. Census Bureau, Statistical Abstract of the United States, 1984 (Washington, D.C.: Government Printing Office, 1983), Tables 30 and 31; Statistical Abstract of the United States, 1991, Table 18.

Table 10.2
Percentage of Population in Age Groups, United States, 2000–2050*

Age group	2000	2005	2010	2015	2020	2025	2050
Under 18	25.7	24.9	24.1	23.8	23.8	23.9	23.8
18–44	39.9**	34.8	33.1	32.6	32.2	31.7	31.3
45–64	22.0	24.9	26.5	26.2	25.0	23.2	22.1
65+	12.4	12.6	13.2	14.7	16.6	18.5	20.3

*2005–2050 percentages are projections. **Percentage is for 1999.

Sources: U.S. Census Bureau, Statistical Abstract of the United States, 2001. Table 11, Residential population by sex and age group: 1990 and 2000; Table 13, Residential population projections by sex and age: 2005–2050. < http://www.census.gov/statab/> Accessed 11/23/02.

old, just as racism and sexism accomplish this with skin color and gender" (see box). Similar to racism and sexism, ageism encourages viewing people not as individuals but as members of a social category (Quadagno, 1999). In American society ageism is connected to the high value placed on youth, and it has increased as the number of older people making demands on the nation's resources has grown. Ageism is more than the attitudes and beliefs held by individuals in a particular society; it is also embedded in patterns of behavior and serves as a social organizing principle (Dressel, Minkler and Yen, 1997). Ageism takes new forms over time. For example, images of the old as vulnerable have recently given way to images of the affluent "greedy geezer," whose selfish drain on society has left younger generations in poverty. In addition, another new form of ageism, based on "the tendency to patronize the elderly and to be overly solicitous" (Quadagno, 1999:6), has also appeared.

Age Categories as Social Constructions

Terms such as *infant, child, teenager,* and *adult* are very much a part of our social reality. They are used to describe such everyday interactions as babies

Ageism and Inequality

To some extent Americans idealize old age. The retirement years are supposed to be the "golden years." Advertisements portray the elderly as carefree, well-dressed, and well-fed. If they no longer live in their family homes, they are pictured as happy members of retirement communities with names like Sun City or Leisure World. In reality, large numbers of elderly people must bear economic, physical, and emotional burdens. Those on fixed incomes can easily fall into poverty, and they may be denied work even if they are able to work. They are discriminated against when seeking housing. They suffer the indignities encouraged by others' incorrect stereotypes about what it is to be old. Political leaders often are insensitive to the needs of the elderly in the policies they create. Eventually the old may suffer technologized deaths in impersonal institutions.

Ageism interacts with other types of discrimination—sexism, racism, classism, and heterosexism—in ways that make the experience of ageism both similar and different across various groups. For example, class, race and ethnicity, sexual orientation, and gender can influence economic dependence in later life. Low lifetime earnings result in lower levels of Social Security. Also, the inability to save or invest in a pension reduces income in later life. A white working-class male will generally have lower lifetime earnings than a white middle-class man; a white working-class woman will not only have even lower benefits, due to lower earnings, but if she is a lesbian, will not be able to collect a pension or Social Security as a spouse. Black men are more likely to experience unemployment and higher rates of disability than white men (c.f., Hayward, Friedman, and Chen, 1996), and are thus more likely to rely on unemployment or disability payments and will also have lower Social Security benefits. The *theory of cumulative disadvantage* takes into account the social categories that increase inequality throughout the life course (Quadagno, 1999). Advantages or disadvantages based on social class, gender, and race early in life carry through to old age.

The intersections of race and class in designating someone as "old" can be seen in the results of a poll conducted by the Americans Discuss Social Security project. The findings reveal that, while people generally feel that old age occurs in one's early 60s, the higher one's wealth, the later the onset of perceived old age. Moreover, African Americans and Hispanics see the onset of old age as occurring in the late 50s (Associated Press, 1998). No doubt class influences this as well. That is, minorities in higher social classes (who have held jobs free of hard physical labor and with adequate health benefits) will not grow old in the same ways as members of racial or ethnic groups who are disadvantaged (Calasanti and Slevin, 2001).

Financial security is a key factor in maintaining a healthy and independent lifestyle in old age. As a group, the elderly have experienced a major decline in poverty since the 1960s, primarily due to the expansion of federal programs such as Medicare. Despite this success, the figures mask a number of factors that not only keep many elderly in poverty but also put certain groups at risk for poverty when they reach old age.

being nurtured by their parents, children playing in parks, teenagers mingling at school dances, and young adults meeting in bars. The use of **age categories** to identify individuals of varying chronological ages appears so natural as to be taken for granted. Surely there have always been and always will be infants, children, teenagers, and adults. But is that really the case? Have such age categories always existed throughout history, or do the definitions of what constitutes the appropriate behaviors of an age category vary by both historical period and from one culture to another?

The answers to such questions become apparent when age categories are considered as arbitrary social constructions rather than fixed biological or chronological divisions. The behaviors underlying such categories ultimately derive their meanings from the social contexts in which they occur. In this section we will focus on the historical origins of four contemporary age categories: childhood, adolescence, middle age, and old age. We will be concerned with how changes in the organization of society have created the context in which people's sense of aging, or subjective experience of the passage of time, has undergone change as well.

The Social Invention of Childhood

As a distinct age grouping, childhood has a fairly short history. It did not exist in the Middle Ages, when the life cycle proceeded directly from infancy to little adulthood to adulthood. Those in the age groups we call children today were then considered to be adults on a smaller scale (Aries, 1962).

Prior to the seventeenth century, adults and "little adults" participated in virtually the same activities. They worked and played together, in continual physical contact with each other. Adults and children played exactly the same games with the same degree of involvement, enthusiasm, and, most importantly, seriousness. Children played games of chance for money, and adults played games such as leapfrog. We could just as well say that the children of the time played *adultishly* as that the adults played *childishly*.

Life was never all fun and games for the young, of course. Both in the United States and Europe, children labored on farms, in homes, and in artisans' shops. Until the end of the nineteenth century, few Americans or Europeans doubted that such labor was beneficial to youth; it taught them industry and thrift and prepared them for future employment. Before 1850, only the most well-to-do could afford to exempt their children from labor in field, home, or factory. However, in the second half of the century, a growing number of affluent middle-class city dwellers and some prosperous farmers were able to delay employment of their children and instead prolonged their education. On the other hand, many more parents—including those who owned, rented, or sharecropped small farms, as well as parents who worked at unskilled or semiskilled jobs in cities—were so poor that they had to put their children to work at a young age (Clement, 1997).

The emergence of childhood as an age category has been associated with the development of the modern family as a particular type of social and emotional arrangement (see chapter 5). This was related to the growth of the new middle class as the effects of industrialization and urbanization intensified, changing the character of American society in the late nineteenth century. The middle class cultivated a new sensibility about children that was based on the idea that they should be protected from contacts with various kinds of "dangerous persons." Children were required to attend schools where they were processed bureaucratically into distinct age-grade groupings, for example.

As childhood came to be viewed as a bona fide age category, a new set of attitudes and values about relations between parents and young children was ushered in. The accepted view today is that parents should not physically abuse their children or treat them in a cold, emotionally distant manner. Children generally are to be protected from the ugly and often brutal realities of what life is "really like."

Adolescence: Between Childhood and Adult Status

Having experienced the agonies and ecstasies of adolescence, you may assume that this phase of the life cycle, like childhood, has a certain timelessness and universality to it. But rather than being an inevitable passage between childhood and adulthood in the lives of all human beings, the adolescent stage is also a fairly recent idea.

The construction of adolescence as an age category in American society can be linked to three social movements in the late nineteenth and early twentieth centuries: compulsory public education, child labor legislation, and separate legal procedures for the treatment of juveniles (c.f., Macleod, 1998). These movements were designed to protect children for increasingly longer periods of their lives. By establishing age regulations in the areas of schooling, work, and criminal violations, social reformers helped mark out precise age categories. Adolescence became recognized as the period between puberty, a biological event, and the ages specified by the law for the end of compulsory education, the beginning of employment, and the limits of special treatment in criminal procedures.

These social movements were a response to the urbanization and industrialization of the United States. Cities came to be seen as places where the young easily fell prey to the vices of sexual immorality, crime, and alcohol abuse. Urban life was considered a "pathological" corruptor of innocent, defenseless youths who were urgently in need of the state's protection. The evils of long hours and hard work for children became more apparent as the need for their services declined.

Between 1890 and 1920, public high schools increasingly became the most central institution in the lives of children we now call adolescents. However, even by 1920 only one child in six graduated from high school (Macleod, 1998). Previously the rhythms of the school year were dictated by the agricultural seasons, with school attendance linked to the need for young laborers on the farm. Now attendance was required, and truancy became defined as a deviant act punishable by law.

The movement to regulate working conditions and set a minimum age at which children were allowed to work outside their own families also helped segregate teenagers from the rest of society and prolong their dependency on their parents. A labor surplus in the post-Civil War period prompted the campaign for child labor laws, which limited the hours, wages, and types of work permissible for youths under a certain age.

The increasing technical sophistication of industrial production called for skilled and disciplined workers. By the 1840s and 1850s, industrialists in the North and Midwest, concerned about urban crime, poverty, and disorder, agreed that schools could provide them with an obedient, law-abiding, and literate labor force (Clement, 1997). Educational reformers geared their arguments to a capitalist economy. Compulsory education would provide a labor force suited to the capitalistic industrial society that was taking shape. Required school attendance and minimum age restrictions kept unskilled labor out of the factory and produced better disciplined and more manageable workers who knew how to follow a supervisor's orders. Some of the constants in nineteenth-century schools included individual competition (e.g., spelling bees), emphasis on respect for private property, and obedience to the teacher's authority (with punishment for misbehaving). The rigid order and strict discipline of nineteenth-century schools served a purpose:

> At a time when the United States was barely one hundred years old, when it had experienced a bloody and divisive Civil War, vast economic expansion accompanied by unemployment, depressions, violent labor disputes, and large-scale immigration of persons from dramatically different cultures, there appeared good reason to quickly train all American children to self-discipline and restraint. (Clement, 1997:90–91)

The creation of a special category of deviance for youthful offenders, juvenile delinquency, furthered the processing of youths as members of a separate category. The first Juvenile Court Act, passed by the Illinois legislature in 1899, became a model for many others during the next two decades. The driving force behind a separate juvenile justice system, however, came from Colorado's municipal judge Benjamin Lindsey (West, 1996). On looking into a case in which a boy had taken coal to sell and use for home heating, he found that many young people facing charges were poor urban children, not criminals. Nevertheless, they were sometimes held in jails with hardened adult criminals for weeks, or even months, before trial. He concluded that it was not a system well suited either for children or for society, and began hearing all juvenile cases separately from adult cases. He also recruited probation agents, mostly from among truant officers, to oversee their lives outside the courtroom. In taking on the roles of parents, however, courts began trying to regulate children's lives more extensively. Guiding them toward respectable adulthood had to mean more than stopping outright criminal activities. Juvenile delinquents, according to the Colorado statute, came to include "not only young thieves and vandals but any boy or girl under sixteen who hung around pool halls or saloons, who walked around the streets at night without a legitimate purpose, or who had a habit of using vile, obscene, vulgar, profane, or indecent language" (West, 1996:67).

The goal was to protect youthful offenders by treating them differently from hardened criminals; the result was another thread in the tapestry of adolescence as a separate age category, distinguished from both childhood and the adult stage.

Pathways to Adulthood

The transition to adulthood has become a thriving area of research in life course studies. *Emerging adulthood* is proposed as a new conception of development for the period in the life course from the late teens through the 20s, with a focus on ages 18–25. Sweeping demographic shifts over the last half of the twentieth century have made the late teens and early 20s not simply a brief period of transition into adult roles, but rather a distinct period of the life course characterized by change and exploration of possible life directions (Arnett, 2000).

One demographic area that especially reflects the exploratory quality of emerging adulthood is residential status. Most young Americans leave home by age 18 or 19. However, as we shall see later in the chapter, the norms about this are relatively loose. A majority of young adults go off to college after high school and spend the next several years in some combination of independent living and continued reliance on adults. About 40 percent move out of their parental home not for college but for independent living and full-time work (Goldscheider and Goldscheider, 1994). About two-thirds of young adults experience a period of cohabitation with a romantic partner (Michael et al., 1995). In fact, emerging adults have the highest rates of residential change of any age group.

School attendance is another area in which there is substantial change and diversity among emerging adults. The proportion of young Americans who enter higher education following high school has risen steeply, from 14 percent in 1940 to over 60 percent by the mid-1990s (Bianchi and Spain, 1996). However, only 32 percent of individuals ages 25–29 complete four years or more of college (U.S. Census Bureau, 1997). College education is often pursued in a nonlinear way, frequently combined with work and punctuated by periods of nonattendance.

An extended period of schooling complicates the transition from adolescence to adulthood (see box). Leaving home for college is perhaps the most potentially dislocating change that middle- to upper-middle-class youths have thus encountered (Holmstrom, Karp, and Gray, 2002).

Why Laundry, not Hegel?

Linda Holmstrom, David Karp, and Paul Gray studied upper-middle-class, college-bound high school seniors and their parents as they were going through the college application process. The seniors they interviewed expected college to be a transformative experience that would affect their identities, a "time for discovering who they *really* were" (see Karp, Holmstrom, and Gray, 1998). They also knew they would experience upheavals in the routines of everyday life as they face changes of place, changes in responsibility for tasks, and changes in familial relationships. Interestingly, their anxiety is focused more on issues such as how to get their laundry done than on whether they will understand thinkers such as Hegel. And although they look forward to the chance to be independent, at the same time they worry about whether they will be able to "cut it" on their own. As one student put it:

> I'll be independent for the first time in my life. I'll be totally dependent on just me and I'll have no one to answer to. That's the rebellious side of every teenager saying, "Oh, good. It's just me now and I don't have to worry about saying, 'No, I'm sorry that I didn't call you and tell you where I was until 3:30 in the morning.'"
> (Holmstrom et al., 2002:446)

On the other hand, the same student continues:

> [My parents] have always taken care of me. They've always been there to help me, to make sure that I got things done, and to give me a little nudge when I needed it, and to keep me going, and to give me support and stuff. Where am I going to get all that now? (p. 446)

These college-bound students see their ongoing transition to adulthood as a gradual, emerging process. College is seen as the next step to full adulthood. Students describe it as a place where you can "wean yourself into independence," "a step . . . halfway between the real world and high school" (p. 449). As one student put it:

> My parents help me; they keep me organized. They cook me dinner. . . . I can always talk to them about stuff, and I won't be able to next year, but then, over the last two years I've met friends that I talk to . . . I can cook good Minute Rice now and then! And I've done all my own laundry. So I've been getting progressively more independent. (p. 446)

Students long for independence but feel comforted knowing that their parents will help them in times of need. They want independence with a safety net—parents are the safety net. It is not surprising that these high school seniors admitted scant knowledge of the logistics of everyday life. Ordinarily, parents simply do not expect them to manage finances, cook, clean, or do their laundry completely on their own. It follows that managing these everyday life tasks would be at the forefront of students' consciousness as they imagined being "on their own" for the first time.

According to Holmstrom, Karp, and Gray, if compulsory public education shaped the "discovery" of adolescence as an age category, the enormous expansion of higher education in the United States over the last several decades has also transformed the way that upper-middle-class youths, especially, make their way into adulthood. Their interviewees' most consistent story centered on the clear parental expectation that children had one primary job in life—to succeed in school. And parents see it as their job to provide all the necessary infrastructural support to guarantee their offspring's educational success.

What these parents are buying with their tuition and dormitory dollars is a particular pathway to adulthood for their children, one that offers "a deliberately gradual transition to adulthood through semiautonomous campus living and deferral of the traditional role transitions to adulthood of self-supporting employment, marriage, and parenthood" (p. 457). For the college student, this strategic delay aims to maximize later opportunities—college attendance provides the most secure route to the skills and credentials necessary for a well-paid and interesting job. As one author points out, "Prolonged dependency may be an emerging strategy for success in the transition to adulthood" (Aquilino, 1999:173).

Crisis and Rebirth in Middle Age

In popular culture, middle age has been portrayed as a time of crisis or trauma in the life cycle. This stage is generally viewed as the period between the ages of 40 and 60, but the social construction of middle age has indefinite boundaries. Although most Americans readily recognize the term "midlife crisis" and pretty much agree that such a crisis occurs on a widespread basis in people's 40s, several studies (see McMillen, 1997) debunk the midlife crisis as an inevitable, nearly universal experience of psychological turmoil.

For example, although more than 25 percent of Americans over age 35 think they have had a midlife crisis, these may be more along the lines of "stressful life events" according to a study by the MacArthur Foundation Research Network on Successful Midlife Development in the United States (Lang, 2001). Most people who told the researchers they had had a midlife crisis—defined as personal turmoil and challenges in people age 39 through 50 brought on by fears and anxieties about growing older—were describing something else. That is, they were talking about stressful life events—situations brought on by specific transitions or events that may or may not be associated with typical aging, such as a life-threatening illness or job insecurity—that had occurred before age 39 or after age 50, rather than the type of turmoil defined as a midlife crisis (Lang, 2001).

And although most people characterize a midlife crisis as a negative thing, many respondents in the MacArthur Foundation study hinted that the myth of the midlife crisis has its good side, in that this time is seen as an opportunity to catch up to where they would like to be or expected to be when they were younger (Lang, 2001).

The meaning of midlife is changing for individuals and families. Defining midlife as the "**empty nest**" period of life is inaccurate for many Americans whose children still live at home—for many, childbearing and childrearing responsibilities have not ended by midlife. The changing demographics of the American population are affecting how midlife is viewed: we are living longer, marrying at later ages, and having children at older ages (Genovese, 1997). In recent years, midlife often has been pictured as "the good years," a time for relaxing and enjoying leisure time after the children are grown. As we have seen with other issues, there are plenty of books to help, such as *How to Survive and Thrive in an Empty Nest* (Lauer and Lauer, 1999), a step-by-step approach to help parents turn their empty nest into an opportunity for growth and positive change.

Other demographic developments have had a considerable impact on both family structure and people's sense of their own aging. In 1920 life expectancy was only 54.1 (U.S. Census Bureau, 1983), so many couples spent their entire married lives raising their children. When the last child was ready to leave home and establish a household, the parents had few years of life left. Today Americans are living longer and more actively well into their 70s, 80s, or beyond.

Women may be relieved, not depressed, to see their children launched; midlife women and men who are at the peak of their careers want to continue to be productive. For some, this time of life may mean concentrating on new interests or new careers. Thanks to "supernutrition" and biotechnology, a new life stage, "middlessence," has appeared, an expanded middle age period from approximately 40 to 60 years of age (Dychtwald, 1999).

However, these rosy vignettes do not apply to all Americans. The aging of the population and increased longevity mean that Americans will spend more years in retirement, which has important implications for financial planning and economic security. For many, whose lives are a constant struggle for survival, economic security remains an unattainable goal. Single mothers who are simultaneously raising their own children and their grandchildren have a full "nest," and extended childrearing years add to their economic and social responsibilities. Other women, who are alone at midlife, may have fewer resources as a result of minimum wage jobs, divorce, or widowhood. Working at low-paying jobs, without health and retirement benefits, does not allow one to save for retirement.

Midlife men also may be insecure financially as a result of low-paying jobs, plant closings, or corporate layoffs. Black men in particular have suffered from the decline in blue-collar jobs offering good pay and benefits. Even many two-income families have not achieved the economic security they expected (Genovese, 1997).

At the turn of the last century, few parents lived until their children reached midlife. Today's midlife adults may expect their parents to live until their 80s or 90s and to need care. Midlife families who face simultaneous care responsibilities for older and younger generations have been described as being part of the "sandwich generation" (Genovese, 1997).

How Old Is Old Age?

The age categories of childhood, adolescence, and middle age do not exist naturally but are social constructions created by humans. Members of all societies do seem to make some kind of distinction between the old and other age groups, but the meanings of old age also vary depending on the historical period and the cultural setting (see Calasanti and Slevin, 2001).

The definition of old age in industrialized nations is closely related to developments in the laws concerning pensions and retirement. In England and the United States, the ages of 60 and 65 have been linked to specific governmental actions defining old age. But before official retirement and pension ages were set, the meaning of old age was subject to much discretion and individual judgment. People were considered to be old when they were getting on in years and unable to support themselves. The label of *aged and infirm* could be applied to people aged anywhere from their late 40s to 80 and older, since ability to support oneself varies with individuals and their occupations.

Inevitably, government finances dictate the "proper" point at which old age and pensions are to begin. The Social Security Act of 1935 established a distinct legal age status for the elderly in American society. The choice of age 65 for retirement was heavily influenced by political and economic considerations. It was understood that providing benefits below age 65 would substantially increase costs and, therefore, might impair the possibility of acceptance of the plan by Congress.

The age for **mandatory retirement** for most occupations was raised from 65 to 70 by an action of Congress in 1978, and it was eliminated altogether by the Age Discrimination in Employment Act of 1986. In recent years efforts to keep the Social Security system financially sound have led to attempts to curtail a trend to early retirement and to prolong the working years. For example, the 1984 National Budget Reconciliation Act further changed the definition of retirement age for future retirees. On a graduated scale, those who retire during the first decade of the twenty-first century will have to be 66 in order to receive full benefits; this increases to 67 by the year 2027. Thus, aging has in a way been redefined through legislation.

Despite the increasing age at which one may receive full Social Security benefits and removal of the legal cap on mandatory retirement, more people are retiring before age 65. The average age at initial reward of Social Security retirement benefits has remained at about 63.5 years since the early 1980s (U.S. Social Security Administration, 1998). However, this early retirement may not have been planned. In a study of the anticipated retirement behavior of the baby boom, Haas and Serow (2002) report:

> The Employee Benefit Research Institute's (2001) retirement confidence study found that during the 1991 to 2000 interval, almost half of the working respondents expected to retire at 65 or later. Yet, 71 percent of retired respondents left the labor force at an earlier age. More than one-third of them retired earlier than expected, typically for reasons beyond their control (e.g., health or changes in the company). (p. 152)

This raises the question of whether workers late in their careers are forced into an earlier retirement than they might wish.

The number of age-discrimination complaints filed with the Equal Employment Opportunity Commission (EEOC) has risen 23.5 percent in the past two years, making this the fastest-growing category of discrimination cases (Knight Ridder/Tribune, 2002). The majority of the cases have to do with unfair termination practices, many from workers who felt pressured into retirement.

Changes in the economy, in particular the downsizing movement, have had a significant impact on older workers. The labor market encourages older workers to move out of the labor force through financial incentives and downsizing. In some instances, downsizing seems to be a "barely disguised form of age discrimination" (Sicker, 2002:61). In one case, in which a company's downsizing resulted in the firing of 1,469 employees, most of whom were just a few years short of entitlement to a full pension, it was estimated that the company saved an average of $326,632 in pension obligations alone per firing (Rosenblatt, 1996).

Although the trend toward early retirement may continue, Haas and Serow suggest that there are factors that may force individuals back to the labor force. It would seem reasonable that more and more older workers would choose to continue their employment and thereby reduce the number of years in retirement for which they may lack sufficient income to maintain a desired standard of living. In fact, voluntary early retirement has leveled off and increasing numbers of older workers have indicated a desire to continue to be active in the labor force (Sicker, 2002).

Definitions of old age may have little to do with the inherent condition of the elderly. Rather, such definitions are a product of competing ideologies, political bartering, and economic conditions. According to one author:

> We have a situation in which aging is increasingly contextualized; that is, increasingly a different experience, depending on health, income, and decisions regarding continuation at work. There no longer is a single progression of steps from birth to death like those portrayed in the "Stages of Life" prints that were once widely distributed. Careers no longer necessarily follow the traditional patterns of long tenure with a corporate entity, followed by a definite period of retirement. Instead, they increasingly are self-managed in response to personal needs or, sometimes, are disrupted by such vicissitudes as mid-career job loss. There is indeed an interval that might justly be called a Third Age for many Americans but hardly for all. (Rubinstein, 2002:32)

The Third Age

The term **third age** has been used to refer to the span of years between retirement age and the advent of age-imposed limitations. For Peter Laslett (1991), whose work is generally associated with the concept, retirement now offers the opportunity to develop a distinct and personally fulfilling lifestyle unconnected with the contingencies of working life. The essence of Laslett's argument is that a combination of demographic change and socioeconomic development has provided the setting for a new generation of retired people who find themselves in a position of greater potential agency (Gilleard and Higgs, 2002). Other authors agree: "[F]or those with adequate resources, adequate health, and few responsibilities, [the third age] provides a context for self-fulfillment, freedom, and purposeful engagement that is largely new in human history" (Rubinstein, 2002:30).

Despite criticisms of "grandiose expectations" and "unpractical idealism," Laslett stuck to his position in the revision of his earlier work (Laslett, 1996:xii–xiii). An increasing number of writers (although not always using Laslett's "third age" terminology) have advocated such a new and more agentic lifestyle, conveying a message that later life is a time of opportunity and "old age" a state to be resisted (Gilleard and Higgs, 2002). The concept has lasting power—the "third age" is certainly reminiscent of Neugarten's (1974) distinction between the **young-old,** those 65 to 74 who generally have good health, adequate financial resources, and support from family members, and the **old-old,** those over 75 who are more likely to have health and economic problems and to be isolated from others.

The Meanings of Age

When age categories are viewed as social constructions, we see that they result from changing human interpretations of the meanings attached to specific phases of the biological life cycle. The behaviors expected of those in various age categories also are products of an ongoing interpretive process reflecting people's continuing attempts to make sense of their dealings with others. In some instances chronological age has a significant effect on the ways people relate to one another, and in others it is far less important. Individuals also hear different messages about the meanings of various age categories, and they respond to these messages in different ways, depending on their social attributes and positions in the social order.

Age Norms in Everyday Life

Many of our daily activities and experiences are prescribed and regulated by **age norms** or social conventions. Older men are expected to marry younger women, for example, but the reverse situation may inspire comment or criticism. The distinctions are often finely grained, such as the expectations we have of a three-year-old and a five-year-old.

Even a few years in age can make a large difference in age attributes and our judgments about what a person can and cannot do or ought and ought not to do, as we noted in chapter 3. In some social circles 18- or 19-year-olds are thought to be too young to marry, but remaining unmarried once one reaches the late 20s may be regarded by parents, relatives, or friends as a cause for concern. Some age norms have been incorporated into law. The

Social Security system was originally based on mandatory retirement at age 65, and 21 has been federally endorsed as the minimum age for drinking alcoholic beverages. Although past surveys found substantial agreement on the ages at which people are expected to engage in specific activities, today there is less consensus about age norms. According to author Gail Sheehy, age norms have shifted to such an extent that "a revolution in the life cycle" has occurred (1995:4). "In the space of one short generation the whole shape of the life cycle has been fundamentally altered" (p. 4). Specifically:

> Puberty arrives earlier by several years than it did at the turn of the century. Adolescence is now prolonged for the middle class until the end of the 20s and for blue-collar men and women until the mid-20s, as more young adults live at home longer [see box]. True adulthood doesn't begin until 30. Most Baby Boomers, born after World War II, do not feel fully "grown up" until they are into their 40s, and even then they resist. Unlike members of the previous generation, who almost universally had their children launched by that stage of life, many late-baby couples or stepfamily parents will still be battling with rebellious children who are on the "catastrophic brink of *adolescence*" while they themselves wrestle with the pronounced hormonal and psychic changes that come with the passage into middle life. (Sheehy, 1995:4)

The norms of aging are deeply embedded in our consciousness and seem to exist "naturally." Nevertheless, like all social conventions, they are arbitrary social constructions derived from societal values and the more specific values of the groups and people with whom we interact. The requirements attached to specific ages therefore may be quite different in various societies and historical eras (see Calasanti and Slevin, 2001). Evidence of the socially constructed nature of age norms can be found in a society's laws and proposed legislation. The attention focused on the juvenile death penalty in the wake of the Washington, D.C.-area sniper attacks that occurred in October 2002 provides a recent example.

Lee Malvo, one of the individuals accused, was 17 at the time of the shootings. After considerable wrangling among the various jurisdictions in which sniper attacks occurred, the decision was made to try Malvo in Virginia. Although the greatest number of sniper killings took place in Maryland, that state bars the execution of those younger than 18. Virginia, however, not only has the death penalty for juveniles, but has used it three times since 1976—the second-highest number of any state (Editorial Desk, *New York Times*, 2002). Legal experts said Malvo's case may interrupt what had become a growing sentiment against executing juvenile defendants. In recent years several states banned the death penalty for people who committed capital crimes while younger than 18. In October 2002 (before the sniper attacks) four U.S. Supreme Court justices said they opposed executing defendants who committed capital crimes at age 16 or 17, stating, "The practice of executing such offenders is a relic of the past and is inconsistent with evolving standards of decency in a civilized society" (Greenhouse, 2003). Then the sniper case hit.

Is There an Age Deadline for Leaving Home?

Since the mid-1980s, changes in patterns of leaving and returning home in the United States, and particularly changes in the age patterning of those transitions, have emerged as important social concerns in the media, among policy makers, and in the scholarly literature. Much of the literature suggests that greater proportions of young adults now live at home with their parents and that fewer have families of their own. Richard Settersten (1998) set out to examine U.S. cultural ideas about leaving and returning home; specifically, cultural age norms for these transitions. He asks the question: "What are the rules in contemporary American society, if any, about the age by which young adults ought to leave their parents' homes or about the age after which they should not be allowed to return?" (p. 1375). In order to answer this question, a random sample of 319 Chicago-area adults were interviewed by telephone.

A large majority of both male and female respondents perceived an age deadline for leaving home. There was nearly complete agreement that both women and men should leave home sometime between the ages of 18 and 25. The reasons given for these deadlines were largely related to the development of self and personality. At the same time, most respondents indicated that there were no consequences for young adults who remain at home beyond the deadline. Returning home, on the other hand, was not at all perceived as an experience that should be dictated by age—in fact, only a fraction of respondents thought an age limit should be placed on returning home.

Age deadlines were cited more often for and by men, for both leaving and returning home, lending support to the idea that men's lives are thought to be more constrained by age and that men are more likely to think in terms of age. This finding is in line with other research, which suggests that age holds more salience in men's lives than in women's (Settersten, 1997). Interestingly, actual behavior patterns contradict these perceptions. Men are not only more likely to remain at home longer, but they are also more likely to return home. This difference is most likely due to the fact that women are more likely to get or be married (White, 1994), which makes their departure more likely and a potential return less likely.

Another trend ran counter to actual behavior. Whereas in the population at large the degree of coresidence with parents is highest for minority groups, white respondents consistently gave later deadlines for leaving home. There were no racial differences with respect to placing age limits on returning home.

The findings generally do not support the assumption that a strong set of cultural timing norms exists for leaving, and possibly returning, home. "Instead, cultural thinking about age and its relation to these events seems relatively loose, particularly in light of the fact that our respondents often did not see any real consequences for staying at home beyond, or returning home after, a deadline" (p. 1396). This leads Settersten to suggest that while these informal age rules may be an important force shaping the life course, their influence, at least for these transitions, may instead be more secondary in nature and more flexible than many scholars have assumed.

So, is your old room at home still available?

According to the Washington, D.C.-based Death Penalty Information Center, the Malvo case can be cited by those who believe that juvenile offenders should not be executed because they "aren't as intellectually mature, they are often led by older compatriots" (Glod and Jackman, 2003). Malvo appears to have been strongly influenced by John Allen Muhammad, 42, the other suspect in the sniper shootings.

In the end it may not matter. A juvenile court judge in Fairfax, Virginia ruled in January 2003 that Malvo could be tried as an adult. That ruling allows prosecutors to seek the death penalty and led to the impaneling of a grand jury which indicted Malvo on capital murder charges January 21. The trial has been set to begin November 10, 2003.

There is a clear relationship between cultural norms, biological processes, and the social context of aging experiences. In some cases even biological processes do not occur independently of social forces and age limitations, as might be expected, but are regulated by the messages people hear from society. Nowhere are the stereotypes of aging more powerful than with sexuality. We continue to link youth with sexuality and age with automatic sexual decline. However, although sexual activity and sexual interest decline over time (c.f., Masters and Johnson, 1966), they do not cease at a specific chronological age. Findings of more recent research suggest that while frequency of intercourse declines over time (c.f., Laumann et al., 1994), sex continues to play an important role in the lives of elderly men and women (c.f., Minichiello, Plummer, and Seal, 1996). In fact, an AARP study reveals that the majority of midlife and older adults sampled consider a satisfying sexual relationship important to their quality of life (AARP, 1999). The minimal investigation of sexuality among the elderly itself reflects ageist assumptions about what scholars deem worthy of investigation, our general "cultural illiteracy" about aging, and long-established cultural biases about the sexless old (Matthias et al., 1997; Weg, 1996).

The age norms in American society number well into the thousands and are constantly changing. An almost endless number and variety of cultural prescriptions about appropriate age-related behavior affect the daily encounters and interactions of people of all ages.

Chronological Age and Experiential Age

Because age norms are social constructions, there are differences between chronological age and **experiential age**, or age as subjectively measured by an individual's range of life experiences. Age norms are closely tied to specific social contexts.

Consider the meanings children attach to slight chronological age differences, for example, and the sharp distinctions they make concerning who may be friends with them. During their early years, children are flooded with new experiences, rights, and obligations. Because of their short biographies and limited life experiences, children are constantly learning and experiencing new things. Age differences of even a few months mean substantial differences in their knowledge. Six-year-olds think they are infinitely wiser than five-year-olds and in a class separate from anyone younger than that. This is in some measure appropriate, since during the early ages children who are separated by only one chronological year do inhabit quite different social, experiential, and symbolic worlds, and a difference of only one year assumes significance.

Parents are constantly setting rules to limit behavior of their children. Largely on the basis of communications with other parents like themselves, they define the rights, expectations, duties, and freedoms appropriate to their different-aged children. Often these judgments are made in terms of the parents' perceptions of their children's physical and emotional readiness to assume certain tasks or engage in certain behaviors. In that sense there is a correspondence between the stages of childhood in the life cycle and the norms for children's behaviors. But parents' decisions about age-related behaviors for their children also emerge from the situation and are made on an individual basis.

Children are not the only ones who attach great value to small chronological age differences in choosing appropriate friends and acquaintances. A one-year age difference also is given considerable significance by college sophomores, who typically have few freshmen among their close friends. At this point in the students' lives, the slight one-year difference corresponds to a very large status difference. The sophomores already know their way around and are wise to the customs, mores, and norms of college life. Because sophomores have experienced events that sharply discriminate them from freshmen, they think of themselves as being much older.

A Symbolic Interaction Approach to Aging

As we noted in chapter 2, the ability to evaluate one's own behaviors objectively from the perspective of others is necessary in order to become a "normal" member of society. A person who acquires that ability possesses the essential components of what George Herbert Mead called *the self*.

Definitions of self incorporate a personal sense of aging. Awareness of reaching middle age, for example, often comes about through recognition of others' definitions of one as middle-aged. Gail Sheehy's midlifers provide examples such as "Students start calling you 'mister.' . . . Your 14-year-old daughter says, 'Mom, how come you're still wearing microskirts?' " (Sheehy, 1995:58). In the words of one of her respondents, a fortyish Manhattan doctor, "A man can look at a woman and tell if she's interested in him as a sexual being. All of a sudden you reach an age where you look at a young woman and—click—you're not even under consideration. That hurts!" (p. 59). It is as though others become mirrors in which we see ourselves reflected, and through these reflections we come to have certain subjective definitions of ourselves.

The symbolic interactionist approach to aging suggests that the adage, "You are as young as you feel" should be amended. More precisely, it should say, "You are as young or old as *others allow you to feel*." Such a reformulation also calls attention to issues of power, constraints, and one's access to social "resources" such as education, income, social status, and physical health. The more of such resources one possesses as one ages, the greater the likelihood that others will respond to you with respect, and consequently the better you will probably feel about yourself. Like any other symbol, age can have a multiplicity of meanings that emerge out of our interactions with others. These meanings are likely to be modified and reinterpreted in the course of interactions, depending upon our own and others' definitions of the situations in which we find ourselves.

The interactionist approach also is attentive to other broad dimensions of the aging process. While the process involves regular, predictable biological changes and chronological stages, it cannot be understood without considering its various social and cultural definitions. The meanings given to chronological age categories vary from context to context and with different individuals. In interactionist terminology, different groups respond to age in terms of different inventories of symbols and create among their members different aging selves. The meanings attached to age vary with people's place in history and the historical times in which they live. Social attributes, such as gender, race, ethnic affiliation, occupation, social class, and marital status, also influence the meaning of a particular age for a particular person. The meaning of being 35 years old is quite different for a baseball player whose career is nearly over than for a corporate manager, or a 35-year-old woman who, having returned to graduate school after a 10-year absence, has now received her Ph.D. and is embarking on an academic career.

Two specific life contexts that affect our notions of aging and our views of self over the life course are work and gender. These contexts will be examined in the following sections.

Effects of Work and Careers on Aging

Our involvement with work helps determine how we experience the passage of time. Because work structures the ways we think about the present and how we anticipate the future, it is a primary source of our sense of aging. Those who pursue different work lives or careers hear different messages about the meaning of age. Ability to do the work may or may not be affected by age, and different career patterns involve varying conceptions of what it means to be on schedule, ahead of schedule, or too late. The ways individuals measure and evaluate their own life progress and their experiences of growing older are a function of where society expects them to be in their occupations at a given point in their lives.

In his voluminous and influential writings on work, Everett Hughes demonstrated the value of conceptualizing a **career** as "the moving perspective in which the person sees his life as a whole and interprets the meanings

of his various attitudes, actions, and the things which happen to him"
(1958:63). This definition of career accords well with the interactionist position. Hughes certainly recognized that, in an objective sense, various occupational careers are established within work organizations, but his definition
also directs attention to another aspect of the career process. On the basis of
communications with others in their work situations, people arrive at subjective, evaluative meanings for the various stages in their own career patterns.

The notion of career is not just a conceptual tool social scientists use to
look at the nature of work. We can also use it as a frame for interpreting
where we are in the life cycle and how the things happening to us at any
point in our lives make sense.

Age Consciousness and Career Structure

Success in a career is closely connected with age. Most careers are
age-graded; that is, we ride an escalator of sorts that travels up the career ladder and are expected to be at a certain point by a certain age. Our careers are
considered satisfactory if we "make the grade" at the appropriate age. As
well as being the measure of success in a career, age is the variable along
which career lines are established. The roles available (and unavailable) to
those in a work organization, and the workers' construction and meaning of
their work commitments, are defined in terms of age. Careers in some occupations involve special contingencies and force a direct **age consciousness**
on participants.

In the corporate world, for example, there appears to be increasing concern about age. A survey of executives and search firms that examined attitudes toward older executives found an increasing tendency for respondents
to consider age an issue in job seekers at or just below age 50 (Marshall,
2000). It is not just that older executives are becoming more conscious of
their age. In fact, 52 percent of respondents said the age-50 issue was a significant concern, an increase from previous years (Marshall, 2000).

In the recent past corporations did not even think of terminating their
managers before 60. Today, men in their 50s in corporate life are in a precarious position. They are "a high-ticket item in an era of downsizing" (Sheehy,
1995:260). The fact is that there is real cause for concern. Between 1999 and
2000, age-discrimination complaints filed with the Equal Employment Opportunity Commission rose to 16,000 from 14,000. On the job, baby boomers
complain of crashing into a "silver ceiling." In focus groups, Clairol showed
before-and-after photos of a man who had had his hair colored, and then
asked participants to describe the man. Consistently, the man without the gray
was viewed as more successful, smarter, and more athletic (Weiss, 2002).

The film industry in particular is one where age consciousness (and ageism) is rampant. Figures for 1998 from the Screen Actors Guild show that
two out of every three roles went to performers younger than 40. While both
women and men over 40 are significantly underrepresented in casting, the
employment figures are worse for women than for men. Thirty-seven percent

of male roles for film and television go to men over 40, while just 24 percent of female roles go to women in the same age group (Millis, 2000). When the focus is narrowed to lead roles, the numbers become even more disheartening for women.

These examples suggest that every occupation generates its own distinctive career path and consequently its own set of symbols and meanings of age. In most occupations people are required to engage in a continual process of interpretation and reinterpretation about their current occupational position and its meaning. Periodically they must assess their success, whether or not they are currently making it, and their chances for eventually doing so. Questions about career success and failure constantly call attention to age. To a significant degree, it is the structure of occupational life that injects meaning into the phrase *growing older*. No doubt such diverse occupations as fashion models, boxers, lawyers, scientists, and strippers generate very different self-conceptions of aging.

Retirement

The life stage known as retirement was invented/constructed in industrialized nations in the twentieth century. Although once a rare event for working men and women, people may now spend as much as a quarter of their lives as retirees, "as life expectancy rises and the age for leaving work falls" (Savishinsky, 2000:30). By the mid-1960s, age 65 had become the age around which retirement clustered in the United States, making it an effective reference point for a variety of purposes. Now, however, the transition is less clear-cut. "The age-graded norm in retirement has become blurred, and the actual range of retirement age has expanded" (Han and Moen, 1999b), making the transition "longer and fuzzier" (Kohli and Rein, 1991) than in the past as retirees from primary career jobs increasingly take up second or third careers. "Thus, the transition itself is now less clear-cut: the boundary separating 'retirement' from 'employment' is blurred, and retirement from one's primary career job is no longer fixed at any set age" (Moen, Kim, and Hofmeister, 2001:56).

Savishinsky's (2000) study of the life stories of a group of men and women in upstate New York finds significant diversity as well as shared dilemmas. One theme that resonates through the stories of many of these retirees is their rediscovery of themselves in the process of making meaning of their experience. In fact, "they work *at* retirement, trying to figure it out and fill it in on their own" (Han, 2001:541). It is the lack of culture—the "cultural lightness of retirement" that "made it so personally heavy to bear" (Savishinsky, 2000:55) for the retirees.

In a capitalist economy, productive achievement is typically associated with earning wages. Thus, as one retires from the workplace, one's personal worth becomes questionable. One is "sidelined," "put out to pasture," or becomes a "has been" (Gergen and Gergen, 2000). Although this displacement is especially important to men, for whom career success is directly entwined with a sense of identity (Gergen, 1992), feminist critics have pointed out that being productive also affects the valuation of the maturing woman (Martin, 1997).

Gender and Retirement

Retirement has typically been studied as an individual, principally male status passage. Today, however, almost half the contemporary workforce is female, and the majority of workers are married to other workers (Moen et al., 2001). Gender has become a key source of heterogeneity in the nature and effects of the retirement process; that is, gendered life scripts and options produce distinctive life course patterns for men and women (Moen et al., 2001). Women and men follow different career paths to and through retirement—women workers in late midlife are less likely to have worked continuously (Han and Moen, 1999a, 1999b). Women tend to experience retirement differently as a consequence of the difference in trajectories and of gendered expectations (Quick and Moen, 1998; Smith and Moen, 1998). For example, women in late midlife may enjoy their jobs and may wish to postpone retirement, feeling they are starting new lives after their children have left home. Husbands in late midlife, however, may be counting the years or months to their own retirement (Moen et al., 2001). Couples increasingly must deal with two retirements, which raises the issue of synchronizing spouses' career exits. Even this is a gendered process—women's retirement is often contingent on that of their husbands (Quick and Moen, 1998).

If employed husbands retire first, wives who are not yet retired are in a *status-dissonant* role relative to traditional gender roles. They may resent their husbands' free time in the face of their own continuing employment, and this resentment may be exacerbated if retired husbands still expect their employed wives to perform much of the housework. If employed wives retire first, husbands who are not yet retired may benefit from their wives' performing most of the household responsibilities. Women in this situation, however, may dislike being thrust into the conventional homemaker role (Moen et al., 2001).

Not only do couples now confront two retirements, but they also must strategize about when each will retire and whether either will take up paid work after retirement (Han and Moen, 1999a, 1999b). The importance of this strategizing is illustrated by the finding that newly retired men and women report increased marital conflict when their spouses remain employed (Moen et al., 2001).

Gender and Aging

Powerful differences between men and women run through the entire life cycle, from birth to old age. Society has imposed standards of acceptable social performance and physical appearance on women that women themselves have been forced to acknowledge if they wanted to achieve a position of value in a male-dominated society. "Because women's worth is so frequently associated with their physical attractiveness, the normal physical changes that accompany aging—wrinkles, weight gain, hair thinning and graying—call into question women's social value" (Furman, 1997:104).

The Double Standard of Aging

From childhood on, females are socialized to place a great deal of emphasis on their physical appearance. The variety of cosmetics that women use to maintain their looks certainly indicates the significance of physical attractiveness for them. Men, by contrast, have traditionally been expected to minimize their public concern with appearance, although there is evidence that this is changing in the wake of corporate downsizing, which appears to be placing pressure on middle-aged men to look younger in order to keep their jobs (c.f., Spindler, 1996).

The response society makes to men's and women's physical attributes is not simply a result of biological functioning but rather a product of cultural, historical, and sociological conditions. Bodily representation and self-presentation are shaped largely through cultural convention and social relations; women in this society are disproportionately affected by these. While loss of physical vigor and decline in health may be experienced similarly by both women and men, the aging body as a means of revealing the self to others has particular significance and consequence for women in U.S. culture (Furman, 1997). In this culture, there is an assumption that attractiveness and older women are mutually exclusive categories. This leads to negative stereotyping, as Furman (1997) found when she asked her students to identify cultural associations with older women.

This was their collective list: domestic (good cooks), nostalgic, interfering, out of shape, bitter, overbearing, frustrated, needy, stubborn, a liability, worn-down, gaudy, wrinkled, more vulnerable to attack, rambling, busybodies, hag, wicked, evil, nag, constant complainer, meddling, gossipy, worrisome, manipulative, martyr, advice-giving, grouchy, fat, "little old lady," bespectacled, moles, crooked, shrinking, widowed, helpless, tea-drinking, arthritic, bingo-playing, liver spots (p. 94).

Furman's (1997) study of older women and beauty shop culture brings to light a constant "reading" of their bodies by older women that is in constant tension with images of youth. One of her respondents, who considers herself lucky in not being too wrinkled, says, "About my appearance, I know I don't look my age. I don't act my age. That's why my age doesn't bother me" (p. 105). For others, who acknowledge that they look old, it's a different story. In one respondent's words: "When I look at myself now (in the mirror), I feel old" (p. 109). Furman explains:

> When Reva looks at herself in the mirror and feels old, she is seeing herself from the perspective of men. This observation is useful but does not go far enough in helping us interpret the experience of *older* women.

> When Reva looks at herself in the mirror and feels old, she is seeing her-
> self from the perspective of men, as would a younger woman as well, but
> also from the perspective of a younger person. Hence she is twice objecti-
> fied, or, perhaps more accurately in this instance, she partakes in the pro-
> cess of self-objectification in two ways: as a woman and as *old* woman.
> As woman she is observed by the internalized male gaze. As older
> woman she is observed by the internalized gaze of youth. We spot here
> another unequal social relation, which, like the male-female relation, is a
> relationship of dominance-subordination. The image and its reading cap-
> tures the social imbalance between youth and old age, especially as it per-
> tains to women. (Furman, 1997:109)

So old women come to be seen as "old bags." And as Furman points out,
"What is a bag but a shapeless, empty container . . . which after use should
simply be thrown away?" (p. 109).

In growing up, males are judged by two sets of physical standards—one
appropriate to boys, and another for men. As boys are socially transformed
into men, society allows them to be judged by a standard that relates to maturity, one which allows for things such as "character lines" around the eyes
and the effects of daily shaving. Females, however, are judged throughout
their lives by one standard of physical beauty—that appropriate to *young girls*.
The cultural image of an erotically appealing woman is commonly one of
youth. As a woman grows further away from this nubile image, she is usually
considered less and less attractive (Bakos, 1999; McQuaide, 1998). In our
society, even young girls are sometimes advised not to frown ("You'll get
wrinkles!"); cosmetics, trendy clothing, and even surgery are used to maintain a youthful appearance for as long as possible. In contrast, the physical
and sexual attractiveness of men is often considered to be enhanced by the
aging process. Gray hair and facial wrinkles may be thought to look "distinguished" on men—signs of accumulated life experience and wisdom. Likewise, while the professional achievements of women may be perceived as
threatening to a potential male partner, it is relatively common for a man's
sexual attractiveness to be closely associated with his achievements and
social status.

The pairings of powerful older men and young, beautiful women reflect
the double standard of aging (I'm thinking Warren Beatty and Annette Ben-
ning). As you might expect, pairings of older men and younger women occur
much more commonly than the reverse. Who would be the female equivalent of Sean Connery, who looks his age (60+) and yet is considered "the sexiest man alive" by readers of *People* magazine? A woman of comparable age
might still be seen as beautiful, as long as she looks considerably younger
than her years, but not "the sexiest woman alive" (Daniluk, 1998).

Given the media's incessant focus on the beauty of young women, it is
no surprise that the medical field has been able to identify a niche and exploit
it. Using familiar biomedical model (see chapter 8) phraseology to turn the
effects of aging—loose and sagging skin, wrinkles, and creases—into pathol-

ogy encourages a view of aging as a medical problem (Haiken, 1997). Cosmetic surgery has become an issue of *needing* a change, not merely wanting it. Surgeons refer to face-lifts, for example, "as something that is needed rather than desired, that may be delayed but not escaped" (Haiken, 1997:172). In the words of a 50-year-old woman interviewed by Gimlin (2000), "There were things my house needed but my feeling was, I needed a face-lift more than my house did" (p. 84). The 125,000 Americans who had face-lifts in 2001 apparently felt a similar need.

In addition, there is the "wildly popular Botox [which] is literally changing the face of baby boomers, its biggest fans" (Weiss, 2002). And in the past five years, sales of anti-aging beauty products have jumped 24 percent, to $374 million.

Despite reports that men are having faces and necks lifted and sagging eyelids corrected to give them a "competitive advantage" in the business world, women continue to be the primary objects of surgical intervention. In addition to the difference in the number of cosmetic surgery operations performed on men and women, marketing strategies are very different for the sexes. For men, cosmetic surgery is presented as a means to enhance job performance and increase chances to compete, while women are targeted in terms of general attractiveness or changes in identity (Davis, 1995).

Like any other physical or social attribute, age acquires its meaning through interaction. To fully understand the aging process, we need to know how people tune in to, interpret, and respond to repeated social messages about the meanings of age. Men and women hear quite different messages about the aging process. At the root of the differing life courses of men and women lies a power differential that operates to age women considerably faster than men, according to the definitions of aging in American society.

Conclusion

Our experience of the aging process depends on where we stand in society—particularly in terms of our age, our gender, and the work we do. We oversimplify the aging process if we think of it only in chronological or biological terms. Age carries no intrinsic meaning. Rather, human beings in communication with one another attach meanings to age. Our feelings about growing up, older, and old are formed by the values of the society at large and by those of the particular groups to which we belong.

Because human beings are not simply objects in nature, or passive receptacles for biological processes associated with the passage of time, we shape the aging process by thinking about it, interpreting it, defining it, categorizing it, labeling it, and attaching values to it. These mental activities have critical consequences for actual behaviors. Chronological age is a symbol subject to continuous human definition and redefinition, and age categories are social constructions which cannot be understood outside the contexts in which they are defined. The norms regulating the behaviors expected of people of various ages are also shaped and defined by people's interactions and communications with others.

Throughout this chapter we have explored how aging identities are formed. Age is certainly one of our most meaningful identity "pegs" or markers. We think of ourselves in terms of the age categories into which we fit at different points in our life. Age, however, is only one dimension by which individuals define who they are to themselves and others. The last chapter of this book examines the issue of identity from a broader, more historical point of view. It will consider some of the features of the modern world that make it increasingly difficult for individuals to answer the question, "Who am I?"

DEFINITIONS

Age categories   Broad designations used to describe people of different chronological ages. The meanings attached to age categories such as childhood and adolescence have varied cross-culturally and in different historical eras.

Age consciousness   Awareness of being a certain age at certain life events.

Age norms   Cultural prescriptions or regulations for appropriate behaviors at particular ages. Chronological age is an important basis for determining how people ought to behave in all societies, but age norms vary across cultures and in different historical periods.

Age status   The roles, duties, obligations, and responsibilities expected of individuals of a certain age. Some age-related cultural expectations are codified into law, such as the voting age and the drinking age.

Age structure   The number of people in different age categories in a society. A society's age structure is determined primarily by birth rates and rates of mortality, and it changes over time.

Ageism   Prejudice and discrimination directed toward older people. Ageism is comparable to sexism (prejudice directed at women or men) and racism (prejudice directed at racial and ethnic minority groups).

Career   The perspective individuals have of their lives as a whole and their interpretation of the meanings of their various attitudes and actions and the things that happen to them. An occupational career is one frame within which people understand and interpret their movement through the life cycle.

Empty nest   The period in the family life cycle after the last child leaves home and childcare and support needs diminish. The lengthening of the empty nest period in recent years has created new life tasks for both women and men.

Experiential age   A subjective measure of where individuals are in the life cycle according to their life experiences rather than their chronological age.

Life cycle   The pattern of broad developmental stages through which all human beings are said to pass as they move through life.

Mandatory retirement   The age at which employees can be forced to retire. In the United States, the mandatory retirement age was raised to 70 in 1978 and eliminated in 1986 by the Age Discrimination in Employment Act.

Meanings of age   The meanings people attach to a particular chronological age will vary according to the individual, the situations in which interactions take place, and the age conventions of the society. Because age categories are social constructions, the meaning of an age varies with the social, cultural, and historical context in which it is defined.

Third age   The span of years between retirement age and the advent of age-imposed limitations.

Young-old and old-old   Two segments of the elderly population, consisting of those between the approximate ages of 65 and 74 and those older than 75.

DISCUSSION QUESTIONS

1. How old are you? Whatever your age, try to describe as many norms as you can that influence what people your age can or cannot do. Think of such categories of norms as proper dress, drinking behavior, involvement in work, and sexual behavior.

2. Into what age category (for example, middle age, late middle age, old age, early adulthood) would you place your parents? Why have you placed them into that age category? Explain the meaning you are giving to that category. How will you know when your parents are no longer in that category?

3. There is an old saying that goes, "You are as young as you feel." Explain why a symbolic interactionist might want to amend this piece of folk wisdom to say, "You are as young or as old as *others allow you to feel.*"

4. Suppose you knew three men, all in their late 30s, who hold quite different jobs. Imagine that one is a professional athlete, the second a lawyer, and the third a machine operator in a factory. How would their respective occupations influence the way they are experiencing the same chronological point in the life cycle? More generally, how might jobs at different points in the class structure produce a different sense of age?

5. We have argued in this chapter that gender critically influences how individuals experience aging. There is a double standard of aging that places women at a greater disadvantage than men as they grow older. What evidence would you submit to argue that such a double standard does, in fact, exist?

6. In earlier times people on average died in their early 40s rather than their mid-to-late-70s, as is the case today. How do you think this demographic fact of life has influenced family and work life? What if the average life span were to become, say, 100? How would such a change influence the structure of family and work life?

REFERENCES

AARP. 1999. *Modern Maturity Sexuality Survey.* Washington, D.C.: AARP.

Aquilino, W. 1999. "Rethinking the young adult life stage: Prolonged dependency as an adaptive strategy." In *Transitions to Adulthood in a Changing Economy: No Work, No Family, No Future?*, edited by A. Booth, A. Crouter, and M. Shanahan, pp. 168–75. Westport, CT: Praeger.

Aries, P. 1962. *Centuries of Childhood.* New York: Vintage Books.

Arnett, J. 2000. "Emerging adulthood: A theory of development from the late teens through the twenties." *American Psychologist* 55(5):469–80.

Associated Press. 1998. "Poll: Young fear aging, elders don't." April 5.

Bakos, S. 1999. "From lib to libido: How women are reinventing sex for grown-ups." *Modern Maturity* (Sept-Oct):54.

Bianchi, S., and D. Spain. 1996. "Women, work, and family in America." *Population Bulletin* 51(3):1–48.

Butler, R. 1969. "Ageism: Another form of bigotry." *The Gerontologist* 9(3):243–46.

Calasanti, T., and K. Slevin. 2001. *Gender, Social Inequalities and Aging*. New York: Altamira Press.

Clement, P. 1997. *Growing Pains: Children in the Industrial Age, 1850–1890*. New York: Twayne Publishers.

Daniluk, J. 1998. *Women's Sexuality Across the Life Span: Challenging Myths, Creating Meanings*. New York: The Guilford Press.

Davis, K. 1995. *Reshaping the Female Body*. New York: Routledge.

Dressel, P., M. Minkler, and I. Yen. 1997. "Gender, race, class, and aging: Advances and opportunities." *International Journal of Health Services* 27(4):579–600.

Dychtwald, K. 1999. *Age Power: How the 21st Century Will Be Ruled by the New Old*. New York: Jeremy Tarcher/Putnam.

Editorial Desk. 2002. "Mr. Malvo, Juvenile." *New York Times*, November 12.

Employee Benefit Research Institute. 2001. *Retirement Confidence Survey*. Washington, D.C.: Employee Benefit Research Institute.

Erikson, E. 1968. *Identity: Youth and Crisis*. New York: W. W. Norton.

Furman, F. 1997. *Facing the Mirror: Older Women and Beauty Shop Culture*. New York: Routledge.

Genovese, R. 1997. *Americans at Midlife: Caught between Generations*. Westport, CT: Bergin & Garvey.

Gergen, M. 1992. "Life stories: Pieces of a dream." In *Storied Lives*, edited by G. Rosenwald and R. Ochberg, pp. 127–44. New Haven: Yale University Press.

Gergen, K., and M. Gergen. 2000. "The new aging: Self construction and social values." In *Social Structures and Aging*, edited by K. W. Schaie. New York: Springer.

Gilleard, C., and P. Higgs. 2002. "The third age: Class, cohort or generation?" *Ageing & Society* 22:369–82.

Gimlin, D. 2000. "Cosmetic surgery: Beauty as commodity." *Qualitative Sociology* 23(1):77–98.

Glod, M., and T. Jackman. 2003. "Malvo indicted as an adult: Teen sniper eligible for execution." *Washington Post*, January 23:B01.

Goldscheider, F., and C. Goldscheider. 1994. "Leaving and returning home in 20th century America." *Population Bulletin* 48(4):1–35.

Greenhouse, L. 2003. "Justices deny inmate appeal in execution of juveniles." *New York Times*, January 28.

Haas, W. III., and W. Serow. 2002. "The baby boom, amenity retirement migration, and retirement communities: Will the golden age of retirement continue?" *Research on Aging* 24(1): 150–64.

Haiken, E. 1997. *Venus Envy: A History of Cosmetic Surgery*. Baltimore, MD: The Johns Hopkins University Press.

Han, S. 2001. Review of *Breaking the Watch: The Meanings of Retirement in America*, by J. Savishinsky. *American Journal of Sociology* 107(2):540–41.

Han, S., and P. Moen. 1999a. "Work and family over time: A life course approach." *Annals of the American Academy of Political and Social Sciences* 562:98–110.

———. 1999b. "Clocking out: Temporal patterning of retirement." *American Journal of Sociology* 105:191–236.

Hayward, M., S. Friedman, and H. Chen. 1996. "Race inequities in men's retirement." *Journal of Gerontology: Social Sciences* 51B(1):S1–10.

Holmstrom, L., D. Karp, and P. Gray. 2002. "Why laundry, not Hegel? Social class, transition to college, and pathways to adulthood." *Symbolic Interaction* 25(4):437–62.

Hughes, E. 1958. *Men and Their Work.* New York: Free Press.

Karp, D., L. Holmstrom, and P. Gray. 1998. "Leaving home for college: Expectations for selective reconstruction of self." *Symbolic Interaction* 21(3):253–76.

Knight Ridder/Tribune. 2002. "Complaints involving age bias are growing fast, EEOC says." *The Baltimore Sun*, July 14:7c.

Kohli, M., and M. Rein. 1991. "The changing balance of work and retirement." In *Time for Retirement: Comparative Studies of Early Exit from the Labor Force*, edited by A. Kohli, M. Rein, A. Guillemard, and H. van Gunstoren. Cambridge: Cambridge University Press.

Lang, S. 2001. "Midlife crisis less common than many believe." *Human Ecology* 29(2):23.

Laslett, P. 1991. *A Fresh Map of Life: The Emergence of the Third Age.* Cambridge: Harvard University Press.

———. 1996. *A Fresh Map of Life.* 2nd ed. Basingstoke, Hampshire: Macmillan.

Lauer, J., and R. Lauer. 1999. *How to Survive and Thrive in an Empty Nest.* Oakland, CA: New Harbinger Publications.

Laumann, E., J. Gagnon, R. Michael, and S. Michaels. 1994. *The Social Organization of Sexuality.* Chicago: University of Chicago Press.

Macleod, D. 1998. *The Age of the Child: Children in America, 1890–1920.* New York: Twayne Publishers.

Marshall, J. 2000. "Age issue cuts both ways." *Financial Executive* 16(5):12.

Martin, E. 1997. "The woman in the menopausal body." In *Reinterpreting Menopause: Cultural and Philosophical Issues*, edited by P. Komesaroff, P. Rothfield, and J. Daly, pp. 239–54. New York: Routledge.

Masters, W., and V. Johnson. 1966. *Human Sexual Response.* Boston: Little, Brown.

Matthias, R., J. Lubben, K. Atchison, and S. Schweitzer. 1997. "Sexual activity and satisfaction among very old adults: Results from a community-dwelling Medicare population." *The Gerontologist* 37(1):6–14.

McMillen, L. 1997. "What happened to the midlife crisis?" *Chronicle of Higher Education* 43(36):A15.

McQuaide, S. 1998. "Women at midlife." *Journal of the National Association of Social Workers* 43:21–31.

Michael, R., J. Gagnon, E. Laumann, and G. Kolata. 1995. *Sex in America: A Definitive Survey.* New York: Warner Books.

Millis, M. 2000. "Coming of age: The plight of actors over 40 in film and TV." *Back Stage* 41(24):28.

Minichiello, V., D. Plummer, and A. Seal. 1996. "The 'asexual' older person? Australian evidence." *Venereology* 9:180–88.

Moen, P., J. Kim, and H. Hofmeister. 2001. "Couples' work/retirement transitions, gender, and marital quality." *Social Psychology Quarterly* 64(1):55–71.

Neugarten, B. 1974. "Age groups in American society and the rise of the young-old." *Annals of the American Academy of Political and Social Science* 415 (September): 187–98.

Quadagno, J. 1999. *Aging and the Life Course.* Boston: McGraw-Hill.

Quick, H., and P. Moen. 1998. "Gender, employment, and retirement quality: A life course approach to the differential experiences of men and women." *Journal of Occupational Health Psychology* 3:44–64.

Rimer, S. 1998. "Tradition of care thrives in black families." *New York Times*, March 15.

Rosenblatt, R. 1996. "Congress examines 401(k) plans." *Los Angeles Times*, July 16.

Rubinstein, R. 2002. "The Third Age." In *Challenges of the Third Age: Meaning and Purpose in Later Life*, edited by R. Weiss and S. Bass, pp. 29–40. Oxford: Oxford University Press.

Savishinsky, J. 2000. *Breaking the Watch: The Meanings of Retirement in America*. Ithaca, NY: Cornell University Press.

Settersten, R. 1997. "The salience of age in the life course." *Human Development* 40:257–81.

———. 1998. "A time to leave home and a time never to return? Age constraints on the living arrangements of young adults." *Social Forces* 76(4):1373–1400.

Sheehy, G. 1995. *New Passages: Mapping Your Life across Time*. New York: Ballantine Books.

Sicker, M. 2002. *The Political Economy of Work in the 21st Century: Implications for an Aging American Workforce*. Westport, CT: Quorum Books.

Smith, D., and P. Moen. 1998. "Spouse's influence on the retirement decision: His, her, and their perceptions." *Journal of Marriage and the Family* 60:734–44.

Spindler, A. 1996. "It's a face-lifted, tummy-tucked jungle out there." *New York Times*, June 9.

Stoller, E., and R. Gibson. 2000. *Worlds of Difference: Inequality in the Aging Experience*. 3rd ed. Thousand Oaks, CA: Pine Forge.

U.S. Census Bureau. 1983. *Statistical Abstract of the United States:1983*. Table 101. Washington, D.C.: Government Printing Office.

———. 1984. *Statistical Abstract of the United States: 1984*. Washington, DC: Government Printing Office.

———. 1997. *Statistical Abstract of the United States: 1997*. Washington, D.C.: Government Printing Office.

———. 2000. *Statistical Abstract of the United States: 2000*. Washington, D.C.: Government Printing Office.

———. 2001. *Statistical Abstract of the United States: 2001*. Washington, D.C.: Government Printing Office.

U.S. Social Security Administration. 1998. *Social Security Bulletin: Annual Statistical Supplement*. Washington, D.C.: Government Printing Office.

Weg, R. 1996. "Sexuality, sensuality, and intimacy." *Encyclopedia of Gerontology* 2:479–88.

Weiss, M. 2002. "Chasing youth." *American Demographics* 24(9):35–41.

West, E. 1996. *Growing Up in Twentieth-Century America: A History and Reference Guide*. Westport, CT: Greenwood Press.

White, L. 1994. "Coresidence and leaving home: Young adults and their parents." *Annual Review of Sociology* 20:81–102.

eleven

SOCIAL CHANGE AND THE SEARCH FOR SELF

Siddhartha, son of a high-caste Brahmin in India, was the central character in a widely read novel by Hermann Hesse that movingly portrayed a difficult quest for a meaningful life. While Hesse's novel was written in the 1920s and set in Asia, Siddhartha's **search for self** has come to represent a central life problem for millions of people in the present urban-industrial or postindustrial nations of Western Europe and North America. This search has led many Westerners to seek membership in organizations such as Asian or neo-Christian religious sects, cult-like groups centered around New Age thinking, and scores of self-help groups. The emergence of such organizations in Western societies has been a response to what Orrin Klapp (1969) aptly called a "collective search for identity."

Every generation, because of its unique historical situation, experiences the world in somewhat different ways than its predecessors. Not having participated in the creation of its social world, each generation is likely to confer new meanings on old familiar objects. Whatever the historical conditions into which people are born, one problem remains constant: Human beings must have a coherent framework of meaning for their lives. In some historical periods the traditional meanings transmitted from one generation to the next adequately perform this function. In other epochs, however, such meaning coherence is not so easily established. The current historical period in the Western world appears to be one in which many individuals experience particular difficulty in understanding themselves.

In this concluding chapter we examine how the matters of personal identity and self-worth have been brought to the forefront of contemporary consciousness in the Western world. We want to explore why the problem of

353

identity has become so paramount in the modern world, the consequences of what some view as the radical individualism of contemporary American society, and the likely shape of future selves.

Symbols, Selves, and Society

Throughout this book we have repeatedly made the point that the selves individuals present to one another are not bestowed by nature. Indeed, a theme in several earlier chapters is that human selves do not exist as independent entities but emerge, are sustained, and are transformed as a consequence of the symbolic dialogues, both verbal and nonverbal, that individuals constantly engage in with others. Clothes, for example, as well as words are symbolic announcements to others of how an individual wants to be viewed.

Central to the interactionist perspective on human life is the notion that people are sensitive to the impressions they make on each other. They go to great lengths to withhold discrediting information about themselves from others in order to appear proper. In our discussions of stranger and intimate relationships in chapters 4 and 5 we stressed the connection between the information people have about others and their ability to role-take with them. We analyzed behavior in public places in terms of the relative scarcity of information strangers have about each other. The measure of trust, risk, uncertainty, and commitment people invest in their relationships is calculated in terms of their faith that others' performances reflect their real intentions and identities.

Sensitivity to others is not distributed equally throughout the social order, as our discussion of the politics of interaction in chapter 6 demonstrated. Those in positions of power can afford to be insensitive to the feelings of the less powerful. Because the ability to role-take is inversely related to power, membership in disadvantaged or relatively powerless groups—for example, women, lower- and working-classes, and minority groups—is conducive to greater role-taking ability. The faces power presents, short of sheer physical force or other forms of coercion, are primarily symbolic. Through facial expressions and the techniques of interrupting, crowding others' space, pointing, and staring, the powerful affirm their status while keeping others under their scrutiny.

Not only are symbols crucial in the communication of power differentials, but, in a larger sense, human social life itself is symbolic, or a social construction. Objects and things have no inherent meaning, only the meanings people confer on them. These meanings are, in the final analysis, arbitrary, since there are always several possible meanings that could be given to them. Whatever the meaning attributed to it, a thing can only be understood within the context in which it is situated.

As we suggested in chapter 2, the symbol-using capacity of human beings makes possible a kind of liberation. Freed from the animal's dependence on instinctual biological impulses, humans can use symbols to bring into reality virtually anything they can imagine. The ability to transcend the world of the here and now through symbolic processes is not without its costs, however. It also heightens humans' awareness that they are destined to die (see box).

The general view of the self as a socially constructed phenomenon suggests that the nature and "shape" of social selves are specific to particular cultures and historical periods. To be sure, a great deal has been written about the fundamentally different place of the individual in American and Asian cultures. Much has been made of the fact that in Japan individuals are expected to subordinate their own interests to those of the group. In America, in contrast, the individual is the key unit of society and the needs of the individual appear to take precedence over group or community interests. As we shall see in greater detail in a later section of this chapter, the contemporary search for self has particular urgency in a society that has always prized individuals above all else. We will need to examine the criticisms of American culture (Bellah et al., [1985]1996; Derber, 2000; Putnam, 2000), arguing that America's radical individualism is the basis for a general unraveling of the society's social fabric. Immediately, however, we need to locate the contemporary search for self within the rise of what might be termed a therapeutic state.

Small Gods and Worms: The Paradox of Human Existence

There is one issue we all must face alone, sooner or later, though we all have an urgent need and desire to avoid it. We must conceive of the reality of our own death and accept it. Elizabeth Kübler-Ross, who has studied attitudes toward death of dying patients and their families, acknowledges that human knowledge has actually increased the fear of dying:

> We would think that our great emancipation, our knowledge of science and of man, has given us better ways and means to prepare ourselves and our families for this inevitable happening. Instead the days are gone when a man was allowed to die in peace and dignity in his own home. The more we are making advancements in science, the more we seem to fear and deny the reality of death. (1997:21)

While Kübler-Ross considers the topic of death in relation to the treatment of the dying and medical science, fear and denial of death have a basis in more fundamental societal attitudes. The essential paradox of human existence is that humans transcend nature but also are a part of it, and death is a natural consequence. Ernest Becker wrote eloquently of this twofold dilemma:

> Man has a symbolic identity that brings him sharply out of nature. He is a symbolic self, a creature with a name, a life history. He is a creator with a mind that soars out to speculate about atoms and infinity, who can place himself imaginatively at a point in space and contemplate bemusedly his own planet. This immense expansion, this dexterity, this ethereality, this self-consciousness gives to man literally the status of a small god in nature, as the Renaissance thinkers knew.

Yet at the same time, as the Eastern Sages also knew, man is a worm and food for worms. This is the paradox: he is out of nature and hopelessly in it. He is dual, up in the stars and yet housed in a heart-pumping, breath-gasping body that once belonged to a fish and still carries the gill-marks to prove it. His body is a material fleshly casing that is alien to him in many ways—the strangest and most repugnant way being that it aches and bleeds and will decay and die. Man is literally split in two: he has an awareness of his own splendid uniqueness in that he sticks out of nature with a towering majesty, and yet he goes back into the ground a few feet in order blindly and dumbly to rot and disappear forever. It is a terrifying dilemma to be in and to have to live with. The lower animals are, of course, spared this painful contradiction, as they lack a symbolic identity and the self-consciousness that goes with it. They merely act and move reflectively as they are driven by their instincts. If they pause at all, it is only a physical pause; inside they are anonymous, and even their faces have no name. They live in a world without time, pulsating, as it were, in a state of dumb being. This is what has made it so simple to shoot down whole herds of buffalo or elephants. The animals don't know that death is happening and continue grazing placidly while others drop alongside them. The knowledge of death is reflective and conceptual, and animals are spared it.

They live and they disappear with the same thoughtlessness: a few minutes of fear, a few seconds of anguish, and it is over. But to live a whole lifetime with the fate of death haunting one's dreams and even the most sun-filled days—that's something else. (1973:26)*

The Therapeutic State and the Problem of Identity

As several observers have noted (see Derber, Schwartz, and Magrass, 1990; Edgley and Brissett, 1999), the behaviors of people in today's postindustrial society are dominated by "experts." Experts advise us on virtually every aspect of our lives. Today, experts follow us through the life course. They are there when we are born and follow us each step along the way, right down to our graves. Many have come to feel reliant on experts to tell them how to maintain their health, how to become educated, and how to raise their children. Experts have become indispensable for repairing the range of technical paraphernalia—for example, TVs, VCRs, automobiles, computers—without which we believe it would be impossible to live. Most important to us in this chapter, however, is that experts now tell us when our "selves" need repair and the proper procedures for doing it. We will trace briefly the context in which we have come to so thoroughly rely on experts.

The Contemporary Concern with Self

While the awareness of death has been present among members of all societies throughout human history, people in tradition-oriented cultures are somewhat insulated from the trauma of death consciousness. In such societies an overarching religious ideology helps to explain life's mysteries. Individuals may know that they are going to die, but they also believe that they know why they are destined to die and where their deaths will take them. Members of nonindustrial, tradition-oriented societies also are fairly secure in the knowledge of who they are. The anxiety occasioned by identity questions is siphoned off, if you will, by the importance accorded to ascribed status characteristics. In such societies, a person's family status pretty well envelopes them and dictates nearly all life experiences:

> In societies with a very simple division of labor, identities . . . are socially predefined and profiled to a high degree. . . . Put simply, everyone pretty much is what he is supposed to be. In such a society identities are easily recognizable, objectively and subjectively. Everybody knows who everybody is and who he is himself. A knight is a knight and a peasant is a peasant, to others as well as to themselves. There is, therefore, no problem of identity. The question "Who am I?" is unlikely to arise in consciousness, since the socially defined answer is massively real, subjectively and consistently confirmed in all significant social interaction. (Berger and Luckmann, 1967:164)

People in contemporary American society are confronted with a very different set of life problems. In the modern world—under the impetus of democratic ideologies, industrialization, and science—many areas of life previously accepted as natural are now viewed as subject to human volition and action. For example, people no longer passively plead for charity; now they expect and demand that governments engage in social welfare activities. Were contemporary Western governments not to do so, large segments of the population would view it as an injustice.

When people come together and collectively act on their definitions of injustice, a **social movement** is born. In Ralph Turner's words, "A movement becomes possible when a group of people cease to petition the good will of others for relief of their misery and demand as their right that others ensure the correction of their condition" (1969:491). Turner argued more than 30 years ago that we were in the midst of a major social movement whose dominant theme was the failure of advanced industrial societies to provide their members a sense of personal worth, that such societies do not foster "an inner peace of mind which comes from a sense of personal dignity or a clear sense of identity" (1969:395). In short, "The phenomenon of a man crying out with indignation because his society has not supplied him with a sense of personal worth and identity" (p. 395) was the distinctive new feature of the era.

The social movements that characterized this period articulated a new definition of injustice, one much broader than the earlier demands for full political participation and freedom from material want. Alienation, previously seen only as a work-related phenomenon, took on a much broader connotation. The term *alienation* used to be associated with such issues as the manager's feelings of loneliness and isolation, the secretary's sense of frustration at being limited to support roles, and the blue-collar worker's lack of job satisfaction (see chapter 7). More recently, **alienation** has been used to refer to a psychological condition in which people are unable to locate a clear conception of self and feel a sense of wholeness. It is in the context of such alienation, as Phillip Reiff (1966) put it some years ago, that the therapeutic state has triumphed.

As the more personalized conception of alienation has become accepted in American society, popular writings by psychiatrists, psychologists, and advice columnists have taken on an influential role. Television appearances have made "mind-tinkerers" such as Dr. Phil McGraw, Dr. Ruth Westheimer, and Deepak Chopra instant celebrities. Their appeal attests to the pervasive anxiety about questions of identity and psychological well-being in society. Such "experts" are constantly dispensing prescriptions for happiness, sexual fulfillment, or mental health.

The movement toward this all-embracing concern with psychological health and personal identity has been accompanied by a corresponding transformation in our "vocabulary of motives" (Mills, 1940), or explanatory schemas of human behavior. When people act in a manner that we consider deviant, our first impulse is to question their mental health and probe their psychological makeup. Are they normal? Why are they doing that? Because of the medicalization of deviance (described in chapter 9), behaviors such as alcoholism, which would have been viewed years ago as evidence of sinfulness or moral degeneracy, are now explained as illness. We use a "sickness vocabulary" rather than a "sin vocabulary." We now ask, "What would make a person do something as sick as that?"(e.g., drink too much). Our grandparents would have had little difficulty in understanding such behavior. For them it was simply *wrong*!

In fact, a therapeutic ethos that sees us in need of "recovery" dominates even the airwaves (Karp, 2001). In her analysis of TV talk shows in which "guests" are encouraged to bare their souls, Kathleen Lowney (1999) uncovers the discourse that currently dominates Americans' thinking about all sorts of deviant or problematic lives: "That people's troubles, often their morally reprehensible behaviors, are propelled by flawed selves that can be—no, ought to be—repaired via therapy" (Karp, 2001:108).

Preoccupied with their dis-ease, large numbers of people in today's society purchase the time and expertise of professionals in order to discover more about themselves. With the aid of the helping professions that have emerged as a major cultural force in the last few decades (among them psychiatrists, psychologists, therapists, and social workers), an increasing proportion of the population has set out to feel better, to "get their acts together," "to get their heads straight." We are in an era that has variously been characterized as the *age of narcissism,* the *me society,* and the *psychological society.* As pointed out in previous chapters, you need only pay attention to the magazines available in your local grocery store, such as *Self* magazine, to conclude that Americans are absorbed with question of self-fulfillment and self-realization.

We might add that self-absorption is consistent with the ethic of consumption and self-satisfaction fostered by capitalism in general and by advertising in particular. In the industrial age, society was primarily organized around the world of work. A person who did not work, for any reason other than physical disability, was defined as immoral, lazy, and worthless. This perspective on work was beautifully captured in Max Weber's notion of the Protestant ethic, or the work ethic (see chapter 7). According to the Protestant ethic, work is intrinsically valuable and an end in itself.

A Consumption Ethic

For sizable segments of the middle class, the work ethic and its moral restraints have been replaced by a **consumption ethic.** The central organizational concern of our time has become less the *production* of goods than their *distribution.* The shift in structure and psychology of modern life has been to an overwhelming concern with the consumption of goods and services. If workers imbued with the Protestant ethic lived to work, now we work to consume. There is even a bumper sticker that proclaims, "I owe, I owe, so off to work I go"!

In the last decades of the twentieth century a new word entered the American vocabulary to describe the young people who embraced this consumption ethic. *Yuppies,* or young urban professionals (and their African-American counterparts, *buppies*), were characterized by the communications media as oriented toward the consumption of such goods as expensive clothing, sports cars, and innovative products of modern technology. The emphasis on consumption has resulted in a paradox. The capitalist system which developed along with the morality of the Protestant ethic required workers who would postpone immediate gratification and who would work at unpleasant tasks for the sake of future rewards. For example, sex had to be foregone and marriage postponed in the interests of industrial efficiency. As the industrial system became more and more technologically sophisticated and productive, it became increasingly unclear what to do with the endless stream of goods, few of which satisfied any genuine needs. A solution was found in the growth of advertising and the transformation of the pleasure-denying work ethic into a self-indulgent society of consumers. The rhetoric of consumption is fostered and sustained by an advertising industry instrumental in creating a seemingly insatiable quest for fulfillment through the ownership of particular commodities (c.f., Ritzer, 1999; Schor, 1998).

The shift toward the social production of consumer-oriented selves has had far-reaching consequences. Since material possessions alone cannot ensure feelings of meaningfulness and satisfaction, many people today find themselves caught up in an endless quest for a sense of significance in their lives. This quest is made even more illusive by the built-in obsolescence of the products produced. There must always be a "better" product in the works, and so the flames of advertising are always available to heat the cauldron of contemporary anxiety.

It is in the context of the broad historical shifts we have been detailing that particular groups and institutions arise to help (some might say exploit) those who are searching for self. In the following section we shall focus especially on two "movements" that reflect the psychological alienation created by life in a mobile, affluent, secularized society subject to rapid change. A great deal has been written about the nature and functions of what has been termed the "new religious movement," and about the "self-help movement."

Buyers and Sellers in the Identity Marketplace

Since the 1960s many new forms of social organization have been devised to provide "services" to those who are trying to increase their self-awareness or are searching for their "real selves." The Esalen Institute, founded in California in 1962, soon became a focal point of the "human potential" movement (McGinn, 2000). The techniques of the human-potential movement included the **sensitivity training** group or encounter group, Gestalt therapy, bodywork and movement therapies, Yoga, Zen Buddhism, and psychodrama. Another development was the rural communes modeled along the lines of nineteenth-century utopian communities which found some favor among young people in the 1970s. Still today, those who are interested in personal growth experiences or consciousness-raising can choose from a wide array of group and individual therapies, ranging from weekend marathons at expensive resorts to years of in-depth analysis. During the 1970s an extraordinary variety of religious and quasi-religious groups flourished in the United States to provide guidance of another sort in the individual's search for self. These "metaphysical" religions (Lewis, 2001), particularly the New Age movement, present the possibility of personal transformation. We will examine this phenomenon in terms of its meaning to those involved in it as well as its significance as a reflection of change in the society.

The New Religions

During the 1960s America was in the middle of a social and cultural revolution. The "hippies" centered in San Francisco's Haight-Ashbury and New York's Greenwich Village were challenging the legitimacy of virtually every American institution. Timothy Leary encouraged young people to expand their consciousness with drugs and, in response, hundreds of thousands experimented with LSD as a route to rediscovery of self. Members of Students for a Democratic Society (SDS), a radical political group protesting

America's involvement in the Vietnam War, regularly took over university buildings across the country, and sometimes forced universities to shut down altogether. In the spring of 1970 the National Guard was called in to stop a student protest at Kent State University, and four students were killed. The scene of American troops killing American students, caught on film and shown over and over again, symbolized the depth of the crisis in the country. During those years hundreds of thousands marched in Washington, D.C. and other cities to end the Vietnam War. At the same time, a Black Revolution was well along the way, and riots erupted in places like Detroit and Los Angeles during which stores were looted and whole city blocks went up in flames as rioters chanted "burn baby burn" (a scene sadly repeated in Los Angeles in 1992).

The political activities of the 1960s were certainly a product of festering injustices in society and a widespread feeling that our purposes in the Vietnam War were wrong. Equally, however, the responses of young people stemmed from the psychological alienation created by life in a mobile, affluent, secularized society which seemed to deprive them of personal meaning. Aside from creating social change, the political involvements of young people during this period satisfied the need to find real engagement in a society that otherwise seemed to provide few opportunities for meaningful life commitments. The events of the 1960s were eloquent testimony both to a political crisis in the country and a cultural crisis of meaning, especially among young people.

When the political furor of the 1960s died down and eventually the Vietnam War ended, the political crisis was somewhat defused. However, the crisis of meaning remained. It is not surprising that many of the disaffected young people who were products of the sixties would be drawn to a variety of new religious groups during the 1970s—groups that promised clear answers to the questions "Who am I?" and "Where do I fit into the world?" The **new religions** of the 1970s were "successor movements" to the broader countercultural activities of the sixties.

Because America has always been a relatively open society in terms of religious expression, religious cultic phenomenon has been an ongoing part of its history (c.f., Jenkins, 2000). But during the 1970s evidence of an infusion of new religious ideologies was visible everywhere. Groups of shaven-headed, incense-bearing, tambourine-playing young people in yellow tunics chanted "Hare Krishna, Hare Krishna" as they persistently pressed flowers or literature on passersby in exchange for donations. Clean-cut, intense, middle-class young people engaged in a variety of business enterprises to support Reverend Sun Myung Moon's Unification Church. Prayer sessions sponsored by the Campus Crusade for Christ proclaiming the approaching coming of the Messiah proceeded next door to assemblies of the Jews for Jesus. Far Eastern religious sects with histories that may go back several thousand years enlisted the support of young, well-educated Americans, many of them from affluent homes.

Evidence indicates that the new religions had wide appeal and touched a large number of lives, directly and indirectly. By the mid-1970s, it had become easy to pursue spirituality outside an established congregation (Wuthnow, 1998), with as many as 10 percent of the population having actually participated in one of the new religions (Wuthnow, 1986). Although this number seems high by any standard, we should acknowledge that the idea of new religions is broadly conceived to include such quasi-religious **personal growth movements** as Scientology and EST (Erhard Seminar Training) along with such **neo-Christian religious groups** as the Unification Church and Far Eastern religious imports such as Krishna Consciousness and Transcendental Meditation.

We have already alluded to the "causes" for the rise of new religious groups during this period, but, as might be expected, their emergence stimulated a huge volume of scientific studies and reinvigorated the sociological study of religion. Since "new religions studies" emerged as a separate area of specialization in the 1970s, hundreds of books and thousands of papers have been written in an effort to understand the nature of new religions and their likely role in the twenty-first century (Melton, 1999). With greater urgency social scientists tried to figure out the basis for the extraordinary receptivity of these groups in both the United States and Europe. Who joined them? How were members recruited? What were the effects on members? Broad theories to explain their proliferation in the 1970s included those that variously stressed (1) the cultural crisis of meaning in America, (2) the loss of community in the United States, or (3) the extraordinary diffusion of identity in a highly fragmented modern world. Such explanations, of course, are not mutually exclusive. They all point to the need to get in touch with feelings and dimensions of self lost in an increasingly impersonal and bureaucratic world. When science and technology portray the universe as barren and bereft of meaning with humans like pebbles on a vast beach, a need is created for people to find explanations that infuse their lives with a cosmic significance. The sociologist Thomas Robbins commented along these lines:

> Personal identity can appear problematic in a highly differentiated society where individuals have multiple limited involvements and interests, some of which must be performed in a "detached" or nonemotionally involved manner. Proliferating new therapeutic movements and mystiques offer to participants a holistic sense of "who am I" which transcends the diverse roles and limited instrumental commitments of participants. (1988:47)

By the late seventies the consciousness began to emerge that new religious groups, especially those that qualified as "cults," constituted a social problem. Important questions began to emerge about the "totalistic" and authoritarian character of such groups as Hare Krishna, Scientology, the Divine Light Mission, and the Unification Church. Parents were bewildered by the religious commitments of their children who, in many instances, would or could have nothing more to do with them. An important stimulus to the "anticult movement" was the disaster in Jonestown, Guyana, in which over 900 members of a group called the People's Temple led by Reverend Jim Jones were murdered or committed suicide. This case created a media explosion on the negative effects of cults and desperate parents were now employing the services of "exit counselors" (Hassan, 1990) to rescue their children from these groups and then "deprogram" them.

While the period since the early 1980s has witnessed a decline in the public visibility of new religious groups, social scientists have a continuing interest in the fate of cults (c.f., Dawson, 1998; Lewis, 2001; Jenkins, 2000) and other spiritual groups (Melton, 2002). The focus of recent scholarship has been on the future of new religions (Melton, 1999), the growth of alternative religions (Niebuhr, 1999), and the continued fascination with the study of those who join these groups (Ayella, 1998). While the number of gurus and their cults may be declining, huge numbers of Americans remain deeply involved in new religions. According to one author, we are seeing the rise or rediscovery of a large number of cults, "grouped around loosely defined and held beliefs, often of a pseudo-scientific nature" (Crone, 2000:17).

At the core of the cult experience is the feeling of community potential that converts get from recruiters (Freie, 1998). According to one author, "People end up joining cults when events lead them to search for a deeper sense of belonging and for something more meaningful in their lives" (Harrary, 1994:20).

Increasingly the attention of social scientists is being drawn to cult-like political groups such as the Christian militia movement (c.f., Abanes, 1996; Barkun, 1997), as well as groups that are part of a "New Age" consciousness (c.f., Heelas, 1996). The conflict in Waco, Texas between Branch Davidians and agents of the federal Bureau of Alcohol, Firearms and Tobacco in 1993 (c.f., Lewis, 1994), and other well-publicized incidents such as the mass suicide of members of groups such as Heavens Gate in 1997 (c.f., Lewis, 2001) resurrected interest in cults. Other areas of interest include women's spirituality (c.f., Borysenko, 1999), and religion and cyberspace (c.f., Zaleski, 1997).

Some of the new religions (e.g., those bitterly hostile to society) appear to have a potential for violence, like Aum Shinrikyo, the Japanese group that used poison gas in the Tokyo subway (Niebuhr, 1999). Although not strictly religious in content, such groups make use of psychological practices that exert strong control over those who turn to them. Such groups may be the contemporary incarnation of earlier cults by providing an overarching system of relevance for those who experience meaninglessness in their everyday lives.

The Self-Help Revolution

The dynamic self-help movement has become an important part of the social fabric of American life. It is not, however, a unified phenomenon that can be categorized easily (Gartner and Riessman, 1998). In many ways, the emergence of self-help and support groups for dealing with virtually every imaginable human trouble represents a combination of many of the elements we have thus far described in this chapter. The self-help revolution reflects the full flowering of the therapeutic culture described at the outset of the chapter. One might say that this has given rise to a relatively new "vocabulary of motives" (Mills, 1940): "that virtually all of us are in need of 'recovery' from one or another psychological problem, whether we acknowledge it or not" (Karp, 2001:107). In self-help groups people turn to others afflicted with the same personal troubles and try, through conversation, to "heal" themselves of what they perceive to be their shared "illness." The illness rhetoric (often implying biological causation) is sometimes joined with a spiritual vocabulary (as in programs like Alcoholics Anonymous) positing that "recovery" requires surrender to a higher power. In short, the self-help phenomenon derives its allure, in part, by combining elements of therapy with elements of religion and science. It is a powerful brew that has drawn the faith of millions.

Group membership has been growing over the last three decades. More than 25 million Americans are estimated to have participated in a self-help group at some point; 10 million in a 12-month period (Kessler, Mickelson, and Zhao, 1997). Today, in any major city, you can attend groups that deal with such diverse problems as alcoholism, mental illness, gambling, spouse abuse, drug addiction, impotence, cross-dressing, and overeating. For example, the Sunday paper in a town of only 40,000 people contained an announcement listing groups such as the following (Edgley and Brissett, 1999:72):

Nicotine Anonymous

Singles Alternative

Co-Dependent Anonymous

Parkinson's Support Group

Smokers Anonymous

SAVES (Sexual Abuse Victims Emerge Survivors)

"Came to Recover"

Concerned Parents

Emotions Anonymous

MENders (for wife beaters)

Sex Addicts Anonymous

Challengers (for the disabled)

Sandwich Generation Support Group

Overcomers (for overweight people)

Alcoholics Anonymous

Al-Anon

AMAC (Adults Molested as Children)

Al-Ateen

TOPS (Take Off Pounds Sensibly)

Narcotics Anonymous

Secular Sobriety

Overeaters Anonymous

ADD (Attention Deficit Disorder) Parents

Community AIDS Network

Although the initial response of mental health professionals to the self-help phenomenon was lukewarm (Powell, 1987, 1990), "the power and effectiveness of self-help is starting to be recognized by government, the human services, the philanthropic community, and by professional helpers who are more and more willing to work cooperatively with self-help groups" (Humm, 1997:5).

Self-help groups bear much in common with the new religions described earlier and consequently serve many of the same functions. These groups, like their strictly religious counterparts, provide integration into a communal network and hold out the promise of personal transformation. People who attend recovery groups, for example, generally acknowledge that their main purpose in becoming involved is to improve themselves (Wuthnow, 1998). In the world of self-help groups, sickness and problems become stable sources of identity,

> creating pseudo-communities for their members, each with a permanent quality about it that people can depend on in a world falling around them. . . . At their best, self-help groups save lives by offering social support to redirect members away from self-destructive habits. At their worst, they are meddling intrusions and trendy clichés that build a consumer culture around drugs, disease, deficits, and infirmities. They offer new selves with which people can identify. (Edgley and Brissett, 1999:197)

Leslie Irvine's (1999) research on Codependents Anonymous (CoDA) illustrates the process at work in CoDA support groups. As in all 12-step support groups, CoDA meetings center on stories. The meetings become a site to examine how "selfhood is a narrative accomplishment, created in the stories people tell about themselves—and this includes the stories that they tell *to* themselves" (p. 1, italics in original). Irvine argues that we learn to tell stories and then become the stories we tell. CoDA members, often reeling from an "uncoupling" (e.g., the breakup of a relationship), "are on a pilgrimage to search for self " (Karp, 2001:111).

The self-help movement may be a response to the huge social upheaval of the last 40 years of the twentieth century. Although a great deal of progressive social change occurred in this period—the civil rights movement advanced African Americans and held the country accountable for the credo that all are created equal; the antiwar movement forever altered the relationship between Americans and those in authority; the women's movement brought masses of women into the workforce and restructured the family and the relationship between the sexes. "While these were all positive, progressive social changes, they came at a cost of social dislocation that could not just be ignored" (Humm, 1997:4). Additional changes occurred as the result of medical breakthroughs (e.g., greater life expectancy) and technological advances that have altered the workplace, our mobility, recreation, and relationships, all with profound social ramifications. "Quietly and assiduously, Americans have been turning to self-help to assist them in making the adjustment to a changed society" (Humm, 1997:4). A positive view of self-help is that it not only provides short-term relief for personal problems, but has the potential to affect the long-term transformation of societal problems. "Self-help values such as anti-elitism, anti-hierarchy, anti-bureaucracy, getting help by helping, and the recognition of peer power have the potential to transform many of the ways in which we live and work" (Humm, 1997:5).

There is another respect in which self-help groups share something in common with new religious groups. Just as people began eventually to document the ill effects of new religions toward the end of the seventies, a self-help backlash has developed (c.f., Edgley and Brissett, 1999). Not everyone is sanguine about the effects of self-help groups. While people may individually feel better through participation in them, their collective effect may be the production of a national mentality in which virtually all of us perceive ourselves as suffering from some sort of illness and as the "victims" of circumstances beyond our control. The dissidents wonder whether claims such as the one made by John Bradshaw, a leader of the recovery movement, that 96 percent of American families are "dysfunctional" trivializes such real abuses as incest by grouping them with an enormous range of experiences somehow deemed as damaging to people. Critics worry that the underlying illness ideology of support groups furthers the view, distinctly a product of the modern world, that individuals do not bear ultimate responsibility for their life problems and personal behaviors. Such a view is rooted in a radical self-absorption that is the logical outcome of a society that has always valued the development and interests of the individual above the greater social good. The sociologist Edwin Schur (1976) pointed out some years ago that increased personal consciousness is too often achieved at the expense of a diminished social consciousness. More recently, a number of authors (c.f., Bellah et al., 1996; Derber, 2000; Putnam, 2000) have written about the self-orientation and excessive individualism that pervades American social character, voicing concern that this emphasis on personal change is conducive to overlooking the need for larger social change (see box).

The growth of self-help groups has always been based on their special ability to meet people's needs for peer support and practical information. While the vast majority of mutual aid groups continue to provide help through face-to-face groups, more and more people are finding it easier and more convenient to have their needs met through participation in online support networks. These online mutual help groups operate via message boards, newsgroups, bulletin boards, chat groups, interactive Web sites, and other online media (Madara, 1997).

It has become impossible to count the number of online mutual help groups, as the number of both mutual help networks and people participating in such groups is increasing dramatically (Madara, 1997). A key feature of these groups has been the ability of any member to offer help and understanding to others. Many people who were previously unable to attend traditional face-to-face self-help groups are among those now participating in online groups. For example, those without local groups or without transportation, those with uncommon conditions or rare illnesses, those with limiting physical disabilities, bedridden individuals, and caregivers with round-the-clock responsibilities are able to participate online (Madara, 1997). Madara gives the example of an individual who found support in the Disabilities Forum on CompuServe, who continues to participate because

> when I suddenly became disabled due to a stroke, I sought out this Forum
> and found many friends, one in particular, who helped me "adjust" to the
> physical and mental aspects of "being disabled." This Forum was a life-

line for me, as I became isolated socially after leaving my job because of the stroke. I could not have coped without all the wonderful people in this Forum and all the helpful support and information. Almost four years later, I still seek out support here and try to help others. (p. 23)

As Madara notes, peer support has long been a key value in face-to-face groups, and online communication enhances this peer equality. In communicating with other people online, there are no signs of social status, age, dress,

---

The Dangers of the Awareness Trap

The search for the real self and meaningful intimate relationships occupies a good deal of the attention and energies of many people in American society. We believe that by increasing our own self-awareness and accepting responsibility for ourselves, we will secure the benefits of "the good life." The trouble with this idea is that people may become so involved in their own search for self that they fail to take into account the built-in sources of inequality and injustice in the social structure that make it more difficult for some people to achieve this goal than others. There are many situations in which no amount of self-awareness will suffice to solve social problems.

A huge industry of personal and spiritual change has grown to help people change themselves. But much of this culture of personal change fuels individualism by propagating the view that we can change ourselves without changing society—"or worse, that the only thing we ever need to change is ourselves" (Derber, 2000:100). But as the well-known sociologist C. Wright Mills (1959) told us in *The Sociological Imagination*, as we probe more deeply into our seemingly *personal* problems, we realize that they nearly always reflect *public* issues that require social and political change. Although self-help groups certainly provide emotional support and interpersonal ties that are invaluable to participants, they rarely challenge the underlying political issues that have shaped the problems of the individual person (Adamsen and Rasmussen, 2001). The insistence that we can do whatever we set our minds to can promote complacency among the privileged and help foster a way of thinking that blames those most wounded by our society for their own problems (Loeb, 1999). According to Paul Loeb, "The most troublesome consequence of this way of thinking is that it exempts even the most powerful economic, political, and social institutions from all responsibility for the state of society" (p. 140). "Is it any wonder," he asks, "that a woman attending a Seattle New Age conference explained that welfare recipients "just need to wake up and realize their mythic selves" (p. 139)?

As sociologists, your authors cringe when we hear simple-minded, feel-good, spiritually based solutions to structurally generated life problems. Certainly it would be, as one of us has said, "a wonderful world . . . if simply cultivating the right attitude really ensured the evaporation of personal woes!" (Karp, 2001:109). But our **sociological imaginations** cause us to know otherwise. And, "while there is nothing novel in the observation that raising personal consciousness is too often accomplished at the cost of a social consciousness, it surely remains a message worth preaching to students" (Karp, 2001:109).

weight, race, disabilities, or other distinctions. Online anonymity makes people more comfortable in sharing sensitive or potentially embarrassing information. There is also something to be said for the ease of participating in an online group. "One need not get dressed up to attend a meeting from home, while the 'doorway out' is always just a mouse click away" (Madara, 1997:23).

The availability of online networks is expanding the variety of mutual help communities as new types of groups develop. Survivors of traumatic car accidents are able to submit their stories as part of the Car Accident Emotional Recovery Circle Web site. Single Disabled Dads can share their experiences in their own section of the disabilities Message Center on AOL (Madara, 1997).

As we noted earlier in discussing the Internet and health (chapter 8), the major barrier to the use of online support networks is the lack of universal access to them. While libraries and schools may provide public use of computers, they are not a substitute for widespread home access. Populations such as the poor, the severely disabled, and the chronically ill and their caregivers stand to gain much from universal access (Madara, 1997).

Individualism, Community, and Commitment

The tension between individualism and community has been an abiding theme of sociological analysis since the emergence of the discipline in the nineteenth century. The development of sociology arose out of the social and ideological upheavals brought about by the French and Industrial Revolutions. From its earliest beginnings sociology was simultaneously a response to, and a critique of, the emergence of a secular urban industrial order in nineteenth-century Western civilization. The rapid development of urban industrial centers throughout the nineteenth century precipitated a still-ongoing analysis concerning the nature of the "social bond"; that is, the connection between the individual and society (see chapter 1). Foremost in the minds of individuals writing about society during the nineteenth century was the contrast between forms of social life rooted in small agrarian societies and the kinds of social relationships characterizing the new urban-industrial world.

The Changing Nature of the Social Bond

Such classical sociological theorists as Émile Durkheim, Max Weber, Ferdinand Tönnies, and Henry Maine may have generated different conceptual models for looking at the emerging urban order in European society, but they fundamentally agreed that the bond between individuals and society had been greatly weakened in modern society. They were unanimous in their view that people were less morally constrained in urban societies, and that their relationships and commitments to community had become far more tenuous. Although each of these writers focused on somewhat different features of the social order, they agreed that while the central unit of earlier societies had been the larger collectivities of family and community, the central unit in their contemporary society had become the individual. Further, as the pursuit of individual gain and personal mobility (as measured by wealth) became ascendant social values, relationships among people became more rational, impersonal, and contractual. Whereas people in earlier agrarian societies related to each other emotionally, with their hearts, those in the new social order related rationally, with their heads.

The social theorists named above viewed these developments with great alarm. They foresaw that the celebration of the interests and needs of the individual over those of the larger society would ultimately weaken society's very core and diminish its capacity to provide meaningful moral guidelines. A moral society, they thought, was one that protected both society and individuals by placing limits on the aspirations of individuals and their ability to act only in a self-interested fashion. Their common prognosis was that a society based on individualism would eventually erode the strength of its major institutions. They feared that the eclipse of community would foreshadow the demise of the family and would in turn precipitate an increase in all sorts of human pathologies—from crime to divorce to mental illness to suicide. In short, these writers warned that a society based on individualism would eventually unravel.

Although these sociologists could not have had contemporary America in mind when they wrote, their analysis appears to apply. Even the most optimistic among us must acknowledge that America has extraordinary problems. Each day the newspaper assails us with more bad news about rates of murder, homelessness, poverty, suicide, drug addiction, robbery, AIDS, teenage pregnancy, illiteracy, and unemployment. In the midst of great wealth, we have increasingly become a nation of "haves" and "have-nots." Racism, sexism, and ageism characterize ever-increasing antagonisms between groups that perceive each other only as adversaries. While it simplifies things too much to pin all of these ills on the consequences of individualism, we must wonder about its causal significance in a society that, more than any other in human history, has made individualism virtually sacred (see box).

Wilding for Fun and Profit

In the spring of 1989 a group of teenagers brutally attacked a woman jogger in New York's Central Park, repeatedly raped her, and left her for dead. When they were later caught and asked why they had committed the crime, one of the youths spoke for several when he replied without remorse that it had been fun, something to do. In fact, the boys had a word for this and similar rampages: they had been out "wilding" they said. The press picked up on the word and a number of urban wilding stories were reported.

In his book, *The Wilding of America: How Greed and Violence Are Eroding Our Nation's Character* (1996), Charles Derber offers a provocative critique of America's culture of individualism in which he argues that wilding is not restricted to the behaviors of a few "pathological" teenagers. Derber maintains that we can trace America's wilding roots to an individualistic, get-your-own-whatever-you-have-to-do ethic that has always been part of the underbelly of the American Dream. By wilding, he means "the epidemic of uncontrolled, unconstrained self-interest that increasingly permeates all aspects of our society, bringing with it enormously destructive consequences to our material, moral, and communal existence" (Derber, in Shapiro and Purpel, 1998:2). According to Derber, this "culture of wilding" has triggered widespread violence that has undermined civic life.

A degraded individualism, especially in the economy, lies at the root of this decline (Derber, 1996). In our market society, the supreme virtue is to concentrate on one's own interests. So chief executive officers of the Fortune 500 companies receive more than 250 times the pay of their rank-and-file employees. Some U.S. firms close down their plants in this country and set up operations abroad where they can hire labor for a pittance. The upshot of all this is that the United States suffers from a huge—and growing—maldistribution of wealth and income. The rich *are* getting richer and the poor *are* getting poorer (Morgan, 1999).

Derber worries that an American Dream that does not spell out the moral consequences of unmitigated self-interest threatens to turn the next generation into wilding machines. Americans could turn, not only on each other, but on society as well—the result of being too self-absorbed to make the commitments and observe the moral constraints that hold stable communities together. Derber already sees abundant evidence that a wilder generation of Americans is assaulting and abandoning society—violence on the streets, family dissolution, chaos in government—all causes as well as consequences of the wilding crisis. "America's culture of wilding, at its extreme, is triggering an epidemic of bizarre and terrifying violence. The new violence constitutes a direct assault on society, undermining the social infrastructure that sustains civilized life" (Derber, in Shapiro and Purpel, 1998:6).

Ernest Morgan (1999) links the tragic school shootings in recent years to a rampant individualism that is a by-product of the greed and exploitation that increasingly has come to characterize American culture. That is, the shootings are but a "tiny symptom of a vastly greater problem" (p. 4). Morgan suggests: "Fundamentally we need a shift from a paradigm of selfishness—of greed and exploitation—to one of caring and sharing" (p. 4).

Derber would no doubt agree. His interviews with about 30 Massachusetts voters find suburbanites, affluent and geographically insulated from the city, who seem prepared to see the cities abandoned if their own comfortable lives can be preserved. Says Derber, "The wilding ethos of the suburbs and the more affluent urban neighborhoods expresses itself less as a frenzied 'antihuman' rage than as an increasingly thick wall that makes the suffering of others emotionally tolerable" (in Shapiro and Purpel, 1998:24). Most of those he interviewed believe that the larger society may be in danger of falling apart, but nonetheless have a remarkable capacity to enjoy their own lives. The fact that "a growing segment of the population is hell-bent on having a good time even as they recognize that the ship may be sinking is one of the most telling marks of the new wilding culture" (Derber, in Shapiro and Purpel, 1998:25).

Habits of the Heart

Although, as we have seen, the sociological analysis of individualism extends nearly to the origins of the discipline, the conversation about its significance in understanding American character and social structure has been reinvigorated through the writings of Robert Bellah and his colleagues. In 1985 they published a book entitled *Habits of the Heart* (reprinted in 1996) that detailed their analysis of the history and consequences of individualism in America. This book has been widely praised as providing lucid, penetrating insights into our current condition. In their book entitled *The Good Society* (1991), Bellah and coauthors continued the dialogue by considering how America's basic institutions have been injured and what must be done to repair the damage done to them.

Bellah and his colleagues begin their analysis of individualism by making reference to the famous writings of a Frenchman, Alexis de Tocqueville, who traveled to the United States in the early 1800s as a sympathetic observer of the first 50 years of our extraordinary experiment with democracy. Tocqueville later wrote two volumes (1835 and 1840) entitled *Democracy in America*, which detailed insights into American character and social structure that remain astoundingly relevant today. Tocqueville centered his writings on the unwritten norms (mores) that seemed to be emerging in the new nation, norms that were part of America's "habits of the heart" as he put it. Tocqueville admired the spirit of individualism that fostered personal freedom, but even at that early point in the country's career, he worried that excessive individualism could separate Americans from each other and undermine the civic spirit so necessary for the success of a democracy.

Bellah and his coauthors extended Tocqueville's analysis by distinguishing two forms of individualism, **instrumental individualism** and **expressive individualism**. Instrumental individualism, the type most noted by Tocqueville, refers to the freedom to pursue financial and career success. This is the kind of individualism celebrated in the maxims of Ben Franklin's *Poor Richard's Almanac,* and in the Horatio Alger "rags-to-riches" stories. Expressive individualism, in contrast, refers to the deep and abiding concerns that Americans have with personal self-fulfillment, with the idea that one of life's missions is to maximize personal happiness by discovering who you "really" are. This second form of individualism is thoroughly consistent with the "therapeutic culture" described earlier in this chapter. Both types of individualism are built upon the kind of personal freedom central to a democratic way of life. The flip side of freedom, however, is loneliness. These authors note that "freedom turns out to mean being left alone by others" ([1985]1996:23).

The essential problem posed by individualism is that it "privatizes" the goals and pursuits of people and thereby erodes the social attachments that provide society's moral anchor. Individualism undermines commitment to community since membership in any community (from the family to local community to nation) implies constraints on the behaviors of people that are perceived to be inconsistent with personal fulfillment.

In the introduction to the updated edition of *Habits of the Heart* (1996), Bellah and colleagues wrote that the consequences of radical individualism were more strikingly evident in 1996 than they had been a decade before, when the book was first published. They observed what they referred to as a "crisis of civic membership," meaning "that there are, at every level of American life and in every significant group, temptations and pressures to disengage from the larger society" (p. xi). This crisis threatens "the confident sense of selfhood that comes from membership in a society in which we believe, where we both trust and feel trusted, and to which we feel we securely belong" (p. xi).

Robert Putnam's *Bowling Alone* (2000) laments the decline in *social capital*—social networks and the norms of reciprocity and trustworthiness that arise from them—at the end of the twentieth century. One of the ways social capital improves our lot is by widening our awareness of the many ways in which our fates are linked. According to Putnam,

> [P]eople who have active and trusting connections to others—whether family members, friends, or fellow bowlers—develop or maintain character traits that are good for the rest of society. Joiners become more tolerant, less cynical, and more empathetic to the misfortunes of others. When people lack connection to others, they are unable to test the veracity of their own views, whether in the give-and-take of casual conversation or in more formal deliberation. Without such an opportunity, people are more likely to be swayed by their worst impulses. It is no coincidence that random acts of violence, such as the 1999 spate of schoolyard shootings, tend to be committed by people identified, after the fact, as "loners." (p. 289)

Laura Pappano echoes this concern in *The Connection Gap* (2001), stating that as a society, we face a collective loneliness. She is not referring to loneliness in the traditional sense—"the lonely one missing out on the party of life, famished for human contact with too much time to wonder what's gone awry" (p. 8). Rather, she is writing about the rest of us: "The overstimulated, hyperkinetic, overcommitted, striving, under-cared-for, therapy dependent, plugged in, logged on, sleep deprived. We are the new lonely" (p. 8).

She continues:

> People talk a great deal about "community" but complain of feeling less and less a part of one. People long for rich relationships but find themselves wary of committing to others. Many of us hunger for intimacy but end up paying professionals to listen to, care for, and befriend us. . . . As a society, we face a collective loneliness, an empty feeling that comes not from lack of all human interaction, but from the loss of *meaningful* interaction, the failure to be a part of something real, or to have faith in institutions that might bring us together. This is what I call the Connection Gap. (p. 8)

Despite the bleak diagnosis of our social ills in the literature we have cited, we should not be hopeless about the future well-being of the society.

Putnam, for example, offers challenges such as the following to those interested in restoring American community in the twenty-first century:

> Let us find ways to ensure that by 2010 the level of civic engagement
> among Americans then coming of age in all parts of our society will
> match that of their grandparents when they were that same age . . .
>
> Let us find ways to ensure that by 2010 America's workplace will be sub-
> stantially more family-friendly and community-congenial . . .
>
> Let us act to ensure that by 2010 Americans will spend less time traveling
> and more time connecting with our neighbors than we do today, that we
> will live in more integrated and pedestrian-friendly areas, and that the
> design of our communities and the availability of public space will encour-
> age more casual socializing with friends and neighbors. (2000:404, 406–08)

The resurrection of a "civil society" requires political and economic policies that stress inclusion rather than exclusion of groups that traditionally
have been disenfranchised. We need to think about economic principles that
will encourage even more civic participation and reawaken feelings of commitment to something larger than ourselves. We need to find ways to refashion an American Dream that has become overly focused on materialism.
This is possible because rampant individualism is a distortion of a cultural
legacy that more appropriately applauds a balancing of individual freedom
and community needs.

In 1991, during the Los Angeles riots, Rodney King uttered a plea:
"Can't we all just get along?" The question remains relevant today. Is it possible for people of different values, races, experiences, and backgrounds to
live together in peace? Pappano (2001) points out that much of what worked
in the past to create a sense of cohesion and community is no longer applicable today. The world and the issues have changed and become more complex. "We are strange new people living strange new lives" (p. 197).
She continues:

> For the middle class—particularly the white middle class—it was easier
> decades ago to forge common ground with neighbors and community
> members, in part because so many people shared the same backgrounds,
> experiences, and values. Our society today is far more diverse, and that
> diversity will only grow. We can see this in our own extended families,
> which increasingly include members of different races, religions, and eth-
> nicities. Likewise, our neighborhoods, our workplaces, our classrooms,
> and our communities are more diverse. Although Rodney King's plea
> was for the cessation of violence, it is not enough to not fight. We must
> find a means for living together, not in silent acceptance but in meaning-
> ful concert. The challenge of connection has, in some ways, grown more
> intense. (p. 197)

This is a complex issue, and the complexity is rooted in our identities.
"We are searching for who we are, caught between the pull of a bland
homogenized culture, in which everyone shops at the Gap and eats at

McDonald's. . . . We have an urgent need to know who we are, where we come from, and why we matter" (Pappano, 2001:197).

Future Selves

We are caught in the midst of a major historical transformation with dramatic implications for our personal well-being as well as that of society. Western culture has passed through two central historical epochs, characterized first by agricultural, pre-urban society and then by urban-industrial society. We now live in a postindustrial society that relies on technological knowledge and is a time of rapid, often confusing social change.

In the wake of such transformations, social scientists have raised troubling questions about the future. Does a modern society, with its emphasis on technical information, services, and consumption, require a different conception of self than the one characteristic of the eras of agricultural and industrial production? Will individuals be able to make the self-adaptations required in a complex, rapidly evolving society?

Measuring Self-Concepts

Some years ago, Louis Zurcher (1977) used a technique called the Twenty Statements Test (TST) to measure self-concepts. Participants are asked to make twenty responses to the question "Who am I?" by completing the sentence "I am" in twenty different ways. They are instructed to write their statements quickly, in the order they come to mind, without worrying about the logic or importance of their responses.

The TST is scored by classifying the responses into categories or modes. Repeated samplings led Zurcher to conclude that the test reveals four central conceptions of self:

The A mode, or physical self.
The B mode, or social self.
The C mode, or reflective self.
The D mode, or oceanic self.

The **physical self** is indicated by responses that refer to actual physical attributes as well as other attributes that involve no interaction with others. A person's residential address would be an example of the latter. The **social self** refers to positions and statuses which clearly locate people in a social structure or social circle. Examples of responses in this mode would include statements like "I am a college student" or "I am an electrical engineer." The **reflective self** is indicated by abstract statements which transcend specific social situations. These responses indicate the behaviors that respondents attribute to themselves. Examples would include such statements as "I am a moody person" or "I am a spendthrift." The **oceanic self** is reflected in statements that are "so vague that they lead us to no reliable expectations about behavior" (p. 46). Statements such as "I am a loving individual" or "I am a person who wants the best for everyone" would be placed in the oceanic-self category.

When Zurcher first administered the TST in 1969, he found that the most frequent mode of response was the C mode, or the reflective-self category. In fact, 68 percent of his respondents fell into this category, in dramatic contrast to the results of an earlier administration of TST by Hartley (1968), which found an abundance of B mode responses in a random sample of University of Iowa students. What sense could be made of such significant differences over time? Zurcher reasoned that perhaps the proliferation of C mode self-definitions in his own 1969 sample was a response to the rapid rate of cultural and technological change in advanced industrial nations. Specifically, the change in self-conceptualization in the 1960s is thought to reflect the social upheaval that resulted from movement from a conservative postwar era to a liberal age of radical demonstrations against the Vietnam War and support of the civil rights movements. Zurcher proposed that a **mutable self**—one in which physical, social, reflective, and oceanic were integrated—would allow a person to assume any of the selves which fit a particular situation.

Today sociocultural change continues at an accelerated rate. We live in a global age of information technology, changing family composition, and the retirement of the baby boomers (Grace and Cramer, 2002:273). Sherry Grace and Kenneth Cramer set out to investigate sense of self at the turn of the century, hypothesizing that this time represented "a state of continued and rapid progress, progress which Zurcher (1972, 1977) and Turner (1976) postulated would lead to a greater detached or transcendental sense of self" (2002:274). In particular, they felt that the Internet and e-mail of our time suggest a self divorced from the ability to reflect through others. According to Grace and Cramer:

> We know too little about the effects of recent social and cultural dynamics (e.g., the effect of the retirement of the baby boomers on the job market for today's youth, the access to information afforded by the information superhighway, and the communication revolution of electronic mail) on current conceptualizations of the self. How would the "millennials" (i.e., those individuals entering university at the turn of the century) conceive of themselves given the current context? (p. 274)

Grace and Cramer recruited 324 undergraduate psychology students to participate in the study. The authors postulated that the predominant mode of self would continue to be C mode (reflective), but that there would be an increase in D mode (oceanic). They also postulated that females would report significantly more social (B mode) self-statements than would males.

Their results show that overall, the preponderant mode of self continues to be reflective (C mode). That is, "the nature of self among students continues to be focused on ways of behaving, moods, feelings, preferences, and dislikes" (p. 277). In fact, these participants have the highest mode of reflective self of any sample published since the 1950s (91.3 percent)! None of the participants had a preponderant mode of physical self; only one participant had a predominant mode of oceanic self. The social self also appears to be declining (8.4 percent).

Although an earlier study (Babbitt and Burbach, 1990) found that females tended to use more social or B category responses, this was not replicated in Grace and Cramer's findings. They had hypothesized that women would provide more social responses since women are thought to be generally more in tune with family and interpersonal aspects of relationships. Their results question that assumption.

Grace and Cramer's (2002) findings make sense in light of the current historical context. As Zurcher (1972) and Turner (1976) argued, the pace of technological advancement and change in our society may be leading to the reflective self. This leads Grace and Cramer to ask, "In future, will this focus on personal affect and evaluation lead to disruption of social group identity and interpersonal relations?" (p. 277).

The Postmodern Self*

In chapter 3 we reviewed the writings of Erving Goffman, who suggested that human beings have multiple selves, that indeed we have as many selves as the situations in which we interact with others. You should remember that such a view of the self raises intriguing questions about the authenticity of social performances, including whether people possess a "true" self that transcends the range of contexts in which we act. While Goffman first raised these questions during the 1950s and 1960s, we think that questions about the fate of the self have become more urgent in the **postmodern world**. The current postmodern world is characterized by information technologies that enormously expand the flow, rapidity, intensity, and volume of communications. These same technologies (from FAX machines to computers to cell phones) also greatly expand the number and range of interactional arenas in which we participate. A geometric increase in the rate of communication has extraordinary implications for the presentation and maintenance of personal selves. "In an emerging postmodern world the construction and maintenance of an integrated self becomes deeply problematic because the social structures necessary to anchor the self have themselves become unstable and ephemeral" (Karp, 1996:186).

In his book of the same title, Kenneth Gergen ([1991]2000) refers to the **saturated self**. He means to convey with this term that the pace of communications and life itself has virtually overwhelmed us and that as a result our selves are "under siege." We may be reaching a point of social saturation that has revolutionary consequences for the ways we conceptualize the human self and its place in the social world. Postmodern life requires us to adopt multiple perspectives on ourselves, making it difficult for us to form a unified, or core self. As we take part in "incoherent and disconnected relationships," we acquire a new pattern of self-consciousness which Gergen calls "multiphrenia," or many-mindedness. Gergen comments:

*For an excellent discussion of postmodernism and the self, see chapter four, "Two Options for the Postmodern Self" in J. Holstein and J. Gubrium's *The Self We Live By: Narrative Identity in a Postmodern World*. New York: Oxford University Press, 2000.

> Under postmodern conditions, persons exist in a state of continuous con-
> struction and reconstruction; it is a world where anything goes that can
> be negotiated. Each reality of self gives way to reflexive questioning,
> irony, and ultimately the playful probing of yet another reality. (2000:7)

Later in the book he summarizes his position by saying:

> So we find a profound sea change taking place in the character of social
> life during the twentieth century. Through an array of newly emerging
> technologies the world of relationships becomes increasingly saturated.
> We engage in greater numbers of relationships, in a greater variety of
> forms, and with greater intensities than ever before. With the multiplica-
> tion of relationships also comes a transformation in the social capacities
> of the individual. . . . The relatively coherent and unified sense of self
> inherent in a traditional culture gives way to manifold and competing
> potentials. A multiphrenic condition emerges in which one swims in ever-
> shifting, concatenating, and continuous currents of being. (2000:79–80)

According to this view, the self is a reflection of the cultural zeitgeist (spirit of
the times). "The protean, fragmented, media- and information-saturated
societies of the West produce, well . . . protean, fragmented, and saturated
selves" (de Munck, 2000:43).

Gergen's postmodern self bears a close resemblance to Goffman's dramaturgical self, in that it is fluid and social, enacted and established in situated
performances. Although upon first consideration Gergen's picture of the saturated self suggests a pessimistic outlook since the intensity of stimuli facing
us is likely only to increase in the future, Gergen notes that it has two distinct
advantages over the traditional self. The postmodern self is highly adaptive to
change—its flexibility allows individuals to cope effectively with the shifting
situational demands faced in performing diverse social roles. And second, it
has liberating possibilities:

> . . . because it is unencumbered by needs for consistency, unity, and
> unvarying authenticity, the postmodern self can be free to play with dif-
> ferent identities, relationships, and commitments, knowing that each is
> valid in different contexts and from certain standpoints. For instance, a
> student can opt to be a "geek" in the afternoon and a "party girl" in the
> evening, trading in a bookish self in the classroom for a boisterous self in
> the bar, without feeling as though these two identities are at odds. (Sand-
> strom, Martin, and Fine, 2003:117)

It may be that the contingencies faced in a postmodern world will require
people to question the ideology of individualism we have described in this
chapter. Faced with extraordinary stimulus overload, we may be required to
redefine ourselves in *relational* rather than individualistic terms. Our sense of
well-being may turn on the realization that our existence is sensible only in
terms of our connectedness to others. In this regard, efforts to cope with an
increasingly saturated self may motivate people to rediscover community as
a central source of personal meaning. Social change in the direction of

greater communality would have a salutatory effect on minimizing the social problems created by excessive individualism.

John Hewitt has observed that in contemporary society our sense of self is much more likely than in the past "to be based on a more or less self-conscious selection of a community as its main support" (2003:137). This self-selected community, or community of choice, provides us with a network of similar others who support our conceptions of self. Even when a community is based on rather narrow criteria of similarity (for example, interest in biking), is spatially dispersed, and "significantly a product of the person's own imagination," a sense of continuity and integration is provided, "linking various situated identities to the social identity it provides" (Hewitt, 2003:137). Most people find limited forms of community in professions, neighborhood, religion, or social movement participation, but do not devote themselves exclusively to any of them. People may also migrate from one community to another, identifying with a number of communities over the course of a lifetime. According to Hewitt, where identification with a community is less than total, personal identity is a more salient component of the self. He explains:

> The contemporary person is thus in many ways a more self-conscious being than the resident of a traditional community. The self is not simply a spontaneous product of a fixed community that surrounds it from birth and that assigns it a place. It is, instead, something that must be found, constructed, or cultivated. (p. 138)

Jaber Gubrium and James Holstein (2000) point out that "personal selves" are being produced in more social settings than ever before. The stories we formulate about our personal selves are increasingly anchored in institutionally produced narratives, or "discursive environments." Discursive environments refer to "institutional domains characterized by distinctive ways of interpreting and representing everyday realities" (p. 103). Examples of discursive environments include schools, health clubs, support groups, recreational organizations, and so on. These environments promote particular ways of representing who and what we are. With more concerns than ever entering the "self-construction" business, today's world could be characterized as being increasingly populated by *institutional selves* (Gubrium and Holstein, 2001). Although many of these discursive environments seem geared to construct problem-ridden selves (comprising a virtual "troubled identity" market), as in the case of CoDA groups, for example, not all identities are medicalized. There are also plenty of environments that feature mainly positive self-images:

> Mountain climbers, cyclists, and go-cart racers, along with martial artists, wilderness skiers, scuba divers, and myriad others, find that the social sites of their activities provide not only recreation but also diverse ways of viewing and articulating identity. Such discursive environments may be just as consequential for self-construction as those that construct and heal the troubled. (Gubrium and Holstein, 2000:104)

Of course, no single discursive environment determines who and what we are. In a postmodern context, the sense of a personal identity is being constructed in more social settings than ever. "A thriving landscape of institutions serves up myriad selves, providing more and more occasions for constructing who and what we are. . . . This amounts to a field of possibilities and constraints that extends well beyond what Mead, or even Goffman, could have imagined" (p. 105). But in contrast to the gloomy conclusions of many postmodern theorists, Gubrium and Holstein offer some optimistic appraisals in their assessment of the implications of this situation for the future of the self (Sandstrom, Martin, and Fine, 2003). Our ability to choose among options in fashioning a self "can be as liberating as it is overwhelming and debilitating" (Gubrium and Holstein, 2000:112). In addition, they suggest that the self is remarkably resilient, so that ultimately it is likely to adapt positively to the challenges of contemporary society. Patricia and Peter Adler's (1999) study of resort workers supports this view. Despite the transience of these "postmodern people" who have "uncoupled themselves from the conventional lifestyles and social structures of society" (p. 53), they have adapted by finding new ways of conceiving themselves:

> In shedding . . . the security of conventional life, they have stepped into a shifting global world where they are, even in the midst of makeshift or professional communities, fundamentally alone. They have looked inward for their source of strength, been resourceful, eschewed the consumerist lifestyle, and forged their own paths. (Adler and Adler, 1999:53)

For these workers, a transient postmodern existence has not resulted in the loss of core self. Whereas many theories of the postmodern self focus on changes that have occurred to the more surface aspects of the self, they have not looked at the deeper aspects of the self, assuming that it has been dissolved, as in Gergen's (2000) portrayal of a fragmented self that eventually becomes "no self at all." As Adler and Adler put it, "In fact, the selves of transient resort workers in the postmodern era have adapted and thrived. . . . Rather than finding themselves fashioned by layers with no underlying core, they have become more mutable: anchored in change rather than stability and impulse-process rather than institution-product oriented" (1999:53). According to these authors, "It seems that the postmodernists' most pessimistic view of the demise of the self has not been borne out; rather, the core self has adapted to contemporary conditions and thrived" (p. 54).

The Tricky Business of Predicting the Future

Even though many of the analyses described in this chapter are grounded in carefully collected data, prediction about the future remains a tricky, highly uncertain endeavor. Social scientists cannot make *absolute* predictions about future norms of social life easily. Few of them accurately forecast the civil rights activities of the early 1960s, the urban riots of the mid-1960s, the women's rights activities of the 1970s, the international terrorist attacks of the 1980s, or the Gulf War of the 1990s. Of course, the terrorist bombings of the World Trade Center and Pentagon on September 11, 2001 rocked the world. And as this final chapter is being written, America is at war with Iraq.

The failure to anticipate such social events does not signal some technical or theoretical flaw in sociological work. It is, instead, affirmation of one of the central messages of this book: Human beings are continually in the process of rearranging their social worlds in ways that they themselves cannot fully predict in advance.

What, then, can we say about the future? The data presented in this chapter and throughout this book justify optimistic judgments about our capacity for adapting to a rapidly changing society. The expansion of the groups described in the preceding sections illustrates a fundamental aspect of social life. When individuals find their lives becoming too impersonal and too rational, they will inject into them some sentiment, some passion. When social life becomes too routinized, people will collectively find ways to experience novelty. Similarly, when they find their lives becoming too unpredictable, they will introduce some routine into their daily activity. Individuals who feel uncertain of their personal identities and are bothered by a diminished sense of self-worth will respond collectively by trying to alter their environments to meet their needs.

In this book we have tried to convey the value of sociology—more specifically of a sociological focus on everyday life—for understanding the mutual transformations in the relationships of situations and selves. In doing so we have stressed certain themes: the balance between social order and freedom; the interplay of individuals and social structures; the interpenetration of macro and micro social worlds. As boundaries for human interaction, these themes are critical if we are to obtain insight into the organization of our daily lives and the likely shapes of our individual and collective futures.

Conclusion

In nearly all the chapters of this book, we have stressed the ways in which individuals' identities are fashioned by the particular social circumstances of their lives. Certainly your sense of self is related to the socialization you have experienced, your family's values and attitudes, your social class, your race or ethnicity, and your gender. We also have argued from time to time throughout this volume that people's consciousness about themselves and the world cannot be understood apart from the particular historical period in which they live. In this last chapter the argument has been that we are now living through a period of history that makes it uniquely difficult to answer the question "Who am I?"

Today's American society is more complicated, more bureaucratized, more impersonal, and more fast-paced than any other in the history of humankind. As a result, there are widespread feelings of anxiety, personal malaise, psychological alienation, and rootlessness. Preoccupied with their *dis*-ease, many people in today's society purchase the time and expertise of professionals in order to discover more about themselves. The helping professions (among them psychiatrists, psychologists, therapists, and social work-ers) have emerged as a major cultural force in the last few decades. For an increasing proportion of the population, professional help is needed to feel better, "to get their acts together," "to get their heads together." It seems a fair characterization that contemporary Americans, in contrast to members of other cultures and historical eras, are uniquely concerned with themselves.

One vehicle for the contemporary search for self consists of the funda-mentalist groups within Christianity; another consists of Eastern religions that have been around for thousands of years but which achieved great appeal especially during the 1970s. We think that their popularity was due in large measure to the efforts of young people to understand their place in the world. These "new" religions were a reaction to the growing rationalization of modern life. The memberships of such religious movements are relatively small compared to the population as a whole, but their significance should not be dismissed. They reflect a deep urge for people to become "pilgrims" involved in a journey into themselves. We suggested that while new religions remain an important locus for the search for self, the proliferation of self-help groups more recently has become a medium for dealing with the dis-ease fos-tered by a therapeutic society that has fundamentally redefined the meaning of "normalcy."

Some observers of the American cultural scene are pessimistic about our collective future. They wonder whether the rate of social change will outrun our ability to cope with it. Other studies suggest a more benign picture of the future, however. Such a view is, of course, consistent with the symbolic inter-actionist perspective that has guided this whole enterprise.

We have maintained throughout this volume that human beings are not merely passive products of culture. Because they are symbolic animals, they have the potential to create cultures that meet their needs. Such a view of human beings provides an optimistic antidote to the idea, underlying much social science, that we are simply victims of our environments. Our distinc-tively human ability to constantly re-create the world includes the possibility of creating a more humane society.

Definitions

Alienation Individuals' feelings of disassociation from the surrounding society. Alienation may express itself as feelings of powerlessness, normlessness, meaning-lessness, depersonalization, or isolation.

Consumption ethic Belief that one's sense of identity and self-worth can be enhanced through consumption of material things. The value of work is regarded as enabling people to pay for the myriad goods and services available in urban-industrial societies.

Expressive individualism The form of individualism focused on the pursuit of per-sonal fulfillment of an emotional sort. Expressive individualism reflects the domi-nant values of a therapeutic culture that prizes self-discovery.

Instrumental individualism   The form of individualism that is primarily focused on a person's financial and career success. Instrumental individualism is reflected in a person's single-minded pursuit of the American Dream of wealth and success, often at the expense of other people.

Mutable self   Louis Zurcher's term for a conception of self which would integrate the physical, social, reflective, and oceanic selves. The mutable self would allow a person to assume any of the selves which fit the situations encountered in everyday life.

Neo-Christian religious groups   Relatively new religious groups which are offshoots of traditional Christianity.

New religions   Religious groups which may be based on principles that are thousands of years old but which have only recently been introduced in their present form in the United States.

Oceanic self   Conceptions of self so vague and general that they lead to no reliable expectations about a person's behavior.

Personal growth movements   Groups devoted to helping individuals gain greater self-awareness and insight into their own motives, behaviors, and life choices. The ultimate goal of members is to increase their personal happiness.

Physical self   Conceptions of self related to individuals' physical attributes and attributes that involve no interactions with others, such as place or residence.

Postmodern world   A term used to describe the current historical period in America characterized by the dominance of information technologies and rapid social change.

Reflective self   Conceptions of self abstract enough to transcend specific social situations.

Saturated self   A term used by Kenneth Gergen to describe problems of identity in the contemporary world. Gergen's notion is that we are so flooded by the rapidity, intensity, and volume of communications in today's world that our very sense of self is in jeopardy.

Search for self   Individuals' attempts to define their personal identity. Organizations such as self-help groups and neo-Christian religious sects and psychotherapy suggest different answers to the question "Who am I?"

Sensitivity training   Group activities designed to increase interpersonal awareness and improve understanding of self and others. Sessions encourage participants to express their feelings about each other openly and to be aware of others' reactions.

Social movement   Attempts to change society, by a group of people which collectively perceives that some aspect of society affects them negatively or results in an injustice to them. They may involve millions of people and have a broad societal focus or be organized around specific issues such as Mothers against Drunk Driving (MADD).

Social self   Positions and statuses such as education or occupation which clearly locate individuals in a social structure or social circle.

Sociological imagination   The ability to see the impact of social forces on our private lives.

DISCUSSION QUESTIONS

1. Which features of contemporary urban-industrial society seem to you most responsible for creating questions of personal identity and self-worth? Name some specific aspects of modern institutions that heighten the problem of alienation.

2. Cite some recent examples illustrating the transformation in our vocabularies of motives from a sin-to-sickness change in explanations of deviant behavior.

3. How do you think about the place of work in contemporary society? Do you consider work as an end in itself or as the means to other ends? Has there been a transformation from a work ethic to a consumption ethic? What part does advertising play in the way people think about work and leisure?

4. Are you personally familiar with any of the new religious groups mentioned? Do you know anyone who is involved in any of these groups? What kinds of people do you think are most likely to join such groups? What functions do you feel these groups perform for their members?

5. Do you see any dangers to society created by the self-awareness, personal growth movement? How might the promise of better and more meaningful lives create an "awareness trap"?

6. Are you optimistic about our capacity to adapt to today's rapidly changing society? What form might such adaptations take? How would you speculate about likely changes in individuals' conceptions of self?

References

Abanes, R. 1996. *American Militias: Rebellion, Racism, and Religion.* Downers Grove, IL: Inter-Varsity Press.

Adamsen, L., and J. Rasmussen. 2001. "Sociological perspectives on self-help groups: Reflections on conceptualization and social processes." *Journal of Advanced Nursing* 35(6):909–17.

Adler, P., and P. A. Adler. 1999. "Transience and the postmodern self: The geographic mobility of resort workers." *The Sociological Quarterly* 40(1):31–58.

Ayella, M. 1998. *Insane Therapy: Portraits of a Psychotherapy Cult.* Philadelphia: Temple University Press.

Babbitt, C., and H. Burbach. 1990. "A comparison of self-orientation among college students across the 1960s, 1970s and 1980s." *Youth and Society* 21:472–82.

Barkun, M. 1997. "Millinarians and violence: The case of the Christian Identity Movement." In *Millennium, Messiahs, and Mayhem: Contemporary Apocalyptic Movements*, edited by T. Robbins and S. Palmer, pp. 247–60. New York: Routledge.

Becker, E. 1973. *The Denial of Death.* New York: Free Press.

Bellah, R., R. Madsen, W. Sullivan, A. Swidler, and S. Tipton. [1985]1996. *Habits of the Heart: Individualism and Commitment in American Life.* Berkeley: University of California Press.

Bellah, R. et al. 1991. *The Good Society.* New York: Alfred A. Knopf.

Berger, P., and T. Luckmann. 1967. *The Social Construction of Reality.* New York: Doubleday Anchor Books.

Borysenko, J. 1999. *A Woman's Journey to God: Finding the Feminine Path.* New York: Riverhead Books.

Crone, H. 2000. "The many opiates of the new age." *Quadrant* (April):15–18.

Dawson, L. 1998. *Comprehending Cults: The Sociology of New Religious Movements.* Toronto: Oxford University Press.

de Munck, V. 2000. *Culture, Self, and Meaning.* Prospect Heights, IL: Waveland Press.

Derber, C. 1996. *The Wilding of America: How Greed and Violence Are Eroding Our Nation's Character.* New York: St. Martin's Press.

Derber, C. 1998. "Killing society: The ungluing of America." In *Critical Social Issues in American Education: Transformation in a Postmodern World*, edited by H. Shapiro and D. Purpel, pp. 5–26. Mahwah, NJ: Lawrence Erlbaum Associates.

———. 2000. *The Pursuit of Attention: Power and Ego in Everyday Life*. 2nd ed. New York: Oxford University Press.

Derber, C., W. Schwartz, and Y. Magrass. 1990. *Power in the Highest Degree: Professionals and the Rise of a New Mandarin Class*. New York: Oxford University Press.

Edgley, C., and D. Brissett. 1999. *A Nation of Meddlers*. Boulder, CO: Westview Press.

Freie, J. 1998. *Counterfeit Community: The Exploitation of Our Longings for Connectedness*. Lanham, MD: Rowan & Littlefield Publishers.

Gartner, A., and F. Riessman. 1998. "Self-help." *Social Policy* 28(3):83–6.

Gergen, K. [1991]2000. *The Saturated Self: Dilemmas of Identity in Contemporary Life*. New York: Basic Books.

Grace, S., and K. Cramer. 2002. "Sense of self in the new millennium: Male and female student responses to the TST." *Social Behavior and Personality* 30(3):271–80.

Gubrium, J., and J. Holstein. 2000. "The self in a world of going concerns." *Symbolic Interaction* 23(2):95–115.

———. 2001. *Institutional Selves: Troubled Identities in a Postmodern World*. New York: Oxford University Press.

Harrary, K. 1994. "The truth about Jonestown." In *Religious Cults in America*, edited by R. Long, pp. 10–20. New York: The H. W. Wilson Company.

Hartley, W. 1968. "Self-conception and organizational adaptation." Paper presented at the meetings of the Midwest Sociological Association, Omaha, Nebraska.

Hassan, S. 1990. *Combating Cult Mind Control*. Rochester, VT: Park Street Press.

Heelas, P. 1996. *The New Age Movement: The Celebration of the Self and the Sacralization of Modernity*. London: Blackwell.

Hesse, H. 1922 (English translation 1951). *Siddhartha*. New York: New Directions.

Hewitt, J. 2003. *Self and Society: A Symbolic Interactionist Social Psychology*. 9th ed. Boston, MA: Allyn and Bacon.

Humm, A. 1997. "Self-help: A movement for changing times." *Social Policy* 27(3):4–5.

Irvine, L. 1999. *Codependent Forevermore: The Invention of Self in a Twelve Step Group*. Chicago: University of Chicago Press.

Jenkins, P. 2000. *Mystics and Messiahs: Cults and New Religions in American History*. New York: Oxford University Press.

Karp, D. 1996. *Speaking of Sadness: Depression, Disconnection, and the Meanings of Illness*. New York: Oxford University Press.

———. 2001. "Recovery in a therapeutic culture." *Qualitative Sociology* 24(1):107–15.

Kessler, R., K. Mickelson, and S. Zhao. 1997. "Patterns and correlates of self-help group membership in the United States." *Social Policy* 27(3):27–46.

Klapp, O. 1969. *The Collective Search for Identity*. New York: Holt, Rinehart & Winston.

Kübler-Ross, E. [1970]1997. *On Death and Dying*. New York: Scribner.

Lewis, J., ed. 1994. *From the Ashes: Making Sense of Waco*. Lanham, MD: Rowman & Littlefield.

———, ed. 2001. *Odd Gods: New Religions and the Cult Controversy*. Amherst, NY: Prometheus Books.

Loeb, P. 1999. *The Soul of a Citizen: Living with Conviction in a Cynical Time*. New York: St. Martin's Griffin.

Lowney, K. 1999. *Baring Our Souls: TV Talk Shows and the Religion of Recovery*. New York: Aldine de Gruyter.

Madara, E. 1997. "The mutual-aid self-help online revolution." *Social Policy* 27(3):20–6.

McGinn, D. 2000. "Self Help U.S.A." *Newsweek* 135(2):42–6.

Melton, J. 1999. "The rise of the study of New Religions." Paper presented at CESNUR 99, Bryn Athyn, Pennsylvania. <http://www.cesnur.org/testi/bryn/br_melton.htm. Accessed 2/1/03.

————. 2002. *Religions of the World*. Santa Barbara, CA: ABC-CLIO.

Mills, C. W. 1940. "Situated actions and vocabularies of motive." *American Sociological Review* 5:904–13.

————. 1959. *The Sociological Imagination*. New York: Oxford University Press.

Morgan, E. 1999. "School shootings: A symptom." *Humanist* 59(5):4.

Niebuhr, G. 1999. "Alternative religions as a growth industry." *The New York Times*, December 25:C1.

Pappano, L. 2001. *The Connection Gap: Why Americans Feel So Alone*. Piscataway, NJ: Rutgers University Press.

Powell, T. 1987. *Self Help Organizations and Professional Practice*. Silver Spring, MD: National Association of Social Workers.

————, ed. 1990. *Working with Self Help*. Silver Spring, MD: National Association of Social Workers.

Putnam, R. 2000. *Bowling Alone: The Collapse and Revival of American Community*. New York: Touchstone.

Reiff, P. 1966. *Triumph of the Therapeutic*. New York: Harper & Row.

Ritzer, G. 1999. *Enchanting A Disenchanted World: Revolutionizing the Means of Consumption*. Thousand Oaks, CA: Pine Forge Press.

Robbins, T. 1988. "Cults, converts, and charisma: The sociology of the new religious movements." *Current Sociology* 36:1–25.

Sandstrom, K., D. Martin, and G. Fine. 2003. *Symbols, Selves, and Social Reality: A Symbolic Interactionist Approach to Social Psychology and Sociology*. Los Angeles, CA: Roxbury Publishing Company.

Schor, J. 1998. *The Overspent American*. New York: Harper Perennial.

Schur, E. 1976. *The Awareness Trap*. New York: McGraw-Hill.

Shapiro, H., and D. Purpel, eds. 1998. *Critical Social Issues in American Education: Transformation in a Postmodern World*. Mahwah, NJ: Lawrence Erlbaum Associates.

Turner, R. 1969. "The theme of contemporary social movements." *British Journal of Sociology* 20:390–405.

————. 1976. "The real self: From institution to impulse." *American Journal of Sociology* 81:989–1016.

Wuthnow, R. 1986. "Religious movements and counter-movements in North America." In *New Religious Movements and Rapid Social Change*, edited by J. Beckford. London: Sage Publications.

————. 1998. *After Heaven: Spirituality in America Since the 1950s*. Berkeley: University of California Press.

Zaleski, J. 1997. *The Soul of Cyberspace: How New Technology Is Changing Our Spiritual Lives*. San Francisco: HarperSanFrancisco.

Zurcher, L. 1972. "The mutable self: An adaptation to accelerated sociocultural change." *Et Al.* 3:3–15.

————. 1977. *The Mutable Self: A Self-Concept for Social Change*. Beverly Hills: Sage Publications.

NAME INDEX

SUBJECT INDEX